READING THE EARLY REPUBLIC

READING THE EARLY REPUBLIC

ROBERT A. FERGUSON

HARVARD UNIVERSITY PRESS

Cambridge, Massachusetts

London, England

First Harvard University Press paperback edition, 2006

Library of Congress Cataloging-in-Publication Data

Ferguson, Robert A., 1942–
    Reading the early republic / Robert A. Ferguson.
        p.   cm.
    Includes bibliographical references and index.
    ISBN13 978-0-674-01338-4 (cloth)
    ISBN10 0-674-01338-7 (cloth)
    ISBN13 978-0-674-02236-2 (pbk.)
    ISBN10 0-674-02236-X (pbk.)
    1. United States—History—Revolution, 1775–1783—Historiography.   2. United
States—History—1783–1815—Historiography.   3. United States—History—Revolution,
1775–1783—Sources.   4. United States—History—1783–1815—Sources.   5. Political
culture—United States—History—18th century—Historiography.   6. Political culture—
United States—History—18th century—Sources.   7. English language—Rhetoric.
8. English language—Style.   9. Criticism, Textual.   I. Title.

E209.F46 2004
973.3′072—dc22   2003067657

For Priscilla, the seemly
raiment of my heart

CONTENTS

ACKNOWLEDGMENTS

Priscilla Parkhurst Ferguson and John Paul Russo have read and commented on every chapter more than once, and the book is immeasurably better for their many suggestions and their expertise in other cultures. Ann Douglas made useful suggestions on "Gabriel's Rebellion" during final revisions. Andrew Delbanco and Charles Capper offered insights that contributed to "The Dialectic of Liberty" and so did many colleagues in the intellectual forum of the Columbia Law School. Lance Banning, Jack Greene, Gordon Wood, and David Womersley gave significant criticism in the early stages of Chapter Two through a seminar under the auspices of the Liberty Fund at Jesus College, Oxford in the Summer of 2001. Margaretta Fulton at Harvard University Press helped me to see the shape of the project at an uncertain stage of its development. The no longer anonymous readers for Harvard University Press, Christopher Looby and John McWilliams, supplied crucial advice in the last stages of revision. It is a richer book for their thoughts. A fellowship at the National Humanities Center in North Carolina furnished some of the time and intellectual atmosphere that every book needs.

Versions of some of my arguments have appeared in various journals and collections, and I benefited from the suggestions of anonymous members of their editorial boards, including aspects of Chapter Two in *Modern Intellectual History*, of Chapter Three in *The William and Mary Quarterly*, of Chapter Four in *The Rhetoric of Law* edited by Austin Sarat and Thomas R. Kearns, of Chapter Five in *Early American Literature*, of Chapter Six in *La Virtù e La Libertà: Ideali e Civilta Italiana nella Formazione degli Stati Uniti* edited by Marcello Pacini, of Chapter Seven in *Law's Stories: Narrative and Rhetoric in the Law* edited by Peter Brooks and Paul Gewirtz, of Chapter Eight in *The Virginia Quarterly Review,* and of Chapter Nine in *Philanthropy and American Society: Selected Papers* edited by Jack Salzman.

The mysteriously joined promise and plight of American culture have driven the author to write this book.

READING THE EARLY REPUBLIC

INTRODUCTION

"The History of our Revolution will be one continued Lie from one end to the other," John Adams complained from his vantage point as the country's first vice-president in 1790. "The essence of the whole will be *that Dr. Franklin's electrical Rod, smote the Earth and out sprung General Washington. That Franklin electrified him with his rod—and henceforth these two conducted all the Policy, Negotiations, Legislatures and War.*" Writing to Benjamin Rush, Adams then evaluated his own account in several ways. "These underscored lines contain the whole Fable, Plot, and Catastrophe," he concluded. "If this Letter should be preserved and read an hundred years hence, the Reader will say, 'the envy of this J. A. could not bear to think of the Truth!'"[1] The puzzles in this comment make it a good place to begin a study of the mysteries in national formations. Why is one of the most successful figures in early republican culture so apparently unhappy with his lot? How do the several audiences for his letter influence what has been said? For beyond his confidential friend and fellow founder, Benjamin Rush, Adams identifies an unspecified reader a hundred years hence. Which of the several ways offered in reading should take priority? Fable, plot, or catastrophe? The substance of the passage raises more questions. Does Adams really believe that the legacy handed down is "one continued lie" or is he simply unhappy with his projected place in it? Where is the truth that he speaks of, and if it is available to him, is it also available to us?

In modern theoretical terms, Adams has given us an example of *habitus,* "the active presence of the whole past" as it comes to us in a reduction of remembering and forgetting. The result is an "embodied history, internalized as second nature and so forgotten as history" in the disposition of the familiar present.[2] Although Adams could not have used these terms, he knew how selective memory worked, including its inevitable eliminations of persons and distortions of events. As he wrote himself, "this My Friend, to be serious, is the fate of all ages and Nations." Why, then, so much exasperation? As the communal celebrations of his own role and elevation to the first vice-presidency had demonstrated, Adams would not be forgotten, and his own pen had been at work to ensure his place in the minds of his countrymen. He ranked officially second among illustrious equals.

True, future readers would misconstrue matters, so strong would be the hold of conventional thought on anyone who might be interested enough to find out. Adams wrote in part to disarm that kind of misunderstanding through his own communicated awareness. He expected, not without reason, that his letter would be preserved. Knowing that any distant peruser would come up with a theory of its truth, he gave enough information through Benjamin Rush for "the continued lie" to be displaced by something closer to Adams's situation. "Do not, therefore, my friend, misunderstand me and misrepresent me to posterity," Adams pleaded with Rush in another letter just two weeks later.[3] Here was the real dilemma, one he shared with all early republicans who wrote. Would his own words of explanation be understood by those who came after him?

Reading the Early Republic is about how that might be done in recognition of the problems involved. Recuperating the past is an impossible undertaking. As historians have recognized, "no account can recover the past as it was, because the past was not an account; it was a set of events and situations."[4] There remains, however, a crucial link to "the past as it was" in this case. In the most literate culture that the world had yet seen, success depended on "the intimate relation between the use of letters and the making of the American Republic." It had been a revolution and national making of writers and speakers as much as actors. Even George Washington would be remembered as much for his two farewell addresses and his presence as a speaker and as an epistolary writer in command of the Revolutionary army as for his military skills. Like many other leaders of the period, he wrote a great deal; the modern edition of his works runs to thirty-nine volumes.[5] From the beginning, the North American colonies were text-oriented cultures through written charters, responses to charters, covenants, compacts, and, not least, biblical exegesis. The language of protest confirmed that orientation in 1776 through endless sermons, petitions, circulars, pamphlets, and more official declarations, bills, and constitutions. Reputation and accomplishment in the early republic rested on the ability to speak and write well. Accordingly, each of the following chapters sketches an aspect of the forgotten dynamism in republican beginnings by retrieving the meaning of words and images through their actual use in a given text or texts—whether book, painting, pamphlet, building, letter, sermon, address, court record, or transmitted oral claim.

John Adams' droll epistolary parody of Franklin and Washington—figures with whom he had major disagreements over the years—can serve to illustrate the complexities in interpreting his times. How should we read the first vice-president and his contemporaries? The list of difficulties in doing so is a daunting one. The texts from the period are artifactual remnants. They have lost their context and do not, in themselves, take into account what has been destroyed or repressed. The language in them is familiar but many of the specific words used had other meanings in the eighteenth century. The word "electrified," for example, would have had a very different connotation in 1790. What did the word signify for Adams, and does it reveal mostly exasperation or does it provide a subtler clue of jocularity in the magical construct that he had so humorously created? As an accomplished participant in the genre of epistolary friendship, Adams *meant* to amuse. The sound and arrangement of words always matters; so does the tone or attitude of mind they reveal, and both lead to another question. What is the attitude of the writer toward his recipients? Words change depending on the audience. Here we have two audiences, and one of them is open-ended. Adams wrote to his confidential friend, a fellow signer of the Declaration of Independence, in a way that he would never have dared to speak or write in public, and yet he also wanted his words to be preserved and heard *eventually* by that distant public reader. What of the art in reaching both audiences? There is, as well, the problem of Adams's several offered alternatives in reading. Fable, plot, or catastrophe? Eighteenth-century writers loved to mix their genres in ways that require special attention to the often ignored question of form.[6]

Understanding Adams' words by themselves is clearly not enough. *Reading the Early Republic* proceeds under the following premises. First and foremost, early republicans used a language that was richer and more nuanced than their inheritors have given them credit for. Not just their words but their sophisticated rhetorical strategies deserve attention. Rhetorical analysis, in this sense, stresses "a study of misunderstanding, and its remedies" and accepts that words lose much of their significance when taken out of their frame of reference.[7] As critics, we must be mindful of Adams' many other writings in approaching this one letter from 1790, and as historians, we must be knowledgeable in studying the peculiarity of his moment. It turns out that Adams frequently expressed frustration over his reputation but just as frequently over his own failings; that he was restless in his largely ceremonial role as George Washington's Vice-President; that he absorbed much of the criticism in Washington's first term that might have been more properly directed at the President; that he and other founders often noted that a true history of the Revolution could never be written; that his own reputation and influence dwindled rapidly in the 1790s under the Federalist party politics of Alexander Hamilton; and that his own fanciful historiography contained elements of truth.[8]

Even so, why should a reader in the twenty-first century want to know any or all of this data? That question is always pertinent in *Reading the Early Republic* and leads to another premise. Montaigne, decrying the tedium of extraneous information in historical writing, once reminded would-be authors to concentrate on "what is worth knowing."[9] That standard applies—not what the writer knows but what the reader will benefit from knowing—and this means, in turn, that an answering relevance must lie in the significance of the truth that Adams tried to convey to Rush. Like any good fable, his touched a nerve. Then as now, some early republican figures loomed larger than the lives they led; others lost credit for what they had done; the birth of the republic appeared a providential success; the heroes in it were said to have accomplished their feats through a blend of technical know-how, God-given insight, and outward show; visual images of their prowess held sway over mundane logistical and economic indicators; and most accounts drew upon a tangle of myth, story, and history that resembled Adams' "fable, plot, and catastrophe."[10]

Exaggeration is a natural by-product of ideological beginnings. Early republicans quickly mythologized their own national formations, and every ensuing generation of Americans has reconstituted the myth for its own appropriation and use, making it that much harder to know the past for what it was.[11] Later leaders have taken what they have needed for immediate use with little regard for historical accuracy or later accountability, turning the founders into a process of authentication that contributes less to the excitement than to the banality of political discourse. At a more structural level, the appropriation of early republican history and thought for institutional legitimation has brought inertia rather than curiosity to understanding of the past. Institutions like to bestow sameness on their members. The desire for individual commitment to the social order encourages solidarity and collective thought over critique and the recognition of difference, and these priorities hold special sway when the example of the founders, akin to ancestor worship, is used to monitor current affairs and guide behavior in the course of later regimes.[12]

These impositions of the present on the past become especially pernicious when they create a false present. We make ourselves better than we are when we confer greatness on what we have inherited. By giving the past a certain prestige beyond its original reality, a citizenry gives itself orders about how to handle the present, and this thought process lends itself to another distortion. By transfiguring the past, we also yearn for it.[13] The result is an unwarranted nostalgia for a better past that never existed. Nostalgia has developed, in fact, into a prominent and sometimes dominant trait in American thought. It thrives in the wake of constant change by substituting for loss. Through it, we try to "re-enchant our relation with the world and pour presence back into the past."[14] All of these gestures are understandable. They are also profoundly antihistorical, and the users of them are cast adrift when it comes to the language and principles of inherited republican thought.

The difficulty in perceiving the early republic can be seen as well in the uncertainties of periodization that it creates. When did the American Revolution begin and when did it end? The answers given to these questions have been subjects of debate from the outset. Conventional understandings assign the first fifty years of national life to the period

from 1776 to 1826, but Adams insisted that he could trace "the feelings, the manners, and principles which produced the Revolution" all
of the way back to Jeremiah Dummer's *A Defence of the New-England Charters* written in 1721, or to the Molasses Act of 1733, or instead to serious implementation of that act in 1757, or to James Otis's
pamphlet *The Rights of the British Colonies Asserted and Proved* in
1763. He gave each of these dates at various points, and felt by 1817
that whatever truth the Revolution contained already had been lost
or squandered "in adulatory Panegyricks, and in Vituperary Insolence."[15] Nor were these merely the musings of a man still embittered
as the one President to have been turned out of office. Most leading
intellectuals in New England shared his despair in 1817.[16]

The very term "early republic" that identifies the period for most
observers reveals a larger problem. No one, it should be noted, ever
talks about a "middle republic" or a "late republic" despite countless
tracts that employ the noun and trace how the nation has developed.
Yet every commentator appears quite certain that the early republic as
an institution and a concept is now past. Notions of periodization are
always suspect but never more so than when they exist in relative isolation.[17] The ideological upshot of a republic that might be aging or
ending is an uncomfortable thought for most Americans; even otherwise objective scholars shy away from assigning trajectories. At the
same time, there is an artificial benefit in declaring "earliness" past.
Many republican successors wish to regard their first origins as frozen
in time and hence clearly visible. The notion of an original meaning in
language is much easier to grasp if it can be said to be fixed or set in
place. Unfortunately for this way of thinking, time and change never
stand still even when they are unobserved. The volatility of thought in
any given moment also works against the idea of single meanings or
what one major critic has called "the Proper Meaning Superstition."
Words have many shifting connotations, where "the remedy is not to
resist these shifts but to learn to follow them."[18] No language was
fraught with more contestation than that used in the early republic,
and the desire to fasten it with one understanding does violence to the
diverse peoples who lived, spoke, and wrote with it.

Reading the Early Republic seeks instead to reinvoke the mystery
and vitality in national beginnings and to recover the dynamism in
language that meant everything to its proponents. Enlightenment
norms implied that history itself could be changed through the dis-

semination of knowledge by the right words delivered in the right place. Debate centered on where the right words were going to be found. If Adams was exasperated by the turn of events, it was because he believed so strongly that the wrong ideas and words were impeding the direction of the country. A bundle of prerogatives and anxieties in 1790, the Vice-President typified a manic-depressive tone found throughout early republican writings even though it is a quality easily overlooked today. Assertions of a colossal destiny ("Dr. Franklin's electrical Rod, smote the earth") vied everywhere with fears of failure and overwhelming feelings of loss ("the History of our Revolution will be one continued lie").

We miss the serious interplay in such commentary because we accept the positive dimension as the historical reality, but "the magic of *e pluribus unum* should not blind us. The literature is indeed that of a people who did not know themselves to a much greater extent than we have yet acknowledged." In consequence, and to a degree still unappreciated, "the literature of the early republic is an anthology of devices for self-persuasion."[19] Indeed, the pressure on language to convey understanding may never have been greater than in this period of American history, and the corresponding subject of choice—the need to protect precarious beginnings—grew overwhelmingly large through competing theories over what protection entailed. The users of that language knew that there would be a high price to pay in history if the experiment failed and that the price would be exorbitant for any writer who had contributed to the ruin of what all considered to be the most important nation on the face of the earth. Early republicans talked compulsively of the children who were watching and of the progeny who would judge them in times to come.

The value in coming to grips with these pressures from long ago is the ultimate premise of *Reading the Early Republic*. If the political truths of the period remain important, they deserve to be seen in the context of the struggle to articulate republican values and in the craft of that struggle. Otherwise they become truisms rather than working propositions, and there is danger in the diminution. For manifestly, the articulation of republican values remains an ongoing issue in the troubled opening of the twenty-first century. This book proposes that many eighteenth-century works of note have been either forgotten or flattened in later ideological manipulations of them and that recovery of their original force brings something of immediate value to current discussions of the United States of America. Indeed, the effort to concentrate on the underlying vitality of early republican texts would seem to be especially important at a time when national leaders claim that "textualism" will lead back to "original meanings" as our surest guide in making current decisions about national directions. Privileging the surviving text over other considerations, legal textualism argues that a text "should be construed reasonably, to contain all that it fairly means."[20] *Reading the Early Republic* accepts this formulation as a challenge. In looking for "all that a text fairly means," we will find that "*all*" turns into an adventure of unforeseen proportions.

CHAPTER ONE

The Earliness of the Early Republic

Few Americans can tell you about a great grandparent, and Alexis de Tocqueville explained why long ago. "Those who went before are soon forgotten," he wrote in his description of the United States, "of those who will come after no one has any idea: the interest of [democratic] man is confined to those in close propinquity to himself."[1] The facts retained about a forebear tend to be a bizarre mixture of reduction and embellishment—a reduction because the rapidly accelerating American present likes to dismiss the relevance of the past, and an embellishment because accounts of ancestors invariably serve immediate ends.[2] The result is a curious paradox. If Americans rarely study their own history, they believe that they already know what they need from the past for use in the present, and the more distant the past, the greater their assumed grasp of its significance.

Nowhere is this paradox more evident than in the contemplation of national origins. Generally scornful of tradition, Americans turn with great frequency to the founding of the republic for easy confirmations. Phrases like "the legacy of the founders," "original intent," "the wisdom of the framers," "the Blessings of liberty," "the first freedom," "the pursuit of happiness," "all men are created equal," "government of the people," and "e pluribus unum" abound in national discourse, and the glib users of those terms presume to know what they mean. Nothing, of course, could be further from the case in practice. When modern wielders of early republican phraseology think they are using the same language, they do so only in a literal sense. The words themselves often held different meanings when first expressed, and every original expression came in a context now lost to easy comprehension.[3] Many misuses of the past are relatively harmless; they fall under the category of national lore, the stuff that allows citizens to define themselves in relation to each other. But manipulations of history for ideological purposes become dangerous when accepted as truths about "the way we were" and hence, as facts about "the way we must now be." Moreover, the danger grows when a manipulator of the past focuses exclusively on the success of national beginnings. Every era must be recognized for its problems as well as its successes if only because subsequent generations always inherit both in refracted form.

Two quick examples from early republican life can clarify the extent to which the American past has become a foreign country.[4] *The Church's Flight into the Wilderness* by Samuel Sherwood, the charismatic pastor of Fairfield, Connecticut, is generally conceded to be one of the most influential sermons preached in 1776. Sherwood drew extended comparisons between the Book of Revelations and Revolutionary America. Biblical words foreshadowed the historical moment in a way that can still be readily understood as typological exegesis. But these same prophecies take on another and stranger quality for the modern reader when they reach for "the kind, watchful providence of God" actually at work in specific events. Sherwood believed that a rainstorm that destroyed shipping in England afforded "incontestable evidence, that God Almighty, with all the powers of heaven, are on our side." Nor was that all. "Great numbers of angels," he concluded, "no doubt, are encamping round our coast, for our defence and protection. Michael stands ready; with all the artillery of heaven, to encounter the dragon, and to vanquish this black host."[5] We can read Sherwood's words and know what they mean, but their emotional impact and philosophical import are now largely lost to us. The point is not just that history was thought to be destined or controlled rather than contingent in eighteenth-century understandings; not even that Providence had taken sides in an earthly contest. Many citizens today still assume that God prefers the American way: "In God We Trust." No, the distinction of importance lies in Sherwood's absolute conviction that God in 1776 had decided to be immanent and imminent in the crisis of American experience and that every earthly participant had better take immediate account of that fact. With this apocalyptic lens in place, the simple recognition of phenomena took on freighted meaning in Sherwood's conception of things, and the addition defined the courage or cowardice with which one faced the world.

Another kind of early republican, Alexander Hamilton, supplies a second example of language only partially understood today. His 1791 *Report on Manufactures* as Secretary of the Treasury became the most prescient document of the period in its articulation of the economic direction the United States would take. The *Report* stressed private finance and technological innovation in the developing nation and the role of government in securing "the confidence of cautious, sagacious capitalists, both citizens and foreigners" to that end. Prosperity depended on the availability of cheap labor for entrepreneurial use. Hamilton accordingly urged "the employment of persons who would otherwise be idle" and he concentrated on two hidden sources. "[I]n general," he observed, "women and children are rendered more useful, and the latter more early useful, by manufacturing establishments, than they would otherwise be." The need for industrialization in an agrarian country demanded that otherwise idle children, particularly those "of a tender age," be put to work in "cotton factories" and "manufacturing establishments."[6] The utilitarian basis of this reasoning is now so intrinsic that it requires no explanation, but no one today would use it to advocate child labor just as no one in 1791 disputed Hamilton's desire to put children in factories.

What changed? More than the relatively new concept of enterprise capitalism supported the early republican vision of child labor. Hamilton's *Report on Manufactures* could project such a plan without protest because eighteenth-century America thought of children as agents of production. Idleness in anyone was an egregious sin. Children were economic resources, first for household assistance and then for farm labor or apprenticeship; they were expected to pull their weight as soon as they were able.[7] There is, as well, another twist to address in the way that language matters in the *Report*. For even though Hamilton wrote before the quantum shift in perception from "an economically useful to an economically useless but emotionally 'priceless' child," his words helped to control industrial practice long after children became the focus of long-term domestic nurture. Laws prohibiting child labor failed to take general effect in the United

States until the 1930s.[8] There is an important lesson here in contemplating any language of the past. Not only do words count; as often as not, they continue to hold ideas in place after their operational significance has changed.

The two examples, taken together, suggest that the power of language is at once boundless and bounded. The written word, a relic from the ideas of time past, must be read as both a current subject for interpretation and the historical object first interpreted.[9] Samuel Sherwood engaged in an act of interpretation that anyone can follow, but he also believed that God's words shined so brightly and directly that they burned off the biblical page to shape the American experience. Similarly, while it is unfair to think of Hamilton as the exploiter of innocent children, his language clearly contributed to a later sense of exploitation as the conception of the child changed in the culture he worked to produce. To avoid creating a false present out of the past in such statements requires concentration. Among other things, we must take into account the vital similarities of Sherwood and Hamilton within their differences as eighteenth-century figures. Sherwood, agonizingly steeped in the evangelical temperament in 1776, and Hamilton, the confident expositor of rational Enlightenment thought in 1791, agreed over more assumptions than they themselves might have realized. It was their significant areas of like-mindedness that made the republic that both sought. To reach this far, however, we must also come to grips with the way religious and secular frames of reference join in conceptions of the period.[10]

It helps, in other words, to think about what rational thought about the material world meant to the Reverend Sherwood and what religious faith did to George Washington's Secretary of the Treasury. At a remarkable moment in *The Church's Flight Into the Wilderness,* Sherwood pauses in mid-revivalist cry to contemplate the possibility of "a free trade" policy on the part of "our honourable Continental Congress" through which "the spirit of liberty might spread and circulate with commerce."[11] From the other side of the coin, *Report on Manufactures* can proceed with such tonal confidence because the economic prospect of the United States had been secured beforehand by God and Nature. Hamilton believed that Christian statesmen erected a proper superstructure only if they first paid sufficient attention to the foundation that Providence had furnished.[12] The seemingly

hard-boiled politician clearly heeded the significance of religious values both early and late in his career, and those values may even have
cost him his life in his duel against Aaron Burr.[13]

There is a final, somewhat puzzling similarity between these very
different men, and it opens into the more obscure singularities of early
republican thought. For while Sherwood and Hamilton appreciated
their impact on others, they despaired over what they saw around
them despite their expressed self-confidence in the success of republican formations. Sherwood knew the time was fast approaching
"when all wicked tyrants and oppressors shall be destroyed for ever,"
but he also gave way to "deep and serious lamentation" over the "awful backslidings and declensions in this land." Somehow the course of
human events was moving steadily downward. "We have, in a great
measure, lost that lively faith, zeal and brotherly love, so conspicuous in the temper and conduct of our pious fore-fathers, and [that]
added such a beauty and lustre to their characters," he protested.
"The true and noble spirit of primitive christianity is scarce to be
found among us; [we] have lost our first love, the love of our espous-
als, and kindness of our youth." A sweeping expounder of human history, Sherwood appeared confused when it came to particulars. "How
has the beauty of this pleasant land of Immanuel been defaced," he
asked, "and its glory spoiled by the little foxes treading down our tender vines; and by the inroads of the wild boar of the wilderness?"[14]
Hamilton complained in parallel terms about his own "odd destiny,"
even though in 1802 he was still the acknowledged leader of the Federalist party and a prominent lawyer in New York. "What more can I
do better than withdraw from the scene?" he moaned in less fanciful
but more poignant terms. "Every day proves to me more and more,
that this American world was not made for me."[15]

The temptation to despair and feelings of loss in such statements
are worth clarifying because they are so endemic to republican discourse in the period.[16] Images of the rising glory of America vied everywhere with the prospect of utter dissolution. The centrally placed
Hamilton's feelings of dislocation raised an open question that every
citizen would ask at some point. For whom *was* this strange new
world of America made? Few observers of early republican life failed
to express anguish over developments at some point in the period. At
one level, intense hope over the new dispensation that America was

supposed to bring to human history produced equally vivid contemplations of failure. At another level, the rapid social pace of change kept everyone unsettled and wondering about ultimate directions. Most Americans were caught up in perpetual surprise by the transformations around them. No one felt in control of the emerging republic for long. Religious and secular thought came together over this problem in part because of the country's slow emergence from a Bible culture with a revivalist stamp, but more was involved. No early republican could understand what was happening without both faith and reason as necessary resources of explanation. There was also a larger problem of orientation: the intellectual resources of explanation themselves were changing—sometimes beyond ready recognition.

Early republicans groped for their recognitions through language that later generations would relegate to convention and civic homily. In reading their words today, we take for granted a reality that they questioned, and we drown their doubts in the certitudes of a later time. They stand for what we require instead of being read for what they needed, and, in consequence, they are always more easily placed than understood. Four separate writings from the central years of the early republican period, 1797 to 1802, will serve here as representative texts to show how a seeming familiarity hides enormous gaps between past and present. More than two centuries of difference are involved when we contemplate Hannah Foster's *The Coquette* (1797), *A Narrative of the Life and Adventures of Venture* (1798), a scribbled passage from 1802 taken from a massive private diary kept across the entire period, and Thomas Jefferson's *First Inaugural Address* (1801). The four texts in question are representative in a variety of ways. They cover vital genres of emerging creativity in 1800 (the novel, the slave narrative, the privately penned communication out of epistolary sensibilities, and the public oration). These same four texts span the powerless and the powerful (women, blacks, a downwardly mobile communal leader, and an ascending president of the United States). All four range across public and private spheres when the distance between those spheres, while vast, was up for grabs. They also share a special way of discussing the problems of their time that lock them together in history and that reveal the republic for what it then was. Finally, and perhaps most important for present purposes, all four have suffered critical amalgamation into an interpretive present from which they deserve to be rescued.

∾

One of very few best-selling American novels from the eighteenth century, *The Coquette; or The History of Eliza Wharton* achieved its appeal through a combination of levels. It told the story of a pleasure-seeking socialite who dies alone in childbirth as a fallen woman, and it strengthened its case as a cautionary tale by purporting through its subtitle to be "*a Novel; Founded on Fact.*"[17] The comparable death of an actual person, Elizabeth Whitman in a Massachusetts tavern in 1788, caused such a media sensation that Foster and other writers easily embroidered the facts into sentimental tales. "You have doubtless seen the account in the public papers, which gave us the melancholy intelligence," a character in *The Coquette* reminds her readers. "But I will give you a detail of circumstances" (LXXI, 161). The best of these salacious fictionalized versions, Foster's account is read today as a feminist protest against "the negation of the female self" in American life through enforced "silence, subservience, and stasis."[18] And the shoe fits. The plot depicts a woman silenced and then discarded by her culture when she fails to meet its rigid sexist standards. But if *The Coquette* supports this kind of interpretation with variations on the theme, it is because literature belongs to inheritors as well as initiators. The original popularity of the novel could not have flowed from the consciousness articulated by late twentieth-century advocates of the gender revolution. Like many another portrait of a lady, Eliza Wharton, the stand-in for Elizabeth Whitman, attracted her first readers because she personified a more general predicament of culture in her own day.

A close definition of Foster's titular term points to an essential contradiction in the novel of first impression. Eliza Wharton doesn't quite qualify for the designation that she is supposed to represent. A coquette in the eighteenth-century conception of the term was "a gay, airy girl; a girl who endeavours to attract notice." Coquetry, the practice, signified "affectation of amorous advances"; the verb, to coquette, meant "to act the lover" or "to entertain with compliments and amorous tattle," and it came from the French root *coquart,* a prattler.[19] Eliza Wharton is manifestly better than that. Far more accurate characterizations of the coquette, so defined, appear as Harriet Simper in John Trumbull's satiric poem *The Progress of Dulness* (1772–1773) and Charlotte Manly in Royall Tyler's play *The Contrast* (1787), both of which would have been known to Hannah Foster.[20] Eliza, by way of contrast, seeks only the pleasure of good company without wanting to control the attention of it. A serious and sought after conversationalist, she is no prattler. She refuses "to act the lover" and resists "amorous tattle" and "affectation of amorous advances" at every turn. Her underlying problem is of a very different sort. In rejecting the advance of would-be lovers, she wants time to slow down instead of having it rush her into decisions that she is not ready to make, a common impulse of early republicans in a rapidly changing society.[21]

Without trying to do so, Eliza Wharton nonetheless occupies the center of attention in her community, and it is important to understand the basis of her appeal. Given the conventions of the time, any acute eighteenth-century observer would have realized that Eliza was doomed from her first moment of speech when she confesses her "*pleasure;* pleasure, my dear Lucy, on leaving my paternal roof" and further admits that she is "all egotism" (I, 5–6). As she goes on to indicate her "natural propensity for mixing in the busy scenes and active pleasures of life" (II, 7), the dullest contemporary reader would have known that her fate was sealed. A self-centered woman who leaves home in the name of pleasure to mix in the busy scenes of life always gets her comeuppance in the imagination of the early republic. Yet much more is at stake in *The Coquette* than the seduction plot.

Foster quickly complicates all of the conventions. Eliza Wharton formally rejects the "term *coquettish*" when it is first raised, claiming accurately that she behaves with "an innocent heart" and "the effusions of a youthful and cheerful mind" in search of acceptable "sources of enjoyment" (II, 7). Her real ambition, as her closest friend points out, "is to make a distinguished figure in the first class of polished society" (XIII, 27). Eliza possesses "an elevated mind, a ready apprehension, and an accurate knowledge of the various subjects which have been brought into view" (IV, 11). It is the pleasure of good company joined in spirited conversation—she terms it "the true zest of life" (XIV, 30)—that attracts her. These elements combine in "'the feast of reason and the flow of soul'" (XII, 25), and they allow Eliza to

engage in her long-term goal, "pleasing anticipations of future felicity" (III, 9). Here, if anywhere, is the early republican intellectual's
secular pursuit of happiness conjoined with the problems of defining
social refinement and attainment in a democratic society. Eliza bespeaks an underlying uncertainty. What kind of well-being can bring
happiness? "Is it not difficult to ascertain," she queries a suitor as she
rejects his own glib words, "what we can pronounce 'an elegant suf-
ficiency?'" She attracts attention because she boldly represents the
new ideal of a materialistic age. Like other Americans in growing
numbers, Eliza seeks upward mobility in a culture where social optimism tells her it should be possible.[22]

The major difficulty, as many have noted, is that Eliza Wharton
lacks attractive choices. Despite its rhetoric, her society cannot fulfill
her hopes. Her two suitors of note are a grasping minister with limited social graces and a rakish army officer. Though very different as
rivals, the Reverend John Boyer and Major Peter Sanford are similar in another way: each is losing ground within his community. They
belong to downwardly mobile occupations in the flux of American
change: the first reaches back to the religious world of colonial times
when ministers controlled their communities, the second owes his status to the fight for independence with its real but now fading martial
glory. Not surprisingly, Eliza falls victim to her Revolutionary heritage rather than the drabber prospect of minister's wife. "My disposition is not calculated for that sphere," she tells her mother, the impoverished widow of a clergyman. She is, however, vulnerable to the
seducing soldier through "love of country," a stance "truly Roman,"
"truly republican," and a woman's duty (XXIII, 44).

This patriotic sentiment is articulated by a Mrs. Richman, the leading socialite of the novel and the person whom Eliza aspires to become and allows to speak for her (XXIII, 44). Mrs. Richman receives
everyone's admiration because she has managed an increasingly difficult feat in 1797. As her name implies, she has secured an envi-
able double in social prestige by marrying General Richman: past military grandeur has been joined to the commercial presence of obvious
wealth. As Eliza explains in noting the health, wealth, taste, refined
disposition, and "favoured dwelling" of the Richmans, "should it
ever be my fate to wear the hymenial chain, may I be thus united!"
(VI, 14). Major Sanford seduces Eliza by pretending to be another
Richman when he is actually "a second Lovelace," which turns Eliza

into "Richardson's Clarissa" (XIX, 36–38). But why is Eliza so susceptible? She wants "for a while, to enjoy my freedom" while all around her want a connection and warn that "a thousand dangers lurk unseen" (XXVI, 50; V, 12–13; XII, 24–25; XXI, 40). Forced to think in terms of connection in order "to repose in safety" (XII, 24)—much in the way that the separate states had to think about a stronger federation—Eliza compares her equally unsatisfactory suitors, the minister to the soldier, and comes up with the question that many early republicans worried about. "Why were not the virtues of the one, and the graces and affluence of the other combined?" she cries in exasperation over a changing world. "I should then have been happy indeed!" (XXVI, 53). Behind this question is a more pointed one raised very early in the novel. Does virtue or rank and fortune secure respect? It is Mrs. Richman who first admits that rank and fortune might predominate (VII: 16).

The novel confirms this perspective when Eliza Wharton comes to weigh the same distinctions: "each felt a conscious superiority; the one [Boyer] on the score of merit; the other [Sanford] on that of fortune. Which ought to outweigh, the judicious mind will easily decide" (XXXIV: 68). But Eliza cannot decide, and Foster's point is that the world itself makes the decision a difficult one. Lucy Freeman, the heroine's main confidante, reveals the nature of the difficulty when she writes to Eliza that "many of our gentry are pleased with the prospect of such a neighbor" in the scandal-ridden Sanford because he is "an accomplished gentleman" and "a man of property" (XV, 31). Sanford "falls" in society only when it is also discovered that he has lost all of his money (LXXII, 164).

Hannah Foster's distaste for this sterile post-Revolutionary setting appears on page after page in her novel. Male figures turn out to be either voyeurs or cads of the first order, and Eliza's female support group fails her time and again, sometimes cruelly. Even successful couples fail to procreate in *The Coquette;* all three children in the novel, including the Richmans's daughter, die in childbirth or infancy. A coquette is always at fault, but Foster distinguishes Eliza and puts a heavier onus on the society that has treated her so shabbily. The military side of Revolutionary success is now either idle or false in the commercial setting of Eliza's world, and the religious underpinnings of morality are increasingly materialistic. The Reverend Boyer will eventually dismiss Eliza in crass commercial terms. She becomes "a subject of speculation in the town," and her character, he delights in

telling her, "already begins to depreciate" (XL: 80, 84). When Eliza
realizes that she is indeed "town talk" instead of its brilliant guest, she
poignantly asks, "how can I rise superior to 'The world's dread laugh,
which scarce the firm philosopher can scorn'?" (XLIV," 99).

The world that Eliza dreads is, of course, the early republic in one
of its ugliest moments. The late 1790s experienced unprecedented
factionalism and vituperation as growing divisions between emerging parties, Federalist against Republican, reached breaking point.[23]
Scholars have traced the republican tropes in *The Coquette*.[24] Eliza's
frequent insistence on her liberty, a vexed term in the political debates of the 1790s, receives a stock rejoinder of the kind that Federalists used to squelch their Republican opponents. How much liberty
should anyone have? "You are indeed very tenacious of your freedom,
as you call it, but that is a play about words," Eliza is told at one
point. The democratically inclined Eliza has overlooked the assurance from those in power that "honor and good sense will never
abridge any privileges that virtue can claim" (XV, 30–31). In Federalist terms, she needs to respect the virtue in reigning authority more
than she has.

Politics as such is a main source of discussion at "parties" in *The
Coquette,* and Foster keeps the double meaning of the term aloft at
every opportunity. When General Richman deplores a division in his
houseguests because they "had formed into parties," he represents
George Washington ruing the factionalism of the 1790s (XXIII, 44).
The divisive lexicon of the times saturates the novel. Worries about
"the unthinking multitude," (XXXI, 62), "corruption" (XIII, 26–27),
"qualms of conscience" (XXXII, 65), "links" in "the confederated
whole" (XXI, 41), the "desired effect" of Christian principles (XLIII,
106), "the severity of censure" (VII, 17), "the false maxims of the
world" (IX, 20), the nature of correct behavior (V, 13; IX, 20), and
the all-important question whether "fancy or reason preponderates"
in decision making (XXXIV, 68) abound in Foster's story. They are
there because they also percolate through early republican society,
dictating the nature of understanding.

The appeal of Eliza Wharton both to characters in the story and to
her first American readers depends on how these republican thoughts
appear in her as personally dramatic but representative features. Eliza
is a synecdoche for America. She is "youth and innocence" freed from
"the shackles" of a previous authority (V, 13). Her desires are the
ones that drive her nation. "Let me then enjoy that freedom which I so

highly prize," she pleads as, like her country, she tries to avoid entangling alliances (V, 13). The answer offered up by Lucy Freeman, the friend who will trade in the valued sobriquet of "freeman" for just such an alliance as "Mrs. Sumner," instructs Eliza to settle for "moderate freedom" through the oxymoron of "dignified unreserve." Notably, Lucy's hackneyed assignations of "those immortal principles of reason and religion" do not translate easily into practical guides of conduct (XIII, 27). Eliza thinks instead with the same uncertainty about standards that trouble her rapidly changing country. She, in fact, *welcomes* change, and it leaves her peculiarly vulnerable to new standards of conduct. Why, she wants to know, should she sacrifice her fancy and happiness to the reason of others, particularly when it is her imagination that first frees her from the past and allows her to go "in quest of new treasures" (I, 5; VI, 15)?

Eliza Wharton has all of the qualities that should attract others. She possesses "an elegant person, accomplished mind, and polished manner," along with youth, charm, and great sincerity of heart in exchange (IV, 10; XIV, 29; XIX, 38). She also knows what others expect of her and plays the part well when she describes herself as "calm, placid, and serene; thoughtful of my duty, and benevolent to all around me" (I, 6). But the reader, with Eliza, is made to see that this conventional world of sacrifice, duty, and decorum is constricting and boring. "I despise those contracted ideas which confine virtue to a cell," Eliza objects with considerable reason on her side (V, 13). She worries about "the restraint, the confinement," in a life based entirely on duty. Hence, she is sympathetic when others complain about "the rigid rules of discretion and the harsher laws of morality" and then tempted by "the greater sources of enjoyment in a more elevated sphere of life" (XIX, 36–37). Those social superiors who can afford to be "extremely refined in their notions of propriety" can also seem irrelevant prudes as the world turns (XIX, 36; V, 13). Like many another early republican in the 1790s, Eliza exhibits ambivalence toward the Revolutionary generation just before her. Her mother is at once a "Poor woman" who cannot possibly understand her daughter's changing situation and the paragon that cannot be reached (II, 7; XX, 39). "You, madam, have passed through this scene of trial, with honor and applause," she confides. "But alas! can your volatile daughter ever acquire your wisdom, ever possess your resolution, dignity and prudence?" The answer is "no," at least on her mother's terms. Eliza jokingly but correctly notes that her aged mother would make a better wife for the Reverend Boyer (XXXIV, 68).

These conflicting impulses place Eliza Wharton on the cusp of early republican preoccupations and uncertainties for all to see. If her first readers know that she will fail, they intuitively share her impulses. Using balance, the favorite metaphor for good government of the times, Eliza announces "my fancy and my judgment are in scales." "Which will finally outweigh," she wonders, "time alone can reveal" (XXVI, 51). The reader does not wonder, but the knowledge that Eliza will fail only sharpens Foster's own balancing act. For while Eliza inevitably falls victim to "the delusions of fancy!" (XXVI, 51), her imagination occupies the space of disappointment felt by many in her generation of Americans. She thirsts for "the independence, which I fondly anticipated" and which the republic claims to give her. She learns instead "We are dependent beings" (LV, 120; LXI, 133). Eliza enters the pursuit of happiness in good faith only to find it unavailable in practice. "I look around for happiness," she observes quietly near the end, "and find it not" (LXII, 135). She fails because she has been thrown by the question of meaningful ambition in the early republic.

Can wealth ensure happiness? (LIII, 114). It cannot, and Eliza in the end accepts the conventional homily that "virtue alone, independent of the trappings of wealth, the parade of equipage, and the adulation of gallantry, can secure lasting felicity" (LXXIII, 167–168). Curiously, though, there are no characters in the novel who are virtuous *without* wealth, and those who *are* virtuous in their wealth appear unrelated to the problems at hand. The envied Richmans are often quoted for their advice in the novel, but they write only two of its seventy-two letters, and each letter focuses rather insensitively on the writer's own high level of self-satisfaction. The General and his wife scribble of domestic bliss in the face of Eliza's obvious misery and of their pride in producing their own "miniature of beauty and perfection," the infant daughter that Foster will kill off (XXXV, 69; XLIII, 97). Their claimed perfection is meant to be suspect, and their lives lack purpose and apparent utility to others. When Eliza rejects their advice, she underlines a larger pattern of great importance to Foster. No one in *The Coquette* ever follows another person's advice even though advice as a narrative device is ladled out by the bucketful.

The cleverness in Foster's reliance on the epistolary form lies here. Current criticism likes to point out that the letter as a device welcomes women's engagement in the writing process, and the use of it is certainly part of the *vraisemblance* that the author needs, but Foster is interested in a larger demonstration. The entire novel is couched in the polished eighteenth-century elocution of the polite letter. Everyone who takes up the pen writes as an accomplished stylist and in complete control of the form. Yet the content of each letter seems to lead only to further division, leaving each writer in a separate and often stranded point of view. There is no republican consensus in the writing out of this plot. The epistolary form always entails a bridge between sender and receiver, and the author who uses it can emphasize either the distance or the bridge.[25] Foster chooses distance. *The Coquette* is manifestly and relentlessly about the hypocrisies of its time.

A final parallel between Eliza Wharton and her culture is particularly difficult to grasp now. An ardent socialite, Eliza always remains the minister's daughter. Foster carefully notes how Eliza's growing worldliness and intelligent reading of serious literature serve to "remind [her] of an awful futurity, for which I am unprepared" (LXII, 135). Current interpretation tends to view Eliza's sudden religiosity at novel's end as part of her silencing in patriarchal terms, and again there is strength in such a reading. Foster's indirection suggests as much. Information about Eliza's final piety comes almost entirely through the language of other figures, and they impose their own questionable interpretations on a figure whom they have turned into everyone's victim. Even so, the Bible culture of eighteenth-century America would have come to a different conclusion.

When Americans of that day were in trouble, the language of religion was a reflex reaction. Secularity and religiosity as explanatory categories were all of a piece more often than not. Only the future would assign clear differentiations. Eliza Wharton, as distinct from her seducer Major Sanford, knows her Bible well.[26] Sanford is an unnatural monster in this world precisely because he despises religion and can use his detachment to place himself beyond the qualms of guilt. As such, he represents a serious danger in this pious society of new republicans who still lack many institutional controls (LXXII, 165; XXXII, 65; LXX, 160). The beginning nation clearly needs religion to hold itself in place. In a criticism often used in the politics of the day, Sanford admits that he has turned himself into "a mere Proteus, and can assume any shape that will best answer my purpose"

(XI, 22). He thus becomes a vehicle for the republic's worst fears about changing standards of behavior. Eliza, by way of contrast, finds order and finally a fixed place through "the greatest consolation," "the infinite mercy of heaven as revealed in the gospel of Christ" (LXXI, 146).

This disparity over religion between two people who have been similarly attached to the pleasure of the moment is important to both the success of the novel and to an explanation of the culture that produces it. In an eighteenth-century understanding, a dying person or a woman on the verge of childbirth was thought to speak only the truth.[27] Eliza Wharton is both. Accordingly, when she tells Peter Sanford that "by a life of virtue and religion, you may yet become a valuable member of society, and secure happiness both here and hereafter," her words deliver a message to Foster's readers (LXX, 160). Eliza's final "composure and peace" against Sanford's obvious despair—"I must become a vagabond in the earth"—tracks a convention in the seduction novel, but it also enlists the power of religion to circumscribe disaster. Foster proves her point by increasing Sanford's anguish in his recognition of the divergence between seduced and seducer (LXXII, 165). "She found consolation in that religion, which I have ridiculed as priestcraft and hypocrisy!" Sanford reveals in his own agony. "But whether it be true or false, would to heaven I could now enjoy the comforts, which its votaries evidently feel." Turning himself into "the pest and bane of social enjoyment," he decides to "fly my country as soon as possible," and he shudders "at the prospects . . . both in this and a coming world" (LXXII, 165–166). In banishing himself from the country, Sanford provides a measure of comfort to all by admitting that the irreligious man cannot be "a valuable member of society." The interesting thing about his distress, however, is the fact that it can only be expressed in the religious terms that he still rejects ("would to heaven," "a coming world").

Critics now look for hypocrisy in the religious expressions of the early republic with its increasingly material orientations. Our own starker sense of separation between church and state has compounded the tendency. In fact, religious terminology is the unavoidable *lingua franca* of social explanation in the period. No one could avoid it, and few tried. Not the degree of religiosity but the variety in religious expression is the key to understanding. The success that Americans today associate with their early heritage further masks the rhythms and tones of this element in eighteenth-century discourse. As *The Coquette* clearly illustrates, religious thought was most important in the first United States when used in response to trouble. The perfidious Major Sanford is a man of many faces, but "confusion, horror and despair," reduce him to just one with religious thought supplying the unities (LXXII, 164–165). The final stance of Sanford embodies a hidden rhetorical factor in need of exploration. Anyone who reads deeply in the period learns that early republicans used religion to voice a terrible sincerity in their frequent sense of defeat.

Defeat for some proved unavoidable despite every ability and drive toward success. *A Narrative of the Life and Adventures of Venture, A Native of Africa, But Resident Above Sixty Years in the United States of America* (1798) supplies a vivid example, and it also reveals ignored strands in the practices of the new nation.[28] The conventions of the slave narrative as they apply to *Narrative of Venture* have been thoroughly explored: the filter of a white amanuensis; the protagonist's original happiness as a child in an African home of milk and honey; the horrors of first enslavement; the deeper horrors of transportation in a slave ship to America; the rampant injustice and cruel punishment inflicted by masters in America who are themselves debased by slavery; the slave's challenge of that punishment; the first freedom of learning to read; the means and attainment of freedom; the doubled perspective of the African-American who gains such agency; the limits of final freedom in a pervasively racist culture; and, not least, the layered significations of creativity in such a narrative as it grows out from under oppression and hegemonic dismissal of the author.[29] *Narrative of Venture* so classically fulfills these dimensions that it is often relegated to them. Like *The Coquette,* however, it is a text that transcends the genres to which it is assigned. A slave narrative and an abolitionist tract, *Narrative of Venture* carries beyond these identifications to portray a more generally shared dilemma of its time.

Broteer Furro, to use the author's name instead of the ones attached to him as a slave by his first and third masters, is obsessed with two themes in the account of his life. He can never stop thinking about either the freedom that was denied him or the money that he needed to buy back freedom on the terms that a republican definition of liberty stipulated. The child Broteer is made "Venture" by Robertson Mumford who, as the steward of a slave ship from Rhode Island, purchases the six-year-old boy off the coast of Guinea for four gallons of rum and a piece of calico as "his own private venture" (pp. 9–10). Not until the age of thirty-six does Broteer finally obtain his freedom by paying his third master seventy-two pounds, two shillings. It is "an unreasonable price" extracted from many years of unrequited toil. In Broteer's summary, "I had already been sold three different times, made considerable money with seemingly nothing to derive it from, had been cheated out of a large sum of money, lost much by misfortunes, and paid an enormous sum for my freedom" (pp. 18–19).

Broteer spends most of the rest of his working adult life buying the freedom of his wife, Meg, and their four slave children, dollar by painful dollar. The psychological result is that everything in Broteer's experience—including his wife ("whom I married for love and bought with my money"), the loss of his son ("for whom I paid two hundred dollars"), and the illness and death of his daughter ("the physician's bill for attending her illness amounted to forty pounds" on top of the "forty-four pounds" for her freedom)—must be calculated in currency (pp. 24, 21–22). No other standard makes sense to the man who must arrange every consideration "in comparison with my interest [in capital]" (p. 20).

Extraordinary energy, capacity, and dedication geared to economic values turn Broteer Furro into a successful capitalist with a peculiar edge. White eighteenth-century Americans could afford to worry about whether or not wealth would destroy virtue, whether material gain would secure or threaten republican liberty. The two notions, wealth and virtue, are instead intrinsically bound together for the struggling slave. Making money by every means possible functions as liberty for the man who would extricate himself and his family. Proper investment provides the only rationale in "this existence of servitude and misfortune" (p. 21). Broteer's "freedom is a privilege which nothing else can equal," but it can and must be measured in "the more than one hundred acres of land and three habitable dwelling homes" that constitute his final sense of worth (p. 24).

Two traumatic incidents stand out in the life, each involving injustice couched in financial terms. Broteer's father, a king of his people, is tortured by the men who enslave him "to make him give up his money." "I saw him while he was thus tortured to death," writes Broteer at age sixty-nine. "The shocking scene is to this day fresh in

my memory, and I have often been overcome while thinking on it."
The writer describes "the old king" as "remarkable" and reports with
pride that his father "thus died without informing his enemies where
his money lay" (pp. 7–8). The second incident takes place in Connecticut, where Broteer is "obliged to pay upwards of ten pounds lawful
money, with all the costs of court" as the loser in a trumped-up law-
suit instigated by a rich adversary who uses his higher station to extract a false judgment. As Broteer explains, his opponent "Captain
Hart was a *white gentleman,* and I a *poor African,* therefore it was *all
right, and good enough for the black dog.*" The comparison does not
end there. "Such a proceeding as this," Broteer observes, "committed
on a defenceless stranger, almost worn out in the hard service of the
world, without any foundation in reason or justice, whatever it may
be called in a Christian land, would in my native country have been
branded as a crime equal to highway robbery" (pp. 23–24).

Several things stand out in these accounts. At age sixty-nine, much
of Broteer Furro's emotional identification remains in Africa even
though his entire experience from the age of eight has been in America. As the slave tells one master when unjustly threatened with ban-
ishment, "I crossed the waters to come here and I am willing to cross
them to return" (p. 16). Broteer's sorrow over the sudden destruction
of his original family and African way of life has never abated, and his
"native country" remains morally superior to the Christian land of
America that continues to cheat him at every turn. Sixty-one years
into his experience in colonial America and the republican United
States, Broteer still sees himself as "a defenceless stranger" in a foreign land. He knows that even his hard-won liberty will not protect
him from injustice in a court of law where all men are presumed equal
but not treated that way. This court case and an earlier one, in which
a local justice of the peace refuses to intervene on the slave's behalf
when beaten for no reason by his master (p. 15), suggest the forgotten
extent of racism at work in Northern states like Rhode Island and
Connecticut, but they are also demonstrations of the prevailing economic frame of reference in early republican law. Neither court is
willing to counter a dominant commercial interest to correct an obvious injustice. If Broteer measures everything in terms of financial
holdings, it is because no other element coheres in a society where
economic power controls him. Everything but money in communal
relations falls under one or another negative category: "the injustice

of knaves," "the cruelty and oppression of false-hearted friends," or, in a far more interesting final grouping, "the perfidy of my own countrymen whom I have assisted and redeemed from bondage" (p. 24).

The decision to invest in the labor of others marks the freed Broteer's own emergence into the marketplace as an independent capitalist. Helpful to his own employees but a prodigious workforce unto himself, he is perhaps unconsciously too stern a taskmaster. At least he is surprised when, after "I purchased a negro man for four hundred dollars," his slave expresses "an inclination to return to his old master" (p. 22). Broteer's later hired help ("two negro men") and his own sons also turn against him sooner rather than later (pp. 21–24). His chosen philosophy of "prudence"—"laying up my money" and buying "nothing that I did not absolutely need" while shunning "expensive gatherings," "spirits," "superfluous finery," and "all kinds of luxuries"—earns him the reputation of "a Franklin." But, alas, not Franklin's success. More than racial prejudice seems to have stood in his way (pp. 21, 3). The joyless determination of the rising entrepreneur alienates the would-be workers around him in ways that suggest a growing problem in the republic.

Broteer Furro as the successful narrator of Venture Smith straddles an apparent division in his adopted culture. The relative significance of commerce (self-interested accumulation) and virtue (unselfish dedication to communal well-being) in the early republic remains a serious theme of debate even today.[30] Broteer is caught in that conflict so intrinsically that there is no way for him to be either one or the other; he is necessarily both, and this contributes to his frustrations. Commerce first made him a slave in direct contradiction to the norms of republican virtue, and the commodification that begins in his slave name requires that everything be viewed through a material gauge. A piece of property, Broteer learns how to adjust his own value downward by appearing discontented to aid a bargain in an engineered exchange for a better master. He soon enters into the corruption of others as they "speculate with me as with other commodities" (pp. 16–17). The debasement of slavery thus becomes a natural symbol of other economic ills. Broteer endures the utter hypocrisy of his three successive masters, each of whom cheats him on the contractual terms that they themselves have set forth. The grasping mentality that they exhibit spreads like a virus through *Narrative of Venture*. Everyone cheats his neighbor in the quest for gain. The bane of commerce, "all kinds of luxuries," infects Broteer's own family. Far from being wise, Solomon, Broteer's prodigal son, loses his life at sea when attracted there by the promise of "a pair of silver buckles" (pp. 20–21). In *Narrative of Venture*, every son is worse than his father.

The same inferiority of the children figures on the plane of republican virtue, where the second generation routinely expresses its inability to match the Revolutionary patriarchs. The "Preface" to Broteer's autobiography, written by Elisha Niles, himself a Revolutionary War veteran, turns "Venture" into a paragon of the Revolutionary generation—"a Franklin and a Washington in a state of nature"—for later generations to emulate. The public persona of Venture "exhibits a pattern of honesty, prudence, and industry" that makes him a perfect example of republican uprightness (p. 3). Even as a child, the slave Venture remains true to his word and honest in all of his dealings, sometimes to his cost (p. 12). The later entrepreneur finds himself in trouble with the law only when he altruistically helps a neighbor as every good republican should (p. 23). Broteer's own virtue leads him to distinguish between "fellow-creatures" and "honest fellow-creatures." Although only the latter deserve dignity and respect, Broteer always gives a benefit of the doubt (p. 23). He suffers betrayal time and again because he takes others at their word until proven wrong and assumes the validity of formal institutions until the moment that they fail him (pp. 22–23). Like Eliza Wharton, Broteer Furro acts in expectation of a better world that never appears. Also like her, he takes final refuge in the forms of religion but with another variant in play.

Generous in his dealings but parsimonious in his holdings, a seeker of equality but a ferocious aspirant, Broteer Furro is not a contradiction so much as the natural product of twisted times. The man who secures his own freedom, coin by hard-won coin, must count everything and everyone by the same measure of success if just because the commercial republic encourages the practice at every turn. He is, nevertheless, better than the avaricious community that has molded him. Broteer gives to others in expectation of a return that rarely comes, and somewhere in the process, his realization of loss begins to swallow his satisfaction in gain. Left only with pride in the path taken, he believes so strongly in his own effort that the failure of his sons must take a singular form. He grieves, "Oh!, that they had walked in the way of their father" (p. 24). The presumed clarity of his own sense of direction leads him to project contradiction as an externality around him. There are, in the end, two different philosophical answers to his developing fear of a meaningless world.

Broteer's first controlling stance in *Narrative of Venture* brings some measure of intellectual salvation. He is *in* but *not of* the world that torments him and, therefore, in his view not responsible for the mayhem visited upon himself and others. Yes, he is *a resident* of the United States, but he is first and foremost *a native* of Africa. The man of sixty-nine holds to the child of six's vision of a better land. Another side of Broteer, though, is more nuanced than that, and this side turns to the most sophisticated speaker available to him in the Bible, Qoheleth, the speaker in Ecclesiastes Or, The Preacher. Broteer's last utterance is also the first of that Preacher: "Vanity of vanities, all is vanity" (p. 24). These words are so startling in final context that the printer of *Narrative of Venture* puts them in parentheses, and they are left out of later editions. What can they possibly mean? The next verses in Ecclesiastes give a clue: "What profit hath a man of all his labour which is taken under the sun? One generation passeth away, and *another* generation cometh; but the earth abideth forever."[31]

To the extent that the Speaker in Ecclesiastes declares himself to be of Solomon, the son of a king, Broteer Furro, also the son of a king and a man who bestowed the name of Solomon on his own first born, seems to be asserting a corresponding right to speak with kingly authority. The voice in *Narrative of Venture* thus becomes an interesting amalgam of African royalty and Old Testament prophecy, with the two cultures entwined in search of truth. Broteer, like the biblical speaker, expresses a profound disillusionment born of experience. He introduces the passage with a bleak admission about his own unadorned prospect: "I am now looking to the grave as my home." Broteer has seen the dark underbelly of early republican life, and he has every reason to reject the progress, destiny, and hope that its mainstream orators want to project. Quietly but firmly, like the Preacher, he finds movement without change, endless labor rather than improvement. The generations come and go, and the earth waits indifferently for each to pass. Philosophical resignation opens a new register in Broteer. "Vanity of vanities, all is vanity" announces the end of struggle and the beginning of rest for a figure who has fought against hopeless odds only to find them truly hopeless despite his own success. Not for another half century will this kind of realization appear again with power in American literature. In 1851 Herman Melville's Ishmael, befuddled in "The Try-Works," will observe "the truest of all books is Solomon's, and Ecclesiastes is the fine hammered steel of woe."[32]

How could an unlettered working man achieve such a depth of understanding? Disappointment can be a profound teacher. When Abigail Adams in the spring of 1776 asks John Adams to "remember the ladies" as the Continental Congress declares independence, her husband "cannot but laugh" at her "saucy" impudence. "Depend upon it," he responds, "we know better than to repeal our masculine systems." One of the drafters of the Declaration of Independence, Adams proceeds to give a complete catalogue of the exclusions that will be upheld in the new nation's "code of laws." "We have been told that our struggle has loosened the bands of government every where," he warns his wife. "That children and apprentices were disobedient—that schools and colleges were grown turbulent—that Indians slighted their guardians and negroes grew insolent to their masters." This catalogue of "discontented tribes," including Abigail's, will be ignored as a matter of policy.[33] Cheated, threatened, robbed, beaten, betrayed, and regularly insulted in America, Broteer knows full well that the promises in early republican rhetoric do not apply to him. No one has to tell him that he is excluded from meaningful consideration nor that the "code of laws" has contributed to his misery. "Separate but equal," the firmest device of exclusion and discrimination in modern America, will borrow its language directly from Adams' first document of republican formulation, the Declaration of Independence itself.[34]

Our third representative text, a diary entry in a journal-keeping era, must be taken as a drop of water in an ocean of prose. Entered on December 30, 1802, it belongs to a colossal document, a continuous, massive record unequaled by any other American writing of the period. The keeper of this journal begins in 1758, well before the Revolution, and ends in 1822—sixty-four years in all, spanning the early republic. He is characteristically splenetic in his perceptions on the next to last day of 1802:

They were first taken in by two up-start lawyers to defeat their own purpose—and F. Ames wishing to shut me out of the meeting so as to enjoy my pew, he harangued them so pathetically about pious forefathers that he cram'd the Priest down their throats, tail foremost—duped by a lawyer.

Civil and ecclesiastical oppression and intrigue triumphant. Harangueing, arrogating, blackguarding in Parish meeting beat the people out of their senses, made them defeat their own wishes and drum good citizens out of the meeting, playing the rogues' march. But some few acted like good men . . . they are handcuffed. And we wanted mutual freedom to go to worship, unhandcuffed.

The rest of the passage, too long to present here, reveals how the many "good men" of this church meeting have been "taken in" by a few of the bad. How could it have happened? Crucial individuals have "mixed with their enemies in meeting," and "acted the turncoat, openly deserting [their] own principles"; they have transformed themselves into "smooth, double faced" traitors. The journalist is more than annoyed. What could have been at stake to unleash such wrath? In fact, the problem at hand involved a frequent source of contention in early republican culture. The diarist has just been defeated in the selection of a minister for the parish, in this case for the First Church of Dedham in Massachusetts.[35]

Ingrown, highly partisan, and miniscule as a sample of the writer's craft, the entry manages to reflect many of the political impulses of its day. The first thing to note about it is the named and thoroughly hated opponent. "F. Ames," *Fisher* Ames, is none other than the brother, neighbor, and adjoining landowner of the writer, Dr. Nathaniel Ames. Nathaniel, sixteen years older than his more famous sibling and an ardent Jeffersonian Republican in 1802, battled through life with Fisher, the highest of high Federalists and the man Jefferson himself despised as "the Colossus of Monocrats."[36] In 1802, every communal issue in Dedham, including the selection of a minister, was shaped by this division into political parties, and the division writ large in the nation led to levels of vituperation, invective, and even violence that would be unimaginable today. The break into national political parties started in the 1790s and reached full force in the first decade of the nineteenth century, fracturing families and localities as well as regions and classes. So bitter were the personal battles between the brothers that Nathaniel refused to attend Fisher's lavish Boston funeral in 1808; he declined even to see "the putrid corpse" back home to its grave.[37]

The diary account of the church controversy in Dedham neatly captures the tones and vocabulary that explain why there was so much trouble when early republicans disagreed. Terms like "turncoat," "double faced," and "mixed with their enemies" were holdovers from standard accusations during the rebellion, and they kept the nastiest of civic allegations, treason, at work into the nineteenth century. Born in 1741, Nathaniel Ames had been shaped by the Revolution. He thought like an old-style Whig in opposition with his assumptions about "oppression," "intrigue," and conspiracy as controlling concepts in the elucidation of events. His suspicion of "the Priest" about to be "cram'd down their throats," was a little more complicated, gesturing as it did back to colonial fears of an Anglican Bishop in America but also forward to ongoing controversies in 1802 over the French Revolution. No event in the period divided Americans more than the failure of republicanism and the emergence of atheism in France; no problem illustrated more clearly the continuing conflation of "civil and ecclesiastical" explanation in American thought.

Meanwhile, the single greatest anxiety of those who sided with Nathaniel Ames came from yet another direction raised in the passage. If the people were virtuous, they were easily "duped." Manipulative demagogues "harangued them" in order to "beat the people out of their senses." Confused by oratory, the people would then be betrayed by timid leaders, "deserting their own principles" in order to curry favor with approaching tyranny. In a Revolutionary understanding, "mutual freedom" was always precarious, "oppression" just around the corner. "Intrigue" was its surest symptom, and one saw it most clearly when a "blackguard" tried to "drum good citizens out of the meeting" in "defeat of their own wishes," leaving them "handcuffed."[38]

Every period has its controversies. Why did early republicans disagree in such unusually volatile terms? To be sure, prevalent anxieties over the fragility of the new nation played a role, but larger ideological considerations were also at stake in divisions that could not be seen for what they were. No one, it seemed, could accept natural disagreement over what everyone knew to be an unprecedented political experiment. In the best known work on ethics of the age, Alexander Pope began by asserting the primacy of reason. In *An Essay on Man,* all other faculties—"*The gradations of* sense, instinct, thought, reflection"—give way to reason. "*Reason alone countervails all the other faculties.*" Pope had to admit that only "thin partitions" divided sense from thought, but reason controlled an inherently "just gradation" that all could depend upon: "The powers of all subdu'd by thee alone, / Is not thy Reason all these pow'rs in one?" It followed that reasonable people would agree with each other if they tried. As Pope again put the matter, "All Discord, Harmony, not understood, / All partial evil, universal Good."[39] The alternative, continuing disagreement, flowed from ignorance or ill will, and this meant that you would find a fool or a knave on at least one side of every controversy. Inevitably, fools and knaves figured everywhere in Pope's satires.

The early republic embraced the conviction that falsehood would be found at the base of every controversy, and it added a corollary based on its own success. One could actually expect to find and weed out the wrong or evil aspects in disagreement. These suppositions came in part from an Enlightenment emphasis on education as the key to republican harmony and progress. Choosing from among the many tracts on education of the period in 1798, the American Philosophical Society gave a prize for "the best System of liberal education and literary instruction" to Samuel Harrison Smith's influential and oft-reprinted essay *Remarks on Education: Illustrating the Close Connection Between Virtue and Wisdom.* "By calling into active operation the mental resources of a nation," Smith wrote, "our political institutions will be rendered more perfect, ideas of justice will be diffused, the advantages of the undisturbed enjoyment of tranquility and industry will be perceived by everyone." Smith's logical outcome was a pedagogical conclusion of the times. "The great result will be harmony." Smith spelled out the basis of his confidence in some detail. "Discord and strife have always proceeded from, or risen upon, ignorance and passion," he announced. "When the first has ceased to exist, and the last shall be virtuously directed, we shall be deprived of every source of misunderstanding."[40] Deprived of *every* source of misunderstanding? What if "the diffusion of knowledge" led instead to greater controversy? Continuing discord left a disturbing possibility. When reason failed to solve conflict, the exasperated disputant had to assume the deliberate malice of others. One could correct human error, but malice presented a more alarming problem, one that drove new world Protestants beyond the scope of reason.

Many battles were joined over where deliberate malice was to be found, and they grew fierce over another ideological conundrum, the ambiguous source of virtue. Early republicans wrestled endlessly with a question that was easy to pose but almost impossible to answer on the basis of an eighteenth-century understanding. Did reason or emotion, sometimes projected as sympathy, supply the better source of virtue?[41] To the extent that virtue was understood to be the calling card of true republicanism, the answer to this question was crucial, and it was here that Enlightenment thought and religious revivalism clashed on the American strand. No word, except possibly the term "liberty," was used more frequently in diverse ways than "virtue" in the eighteenth century, and its multivalent meanings led to a basic divide in how one thought about civic behavior.

The Enlightenment stress on reason found virtue in the workings of good government. It concentrated on the willingness of leading early republicans, mainly property owners, to sacrifice their own interest in the name of the common good. Religious revivalism wanted instead to find virtue in the purifying acts of God watching over his chosen people—a people that had to be virtuous through faith for God's promises to take effect. The Enlightenment orientation turned largely upon a delicate balance in mechanics, and it called for an elite understanding imposed from above; the religious impulse depended on a general level of collective devotion that would ensure communal well-being from below. The Revolution succeeded in the 1770s and early 1780s because these alternatives remained more in harmony than in conflict. Divisions arose in the 1790s when new conflations of religious and political understanding added fuel to the flames of democratization.

Did one trust the destiny of the new nation to the wisdom of established leadership or to the will of an increasingly suspicious people? Early republicans could answer this all-consuming question in either religious or political language without seeing much difference. The result was an unbridled confusion of terms when debate occurred. Republican leadership could be virtuous either through knowledge acquired or through the guiding hand of providence; the American people could exercise their will through innate reason, the cleansing power of sympathy, or their recognition of God's plan for America. Progress could be the result of an orchestrated republican harmony, or the discovery of millennialist patterns, or any combination thereof.

Frustration and defeat could be explained by ignorance or sin, sordid ambition or cosmic malice—or all four. Some saw polarities; others strained for connections. Every side of the question about republican well-being reached for linkage but from a variety of directions, and each articulation of the issues lent itself to misinterpretation even though every speaker or writer seemed to assume that clarity was a given easily achieved.

Nathaniel and Fisher Ames personified these differences.[42] They shared a basic family rigidity that made each "a zealot in politics" in his own way, allowing each to divide the world into contrasting versions of heroes against villains, angels against devils. Nathaniel trusted to God over the power of reason; Fisher concentrated on the superintending power of reason in this world. Virtue for Nathaniel came from the people; Fisher thought it "diffused through society" from above. Nathaniel feared the people would lose everything if they did not immediately exercise their sovereignty through suffrage; Fisher warned that the popular vote would be *"the ruin of the wise, rich and good."* In the 1790s Nathaniel found himself "amazed at the growing insolence of our public Servants"; Fisher argued that "the Government must display its power *in terrorism.*" Nathaniel thought of Thomas Jefferson as one of "the old Patriots" and welcomed his presidency with the words "it is hoped treason will not be so triumphant as in the last [administration]"; Fisher criticized Jefferson as "our illustrious Caesar" and another Bonaparte. Nathaniel in the election of 1800 foresaw "the eradication of hierarchy, oppression, superstition, and tyranny over the world"; Fisher saw instead "visions of horror," "the barbarous dissonance of mingled rage and triumph in the yell of an infatuated mob," and "the control of the fiercest and most turbulent spirits in the society."

There was, in short, no place for middle ground in the suppositions of either brother, no room for compromise when Fisher Ames and his supporters wanted a high federalist minister for their church in 1802. The *New England Palladium* had summarized the stakes for both sides as well as the fusion of ecclesiastical and civic discourse when it warned "should the infidel Jefferson be elected to the Presidency, the seal of death is that moment set on our holy religion, our churches will be prostrated, and some infamous prostitute under the title of the Goddess of Reason will preside in the sanctuaries now devoted to the

most High."[43] Where one stood on this issue determined one's friend-
ships, one's social engagements, one's business possibilities, and occasionally one's safety in the town of Dedham.

The passage from Nathaniel Ames' diary resonates at another level
when this background is taken into account. Losing the family pew to
Fisher involved more than a petty quarrel. The placement of the pew
that one rented in the First Church of Dedham assigned communal
status. When the church was built, the father of the brothers won the
third best pew on the basis of his wealth and acknowledged position
in the community. Nathaniel Ames, Sr.'s standing as a leading physician, writer, and landowner in the region also determined his sons'
rank in class when they entered Harvard College. So when Nathaniel
as the older and, therefore, inheriting brother wrote that Fisher
wanted "to enjoy my pew," more than a good view of the minister
was implicated.[44] To be "handcuffed" signified downward social mobility, and Nathaniel felt it keenly. He often complained in his journal
that his politics had injured his medical practice, his social possibilities, and even his domestic life. Others in his life were inclined to agree
with him.[45]

A final key to Nathaniel's bitterness over lost status in the passage
is even more significant, and it comes through his seemingly gratuitous reference to "upstart lawyers," a frequent frame of reference in
the journal. In Nathaniel's own lifetime, the move from colonial to
early republican culture witnessed and encouraged the complete ascendancy of the legal profession in the direction and formulations of
government and society. Lawyers took the place of crown agents in
the Revolution and, almost as quickly, supplanted indigenous merchants, landowners, ministers, other professional men, and established families in the articulation of early republican norms. They did
so with remarkable rapidity and assertion. A doctor like Nathaniel
Ames could easily feel shoved aside by lawyers like Fisher Ames, with
a good deal of reason and evidence to support the claim. The journal
records "the tyranny that drove us to withdraw" in tones that suggest
lost agency. Nathaniel described his technically voluntary departure
from the First Church of Dedham as more than that; it was a removal,
"my excommunication!!!"[46]

All of these elements point to a more subtle frame of reference that
is difficult to place but essential to a complete understanding of the
passage and the slow emergence of a new and unique American voice

that will soon come into its own in republican culture. The uses of national identity, then and now, always include an appropriation and re-
construction of some kind. But to what end? Nathaniel Ames saw the
problem clearly. Not much of a speaker himself, he watched his more
gifted brother control the controversy in the First Church of Dedham
through a brand of oratory that would continue to flourish throughout the century. "F. Ames wishing to shut me out of the meeting so as
to enjoy my pew," the journal entry runs, "he harangued them so pathetically about pious forefathers that he cram'd the Priest down their
throats, tail foremost."

In Nathaniel's account of the event, a patriotic invocation of the
founders disguises naked ambition and personal gain. He also finds a
layer of false piety in his opponents, one that hides demonic influence.
The imp-like "tail" of the priest, positioned in the throats of the
people, denotes the silenced, even gagged position of a citizenry held
in passive reception by an eloquent speaker making bogus use of
their "pious" heritage. There is no need to explore the accuracy of
these claims to establish their significance. Scatological sarcasm, satiric force, a quieter wit, ironic distance, and spite all vie for control of
the passage. They also work together. The passage foreshadows an alternative and ultimately more candid voice in the culture. Here are the
beginnings of a counterstatement to what power and conventional
wisdom always claim for themselves. The mellifluous tones of the
platform orator meet their match in the puncturing, always searching
point of the humorist's foil.

No humorist (a singular lack in the otherwise complete eighteenth-
century man), and no orator either, Thomas Jefferson nonetheless
provided the early republic with its democratic vision and trajectory.
He did so first in words and after in the exercise of power as the country's most accomplished writer and political leader. No other figure
in the impressive pantheon of the founders comes close to matching
this dual achievement of shaping expression and guiding institutions.
A Summary View of the Rights of British America (1775), The Declaration of Independence (1776), *A Bill for Establishing Religious
Freedom* (1777, 1779), *Report on Government for Western Territory*
(1784), *Draft of the Kentucky Resolutions* (1798), and the *First Inau-*

gural Address (1801) set the agenda of both debate and resolution in the new nation. With those documents in place, Jefferson and his immediate protégés, James Madison and James Monroe, controlled the executive branch of the federal government for the first twenty-four years of the nineteenth century. There is no other influence remotely like it in the history of the United States.

Jefferson's preeminence presents a very different problem in interpretation. The man and his writings have been analyzed endlessly with every nuance and contradiction examined and contested. Scholars and politicians alike will always have more to say about Thomas Jefferson, and it will be said with little hope of a culminating consensus. But if accord remains impossible, lost elements in the Jeffersonian legacy still need to be recovered, never more so than in the fourth representative text, Jefferson's *First Inaugural Address.* The address itself was celebrated as a masterpiece in its own time and has been hailed regularly ever since.[47] But if that is the case, how can such a central document of the republic be thought of as even partially lost? The question turns on a particular problem in analysis. For as famous as Jefferson is in American culture, selected words from his pen are even better known—so well known, in fact, that they dominate consideration of what he wrote, leaving us with disembodied or extra-textual statements. The line, for example, that every critic places at the heart of the *First Inaugural,* the line that dominates general understanding, the only line that even learned observers tend to remember, is "We are all Republicans, we are all Federalists." Jefferson's address thus becomes the great work of conciliation after the "revolution" of 1800, a term that Jefferson himself used to describe "the momentous crisis" in the transfer of power from the Federalist administration of John Adams to his own.[48]

What, then, has been lost? More than the Declaration of Independence, Jefferson's *First Inaugural* provides the crux of American republicanism. It contains the frankest, most explicit, most concise assertion of civic principles that the society has been able to produce. It is, as one early twentieth-century critic argued, "to good government what the Sermon on the Mount is to religion."[49] Praise of Jefferson's political performance only begins to touch the continuing usefulness of the document that he left behind him. Three elements stand out in coming to grips with that utility: Jefferson's warnings to his country, his catalogue of republican values, and the overarching form that vitalizes an entire genre in American speech and reception. Only

Abraham Lincoln's *Gettysburg Address* and *Second Inaugural,* which follow in the genre, can compare as presidential utterances with Jefferson's accomplishment, and the *First Inaugural* is a better guide to national well-being than either of them.

Jefferson's warnings seek to encourage instead of alienating his audience; they appear alongside his auditors rather than from on high. *The First Inaugural,* as befits the author's claims about democracy, speaks to "FRIENDS AND FELLOW-CITIZENS" in that order, rather than the official hierarchy of government functionaries who were present on the occasion, and its first admonition addresses a common fear. Every American sees "a rising nation" that is "advancing rapidly to destinies beyond the reach of the mortal eye." No one, that is, can tell where the country is going. Jefferson responds to this prevalent fear by asking citizens, who must "shrink from the contemplation" as much as he does, to put their trust with him in the "high authorities provided by our Constitution." Jefferson is not the first to suggest that a text can supplant and even correct unordered space, but he is among the first to claim that in such a text he can "find sufficient recourses of wisdom, of virtue, and of zeal on which to rely under all difficulties" (p. 492). No problem is too great for the Constitution to handle. Jefferson uses the recent turmoil and extreme antagonisms between Federalist and Republican to prove his case. The bitter change of power into a new order has been negotiated peacefully through successive filters of legitimacy that all accept, "decided by the voice of the nation" *and* "announced according to the rules of the Constitution" (p. 492).

A second warning concentrates on that emerging new order, the winners in 1800, with a reminder of what it will take to "unite in common efforts for the common good." The will of the majority is a "sacred principle" in the republic, and Jefferson will push it ever further along the continuum toward democracy, but the majority's will "to be rightful must also be reasonable." Jefferson hammers the point home in a context that will take centuries to prove. "[T]he minority possess their equal rights, which equal law must protect," he maintains, "and to violate would be oppression" (pp. 492–493). These words from a slave owner participate in the general hypocrisy of early republican ideology, but they do not prevaricate; where equal protection under the law does not exist, there oppression will be found.

Jefferson's third and final warning speaks to anxieties in the twenty-first century as truly as his own. Some, he knows, will never see the common good that he espouses and will seek to destroy rather than build. What is to be done with them? "If there be any among us who would wish to dissolve this Union or to change its republican form," he advises, "let them stand undisturbed as monuments of the safety with which error of opinion may be tolerated where reason is left free to combat it." There are no "angels" in government to make decisions about who should be allowed to keep the rights guaranteed to all or when some should forfeit those rights. It is much safer, in consequence, to trust to "the full tide of successful experiment" and to the extant forms of "a government which has so far kept us free" than to engineer special arrangements for opponents or more intricate laws to control dissidents. A product of the Enlightenment, Jefferson puts great trust in the power of reason to identify mischief before it ripens into disaster, but he does not forget to identify the risks involved. "Sometimes it is said that man can not be trusted with the government of himself," he admits. "Can he, then, be trusted with the government of others?" (p. 493).

The speaker's response to his own question is a complicated "yes." We, the people, can hope to govern ourselves by "entertaining a due sense of our equal right to the use of our own faculties" while keeping in mind "the honor and confidence from our fellow-citizens, resulting not from birth, but from our actions and their sense of them." Success cannot be guaranteed or even promised, but it must be given a chance. If the equality and communal effort that represent republican virtue fail, they will give way to hierarchy and personal privilege, and all will be lost. That is why the American experiment is "the world's best hope" and not a certainty. The trick, if it can be called that, is to convince each citizen to treat "public order as his own personal concern" (pp. 493–494).

Jefferson talks a great deal about "happiness" in the *First Inaugural*. He believes that an intrinsic connection between personal and collective happiness will sustain the required tie of cooperation between the private and public spheres for a government of the people to flourish. Often accused of a superficial optimism, he explains the connection quite poignantly and from an unexpected direction. His key is the misery in the world that he has seen and experienced. "Let us, then, fellow-citizens, unite with one heart and one mind," he pleads. "Let us restore to social intercourse that harmony and affection without which liberty and even life itself are but dreary things." The stipulated dreariness in life comes not from the "the agonizing spasms of infuriated man, seeking through blood and slaughter his long-lost liberty," though Jefferson alludes to that record of unhappiness, but from the personal misery that individuals bring upon themselves every day through their own quarrelsome natures (p. 493).[50] One need only contemplate the petulance of Nathaniel and Fisher Ames and the acknowledged unhappiness that it brings to both of them to grasp Jefferson's point.

The new president's personal catalogue of "the essential principles of our Government" follows hard upon his three warnings and their projected solutions. "I will compress them within the narrowest compass they will bear," Jefferson promises, "stating the general principle, but not all its limitations" (p. 494). Fifteen controlling principles then appear in less than a paragraph, supported by the claim that "they should be the creed of our political faith, the text of civic instruction, the touchstone by which to try the services of those we trust" (pp. 494–495).

Jefferson relies here on one of his greatest gifts as a writer. In an age of bombast and much declamation, he understood the power of simplicity and concision. He was fully aware, even committed to "those distinctions, which eloquence of the pen and tongue ensures in a free country," but he never forgot that, in listening to George Washington and Benjamin Franklin, "I never heard either of them speak ten minutes at a time, nor to any but the main point which was to decide the question." "Amplification is the vice of modern oratory," he would later complain, adding that "speeches measured by the hour, die with the hour."[51] The entire *First Inaugural* contains under 2,000 words. Just six paragraphs in all, the address took less than five minutes for its author to deliver. Jefferson made his principles memorable through ease of form. Indeed, they had to be more than memorable to fulfill his assigned triptych of "creed," "text," and "touchstone." The fact that he aimed for all three also illuminates the overall structure and tone of his performance.

A mere list of Jefferson's principles therefore fails to do it justice. Consider instead the actual form presented below, with numerals added in brackets to assist further analysis (pp. 494–495):

[1] Equal and exact justice to all men, of whatever state or persuasion, religious or political; [2] peace, commerce, and honest friendship with

all nations, entangling alliances with none; [3]the support of the State governments in all their rights, as the most competent administrations for our domestic concern and the surest bulwarks against antirepublican tendencies; [4] the preservation of the General Government in its whole constitutional vigor, as the sheet anchor of our peace at home and safety abroad; [5] a jealous care of the right of election by the people—a mild and safe corrective of abuses which are lopped by the sword of revolution where peaceable remedies are unprovided; [6] absolute acquiescence in the decisions of the majority, the vital principle of republics, from which is no appeal but to force, the vital and immediate parent of despotism; [7] a well-disciplined militia, our best reliance in peace and for the first moments of war till regulars may relieve them; [8] the supremacy of the civil over the military authority; [9] economy in the public expense, that labor may be lightly burthened; [10] the honest payment of our debts and sacred preservation of the public faith; [11] encouragement of agriculture, and of commerce as its handmaid; [12] the diffusion of information and arraignment of all abuses at the bar of the public reason; [13] freedom of religion; [14] freedom of the press; [15] and freedom of person under the protection of the habeas corpus, and trial by juries impartially selected.

Like a comparable list in the Declaration of Independence, the order of principles here is designed to reel listeners in and then to release them with every intellectual comfort in mind. No early republican could disagree with the five initial claims of equal justice, peace in international relations, the two balanced principles of federalism, and the right of election. The final four—the diffusion of information and arraignment of abuses, and the three freedoms of religion, press, and person—are similarly uncontroversial.

Cleverly, the politician at work within the statesman, Jefferson hides his democratic agenda in the middle six principles with tones that discourage debate. "Acquiescence" to the majority in principle six, already qualified in his earlier warnings, has been a basis of alarm in the election of 1800 but not against the worse alternative of "despotism," which is raised here. Principles seven and eight refer obliquely to the use of military force by previous administrations to quell disturbances, but they are couched in conventional rhetoric against standing armies, and everyone accepted the overriding need for civil control of the military. Principles nine, ten, and eleven supply comparably indirect challenges to the expansive budgets, high debt management, and commercial emphases of the Federalists by under-

lining frugality of government, the payment of its debts, and the reduction of commerce to the "handmaid" of agriculture. Again, however, Jefferson employs the lightest touch possible while making his
points. "Honesty" in financial dealings, "preservation of the public
faith," and "encouragement" of all economic endeavours may sound
like bromides, but in context they are disarming qualifications that
put off challenge. Notice the careful juxtaposition of strict and re-
laxed intonations throughout the list: "exact justice" but "honest
friendship," "constitutional vigor" but "peace at home and safety
abroad," "jealous care" but "a mild and safe corrective of abuses,"
"absolute acquiescence" but the final litany of "freedoms." It is no
wonder that opponents complained bitterly of the "lullaby effect"
and tried to evade the "comforting words and general professions
that mean nothing" of the address.[52]

The welcoming tones and moderations of authority that pervade
the list of principles appeal back to an earlier expression of confidence
in government. By accepting so many heartfelt limitations, Jefferson
will preside over "the strongest Government on earth," "one where
every man, at the call of the law, would fly to the standard of the law"
(p. 493). Law, as Jefferson had expressed it and reformed it in *Notes
on the State of Virginia*, represents the surest antidote to corruption in
human affairs.[53] The *First Inaugural* assumes that a wise rule of law,
in this case the Constitution properly administered, will bring out the
better self in every citizen: "all will, of course, arrange themselves under the will of the law" (p. 492). In return, "a wise and frugal government" will restrict itself to three main duties under law. It will, first,
"restrain men from injuring one another," second, "leave them otherwise free to regulate their own pursuits of industry and improvement," and third, "not take from the mouth of labor the bread it has
earned." This, in Jefferson's view, is "the sum of good government"
(p. 494), and as simple as it sounds, his successors have experienced
considerable difficulty in following it. The art of administering good
government is comparably simple. Jefferson expressed it long before
in *A Summary View of the Rights of British America*, where his peroration asserted "the whole art of government consists in the art of
being honest."[54] In the difficulties that he will face as chief executive
of the country, perhaps "through defect of judgment," Jefferson asks
only that his sincerity not be questioned. "Honesty," as noun and
adjective, appears five times in this short address, twice within the fif-

teen principles of government. A dozen other expressions, including "trust" and "confidence," depend upon its presence.

The idealism in these abstractions never drops down to explain the difficulty in remaining honest in politics, but Jefferson offers a hidden parable of political growth through the speaking "I" of the *First Inaugural* to show how integrity in office might be maintained. The first person singular pronoun appears twenty-one times in the address, an unusual repetition for the age. Although Jefferson's first uses wallow a bit in the stock humility of entering upon high office ("I shrink from the contemplation, and humble myself before the magnitude of the undertaking"), he raises the convention only to make more of it. The Jefferson who worries about incapacity at the beginning of the address ("[I] declare a sincere consciousness that the task is above my talents") will, by the end, confidently assume the presidency with "experience enough in subordinate offices" to see his way clearly ("I repair, then, fellow-citizens to the post you have assigned me") (pp. 492, 495).

The parable acts out a simple reversal in dramatic terms. Jefferson demonstrates that more than experience has given him the confidence to proceed. Like the citizens whom he will lead, he has been calmed and encouraged by "the bright constellation" of principles that he has just explained. These fixed points of light have "guided our steps through an age of revolution and reformation." Everyone can now see where darkness previously reigned (p. 495). In turn, the brilliant constellation of principles illuminates a corollary structure in the joined endeavor of leaders and led, governors and governed, elected and electing, all of whom are rendered visible in the recognition and trust that they give each other. "Let us, then, with courage and confidence pursue our own Federal and Republican principles, our attachment to union and representative government" (pp. 493–494).

The choice of metaphors performs a telling gesture in the Enlightenment figure. With his enunciated list of principles transformed into "a bright constellation," Jefferson quickly projects his own sight into one of extensive scope. In the penultimate paragraph of the *First Inaugural*, he twice claims to hold the largest view, and it is an answer to coming controversies. "When right," he observes, "I shall often be thought wrong by those whose positions will not command a view of the whole ground." The real problem, he suggests, will be the narrower perspective of his critics! In anticipation, the new president asks for "support against the errors of others, who may condemn what they would not if seen in all its parts" (pp. 495–496). To see far enough is to find the truth in an Enlightenment understanding. The whole thrust of Jefferson's address is to claim the horizon.

The sleight of hand in the claim is, by definition, invisible to the naked eye. How does Jefferson get away with the assumption that his list of fifteen principles is complete? Why can he further assume that they create fixed beacons of light that will guide republican steps into a prosperous future? Jefferson mixes the memory of his oldest auditors, the gathered official worthies around him who experienced the Revolution, with the historical consciousness of the new generation that is coming after. He seizes what critics have called *les lieux de mémoire*, the sites of memory, the crux where memory becomes history, "where memory crystallizes and secretes itself . . . at a particular historical moment, a turning point where consciousness of a break with the past is bound up with the sense that memory has been torn."[55] The early republic has moved through "an age of revolution" into one of "reformation," from the successful break with England into the ongoing process of developing a democratic society. The comfort zone for Jefferson's anxious immediate auditors, half of whom have been on the other side, comes in his assertion that "the essential principles" have remained *the same* "through an age of revolution and reformation" (p. 495). Certain that something has indeed been torn, Jefferson's opponents *want* to believe that the same principles of government are in place and will guide and control the new administration. Even an inveterate foe like Alexander Hamilton thought in these terms. He described Jefferson's speech "as a pledge to the community that the new President will not lend himself to dangerous innovations, but in essential points will tread in the steps of his predecessors."[56]

Jefferson has protected his claim of totality in other, more tactical ways. He begins by noting that "the essential principles of our Government" will be presented *only* in their generality *without* their limitations (p. 494). The items on his list thus take on an established spirit of comprehensiveness. His goal is to cover, one at a time, each recognizable dimension in the republican experiment: equal justice, the balance between governmental institutions (within levels and between them), constitutional safeguards in a rule of law, peaceful intentions at home and abroad, popular suffrage, responsible expansion, majority rule with minorities protected, the restraint of necessary military power, the exercise of fiscal responsibility, the diffusion of knowledge through information and education, the safeguarding of the essential individual freedoms from time out of memory, and, far from least, common prosperity encouraged and to some extent engineered.

No central republican aspiration is left out of this catalogue of principles. The auditor or reader, whether early republican or twenty-first-century American, can think of qualifications but not so readily of additions. The compact form of the single paragraph adds to this sense of entirety. The paragraph doesn't exclude, but it can and does stand alone, and the stylistic ease in the compilation further compounds the difficulty of reaching beyond it. Admittedly, there have been many instances in the events of the United States when one or more of Jefferson's principles have been violated, but even here the notion of totality is at work. The interesting thing about the fifteen principles is that they have rather successfully protected one another when violations have occurred. Historically as well as philosophically, they belong to an intrinsic whole beyond a sum of parts.

Significantly, a more strategic mechanism administers these tactical assurances in "the creed of our political faith." One sees this higher level when Jefferson insists that his list of principles belongs to an age of reformation as well as the age of revolution. The many social innovations and geographical expansions of the post-Revolutionary context were the real sources of controversy in 1801, and Jefferson, a child of the Enlightenment, understood that most of his early republican peers were trying to control their anxieties about the future with a very different explanation of unending, positive change. His choice of the term "reformation" is a calculated one. Reformation plays upon the thought processes of a reform Protestant society entering the nineteenth century, and Jefferson's deliberate manipulation of those processes is extensive. His acknowledged role as the architect of "a wall of separation between church and state" doesn't stop him from relying heavily or movingly on religious terminology and forms in his assumption of civic power.[57]

The *First Inaugural Address* is nothing less than a secular sermon in the emerging civil religion of the American republic.[58] Loosely but clearly, Jefferson tracks the familiar mode of the election-day sermon to instill belief in his auditors and faith in the emerging democratic republic. Instead of kneeling figuratively before God, the speaker opens by prostrating himself before the people "here assembled." Their "presence," together with "the favor with which they have been pleased to look toward me," allows a demonstration of *vox populi, vox Dei*: the voice of the people is the voice of God. The speaker, "grateful" for the people's expression, makes much of "the greatness" of their charge in order to "humble myself" before them and it (p. 492). The principles that he announces are repeatedly "sacred" (pp. 492, 495). Central to the "blessings" that he recounts is a "benign religion, professed indeed and practiced in various forms, yet all of them inculcating honesty, truth, temperance, gratitude, and the love of man; acknowledging and adoring an overruling Providence, which by all its dispensations proves that it delights in the happiness of man here and his greater happiness hereafter" (p. 494). Tonally, the address moves from an expression of personal fear and humility toward the certainty of collective salvation. There is talk of the transcendence, devotion, and faith that will make that salvation possible. Most telling of all, Jefferson completes his inaugural in the patent tones of benediction: "And may that Infinite Power which rules the destinies of the universe lead our councils to what is best, and give them a favorable issue for your peace and prosperity" (p. 496). The closing "Amen" of this secular prayer is necessarily implicit but transparent to an audience steeped in the forms of religious service.

The conflation of religious and secular explanation is as much a part of Jefferson as it is of the other writers examined here. We get nowhere in understanding either his words or his philosophical self-confidence without first unraveling the nature of the connection. Jefferson chose as the motto for his personal seal "Rebellion to tyrants is Obedience to God." Called an infidel, he spent considerable time while President editing the gospels in an attempt to find the true words of Jesus. The writer who insists that morals are just as important to a country as manners and habits thinks not just of Montesquieu's political theory but of cosmic design. Human beings were "endowed with a sense of right & wrong" by "He who made us." Jefferson believed, in consequence, "that men are disposed to live honestly," and assumed "the happy truth that man is capable of self-government and only rendered otherwise by moral degradation designedly superimposed on him by the wicked acts of his tyrant." People were innately good; society made them evil, and society could be changed. Jefferson's views depended absolutely on the benevolent design that he found implicit in nature. Days before he died, he wrote that "the general spread of the light of science" and the "opening to the rights of man" were planned and joined by "the grace of God."[59]

Most serious American intellectuals give way to disenchantment over the national experiment if they live long enough in its flux of change. Jefferson affords the great exception. "I have much confidence that we shall proceed successfully for ages to come," he wrote late in life. He was certain as late as 1817 that Providence, to use his favorite term for the Deity, had literally *provided* a setting and context for national greatness through "the moral construction of the world." Despite every disappointment, he held to "belief in the future result of our labors." Belief, in this case, also controlled temperament. "My theory has always been," he concluded, "that if we are to dream, the flatteries of hope are as cheap, and pleasanter than the gloom of despair."[60]

❧

The nature and degree of Jefferson's achievement bring us back to the singularity of his age. Better novels, more nuanced slave narratives, and more cohesive diaries—all beyond the scope of the early republicans that we have examined—appear later in American literature, but no subsequent speech has ever quite matched Jefferson's *First Inaugural Address* in grace of presentation, explanatory power, scope, and simple conviction. Every writing examined here has told us more about what the age believed, how it thought, and where it could be creative. The *First Inaugural* reminds us of something else. It reveals our own limitations. We lack the capacity to create political oratory in the same way today because we no longer believe and think in quite the same way. The leading scholar of the Revolutionary period, Gordon S. Wood, has summarized this problem appropriately when he writes "somehow for a brief moment ideas and power, intellectualism and politics, came together—indeed were one with each other—in a way never again duplicated in American history. . . . We know that something happened then in American history that can never happen again."[61]

There is, however, a matchless irony in Jefferson's achievement. His ability to mask the anxieties of his time has left us with an impoverished view of the period. We accept his vision without being able to duplicate it in part because he has simplified its problems to deliver a larger message. The Apostle of Democracy's ideology of republicanism obscures the hampering weight of the times. Hannah Foster's *Coquette,* Broteer Furro's *Narrative of Venture,* and Nathaniel Ames' diary are all burdened by that weight with its anxieties and problems, and they too address the reader across the centuries. Even the most time-bound of the works before us, Nathaniel Ames' journal, wonders about the readers who will "see this in future time." Ames, in fact, offers a warning in direct address: "do not despise old times too much, for remember that 2 or 3 centurys from the time of seeing this, you will be counted old-time folks as much as you count us to be so now." There is considerable bite in this warning: "do not think yourselves so much wiser than we are as to make yourselves proud, for the last day is at hand in which you must give an account of what you have been about in this state of probation." The entry ends with a marvelously abrupt descent into the quotidian of Ames' own moment: "Dinner is ready," he scribbles to the ages, "I must leave off." [62]

The terminology of the eighteenth-century journal is slightly different and a little quaint today with its talk of "probation." Even so, the youthful Nathaniel, writing all the way back in 1758, hits a permanent mark in the human condition when he says "you must give an account of what you have been about," an injunction that applies to each generation before its inevitable last day is at hand. The writings of our ancestors are intended acts and sometimes desperate cries of communication. Because these same ancestors helped to define us, their writings are there for use. In order to give our own account of what we "have been about," we should first know what our intellectual forebears had to say. Knowing, of course, is not as easy as it sounds, but there are ways around our limitations in thinking about the applicability of the past. How should we use our vantage point?

The juxtaposition of Jefferson's inaugural against a series of more obscure works in fiction, autobiography, and journal-keeping are representative of the early republic in two final ways that further "a methodology of contextual reading." [63] On the one hand, Jefferson, Foster, Furro, and Ames delineate the breadth of utterance to a more-or-less common audience. Their mutual dependence on religious discourse and their need to discuss a certain brand of political conflict indicate as much—even though they use the same words to persuade that audience of different things, with very different purposes in mind, and with different generic considerations in control of their projects. The effort here has been to show the relations between these different statements without denying their separate integrity. The goals have been to find the general base of language to be relied upon in approaching the period and to show how early republicans actually talked on their own terms and what they thought it important to try to say to each other. There is a specificity of equipment in early republican speech that we need to master to approach their lives and thoughts. On the other hand, the actual juxtaposition of these texts underlines a symbiotic tension between them along a universal textual divide. Some works are designed to affirm or deny; others, narrating with an alternative kind of rhetorical complexity, identify a predicament or placement in cultural understanding. We ignore the utility in this tension at our own peril. The generic alternatives valued in a given period can take us beyond the constraints upon imagination that our own social situation imposes. Differences in the texts of the same era begin in the complexity of their own moment; they also bring us into contact with subterranean similarities that might otherwise go unrecognized.

It is impossible to approach either the past or the present without preconceived notions, but we can reach beyond ourselves by heeding a past as rich and as valuable as the present. What was it that early republicans wanted to say to each other and were capable of understanding? How do their words and thoughts shape our own subsequent understanding of a language that is at once mutual and different? The words at risk, the same words repeated in different contexts, have mundane uses as well as exalted meanings. They give us Thomas Jefferson addressing the nation but also Nathaniel Ames rushing to dinner as he grumbles about the distant future. We have to keep in mind the whole range of communication. The meanings of republican formation also contain the means of simple living. Both take on an added explanatory force when we, like William Butler Yeats, "lie down where all the ladders start, / In the foul rag-and-bone shop of the heart."[64]

CHAPTER TWO

The Dialectic of Liberty

Liberty in the eighteenth century was simultaneously the most cherished right that a people could possess and the most volatile term of distinction in political debate. "There is no word that admits of more various significations and has made more various impressions than that of liberty," Montesquieu had written in 1748. By 1776, all parties in the English-speaking world assumed "there is not a word in the whole compass of language which expresses so much of what is important and excellent"; most agreed that "the sound of that single word, LIBERTY, should be equal to an army of other words."[1] Liberty, in consequence, emerged as the term of choice in every disagreement, spawning quite literal armies of words in the pamphlet wars of the Anglo-American conflict. Since liberty covered all that was right, it could just as easily be turned into anything that was needed, and the same writer often used the term in a variety of ways without distinguishing between connotations. Liberty could signify an exact or identifiable right, a loose encomium, a term of worship, membership in the British empire, a personal possession, or the simple enjoyment of property. It also appeared as a badge of virtue, a distinction between peoples, a divine guarantee, a natural law, a political goal, participation in government, an affirmation of security, and not least, as the very worst of apprehensions. The eighteenth century made an absolute claim upon liberty as a concept but feared the relative continuum that it contained. Thus, in *Johnson's Dictionary* from 1755, the first meaning opposed liberty to slavery while the last raised vague alarms over permissiveness; *to take a liberty* led to "exorbitant liberty" and the danger of "license."[2]

No investigation can hope to clarify the myriad confusions over liberty. Eighteenth-century rhetoricians approached the concept from different directions, deliberately conflated the various possibilities, and allowed the term itself to change under the pressure of events. Many of these confusions are of special interest to historians and philosophers of the period. When, for example, Patrick Henry supposedly uttered "give me liberty or give me death" before the Virginia Convention in 1775, the now-famous juxtaposition, liberty or death, already formed a familiar phrase throughout the Anglo-American world. Did Henry actually say these words or not? Insertion of the sentence may have come later through Patrick Henry's first biographer William Wirt.[3] Debates of this kind over the historical record are real ones, but they tend to miss a larger problem at the source. Given universal resort to the term, what are the actual roots of discourse on liberty in early America? The eighteenth century experienced a strategic and now largely hidden conflict over the idea of liberty itself—a conflict with significance for the modern body politic. The evolution of liberty in early America involved two main competing sources and the sudden dominance of one over the other, though the competition between them and conflicting use continue to this day. Arguments over liberty still flow from this dialectic over original meanings.

In effect, two competing modes of thought established a republic based on liberty in America. The first mode, new world Protestantism, provided the oppositional platform from which insecure provincials challenged their mother country. Clergymen were the rhetorical masters of an eighteenth-century American Bible culture, and they used their knowledge to produce the moral differentiation, the dissenting vocabulary, the prospect of union, and the weekly indoctrination from the pulpit that colonials needed in order to come together against the power and hegemony of the British empire. Not for nothing did the loyalist historian Peter Oliver name the ministry "the black regiment" with "so active a Part in the Rebellion."[4]

The second contributing mode of thought drew upon the American idea of law. The idea itself came through English common law and the legal treatises of the European Enlightenment, but Americans quickly made these sources their own. Less independent in voice than its religious counterpart, American legal thought was just as vibrant in developing oppositional terms through a language of rights, and it triumphed in the actual making of the republic. For while ministers gave Revolutionary Americans much cf their moral and intellectual courage to fight, lawyers defined the event and capped its directions.

The movement toward legal explanation had concrete manifestations. 1776 and 1787, the touchstones of Revolutionary achievement, took their meaning from the seminal legal documents that lawyers wrote in those years. Another lawyer would then complete this text-oriented basis of achievement by assigning these documents their ultimate place in an American ideology of liberty. Under enormous pressures in the 1860s, Abraham Lincoln took the Constitution of the United States of America, the "*picture of silver*," and made it the frame of an earlier, all-important "apple of gold," the Declaration of Independence.[5] Through this established centrality, the Declaration became the symbol of American liberty. Lincoln's version of it privileged a national understanding of equality and turned its claim about the pursuit of happiness into an opportunity for all in republican life.

In this way law trumped religion in the process of national formations. Wasn't it logical, after all, for *early republican* lawyers to replace *colonial* ministers when it came to shaping the republic?[6] Many have said so, but the chronological argument falters over the issue of origins, and it fails altogether in assessing how liberty is employed as the lynchpin of choice in cultural understanding. When in crisis, the sometimes loosely joined United States of America have needed all of their intellectual resources, one of which has been "In God We Trust."[7] The same lawyer who completed the textual formations of the republic of laws also saw more forcefully than any other leader the need for providence in articulating the promise of America. In the crucible of the Civil War, Lincoln held the nation to religious understandings in his Gettysburg Address and Second Inaugural. One of his last acts would be to urge his cabinet to devise an amendment that would bring God into the fabric of the Constitution.[8]

The recognition that religious explanation joins legal explanation in the construction of American liberty leaves many questions unanswered.[9] If the religious sources of liberty are powerful and significant, *why* did they disappear from civil discourse so rapidly in the early republic? *Where,* in the continuing dialectic, are the religious contributions to civil and political liberty in American life? *How* did religious and legal sources of liberty interact to produce a distinct American understanding? *What*, if anything, does a closer look at religious explanation restore to a balanced understanding of American liberty? The following four sections take up each of these questions in turn and in order of difficulty.

ॐ

The abrupt removal of religious voices from controlling political discourse in the post-Revolutionary era remains one of the neglected stories in American history. How did it happen? There are essentially three reasons for ecclesiastical disenfranchisement, and each reflects a corresponding strength in the legal temperament. First, the rapid rise of the commercial republic undercut the ministry on both financial and rhetorical grounds even as it enhanced the legal profession. Second, the doctrine of separation of church and state—with enforcement by the legal profession—effectively silenced the ministry on a variety of issues crucial to republican formations. Third, secularization in the early republic provided alternatives to what had been dominant religious explanations of human behavior and external phenomena. A variety of disciplines—science, psychology, economics, history, as well as law—all challenged religious exegesis. Even so, legal thought was most crucial in co-opting political interpretation from the pulpit, and it is important to understand why. "The Evangelical Basis" and "The Legal Mentality" were at once compatible and conflicting modes of explanation in the early "life of the mind in America," but how they joined and where they departed, as well as the ongoing struggle between them, remains to be worked out.[10]

Because the three factors undercutting the clergy reinforced each other in the aftermath of the Revolution, the result was more than a simple acceleration of effects. Financially, ministers lost ground while lawyers grew rich on the settlement of wartime disputes and the land transactions of continental expansion. The dis-establishment of religion also cost ministers dearly; it eliminated state support, leaving them to their congregations on fixed salaries that dwindled during inflationary cycles.[11] Intellectually, commercialism reduced the power of the pulpit in more obvious ways. The presumed moral superiority of America over England during the Revolution had been the special province of ministers who emphasized American simplicity, public-mindedness, sacrifice, and piety over British materialism, cynicism, and depravity. The byword of warning from every Revolutionary pulpit in the land had been "luxury." Ministers turned luxury into a two-headed monster feeding on corruption and lost spirituality, supreme dangers to a virtuous republic fighting for its God-given rights against a British empire seeking taxes for its own gain. But if these warnings bolstered the Revolution, they played less well in the increasingly material culture of the early republic. Instead of uniting against a common external foe, the theme of luxury as vice reminded early republicans of growing differences in their own more complicated moral landscape.[12]

The dis-establishment of religion also translated into clerical exclusion through enforcement of the doctrine separating church and state. For lawyers like John Adams, the earliest understanding of religious freedom involved more than freedom of conscience; it meant opposing clerical authority in the state in all forms, or, as Adams put the matter himself, it meant "deriding . . . the ridiculous fantasies of sanctified effluvia from episcopal fingers."[13] Lawyers like Adams and Thomas Jefferson worked ceaselessly to implement their suspicion of ecclesiastical authority by insisting on the exclusion of religious leaders from all governmental questions.[14] By the Federal Constitutional Convention of 1787, the lawyers who framed the republic would regard the prospect of an official chaplain with disdain.[15] The pattern of exclusion did not end there. With the doctrine of separation of church and state firmly in place, American law would eventually displace or qualify most vestiges of public religious explanation. American courts today restrict religious expression in the civic sphere whenever the secular interest of the state is thought to be present.[16]

Nothing proves the rivalry between legal and religious thought in America more conclusively than the continuing clumsiness of American law in dealing with religious issues. With some exasperation, Justice Byron White complained in 1973 that "one cannot seriously believe that the history of the First Amendment furnishes unequivocal answers to many of the fundamental issues of church-state relations." "In the end," he added defensively, "the courts have fashioned answers to these questions as best they can."[17] Their best, however, has not been good enough for most critics. Leading legal commentators describe an "Alice in Wonderland" quality in Supreme Court interpretations of the religious provisions of the First Amendment of the Federal Constitution. As Leonard Levy has observed, "the Court exercises a freedom almost legislative in character, bringing us close to the intolerable, a Humpty Dumpty Court," where language means whatever the Court says it means.[18] Others find "little doctrinal stability," an "ahistorical manner," "inattention to original meaning," and willful inconsistencies in the judiciary's methodological approaches to the different religion clauses of the First Amendment.[19] Recently, both legal confusion and cultural acrimony achieved new heights when, in June of 2002, the United States Court of Appeals for the Ninth Circuit decided that reciting the Pledge of Allegiance in public schools was unconstitutional because the Pledge includes the phrase "one nation under God."[20] The trouble, of course, is never over religion per se but over the use of religious expression in public discourse, and even these difficulties belong to a longstanding dialectic in which law and religion have shared the national arena and intellectual affinities within it.

Harder to appreciate but much more decisive in the rivalry have been the linguistic homologies that allowed eighteenth-century law to subsume religious thought. Law took the place of religion in early republican civil discourse through structural equivalencies. A guiding providence could be found in Nature as "Nature's God" and, therefore, in something called "the law of nature." It followed that fundamental rights once sacred because they were "antecedent to all earthly government" and "derived from the great Legislator of the universe" could enter legal lexicons instead as inalienable rights, or as natural rights, or even as man-made rights—so long as they began before recorded time, from time immemorial or time out of memory.[21]

Eighteenth-century religious understandings found little to fault in these easy transitions. Patriots, most of whom were also believers, welcomed progress in their legal rights as part of a divine plan. Intellectually and methodologically, they saw significant and comforting correspondences in the forms of presentation: scripture to precedent, dogma to doctrine, liturgy to procedure, sin to crime, the voice of God to the voice of the people. There were good reasons for their presumed familiarity. Each parallel and resemblance referred back to Western legal origins in religious thought, and every lawyer's use of them took the form of professional instinct. European law carved its own emerging independent place out of medieval Christian conceptions of authority and organization. The law took what the Church could give it—often a great deal—and it continued to take at every available opportunity.

The many parallels remind us that the shift towards legal explanation in the early republic should not be overstated. Ministers remained extremely active in celebrating "the sacred cause of liberty," in shaping "visions of a republican millennium," and in crafting the so-called Second Great Awakening, a revivalist event that reached many Americans in the 1790s.[22] Religious fervor may even have increased within the general culture. Nevertheless, religious discourse had much less to do with civic identity in the early republic than it did in the colonial period, and it fell increasingly under the rhetorical sway of natural legal rights.[23]

One can go further. The proficiency with which the law superseded religion in republican formations has created a conceptual divide in the history of ideas.[24] On the one hand, religious displacement from civic discourse has made it harder to determine how early Americans actually thought about the public sphere. On the other hand, the ease with which the law supplanted its philosophical rival has made it just as difficult to differentiate what remains from what has been displaced in public understandings.

A minor incident within a major historical event can signal the dimensions of the problem. The most daring American military campaign in the course of the Revolution—a campaign doomed to failure from the outset—involved the American invasion of Canada in 1775 with the conquest of Quebec as its goal. The Reverend Samuel Spring, Chaplain of the Revolutionary Brigade that marched on Quebec, tells us that just before the expedition set off he gave a rallying sermon to the massed troops over the grave of George Whitefield, the leading revivalist and acknowledged firebrand of the Great Awakening in the 1740s. But Spring did more than preach. Eyewitness accounts reveal that he descended into the grave to remove the collar and wristbands of Whitefield, who had died five years before, and that he solemnly distributed pieces from the articles of clothing to the officers of the expedition in a pledge and guarantee of their righteous cause.[25]

Quebec had been targeted in the first place because of negative colonial reactions to the Quebec Act of 1774, in which Parliament validated Roman Catholicism in Canada. Many American patriots saw the Quebec Act as a jesuitical plot and their own responses as the struggle of liberty against arbitrary power and papal tyranny. To take Quebec would mean to secure the continent for a Protestant vision of this world—and the next![26] Whitefield, the great itinerant preacher

who won converts in mass revivals all over America, stood for three
other useful propositions: first, the intercolonial character of the
Great Awakening and, hence, the projected unity of the new Revolutionary brigade; second, God's imminent involvement in a colossal
American destiny, which certified the connection between political
and religious rights; and third, the power of the religious voice in
American thought, which made ministers guardians of political liberty in America. Not the least officer to receive the talismanic touch of
Whitefield's clothing was Aaron Burr. It would be difficult to find a
more secular mind in the early republic than that of Burr, who fought
bravely in the Revolution but resisted religious conversion at all
points in a long and tempestuous life. Even so, Aaron Burr was the
grandson of Jonathan Edwards, the greatest of American divines, and
he would have known the relevance of Samuel Spring's conviction and
the reasons for it.

There is a balance within the dialectic to be struck here. Religious
fervor reached unusual heights in Revolutionary America, levels that
no culture could maintain indefinitely, but the larger point in raising the Spring incident should not be missed. Early Americans had
no choice but to think through a religious frame of reference; it was
the mental equipment that people brought to daily life, and it was
the ordering device for larger conceptions of history and communal well-being. Furthermore, the root of this conception required the
thinker to accept a premise that Samuel Adams, the organizer of Boston mobs, gave most succinctly. In words that came from many lips
throughout the crisis, Adams claimed "The Religion and public Liberty of a People are intimately connected; their interests are inter-
woven, they cannot subsist separately; and therefore they rise and fall
together."[27]

What did it mean to think that public liberty and religion would rise
or fall so certainly and precipitously together? Although the first radical dissenters in religion colonized America for a variety of reasons
(including commercial gain), their eighteenth-century descendants
gave priority to one motivation only. By 1765, the first settlements in
America stood for a single-minded quest for religious liberty, install-
ing a vital *first* freedom on the American strand. In this eighteenth-
century narrative, while "the first place is due religion," it was "a love

of universal liberty" that supplied the real motivation for settlement, thereby joining the first Puritans to the Sons of Liberty a century and a half apart. The connection, however artificial, was ideologically momentous; it created an account that was at once legally correct (based on historical precedent) and religiously sound (part of God's plan). John Adams summarized the premises involved: "I always considered the settlement of America with reverence and wonder, as the opening of a grand scene and design in Providence for the illumination of the ignorant, and the emancipation of the slavish part of mankind all over the earth."[28]

The same narrative conveniently put the colonies and the colonial speaker at the center of human history. John Adams assumed that Americans knew the most about the inevitable spread of liberty because either a new kind or a special degree of liberty—they amounted to the same thing for Adams—had been born in America. Colonials of all persuasions easily accepted this flattering account, although it was a European, Hector St. John de Crevecoeur, who offered up the most graphic expression. Re-shaping an ugly image to explain how religion worked to the unique benefit of America, Crevecoeur thought he knew why religious belief would lead to harmony instead of persecution in "the most perfect society now existing in the world." Religion resembled gunpowder. In Europe, where it was confined, it tended to explode; in America, spread to the four winds, the gunpowder of religion burned harmlessly but with a glorious flame for all to enjoy.[29]

As secular statements, the claims of Adams, Crevecoeur, and many others sound like naive exercises in self-aggrandizement, and so they were. They allowed everyone who believed them to feel important. But the same claims were also central to unifying formations, and behind them was a religious fervor that lent sincere conviction to mere assertion as well as place to provincialism. In 1742 Jonathan Edwards, the greatest philosopher of early America, supplied an elaborate rendition of the free society in America and what it meant for the world and beyond. The earthly fulfillment of this society added an electrifying dimension to divine promise. "The days are coming when the saints shall reign on earth," observed Edwards in a direct appeal to civic leaders. All Americans were meant to unite in "a strange revolution" that would "renew the world of mankind." For Edwards, "the *New Jerusalem* . . . has begun to come down from heaven," and it would come down first in America. Since "*America* was discovered about the time of the reformation," and since "[only] *America* has received the true religion of the old continent, the church of ancient times," it followed from both scripture and history that "God intends it as the beginning or forerunner of something vastly great." "This work will begin in *America*," Edwards insisted, and he already saw "the first fruits of that glorious day."[30] Elsewhere, he drew intricate analogies between church and community, calling upon both "visibly to unite, and expressly to agree together, in prayer to God for the *common prosperity;* and above all, that common prosperity and advancement, so unspeakably great and glorious, which God hath so abundantly promised to fulfill in the latter days."[31]

One did not have to be a revivalist to emphasize the intrinsic connection of religious and civil liberty in the organization of society. In *A Discourse on the Christian Union* from 1760, Ezra Stiles, a more conservative minister and also president of Yale College, called on all Americans to "stand fast in the liberty wherewith the gospel has made us free." Stiles drew explicit analogies between "the *equality* and *independence* of every congregational apostolic church" and a corresponding freedom in harmony of "the thirteen provinces on this continent." What were churches if not little colonies? Stiles argued that "the same principles may take place in confederating a multitude of lesser bodies, as in confederating larger bodies, such as provinces, cantons, and kingdoms."[32] The American Revolutionaries of the 1770s learned how to translate the confederating premises of religious liberty into direct political action. The premise they shared with Edwards and Stiles left no need for disagreement: a religious people deserved to be free.

Thus far, the religious components of liberty in eighteenth-century America can be traced with some assurance. But how many eighteenth-century Americans listened to ministers who preached like Jonathan Edwards and Ezra Stiles? Even if they listened, and even if church-going was the major social activity of the time, did Americans act upon such statements? Was New England the main source of such language or did the revivalism in other sections, particularly in the western areas of every colony where few sermons were printed, also trigger visions of an America that challenged European hegemony? In the absence of available evidence, historians tend to disagree over these issues and take the debate into the intricacies of denominational, class, and regional difference. If, however, the investigation turns less on levels of belief and more on the formation of general political understandings, a broader connection can be seen. The radical dissenting basis of religion in America, roughly seventy-five percent of the population as opposed to less than ten percent in England during the eighteenth century, made a difference in the approach to politics.[33] How much of a difference? That is the obvious question that remains.

A good answer must carry beyond the articulation of religious liberty as such and toward a more general and philosophical conception of liberty from a religious perspective. One of the shrewdest observers of the times, Edmund Burke, gave a celebrated summary of the American situation before Parliament in 1775:

> Religion, always a principle of energy, in this new people, is no way worn out or impaired; and their mode of professing it is also one main cause of this free spirit. The people are protestants; and of that kind, which is the most adverse to all implicit submission of mind and opinion.[34]

A great deal lay behind Burke's assertions and recognition of a "free spirit" and "principle of energy," particularly in his related implication that both characteristics flowed from religion and toward a political stance about authority. Burke saw the religious temperament that would attach certain ideas about liberty to republican inceptions.

Dissenting Protestantism in America—"adverse to all implicit submission of mind and opinion"—measured temporal authority in severe terms. Worldly leaders were suspect, and that suspicion led toward expansive notions of civil liberty for the subject and an implied equality of consequences for all. American ministers never seemed to tire of noting that kings and counselors went down in the end just like ordinary people. Three of the most renowned rejoinders to authority in colonial America took this route, all from ministers who raised conceptions of liberty through the deaths of kings: they were Benjamin Colman's *Government the Pillar of the Earth* in 1730, Jonathan Mayhew's *A Discourse Concerning Unlimited Submission and Non-Resistance to the Higher Powers* in 1750, and Samuel Davies' *On the Death of His Late Majesty, King George II* in 1760.

Benjamin Colman, pastor of the prestigious Brattle Street Church in Boston, preached his greatest sermon before the civil authorities of Massachusetts. He began by proclaiming that any speaker filled with the Spirit had the right to address "nobles and rulers, captains and the mighty men" in order to "lay 'em low before God." He finished by boldly denouncing all temporal authority as ephemeral and suspect in the best of circumstances. Colman took his text from First Samuel: "For the Pillars of the Earth are the Lord's, and He hath set the World upon them." The leaders in front of him were God's earthly pillars, but every one of these leaders would soon "moulder into dust"; that is, if God's "pleasure" didn't actively destroy them first ("he disposes of them as he pleases"). The Godly ruler was to be obeyed, but what of the ungodly ruler? Colman placed his own trust in Samson, the warrior who tore down the pillars of the Philistines. *"Put not your Trust in Princes,"* he thundered. "We must not look too much at the loftiness of any, nor lean too much on any earthly pillar."[35] The rhetorical power in Colman's challenge had several prongs. Clearly, a minister in colonial America could use the veil of scripture to say what no secular speaker would dare to utter, and this level of freedom of speech belonged, at least by implication, to any one of God's vessels when properly inspired. Then too, and even when trivialized, civil authority had no rhetorical counter to a minister who questioned the secular world through the guiding hand of providence.

Jonathan Mayhew took up the problem of the ungodly ruler with a vengeance. The gist of Mayhew's position in *A Discourse on Unlimited Submission* came in a single sentence where he announced the right to "speak freely" in America. Speaking freely for Mayhew meant choosing between polar opposites. True Protestants lived "on the side of liberty, the Bible, and common sense, in opposition to tyranny, priestcraft, and nonsense." Common sense was the unusual term in Mayhew's otherwise conventional Protestant understanding of the Reformation, and he wielded it much as Thomas Paine would twenty-six years later. For a leader of the liberal reform clergy in Massachusetts like Mayhew, common sense clarified scripture *and* liberty; both came directly from Heaven and reached all of the way down to the people's earthly capacity, enabling them to act as proper judges when a ruler oppressed them. The execution of Charles I was Mayhew's announced theme, but it served in *A Discourse on Unlimited Submission* to claim a general liberty for overthrowing ungodly rulers. Liberty, in this sense, defined the people's right to rebel when their reason told them it was just. In Mayhew's words, "for a nation thus abused to arise unanimously and resist their prince, even to the dethroning him, is not criminal, but a reasonable vindication of their liberties and just rights." *A Discourse on Unlimited Submission* provided a stunning reversal of ordinary political implications. Suddenly, not the attempt to resist but the failure to resist constituted "treason"—treason not just "against the whole body politic" but "against God."[36]

Samuel Davies' eulogy for George II in 1760 applied the patterns of Colman and Mayhew to another aspect of liberty, one that would figure prominently in Revolutionary rhetoric. The Virginia evangelist and new President of the College of New Jersey carefully chose an ambiguous text from Second Samuel for his sermon, "How are the Mighty fallen!" George *was* mighty, but he *had* fallen. Davies used the phrase first to dance a little over the body of George, reminding his auditors, much in the way that Benjamin Colman had, of the triviality of earthly power: "a throne is only a precipice, from whence to fall with greater noise and more extensive ruin into the grave." Everyone knew that George II had been a good monarch. Davies noted the fact but cleverly turned his catalogue of the dead king's virtues to other purposes. The real question was whether a successor, George III, could rise to the same level, and this uncertainty, like the ambiguity in the scriptural text, supplied another opening. The people, Davies observed, had the right to judge between a good and a bad king; for only a king who preserved liberty and the Protestant religion together would find willing obedience in America. In a remarkable addition, he then turned to the subject of *how* the people would exercise their judgment.

Davies' description of the people's solid happiness under George II allowed him to take the logical step toward a *right* of happiness. George II had known "the generous, disinterested, god-like pleasure of making multitudes happy." The colonies, by enjoying his success, "a long and delightful experience" in a "happy reign" of thirty-four years, also had grown accustomed to it. Again and again, Davies emphasized the happiness of the people. "Happy!," he warbled, "thrice happy, to live under a reign so gentle and auspicious!" Obviously, no one could raise a circumstance of life so intensely without contemplation of the opposite condition. What if the people were *not* happy? Repeating the many virtues that George III would have to live up to in George II, Davies raised new worries that would soon become a refrain in America. There was always the danger of "evil counsellors" and "mischievous influence." He closed on an ominous note that would be long remembered. "We can be certain," Davies warned, "of almost nothing but what is past." The gloom in this cautionary note brought the subject of liberty to the edge of a curious inversion. The pursuit of happiness as a positive right would prove most immediately useful to experts on unhappiness.[37]

Gad Hitchcock, pastor of Pembroke Church in Boston, would be that expert in 1774, when he preached what he called his "moving sermon." The performance was moving because his nominal host, General Thomas Gage, the new military governor of Massachusetts, stalked out in the middle of it with retinue in tow. Hitchcock copied other ministers by carefully cloaking himself in the veil of scripture. His text came from Proverbs 29:2: "When the righteous are in authority, the people rejoice: but when the wicked beareth rule, the people mourn." In a performance filled with suspense, Hitchcock steadfastly clung to the sorrows of his people, leaving to his audience the implied conclusion of evil rulers. "The people mourn!" he repeated over and over again in tones of drawn-out sadness. "It is, however, certain that the people mourn!"[38] The adroitness in this strategy lay in the impossibility of a response. If the people were the best judges of their own happiness, and if the people were *supposed* to be happy and they were *not* happy, who but their leaders could be at fault? Unhappiness became its own sufficient indictment.

The pursuit of happiness as part of liberty had many logical philosophical sources, but Christian theology offered the prospect of something more, *complete* happiness. Its radical Protestant variants in colonial America added both the certitude of typological verification (Biblical scripture carried into contemporary historical parallels) and millennialism (the conviction that God's plan included a thousand-year reign of happiness on earth). Put another way, religion in America knew what to do with happiness as a realizable social goal. The relevant biblical quotation that appeared everywhere on Revolutionary lips came from the fourth chapter of the Book of Micah. The passage in question began with a still acclaimed notion of peace ("they shall beat their swords into plowshares"), but the emphasis in eighteenth-century understandings fell upon the personal happiness that would result therefrom: "they shall sit every man under his vine and his fig tree; and none shall make *them* afraid; for the mouth of the Lord of hosts hath spoken *it*."[39]

The passage offers an interesting example of the dialectic of liberty at work in American understandings. The farmer secure on his own land joined Lockean, common law, continental legal, and religious notions. Inasmuch as security through the right of property appealed to every commonwealth theory of government and law, the passage welcomed recognition on both sides of the Atlantic.[40] That said, a more expansive reading necessarily put the emphasis in the quotation squarely on "every man," not just the landowner, and this more general vision of propertied ease played better in boundless America, where the religious context of the passage added to that significance. The figure under his own vine and fig tree was important because he was *unafraid*. He had achieved *tranquility*. Montesquieu gave the popularly cited legal version of the definition in *The Spirit of the Laws*. "The political liberty of the subject," he wrote, "is a tranquility of mind arising from the opinion each person has of his safety."[41] There was a paradox in the definition that only a religious perspective could solve. In a legal or political frame of reference, the notion of tranquility vied directly with a contrary "country or Whig" impulse, the constant need for vigilance. How could anyone be tranquil in the enjoyment of liberty while remaining ever alert against the many dangers that threatened?

Although a religious temperament also required eternal vigilance, the focus of attention involved more manageable sources and a different mechanism of control. The secular lover of liberty worried about a plethora of external pressures on liberty—tyranny, faction, luxury, the ignorant multitude, minority interests, Indian attack, imbalance in government, economic failure, foreign invasion, civil war, incompetent leadership, dissident groups, individual traitors, and so on. The list was endless and largely beyond the observer's control. True, the enlightened observer could turn embattled participant, but then all sense of ease and tranquility would be lost. By way of contrast, a religious temperament lumped every difficulty into one comprehensive category: *sin*.[42] The category itself was large but ideologically under control. The first directive against sin asked each person to look within; only then, did one reach for the external world and blame it for one's troubles. The message from the pulpit was simple. Solve the inner problem of sin and everything would follow in combinations of the godly people of America coming together. In the crisis of the Revolution, minister after minister intoned with the tranquility of conviction, "if God be for us, who can be against us?"[43]

In America, the new-found biblical man who sat unafraid under his own vine and fig tree became a comprehensive symbol of liberty because "God hath spoken it." Here again, civil or legal and spiritual liberty were inseparable but with primacy given to a religious frame of reference. Nathaniel Niles, minister and lawyer, displayed just how this conflated conception of liberty would operate in a crisis with *Two Discourses on Liberty,* a sermon delivered in the North Church of Newburyport, Massachusetts, just after the British closed Boston Harbor in 1774. Liberty was the highest earthly good, but Niles substantiated the claim by proving that civil liberty depended on spiritual liberty: "the former without the latter, is but a body without a soul." Because the civil and spiritual elements were inseparable and the blessings of Heaven, liberty was a duty as well as a right: "it is a loan of heaven, for which we must account with the great God." The individual Christian was to unite with the whole in a cosmic vision of America's struggle with England. Niles's constitutive metaphor for union made the individual a drop in the river of God. "The smallest particles have their influence," he observed. God would take care of the whole if each of his servants exercised a part in proper godliness. If you accepted God, then it was spiritual liberty that united America.[44]

It is almost impossible to exaggerate the confidence with which the religious view of liberty celebrated itself, galvanized colonial Americans, and clarified each stage of America's uncertain struggle with England. The vast majority involved in that struggle still believed that cosmic forces dictated the nature and degree of civic well-being. Specific historical events contained an equally specific spiritual significance—all pointing in Revolutionary rhetoric toward the spread of liberty. "This was from God," ran a typical explanation from the pulpit when Parliament repealed the Stamp Act, "that God who made us free, who gave us our birth-right *liberty.*"[45] Ministers regularly bolstered their anxious flocks with declarations that only authentic religion could make a citizen bold or a soldier brave; only such a person would grasp the true nature of liberty.[46] Similar assumptions held sway in the Revolutionary Army. When Ethan Allen, elected leader of the Green Mountain Boys of New Hampshire, demanded the surrender of Fort Ticonderoga by its British commander in 1775, he did so "in the name of the Great Jehovah and the Continental Congress."[47]

Above all, the religious voices in America could boast a comprehensible arrangement of liberty. God's plan of happiness had been designed specifically for godly communities, and that plan could be known.[48] Knowing it, and then speaking it, was the best assurance of communal happiness in the very near future. Revivalist Joseph Bellamy's sermon on the coming millennium established a trend of thought for thinking about the future. It was so immensely popular in the 1760s and after because, in resorting to biblical parallels, it guaranteed the completion of God's plan of happiness despite the uncertainties of history. The Bible clarified the history to come when read with proper expertise before a believing community. Bellamy carefully charted the prophecies, and they made it "perfectly rational to conclude, that all things are only preparatory, as an introduction to the glorious day."[49]

What happened to this confidence and control of American destiny as seen through a religious conception of liberty and collective happiness? After the Revolution, ministers maintained the spiritual keeping of their congregations, but they lost the capacity to represent the gathered community in political thought. Benjamin Colman's crumbling pillars in *Government the Pillar of the Earth* back in 1730 gave a clue as to what would occur. The confidence of the ministry to speak on civil affairs came from a premise that Colman rendered there with great precision. "As government is the pillar of the earth," he preached then, "so religion is the pillar of government."[50] Americans stopped believing that statement in quite the same way as they went about the formation of republican institutions. Religion remained a concern and for many a central concern, but it was no longer the pillar, no longer the explanatory tool, no longer the primal voice of liberty. Ministers had ceased to be the guardians of social well-being. The keeping of liberty, once a joint responsibility, had passed rather suddenly to the legal mind in America. Something, however, had been lost in the process, and at crucial moments communal sense of that loss would lead to resurgence in the religious side of the dialectic. Religion spoke to the people in a way that law never could. For while the law possesses many virtues, it smells of the lamp, of calculation and reason, of an elitist response; none of these elements ever tells the wistfully searching subject much about happiness.[51]

What difference did passage to a more secular discourse on liberty really make? Legal rhetoric had its own place in colonial oppositional politics, and each of the freedoms just noted in religious discourse—

freedom of religion, freedom of speech, the emerging ideal of equality, even the pursuit of happiness—were entrenched in careful legal argument well before the Revolution. Moreover, lawyers quickly inscribed each liberty in the republican framework. The seventeen state constitutions written during the Revolution, along with the Articles of Confederation, the Northwest Ordinance of 1787, and the Federal Constitution from the same year represented the greatest collective intellectual accomplishment of the age and an achievement in lawmaking that has not been surpassed by any other.[52] The question, then, remains a serious one. What, if anything, has been lost to discussions of liberty by removing religious voices from the fundamentals of civic discourse?

Religion and law were competing frames of reference in the eighteenth century because they thought very differently about common conceptions of authority and legitimacy. If religion demanded a higher faith and the truth of revelation, the law placed its own narrower faith in human artifice and the power of argument. Religion, particularly in its revivalist mode, touched the affections and called on Heaven; law insisted on reason and sought answers in human behavior. Religion assumed divine protection; law protected the rights of those who held proper standing within its rules and who knew how to complain when those rights were infringed. Religion ordered the cosmos; law decided individual cases in dispute. Religion sought all-or-nothing answers; the watchword in every legal answer was balance. Religion searched for the spirit in the word; law classified words for use. These and other distinctions can be exaggerated, but even as approximations they led eighteenth-century proponents of each framework to regard civil liberty in different ways.

Although eighteenth-century law agreed with religion in making liberty an absolute value, it approached the subject in more instrumental ways. Civil liberty and social happiness in a legal understanding depended less on abstractions like virtue and righteousness and more on a well-made constitution and a proper set of laws.[53] The degree of civil liberty to be sought became, in consequence, less a cosmic aspiration and more a calculation of what a culture could bear to receive within its available conformities and conventions. Liberty could thrive in a legal understanding only in keeping with existing communal customs.[54] Philosophically, the legal notion of civil liberty rested on a cautious, nearly redundant foundation. Liberty existed where it could be tolerated; it depended on a rule of law, which is to say on the degree to which ruler and ruled agreed to be governed.[55]

All of these tactical considerations meant in practical terms that the law recognized civil liberty through a strict enumeration of values in context, and the context in colonial America was English common law. As Englishmen, eighteenth-century Americans claimed the right to life, the right of habeas corpus, the right of free speech, the right to a public trial before a jury of one's peers, the right of property, and the related protections of the British constitution. They also understood that these rights extended somewhat vaguely to a larger right to resist oppression. But this last right remained abstract, and it was further qualified by uncertainty over the meaning and import of the term oppression and by the assumption that the British constitution provided the perfect vehicle of liberty for those subjects fortunate enough to fall under its sway. Notably, the clearest justification for resisting oppression in eighteenth-century Anglo-American culture came from the one nonlawyer to contribute greatly to an English concept of law, John Locke, though even Locke, at the end of *The Second Treatise of Government,* qualified the right of resistance, and claimed limited ground for it through natural law, eschewing all argument based on English common law and the ancient constitution, an extraordinary absence in the political theory of the times. Only "a long train of Abuses," language repeated in the Declaration of Independence, should arouse the people. Locke wrote in careful circumlocutions and only about "Cases whereby a King may Un-king himself."[56]

The triggering term for action, oppression, was what would now be called a floating signifier in the legal rhetoric of the eighteenth century. The point on the continuum between unwarranted intrusion, which called for redress, and oppression, which might justify resistance, was identified in different ways. In the English-speaking world of the eighteenth century, it could be treason to talk too much about the distinction or to define the line too finely. The American Sons of Liberty would try to handle the problem by removing all middle ground between the polarities of liberty and slavery to justify their rebellion.[57] Here, of course, was the answer to Samuel Johnson's celebrated jibe: "how is it that we hear the loudest yelps for liberty among the drivers of negroes?"[58]

The two greatest discursive productions of the legal mind in America during the Revolutionary period were John Dickinson's *Letters from a Farmer in Pennsylvania* and the collaboration of Alexander Hamilton, James Madison, and John Jay in *The Federalist*.[59] The two pamphlet series—twelve letters by Dickinson in 1767 and 1768, eighty-five by Hamilton, Madison, and Jay in 1787 and 1788—illustrated the propositions noted above, but they also did more. Written at the beginning and the end of the Revolutionary period, they reflected the problems and the continuities of American legal attitudes toward liberty. As Dickinson's letters awakened the colonies to a qualified but sustained spirit of resistance, so *The Federalist* formalized the final accomplishment of republican formations in the ratification fight over the Federal Constitution. Dickinson, though unwillingly, brought Americans to the edge of rebellion; *The Federalist*, quite willingly, capped the Revolution in the name of a new order.[60] Together, they were central in placing legal restraints on the concept of liberty in contradistinction to the more open-ended avowals of religious thought.

Dickinson was "the penman of the Revolution," centrally involved in every major formal intercolonial document of law from 1765 to 1787 (including the Congressional Resolution against the Stamp Act in 1765, the Declaration of Independence, the Articles of Confederation, and the Federal Constitution). Nevertheless, he was known best in the eighteenth century for *Letters from a Farmer in Pennsylvania.* His *Letters* galvanized American opposition against "taxation without representation" as no other writing. The first of many American pamphleteers to assume an agrarian guise, Dickinson wielded the persona with such success that he was known thereafter as "The Farmer," though in life he was a dynamic lawyer and leading cosmopolite in Philadelphia.[61] *Letters* offered the best technical legal explanation of the colonial right to resist taxation imposed by British authority. Dickinson could accurately boast that he possessed "a greater knowledge in history, and the laws and constitution of my country than is generally attained by men of my class."[62] He then confirmed it by festooning his arguments with detailed footnotes from acts of Parliament and leading authorities in English and continental law. But this legal erudition, based on four years of study at the Middle Temple in London, would prove a straitjacket as well as a resource on the subject of liberty.

Dickinson's commitment to liberty came through the British constitution and common law, and that commitment restricted him to a theory of resistance *within* the comprehension of the British empire. Although every letter from the Farmer summoned Americans to resist British encroachments, he insisted first that "the cause of *liberty* is a cause of too much dignity to be sullied by turbulence and tumult" (III:17), and second, that resistance by force could be justified only when "the people are FULLY CONVINCED that any further submission will be destructive to their happiness" (III:18). Even then, Dickinson refused to contemplate formal rupture between England and her colonies: "we are as much dependent on *Great Britain,* as a perfectly free people can be on another" (II:8). "[W]here shall we find another *Britain* to supply our loss?" he asked, deploring the possibility of separation. "Torn from the body, to which we are united by religion, liberty, laws, affections, relation, language, and commerce, we must bleed at every vein." For Dickinson, only "the constitutional modes of obtaining relief" applied (III:19–20). "Let us behave," he concluded, "like dutiful children, who have received unmerited blows from a beloved parent" (III:20).

The Farmer's reliance upon Anglo-American law held him to a balance that he realized might become impossible. He pleaded for a spirit in which "it will be impossible to determine whether an *American's* character is most distinguishable for his loyalty to his Sovereign, his duty to his mother country, his love of freedom, or his affection for his native soil" (III:18). Liberty was Dickinson's overriding concern, but the exercise of freedom was only one of a number of variables to be factored into an equation. Later, this balancing act would help to prepare early republicans for the concept of dual sovereignty; at the moment, circumstance and legal theory were already pushing Dickinson and his readers off the intellectual tightrope that he had designed so carefully. As English commentators like Samuel Johnson would point out, the rights of Englishmen came with legal obligations: the assertion of the former included accountability to the latter. "[I]t seems to follow by consequence not easily avoided," wrote Johnson, "that [our colonies] are subject to English government, and chargeable by English taxation." By resorting to English rights and English law to support their right to object, the colonies remained under those laws and could not pick and choose between them. In Johnson's withering summary, "these lords of themselves, these kings of *me,* these demigods of independence, sink down to colonies, governed by a charter."[63]

Acceptance of English law left Dickinson with another problem.

Over and over, *Letters from a Farmer in Pennsylvania* posed a leading question to which there was no answer. Where was colonial unity when it was most needed (II:14, IV:24–25, VI:36, VIII:46–47, X:65–67, XI:77)? Dickinson complained that the colonies in 1767 were not opposing Parliament's newest incursions against colonial liberties with anything like the unified zeal that led them to thwart the Stamp Act just two years before, and this was true even though the new Townshend Act of 1767 (with its duties on glass, paper, and other imports) and the equally new Declaratory Act (insisting on Parliamentary supremacy over the colonies in all matters) were as dangerous to American liberties as the Stamp Act had been. He feared that *"we have already forgot the reasons that urged us with unexampled unanimity, to exert ourselves two years ago"* (XII:81). Americans needed to recover what had been lost. They had to realize anew that their liberty could only be secured through unified opposition (X:67–68).

Not surprisingly, communal unity proved much harder for Dickinson to project than it was for reformist ministers, who orchestrated continental harmony through their vision of a religious liberty peculiar to the new world. For the Farmer, the politically unified opposition to the Stamp Act had been "unexampled." Colonial solidarity of any kind was a rarity and hardly the norm in a British empire where colonies dealt with the mother country far more frequently than with each other. Dickinson's stress upon chartered membership in that empire only underlined the issue. The British Constitution secured English liberties everywhere in the empire but *through* Britain, *through* British government. Dickinson could call for colonial unity all he wanted, but his own theories forced him to admit "these colonies are dependent on *Great-Britain*" and "[Britain] has a legal power to make laws for preserving that dependence." Power was not the end of the matter. Dickinson accepted that Parliament possessed the legal right and the political duty "to preserve [colonial] dependence, and the connection of the whole in good order" (V:27–28).

An orientation in common law gave strength to legal resistance but undermined more radical assertions of liberty. A telling simile exposed Dickinson's predicament. "The *legal authority* of *Great Britain*," he wrote at the end of *Letters from a Farmer in Pennsylvania*, "may indeed lay hard restrictions upon us; but like the spear of *Telephus*, it will cure as well as wound (XII:81)." In classical mythology, Telephus can only be healed by the rust of the spear that wounded him, and Dickinson's legal cures contained such a wound. The common law revealed the nature of Parliamentary abuse, but it, in its healing powers, could not be used to challenge the supremacy of British authority under the constitution.

The dilemma for the colonial legal mind in the act of resistance can best be seen in the controlling legal text of the era, a text that had a phenomenal impact on American culture generally.[64] William Blackstone's *Commentaries on the Laws of England* (1765–1769) unified law, nation, and history around a proposition taken from Montesquieu's *Spirit of the Laws,* a source that doubled the credibility of the basic claim in Anglo-American legal circles. In Blackstone's words, "a learned French authority [Montesquieu] . . . hath not scrupled to profess, even in the very bosom of his native country, that the English is the only nation in the world, where political or civil liberty is the direct end of its constitution." All of English history, in Blackstone's view, had to be read as the recovery of ancient liberties and rights through the evolution of a proper constitution that had achieved final perfection in the Glorious Revolution of 1688. That constitution had achieved permanence—"ESTO PERPETUA!"—because it *was* proper and perfect for all concerned. No matter how dire the problem, every grievance could be resolved by constitutional remedy. "The vigour of our free constitution," Blackstone explained, "has *always* delivered the nation from these embarrassments [attacks on liberty], and as soon as the convulsions consequent on the struggle have been over, the balance of our rights and liberties has settled to its proper level."[65] Always? The common law tied everyone to its common solution: remonstrance, yes; rebellion, no.[66]

Lawyers more radical than Dickinson worked to solve this legal dilemma. As resistance mounted, they found it expedient to tie English rights to natural rights, and they were helped by the fact that natural law functioned as a parallel source of liberty in the eighteenth century, rendering the connection to English liberties plausible.[67] James Otis, the lawyer whom John Adams termed "the earliest and the principal founder" of the Revolution, showed the way in *The Rights of the British Colonies Asserted* (1764).[68] Otis realized that a guarantee of rights through the colonial charters would always remain unstable. Parliament could revoke the charters of colonial rights whenever it wished to do so; that was what Parliamentary supremacy meant. It could not, however, touch English rights deemed natural, and Otis used the distinction to declare "every British subject born on the continent of America or in any other of the British dominions is by the law of God and nature, by the common law, and by act of Parliament (exclusive of all charters from the crown) entitled to all the natural, essential, inherent, and inseparable rights of our fellow subjects in Great Britain."[69]

Much of the subsequent success of Revolutionary rhetoric depended on how well lawyers manipulated Otis' grab bag of legal authorities on liberty. There were legal rights, they began to insist, that didn't need to be written out. As the Massachusetts Stamp Act Resolves argued in 1765, these rights were "founded in the Law of God and Nature," and they were "the common Rights of Mankind."[70] Matters came to a head in 1774 when Congress debated whether to rely on natural law as well as British law in its responses to the Crown, and John Adams, who often saw farther than others in the 1770s, came up with the winning argument. Asked "whether we should recur to the law of nature, as well as to the British constitution," Adams announced himself "very strenuous for retaining and insisting on it, as a resource to which We might be driven by Parliament much sooner than We were aware."[71] The balance would tilt toward natural law and away from British rights in the Revolution. But while Adams and other Revolutionary lawyers raised natural law in defense of liberty at each turn in the contest, every use carried them back to a rival frame of reference. Arguments based on natural law turned in the end on a religious conception of liberty and that conception, based on the order of the universe rather than on contextual exposition, would force lawyers to be more open-ended and vague about liberty and claims of rights than the legal mind could long accept with comfort.[72]

To the extent that a benevolent natural world was essential to the concept of inalienable or inherent liberty, it depended on the presence of a design antecedent to human society. Somewhere, somehow, there had to be an earlier force in the universe that sustained natural rights for those rights to have universal validity beyond a British frame of reference. There was, in fact, no real alternative for an eighteenth-century American who wanted to sustain challenges to British authority. If the universal order proved to be arbitrary in its treatment of individual human beings, then who could argue against the presence of arbitrary authority in England or, more particularly, against the exercise of that authority elsewhere? The rights of Englishmen in America meant so much more if the British sovereign who professed to rule by divine law was concurrently bound by God's will in a way for anyone to observe through the design of nature. Accordingly, ministers confirmed the design of nature as part of God's plan, while lawyers made it visible and practical with the claim that natural law constrained civil law. The Reverend Samuel West, among others, affirmed that the law of nature prevented "anything that is immoral, or contrary to the will of God, and injurious to their fellow-creatures." Natural law remained as "unchangeable as the Deity himself, being a transcript of his moral perfections."[73] For James Otis, who thought "*a lawyer ought never to be without a volume of natural or public law, or moral philosophy, on his table or in his pocket,*" the same hold of natural law over human action in society opened an argument that many would use. Since government had "an everlasting foundation in the *unchangeable will of god*, the author of nature, whose laws never vary," violations of natural law were illegal. "If such a proceeding is a breach of the law of nature," Otis wrote, "no law of society can make it just."[74]

These arguments, endlessly repeated in a variety of forms, served the Revolution well, but they raised substantial problems in the peace that followed. The right of the people to turn natural law against positive law applied just as easily to political authority under the Articles of Confederation as it had previously under the British crown. The new rulers in America soon found that open-ended ideas of liberty under natural law were hard to control, and they were especially alarmed by the exaggerated sense of rights that followed therefrom. A reallocation by the legal mind was already evident in 1778, when Theophilus Parsons penned his criticisms of a proposed constitution for Massachusetts. *The Essex Result,* written by a man who would become Chief Justice of the Supreme Judicial Court of Massachusetts and who would be known throughout New England as "the giant of the law," prefigured much that would happen in the Federal Convention nine years later, right down to a first articulation of the theory of checks and balances and the naming of an ideal bicameral legislature as "the house of representatives" and "the senate."[75]

The Essex Result sought to curb domestic unrest, the unfortunate by-product of Revolutionary zeal. Parsons worried about the rise of "the artful demagogue, who to gratify his ambition or avarice, shall, with the gloss of false patriotism, mislead his countrymen." Why were the people in danger of being so easily misled? Caught up in the rhetoric of the times, they tended to exaggerate their own role when "the voice of the people is said to be the voice of God." "No man," Parsons observed, "will be so hardy and presumptuous, as to affirm the truth of that proposition in its fullest extent." A "false patriotism" had grown from inflated conceptions of liberty, and the combination was preventing a proper legal balance from emerging in the new order. "The idea of liberty has been held up in so dazzling colours," Parsons complained, "that some of us may not be willing to submit to that subordination necessary in the freest States." In short, the people had lost their proper sense of place under the restraints of wise leadership ("gentlemen of education, fortune, and leisure"). Constitutions and the law were *for* the people but not *by* them. "We are to look further than to the bulk of the people," Parsons wrote, "for the greatest wisdom, firmness, consistency, and perseverance." Direction had to come from above if the laws were to be "wisely and consistently framed," and Parsons was direct about what this meant. A further enumeration of constraints had to regulate civil liberty.[76]

The authors of *The Federalist* agreed with Theophilus Parsons' assumptions in *The Essex Result* and wrote in 1787 to implement them through the ratification of the Federal Constitution. Like Parsons, they roundly condemned "a zeal for liberty more ardent than enlightened."[77] They feared the passions of the people, planned to have those passions "controlled and regulated by the government" (49:331), deplored the loss of a "spirit of moderation" in public discourse (37:225), and wanted to establish a new "requisite stability and energy in government" against "the inviolable attention due to liberty" (37:227). Like Parsons, they found their answers in the proper design of strong government: "the genius of the whole system; the nature of just and constitutional laws" (57: 373, 1:5).

The intellectual affinities between *The Essex Result* and *The Federalist* flowed from a mutual source, the legal temperament of the period. Alexander Hamilton, James Madison, and John Jay can be distinguished from each other, but they shared this temperament to an extraordinary degree in *The Federalist*. They agreed that a stronger legal union would be necessary to "repress domestic faction and insurrection" (9:51); also that their legal knowledge had prepared them to design "the more perfect structure" or "proper structure" so definitely needed (9:48, 10:62). Abstractions like republican virtue,

enlightened reason, and natural law were dangerous enthusiasms not
to be trusted in the business of forming "a more perfect union"
(10:53–58, 49:329, 51:340).

The Revolution had been a success but mistakes had been made in
the aftermath. "Is it not time," Hamilton sneered, "to awake from the
deceitful dream of a golden age, and to adopt as a practical maxim for
the direction of our political conduct that we, as well as the other inhabitants of the globe, are yet remote from the happy empire of perfect wisdom and perfect virtue?" (6:33). Madison made it equally
clear that anyone who trusted to "reverence for the laws" and "the
voice of enlightened reason" as constraints was dreaming of "a nation of philosophers . . . as little to be expected as the philosophical
race of kings wished for by Plato" (49:329). Only a strong government "framed with singular ingenuity and precision" could hope to
hold the passions of the people in place (49:332). "If men were angels," cautioned the ever-practical Publius, or "if angels were to govern men, neither external nor internal controls on government would
be necessary." Fortunately or unfortunately, there were no angels in
human affairs. "In framing a government which is to be administered
by men over men," strict design and meticulous controls were the essential ingredients. A careful balance of "opposite and rival interests"
with an even more careful "subordinate distribution of powers" had
to supplant "the defect of better motives" (51:337). Republican lawgivers could not afford to trust to the ideals of the day. They were to
remember instead that "the ordinary administration of criminal and
civil justice" formed the "great cement of society" (16:103) and that a
government for the people had better be "tolerable to their prejudices" before it could hope to be "best suited to their happiness"
(38:234).

The legal temperament behind *The Federalist* espoused such views
with an assurance born of the secular Enlightenment in American
thought. Hamilton, Madison, and Jay wrote with extraordinary confidence. Faced with the unprecedented prospect of a continental republic, they nonetheless believed that they personally held the important answers to the problem at hand.[78] The intellectual quality of their
self-assurance is easy to miss because, as men of affairs, they appeared
impatient of theoretical assertion and moral abstraction.[79] The combination, an impatience based upon practical certitude, meant two
things. First, the authors of *The Federalist* were quick to dismiss their
primary intellectual competitors in eighteenth-century thought, the

clergy. To be sure, all three authors of *The Federalist* paid lip service to the "Almighty hand" that guided them, but they were adamant in linking religious zeal to faction and in discounting moral and religious arguments as a source of political definition.[80] Second, they were just as quick to propose the legal temperament as the best guide of republican destinies. "Federalist No. 35," ostensibly on taxation, gave several pages to "the man of the learned profession" as the best arbiter and most objective leader in a political dispute (35:214–215).[81]

In sum, *The Federalist* did more than cap the Revolution by calling for the ratification of the Federal Constitution; it confirmed, once and for all, the dominance of legal over religious explanation in civic discourse. Learned contrivance, practical artifice, and hard-headed institutional planning were the keys to a new mental adventure where those engaged knew they were neither angels nor under the control of angels. Philosophically, in dismissing the relevance of angels, Publius expressed the shift in a single sentence. "But what is government itself," he asked, "but the greatest of all reflections on human nature?" (51:337). The priorities established here reached well beyond *The Federalist*. What were the implications of calling Government *"the greatest of all reflections on human nature"*? By insisting that the best focus of human endeavor belonged to the study of institutions and worldly behavior, Publius carried Americans toward a new balance in the conception of liberty. Henceforth, liberty would appear more in the guise of governmental prescription, enactment, and protection and less forcibly as an assertion of abstract, inalienable right.

The priorities of *The Federalist* bring the inquiry back to the original question of this chapter. If the eighty-five letters of Hamilton, Madison, and Jay represent the nation's most influential exposition of constitutional protections, they also remain the touchstone text in placing liberty under the constraints of government. What then, if anything, has been lost—or gained—in the conception of modern liberty? The benefits achieved in contemporary liberal society are perhaps too obvious to list; prosperity and the legal emphasis on individual rights have granted the majority of American citizens the freest opportunity in history to pursue their happiness. It follows that the general idea of gain should be kept in mind to protect the inquiry about loss from misrepresentation. The corresponding idea of loss, in turn, should be

approached with caution. The primary question—"what then, if anything, has been lost?"—has nothing to do with nostalgic impulses or
with a projected act of recovery or rescue. Meaningful responses must
concentrate instead on the historical construction of liberty as an idea
and its relation to ongoing American understandings.

The farthest reaching legal definition of liberty in eighteenth-century America came from an English source. Blackstone's *Commentaries on the Laws of England* declared that "liberty, rightly understood, consists in the power of doing whatever the law permits."
These words implied that legal enactment defined the scope of liberty,
and the writer of them was notoriously quick to reconfigure personal
rights as civil obligations.[82] Still, Blackstone necessarily thought in
eighteenth-century terms. He *automatically* assumed a fundamental
law prior to all human intervention, accepting what critics now call
"a preinterpretive concept of law."[83] As he put the matter himself,
"the principal aim of society is to protect individuals in the enjoyment
of those absolute rights, which were vested in them by the immutable
laws of nature. . . . Hence it follows, that the first and primary end of
human laws is to maintain and regulate these *absolute* rights of individuals."[84]

Blackstone agreed with John Locke in presenting "the natural liberty of mankind," and, like Locke, he had little difficulty in finding
liberty "posterior to the formation of states and societies," mediate
to common human understanding, and traceable to God. "This natural liberty," Blackstone wrote, "consists in a power of acting as one
thinks fit, without any restraint or control, unless by the law of nature: being a right inherent in us by birth, and one of the gifts of God
to man at his creation, when he endued him with the faculty of free
will."[85] Eighteenth-century participants, whether governors or governed, made these assumptions facts by applying simple reason to the
law of nature. In Lockean terms, "Reason, the common Rule and
Measure, God hath given to Mankind" unlocked the secrets of a natural order that defined acceptable human behavior and formed discernible law ("it is certain there is such a Law, and that too, as intelli-
gible and plain to a rational Creature, and a Studier of that Law,
as the positive Laws of Common-wealths, nay possibly plainer").[86]
Much followed therefrom. As long as such premises on natural law
remained in place, liberty as a basic conception was inalienable or, to
use Blackstone's language, it belonged to "absolute rights . . . which
every man is entitled to enjoy whether out of society or in it."[87]

But what if Nature turns out *not* to be mediate? What if human reason fails to discern a liberty prior to formal institutions? What if law rests entirely on its own language and protest against it must be mounted through its own enactments? If these revocations become accepted truth, then Blackstone's definition—liberty consists in the power of doing whatever the law permits—takes on some negative connotations, and the user of it comes perilously close to the predicament that John Dickinson faced in *Letters from a Farmer in Pennsylvania*. You cannot defy a legal regime if you accept its values as your restrictive gauge of meaning. You must be able to stand outside to rebel against. You need a preinterpretive concept of law to challenge legal interpretation.[88]

It should be clear that American law has reached most if not all of the positions raised in the interrogatives of the last paragraph. Few observers today, with a vastly extended and complicated conception of the universe before them, regard Nature as mindful of (or patterned for) specific human needs. Neither philosophers nor lawyers celebrate common reason now. In the words of a frequently cited contemporary source, "technically, of course, reason alone can't tell you anything; it can only connect premises to conclusions."[89] Even less modern credence has been given to a concept of liberty based on a prior state of nature. Contemporary theorists generally discount natural law as the undergirding force in legal thought. We now live in an age of rampant legal positivism. Most legal systems in the world today accept an exclusive hegemony of their own devising and turn to their own empirical structures for the solutions to even epistemological problems. Legal positivism projects its own morality, resisting all other criteria: "at the very heart of its case, [it] affirms the reality of legal obligation, based on nothing more than the actual law in effect."[90]

Does one need an external gauge to justify and safeguard fundamental rights? An argument in response must remember the balances involved. Legal positivism protects fundamental rights vigorously and with great accuracy through the formal stipulations of its own system. Many fundamental rights—for instance, the right to life, to a prompt public trial, to a jury of one's peers, to free speech, to protection from false imprisonment, to freedom of religion, and to a free press—welcome in their tangibility the specificity of statute and case law. As long as one accepts the proposition that positive law coincides with a just social order—a proposition that most Americans have been willing to acknowledge through their history—the problem of articulating and safeguarding fundamental rights remains internally consistent and manageable. From the other side of the coin, natural law as a preinterpretive concept of law hardly represents a panacea in any discussion of rights. In the eighteenth century at the height of its intellectual legitimacy, natural law came into play as a legal remedy only in extreme cases or in a time of crisis. Lawyers had many reasons even then for not trusting to its loose constructions and potential excesses.

But none of these considerations quite reaches the interactive complexity of American law and religion over the idea of liberty, and there remains the question of how origins now lost or diminished must figure into the equation. Within American law, liberty is a very different kind of fundamental right than others. Less tangible and hardly ever a legal remedy on its own, liberty functions rather as a comprehensive reminder of all legal remedies. When modern legal interpreters talk about liberty, they instinctively employ a language that pulls them beyond the specificity of legal determination. For instance, when Justice Brandeis describes a right of privacy as intrinsic to liberty in *Olmstead v. United States,* he discusses "conditions favorable to the pursuit of happiness" and "the significance of man's spiritual nature, of his feelings and of his intellect."[91] When liberty comes up in another context, Brandeis' colleague Justice McReynolds admits that the Supreme Court cannot really "define with exactness the liberty thus guaranteed," but he knows that "without a doubt, it denotes not merely freedom from bodily restraint, but also the right of the individual to contract, to engage in any of the common occupations of life, to acquire useful knowledge, to marry, establish a home and bring up children, to worship God according to the dictates of his conscience, and generally to enjoy those privileges of happiness by free men."[92] The striking fact about such comments is that they assume and depend on a spiritual level of explanation. These and other courtroom formulations of liberty need the kind of terminology—happiness, feelings, conscience, spirituality—that they would otherwise reject as insufficiently analytical or vague. They assume the individual worth and desirable well-being that religion supplies.

The value of natural law in eighteenth-century discussions of liberty resided largely in its integrative evaluative function on this ethical plane of explanation. It was ethical in its assurance of the harmonies that correct human behavior could be expected to reach. It was integrative in that it supplied a standard against which the legal system of that day could be tested.[93] The cultural power of that standard should not be underestimated. Revolutionary Americans regarded small intrusions as absolute challenges to liberty through their immersion in natural law norms. They were not prepared to obey a law of the state contrary to reason or against the ordained consent of the governed.[94]

How would contemporary Americans respond to a similar intrusion today? Surely not with the rubrics of natural law. The quiescent response of public opinion and political opposition in 2002 to the federal government's anti-terrorist policies—"sweeping claims of unbridled executive authority to hold secret deportation hearings, label and incarcerate 'enemy combatants' without access to lawyers or judges"—offers a case in point. What might have formerly led to general protest against the invasion of the fundamental right of habeas corpus has been fought out instead on the highly technical level of a federal judiciary that asks the government to show the courts what it is doing.[95] The nature of protest has changed to match a larger shift in the understanding of what law has become.

The philosophical problem raised in the loss of natural law as a viable resource for objection to positive law has been stated quite simply: "no intrinsic quality of law ensures its morality in the manner of natural law."[96] The loss is significant because acts of resistance demand a moral imperative. To resist the overwhelming authority of the state requires a special cognizance on the part of an actor who undergoes an unknown level of risk. "Why am I willing to hazard this much?" a resisting person must ask in order to achieve the inner coherence necessary to perform against a far more visible establishment. That coherence requires an element of inner spirit. Significantly, the patterns of resistance against state imposition in American history have tended to pit religious morality against established law. The abolitionist movements of the antebellum period, the right-to-vote protests after the Civil War, the prohibition movement in the first decades of the twentieth century, the anti-war and civil rights movement of the 1960s, and the anti-abortion protests of contemporary times have all relied heavily on religious impulses to make their cases. Are the alternative explanations that religion has always given to the concept of liberty still available? Yes, they are. In a crisis, belief in a collective or communal happiness appeals at least as much as the protected conditions that allow the individual pursuit of it. As the remarks of Justices Brandeis and McReynolds have just demonstrated, the language of religion remains a resource.

Even so, the dialectic of liberty is not the same. Legal positivism has become profoundly secular in its impulses and trajectory, and there are severe limits to what it will allow itself to receive from outside its frame of reference. On its own terms, positive law cannot go beyond the experience of freedom within its immediate domain, and it rejects ethical challenge to its carefully reasoned internal coherence.[97] The basis if not the dimensions of this intransigence began almost in the same moment that Publius wrote *The Federalist.* Alexander Hamilton and his colleagues sought to strengthen the uncertain normative footing of positive law in their own time. In practical terms, their orientation required them to present the Federal Constitution in an attractive enough stance to secure moral sanction through the consent of the people. In legal terms, it meant preserving while at the same time curbing individual liberty in order to increase the ability of the state to make law.[98] Since then, the power and authority of the state to make and enforce law have increased a hundredfold while acceptance of liberty as a rhetorical guide to action has dwindled.

Liberty today is all too often an abstraction taken for granted in American discourse. Success has not bred contempt, but it has discouraged articulation in the face of change. Liberty is the lightly tongued given, like the air we breathe. Vigilance in protecting it is no longer a communal calling card. After all, the problem of preserving liberty while guarding the authority of the state can seem hopelessly abstract so long as the state is understood to be just. But what if the state grows unjust, or wrong, or simply misinformed? To what extent would the legacy of Revolutionary leaders who spoke a vaguely familiar but very different language more than two hundred years ago suffice in response? Somewhere in the dialectic of liberty, a republic defined by the right of revolution has been replaced by a modern nation state where the test of membership has become loyalty.[99] The members of that nation state should think more about what this institutional metamorphosis means in practice, and the intricate eighteenth-century root system in the liberty tree is a good place to begin. The suggestion here is not of return but of useful realization. Liberty, always a vexed value, is best protected by knowledgeable debate over its many meanings and applications.

CHAPTER THREE

The Commonalities of *Common Sense*

Historians always note the great impact of Tom Paine's *Common Sense* in 1776, and critics agree in calling it "one of the most brilliant pamphlets ever written in the English language." Yet, despite the frequency of these claims, they are rarely brought together as mutually informing insights or controlling premises.[1] On the one side, the twin appeals of the pamphlet—the historical assertion of immediate impact and the literary assessment of timeless merit—make it an extraordinary source for gauging how Americans think about themselves and their country, then and now. On the other side, the same unique combination of instant effect and lasting influence welcomes rhetorical analysis, turning *Common Sense* into a seminal text for thinking about the art of persuasion in American life. What is more, precisely how the pamphlet persuades its readers is an object lesson in the workings of modern democratic culture. The way Americans have absorbed *Common Sense* into collective memory remains an untold story in ideological formations.

There is, in fact, no other written production in American culture quite like *Common Sense*. No other text by a single author can claim to have so instantly captured and permanently held the national imagination.[2] At a time when the largest colonial newspapers and most important pamphlets had circulations under 2000, *Common Sense* achieved between 120,000 and 150,000 copies in its first year alone. It was the first truly American best-seller. Hundreds of thousands of Americans, perhaps a fifth of the population in all, either read *Common Sense* or had it read to them during the course of the Revolution. Paine could credibly boast that his work had achieved "the greatest sale that any performance ever had since the use of letters."[3]

Other leaders of the Revolution were almost as extravagant in their praise, and their comments convey another quality, the innate vitality in Paine's words. George Washington called *Common Sense* "unanswerable" and found it to be "working a powerful change . . . in the minds of many men." Benjamin Franklin thought its effect "prodigious." Benjamin Rush wrote that "it burst from the press with an effect which has rarely been produced by types and papers in any age or country."[4] When modern scholars test these earlier assessments, they agree that Paine "transformed the terms of political debate" and "forged a new political language."[5] And there are good reasons for such glowing appraisals. Much of the terminology of national discourse, including the term "United States of America," can be traced to Paine's Revolutionary writings.[6] The rhetorical patterns initiated in *Common Sense* have become intrinsic to American political speech, and they are now permanently embedded in the expressions of identity on which the culture depends.

The originary powers of *Common Sense* remain crucial rhetorical ingredients for another reason: they made the pamphlet all things to all people. Every brand of American politics finds some justification in its pages, and the glass that Paine so beguilingly offers can be either half empty or half full as each occasion or cause commands. The bold hardihood of a continental union and the utter fragility of that union both receive first expression here: "now is the seed time of continental union," but also "the least fracture now will be like a name engraved with the point of a pin on the tender rind of a young oak."[7] Here as well for the first time is the daring prediction of a legitimating national constitutional convention, but this optimism appears against a deliberately gloomy backdrop, "the precariousness of human affairs." *Common Sense* inaugurates both sides of a never-ending debate in American federalism. It demands a stronger union ("The Continental belt is too loosely buckled") while also recognizing the hold of local identities ("the force of local prejudice").[8]

Common Sense succeeds in having it both ways on debates that will consume the later body politic. The pamphlet famously resists government and authority, making them necessary evils, but it simultaneously lauds both in its new plan ("the glorious union of all things") and in its exaltation of a proper order ("in America THE LAW IS KING").[9] Revolutionary Americans learn that, like Noah, "we have it in our power to begin the world over again," but they also receive the first in a whole series of stock political warnings: their house, when divided against itself, will not stand; their virtue, because not cultivated, will disappear; their common sense, as it becomes less vigilant, will tumble before "the mind of the multitude," and so on.[10] Not least, Paine's assertions of strength in unity must be read against a counter proposition: danger lurks everywhere from a hidden enemy within.[11]

A manic-depressive quality governs such prose—a quality that has become standard fare in American politics.[12] Paine, the pamphleteer, instinctively knew what the more philosophical thinkers of his day failed to grasp. He saw that material success in the secular state might be boring instead of dramatic, that the result might prove hollow or even comic rather than enlightened. In celebrating the promise of America, he realized that communal well-being might best be appreciated in a context of crisis. The presumed glory of America could be made to matter more if the country itself seemed to teeter on the very edge of ruin and chaos. Danger, properly conveyed and then overcome, would carry mere prosperity toward the realms of higher accomplishment.[13]

These and other ambiguities shape the rhetorical stances as well as the themes of later generations. *Common Sense* insists that "the cause of America is in a great measure the cause of mankind," but it also orders Americans to protect themselves from the rest of the world.[14] Paine blithely punctuates his claims of reasonableness and disinterestedness with other, disconcerting demands for revenge.[15] Sometimes a lofty civic virtue appears as the linchpin of American endeavors; at other times, the practical world of commerce appears to dominate the writer's expectations; and at still others, market forces are definitely the enemy. Greater wealth will help to defend the new republic, but Paine also warns that it will encourage "the trembling duplicity of a spaniel" in leaders who will have more to lose.[16]

The conflict of alternatives in *Common Sense* can be quite direct. Paine congratulates Americans for their "spirit of good order and obedience" on one page and condemns them for their dangerous lawlessness on another.[17] Even as he castigates his opponents for "intermingling religion with politics," his own narrative constantly conflates biblical and secular imagery and explanation.[18] Thematically, the stakes on the table always seem to be at their highest when Paine pauses to claim methodologically that he actually writes to avoid exaggeration and hyperbole.[19]

Such extremes in theme and tone are everywhere in the pamphlet, and they are important beyond themselves. They help to explain how the widest range of readers could be pulled into Paine's orbit, and they identify the birth of a distinctively American voice in politics. More immediately, these extremes need to be incorporated into a larger philosophical and rhetorical frame of reference, for when they are not they become seeming contradictions in terms, blocking awareness of the underlying consistencies and overall aesthetic integrity of *Common Sense*. J. G. A. Pocock conveys the frustrations that many readers bring to these problems when he claims that *Common Sense* "does not consistently echo any established radical vocabulary" and that Paine himself "remains difficult to fit into any kind of category."[20] As often as not, the seeming inconsistencies in the work are often traced, verified, and then tied to the more apparent irregularities in the author's life.

Paine has been called a raucous haranguer (too embittered to think about style), a journalist shopping the ideas of others, a propagandist rather than an original thinker, and an opportunist of expression instead of a philosopher of thought. Even his most careful defenders tend to speak disparagingly of his weakness in argument and his deficiencies in intellectual originality.[21] But while many of these criticisms apply to the man, they divert attention away from his text, and they tend to disregard the overarching craft of the writer. The impressive things about *Common Sense* are intrinsic to the rhetorical structure and narrative pace of the pamphlet. Paine orchestrated ideological unities out of fragments, and he knew how to wrap his readers in the sincerity of his claims.

The strength of the work can also be seen in an oddly compelling historical fact from 1776. Paine was the only figure in the pantheon of Revolutionary leaders to achieve his place entirely through authorship. Whatever they wrote, the other republican founders owed something to their original station, their prowess in the field, their political accomplishments, their subsequent positions, their good fortune in

events, their families, their regional affiliations, their wealth, their political alliances, or their location within some other grouping. Paine
stood alone in this regard. Now a citizen of the world, he was then
an isolated, impoverished immigrant who gained attention wholly
through his writings. An embarrassment in every political position
that he would later fill, he possessed powers of expression that were
clearer and bolder than those of his contemporaries, and, to their
credit, they realized as much. In the words of Thomas Jefferson, "no
writer has exceeded Paine in ease and familiarity of style, in perspicu-
ity of expression, happiness of elucidation, and in simple and unas-
suming language."[22]

There is, however, another level of complexity to be dealt with in
the acknowledged power of this writer. Gifted beyond other Revolutionary propagandists, Paine nonetheless created far better than even
he knew, and the language that he used took on a life of its own. The
story that Americans have received is far more potent than the one
Paine originally tried to tell, and here, once again, the embattled personality of the writer has gotten in the way of a deeper understanding.
The political maverick who wrote can be deciphered readily enough,
but that individual does not begin to explain the received product that
shattered the traditional Anglo-American mold for pamphleteering in
1776.

Paine gave many commonly available stories a new form and energy. The man who added the final "e" to his name only as he reached
America wanted to see himself—and everything else—afresh. He
strained to marshal affinities that he could only intuit, and he raised
still vaguer proclivities toward the surface of conscious articulation. It
is easy to suggest that the strengths, frustrations, and eccentricities of
the writer tallied with the felt necessities of his times. But in another
sense, Paine stimulated previously unforeseen possibilities, changing
the very nature of the political reality that he saw around him. The
uncanny aspect of Paine's creativity occurred in this area. He grasped,
in recognizable literary form, the emerging ingenuities that the new
politics would require.

To study all of these spheres of implication at once presents problems in analysis. How does one measure the overlapping but still concentric circles of production that have made *Common Sense* a seminal
text? Separating the pamphleteer who knew what he was doing from
the author of heightened magnitudes is to make an artificial distinc-

tion, but it reveals the craft in Paine's writing, and it clarifies the relation of ephemeral pamphlet to timeless literary work. The following three sections adopt a tiered approach but with two synchronous aims always in mind. These twin aims might best be expressed as questions. How does *Common Sense* galvanize an enormous audience so quickly and so permanently? How do the different and often conflicting components in colonial understanding and imperial design generate a new form of communal understanding in consensual nationhood?

The first section below explores the historical Paine, the disaffected member of the Anglo-American empire who knew many things about his various eighteenth-century audiences and who possessed a broad but explicable range of devices for persuading them of his own purposes. In his *Rhetoric,* Aristotle observed "it is not hard to praise Athenians among Athenians." Paine comparably knew how to praise Americans in America and, thereby, to establish popular identifications with his arguments.[23] But more was at work for the disenchanted emigrant who carefully kept the identity of "an Englishman" in the first edition of *Common Sense.* In 1776 he was peculiarly situated to make the most of his disaffections, but he was able to do so without sacrificing either the identity or the rhetorical platform available to him as an Englishman with an Englishman's rights.[24] There is real genius in his manipulation of these combinations—a genius born of conscious risk and dislocation, the very elements that he had to convince British Americans to adopt.

A second section scrutinizes the pamphlet itself for its literary elements of tone, style, symbol, form, and metaphor, and for the relation of literary import to political content. These factors, often referred to but rarely examined in detail, give *Common Sense* much of its practical punch with audiences of all periods. They explain why the pamphlet is such a complex performance despite the simplest of dictions and organizations. In their combined effect, these literary elements also force a dramatic reconsideration of a central debate in rhetorical theory. For manifestly, Paine finds his innermost power in his manipulation of an ancient rhetorical conundrum or uncertainty.

Classical and modern rhetoricians alike have always argued over the proper dimensions of their art. Is successful language, they want to know, about encouraging the recipients of that language to feel a given way or must that language necessarily go further and persuade an audience to act a certain way in order to be considered effective?[25] Paine solves this conundrum by stepping into the continuum of perception between feeling and action. Feeling, properly claimed, becomes action in *Common Sense*. The pamphlet celebrates an orchestrated solidarity of the right-minded in a new type of participatory republic. This idea of the right-minded rests on its own excitement, sufficient unto the moment, but the potential discrepancy between political expediency and philosophical explanation remains great. Paine's account presents a troubling first image of the citizen *en masse* in the modern nation state.

A third section of the chapter carries the historical figure of the first section and the literary analysis of the second into another dimension, into the imaginative domain of storytelling. Paine seems to have deliberately sought a place and, hence, a rhetorical stance at the farthest edges of the Anglo-American empire, a world in which he had failed miserably until emigrating to America. Somehow, after a scant twelve months in colonial Philadelphia, the so-named city of brotherly love, he taught himself to write a previously unimagined story about a better and decidedly new world. The positive appeal of that story is clear enough to all—"we have it in our power to begin the world over again"—but much of its force comes from more unsettling and darker factors. Paine re-fashions a conventional, hackneyed political account into an electrifying tale of basic affections and primal hatreds. Americans easily forget that their republic began in feelings of fear, betrayal, anger, and self-righteousness—the feelings that the Revolution required of its participants. Half of a single sentence from *Common Sense* parades all four emotions at work: "there is no punishment which that man will not deserve, be he who, or what, or where he will, that may be the means of sacrificing a season so precious and useful."[26] Tom Paine learned to wield these negative sentiments to stunning effect, and current Americans have been left with the patterns of his success.

Every culture has five or six stories that it tells itself over and over again as part of a pattern in self-recognition and sought-after cohesion. *Common Sense* clearly provides one of those stories in the United States of America. Recent theories of nationalism, with their recognition of the power of language in the ritualistic reiteration of national formations, permit an additional claim.[27] Paine's story of love and hatred comprises an inexhaustible source in the reservoir of national energies, and when that story is used or repeated in all or in part, it demands of its participants some acceptance of its implications in the ritual performance of national consciousness. Is it an accident that succeeding generations of Americans always reach so promptly for the language of crisis that Paine helped to instill in their forebears? Should the search for internal enemies in times of trouble, whether those enemies are real or imagined, surprise anyone? Here, as well, are the commonalities in *Common Sense.*

Controversies about *Common Sense* abound in part because the facts about its author are tantalizingly scant.[28] Thomas Paine was born in 1737 at Thetford, a Whig stronghold in Norfolk, England. He grew up as the son of a Quaker father, a stay-maker for the corset industry, and an Anglican mother, the daughter of a local attorney. Paine was raised in both faiths but confirmed in the Anglican church, though he rejected, by the age of eight, the basic tenet of Christianity, the sacrifice of the Son by the Father. As he would later summarize his youthful conclusions, "any system of religion that has anything in it that shocks the mind of a child cannot be a true system." An early free thinker, he was raised in a solid denominational setting; he knew the Bible well, better by far than any other writing.[29]

Into middle age Paine experienced "almost unrelenting failure."[30] The corset trade of his father, a life at sea, teaching, possibly the Methodist ministry, shopkeeping, and government service all attracted Paine, but he floundered in each vocation more than once. These experiences took him from town to town, including Dover, Sandwich, Lewes, and London as well as Thetford. By 1774, the year that he left for America at the age of thirty-eight, Paine had descended into bankruptcy with two dismissals for cause from government service and two failed marriages behind him. The separation settlement from his second wife paid for his voyage to America, during which he nearly died of typhoid fever. Notably, his first ambitions on arriving in America were neither political nor daring in scope. He hoped to open a school, and yet within thirteen months he had written *Common Sense* and emerged as the personage that John Adams and other Revolutionary founders would marvel over, a man with "genius in his eyes."[31]

The intellectual background of these early events was just as vague and unprepossessing. Paine received a limited education from grammar school between the ages of eight and thirteen but no formal schooling thereafter. Newtonian science interested him more than politics as a young man, and he attended public lectures in London on the subject, meeting, among others, the writer and poet Oliver Goldsmith and making scientific connections that led him eventually to Benjamin Franklin.[32]

Even so, some formal political sentiments can be traced as early as 1772, when Paine wrote against administrative abuses in his earliest known composition, "Case of the Officers of Excise."[33] Between 1768 and 1774, Paine also learned something of the "Wilkes and Liberty" campaign when John Wilkes, a popular political figure who fled England after being convicted of seditious libel in 1763, returned to create new controversies by regaining his lost seat in Parliament. The Wilkes campaign focused on freedom of the press, ministerial corruption, and Parliamentary reform—all favorite subjects of the later writer—and it drew from the rapidly evolving public sphere of radical coffeehouses that materialized in eighteenth-century England. Paine would have had some access to these institutions in the towns where he lived, especially in London and Lewes, but the extent of his involvement remains uncertain, and his poverty would have kept him a peripheral figure in their controversies.

Paine's personal readings from the period remain largely a mystery; they were certainly unsystematic and often superficial, with the possible exception of close newspaper reading. The deeper parallels that scholars like to draw between John Locke, other political theorists, and *Common Sense* falter in the face of Paine's admissions. "I have never read Locke nor even had the work in my hand," he wrote in 1807, "and by what I heard of it . . . I had no inducement to read it."[34] At the same time, Paine could brag of a perfect memory for everything he did read, and he frequently claimed prodigious intellectual capacities. "I seldom passed five minutes of my life, however circumstanced, in which I did not acquire some knowledge" ran a typical assertion.[35]

This mixture of dreary biographical fact and personal bombast has encouraged scholarly license when dealing with the intractable but fascinating problem of influence. If the boasts of the self-made man are allowed to dominate the paucity of actual data, the possibilities quickly become open-ended and conflicting. Historians in search of handy correlations have turned Paine into the consummate intellectual blotter. Whatever he touched, he can be seen to have absorbed; whomever he mentioned, he can be said to have mastered.

Virtually every fact just noted has been magnified to secure some interpretation of *Common Sense*. The Whig political orientations of towns like Thetford and Lewes and Paine's Quaker background have been variously tied to the writer's oppositional politics, anti-establishment courage, and moral fervor.[36] Just as the religious split between the Quaker father, whom Paine admired, and the Anglican mother, whom he never mentioned, has been offered to justify his later animosity toward an Anglican "mother country," so Paine's failures in marriage have been raised to explain the writer's frequent familial metaphors.[37] Predictably, the negative experiences of the excise officer have provided an especially convenient handle for interpreting the later Revolutionary's zeal in a righteous cause.[38]

The puzzle of Paine's sudden triumph in America has made such speculation unavoidable. Do the unhappy experiences of the corsetmaker and shopkeeper refine artisanal angers and class affiliations in the pamphleteer?[39] Can the young Englishman's interests in Newtonian science explain and justify his later optimism about human nature and natural rights?[40] Either way, the radicalism of the coffeehouses and Paine's presumed newspaper reading have emerged as favorite repositories for whatever philosophy one wants to find in *Common Sense*, from Whig "country" or party rhetoric, to the Scottish moral sense school, to the social compact of Locke, to the denominational agenda of deism, to utilitarian notions of happiness and prosperity.[41] In the absence of hard evidence, any one of these distinct frames of reference can be found "in the air" of Paine's England.

But none of the particulars of influence—nor, for that matter, the sum total of them—produces the author who stunned the world. Even if the reductionism of a single or paramount claim is avoided, the alternative, a collation of relevant influences, still leaves us with the unoriginal thinker rather than the creative writer. Indeed, the distinction itself is worth a pause in rhetorical analysis. Rhetoric trades upon the memorable utterance to achieve a peculiar kind of originality. The speaker or writer takes what is plausible to an immediate audience and turns that recognition into something unforgettable. The Massachusetts Whig, Joseph Hawley, captured the essence of this quality when describing his own reading experience of *Common Sense*. "Every sentiment," he wrote in 1776, "has sunk into my well prepared heart."[42] An anonymous contributor to the *New York Journal* found himself galvanized in the same way, explaining "you can scarce put your finger to a single page, but you are pleased, though it may be, startled, with the sparks of an original genius. . . . It treats of the most important subjects to America . . . exciting and calling forth to public view, the thoughts of others."[43]

Rendition provides the potency in thought. Platonic ideas may epitomize the highest form of knowledge, but they are disembodied abstractions and lack two central ingredients for securing themselves in collective memory. They lack "the timing" that place or context supplies and "the agency" that individual people give to observable experience. Ideas, in short, require concrete expression, and the set of records that we hold about ourselves come through the timing and agency that stories grant—"stories of all kinds, true, embellished, invented."[44] To tell such a story in 1776, Paine had to know how to comprehend and manipulate the milieu of his audience, and so the issue comes back again to the basic puzzle. How did Paine understand the hearts and minds of his new and still inchoate American auditors so quickly, and what gave him the ability to express their sentiments so well?

For part of the answer, the admittedly scant record of biographical facts can be used with more literary purposes in mind. There are patterns in the early life of Paine that clarify the transition of the transplanted Englishman. Note, for example, the degree of mobility that Paine enjoyed along a number of fronts—geographical, religious, vocational, and social. While his movements from town to town, from denominational affiliation to affiliation, from job to job, from oral protest to published dissent, and even from one familial context to another were all part of a record of failure, they also distinguished him from the earlier, more restricted world of place of a previous or seventeenth-century Englishman of his class, and they gave him comparative frames of reference with which to work. Note, as well, that the obscure Paine managed to meet and mingle with such acknowledged great men as Oliver Goldsmith and Benjamin Franklin.

Paine in his mobility illustrated something fresh afoot.[45] The Anglo-American world of the eighteenth century did not discourage unlikely figures with "genius in their eyes." In fact, it expected them as part of its peculiar quest for knowledge, and its leaders, figures like Gold-

smith and Franklin, kept themselves on the lookout. The Enlightenment motto—*"Sapere aude!!"*—"Have the courage to use your own
understanding!"—meant that fresh knowledge might come from anywhere and anyone.[46] Meanwhile, the rapid spread of print technology
in England and America dictated the logical avenues of communication for the dissemination of that knowledge. The linked result, any
good writer with access to a printing press, made these innovations
tangible and exhilarating. From the moment that Paine wrote and
published his first essay, "Case of the Officers of Excise" in 1772, he
became a member in good standing of what was called "the republic
of letters."[47]

The eighteenth-century version of the republic of letters gave Paine
his basic stance in *Common Sense*. Its membership consisted of self-
consciously equal or "world-historical men of letters." Its message involved a critique of church and state, both of which it challenged by
assuming an "autonomous order of mind" that could be liberated
from custom, superstition, locality, and unwarranted hierarchy. Its
medium was print, the very source of its existence, and its mode
was the occasional essay or pamphlet, through which it took on specific historical situations, often questioning the exercises of authority
within them. Inasmuch as Paine reached maturity as the republic of
letters became a "third realm" alongside the two more established
realms of Church and State, his optimism and success become easier
to see and explain. He wrote as a leading pamphleteer in the age of
pamphleteering.

The self-confidence with which Paine rode the crest of this historical wave sustained *Common Sense*—a source of vitality easily overlooked because the same concatenation of historical ideas and events
allowed Paine to ignore the ocean of history beneath him. The rising
third realm of the republic of letters was a historical phenomenon that
questioned previous interpretations of history and assumed that history itself might be made over or changed. Thus, the mantra of *Common Sense*, repeated in some form on almost every page, advised everyone to ignore the past by accepting the present. In its sharpest
expression, it read: "a new era for politics is struck; a new method of
thinking hath arisen. All plans, proposals, etc. prior to the nineteenth
of April, i.e. to the commencement of hostilities, are like the alma-
nacks of the last year; which, though proper then, are superceded and
useless now."[48]

Paine's ingenuity in re-fashioning already established or conventional themes took a similar form. He refurbished stories by removing, dismissing, or at least disarming the domineering pasts that controlled narrative development. Most political pamphlets of the period began with a tedious review of the history of government, and *Common Sense* followed the model in its own introduction, "Of the Origin and Design of Government in General."[49] Paine, however, re-cast the whole discussion by boldly challenging the legitimating histories of governments, which he pronounced to be false and bloody. His convenient tool of entry was a more optimistic pre-history in social contract theory. "Society is in every state a blessing," he began, "but government even in its best state is but a necessary evil."[50]

While Paine also brought the biblical story of the fall into this introduction, he did so to rob it of its customary constraining inflections. Governments did not protect the race from its own fallen nature, as the realms of Church and State would have it; they represented the fall itself, and they actively repressed the human good that would otherwise flourish in social interaction. "Government, like dress, is the badge of lost innocence;" Paine warned, "the palaces of kings are built on the ruins of the bowers of paradise."[51] The implications for Americans choosing between their king and their independence were mesmerizing. You could be fallen and naturally depraved and, thereby, subject to the crown under previous historical conceptions of identity, or you could find yourself to be socially integrated in your natural goodness and, therefore, deserving of ever greater dimensions of freedom. These new dimensions could be disconcerting but not if you accepted your place in the new order.

Consider, for a moment, the alternative rhetorical predicament of the American loyalists, who necessarily tied themselves to a familiar but increasingly problematic old order. "When a Reconciliation is effected, and things return into the old channel," wrote the Episcopalian minister Charles Inglis, in direct response to *Common Sense*, "a few years of peace will restore everything to its pristine state." Everything? What pristine state? Were Inglis' conditional hopes for the past any easier to believe than Paine's aggressive predictions about the future?[52] In a master stroke, Paine grasped that Americans must be forced to choose between a brilliant future and a manifestly duller past, and for that choice to be made absolute, he saw that all of history had to be refigured and collapsed into a fresh sense of the present.

Paine accepted that assignment with unflagging energy and ingenuity in *Common Sense*. For while he clearly sanctioned the conventional Whig Theory of History, affirming a struggle for human rights since the Norman conquest, he also rejected its backward-looking assumption of an ancient Anglo-Saxon golden age.[53] There must be no pristine past to reach for! The present and the future had to be the only keys to an effective understanding. True, William the Conqueror had been a singular figure—"a very paltry rascally original," "a French bastard landing with an armed banditti and establishing himself king of England against the consent of the natives"—but every other king in history, no matter how benevolent, helped the Conqueror to put "the world in blood and ashes." Exalting monarchy in any form contributed to false history and a dangerous psychological confusion about liberty.[54]

Paine, the disenchanted Englishman, knew what American colonials could never quite admit to themselves as imperial subjects in need of a usable past. He saw that a belief in monarchy was the mortal enemy of common sense in representative government and that it had to be answered directly. This insight turned the whole long second section of *Common Sense*, "Of Monarchy and Hereditary Succession," into a battle over the true nature of sovereignty, and it put basic ideas about history up for grabs in the process. When Paine attacked the accepted notion of "an honorable origin" for kingliness, he reduced the intricacies of Anglo-American debate about the king and his ministers to a more elemental level. Contention was no longer about failures in policy but rather "the natural disease of monarchy."[55]

To be sure, the world was still absolutely geared to royal sway. To break this orientation, *Common Sense* had to show not just that monarchy had grown evil, but that it had always been so: "it is more than probable, that could we take off the dark covering of antiquity, and trace them to their first rise, that we should find the first of them nothing better than the principal ruffian of some restless gang, whose savage manners or pre-eminence in subtlety obtained him the title of chief among plunderers." Here, in a nutshell, was a conversion experience for the enlightened citizen. Only with such a bold claim could Paine turn his readers away from the familiar past and toward an uncomfortable but promising present. Paine's conclusion to the section drove the point home. "Of more worth is one honest man to society, and in the sight of God," he declared, "than all the crowned ruffians who ever lived."[56]

Paine employed similar revisionist strategies to guide the remaining sections of *Common Sense,* "Thoughts On The Present State Of American Affairs," and "Of The Present Ability Of America, With Some Miscellaneous Reflexions." His message was the same: the past could not be allowed to determine the present. If Paine could argue that "the nearer any government approaches to a republic the less business there is for a king," he could also add "there is something very absurd, in supposing a continent to be perpetually governed by an island . . . they belong to different systems: England to Europe, America to itself." Geography and the force of gravity were no different than republican politics when it came to transforming the past. "In no instance hath nature made the satellite larger than its primary planet," Paine contended. Why, then, should America revolve around England? Something had to be terribly wrong when the course of history "reverses the common order of nature."[57]

These arguments may seem merely glib today, but they were trumps in an integrated pattern of play in 1776. With the formal discourses of eighteenth-century political science, cartography, Newtonian physics, and natural law in place, Paine inserted a separate but unifying rhetorical flourish, one that domesticated all of knowledge in the blink of an eye. Permeating everything, in a trope that appeared with ever-increasing frequency in *Common Sense,* was the eighteenth-century paradigm of the household, and once again, the pamphleteer wrote transgressively. Rooted patriarchal authority was a dangerous symbol for Paine with its obvious, traditional parallels to absolute monarchy. Since he could hardly leave these familiar associations in place, he attacked head-on with a narrative based on the increasingly popular ideas of sentiment and nurture. What, after all, was authority without love? Loyalty without a reciprocating consideration? The traditional sway of the parent meant nothing when, instead of "tender embraces," one encountered "the cruelty of the monster." England was an "unnatural," even a "false" progenitor. In Paine's elaboration, "the phrase parent or mother country hath been jesuitically adopted," and anyone who still so approached England stood condemned, "unworthy the name of husband, father, friend, or lover."[58]

The relationships so named—husband, father, friend, and lover—forged a new family. Sequentially, the term "husband" led Paine's catalogue precisely because it subsumed and codified the succeeding roles. Husband led to father, friend to lover, or all in one, and all four categories bespoke the paramount goal of parenting and nurturing a new republic. Not the distant and disinterested parent in Europe but the American child in a united family was Paine's subject—so much so that childhood, and especially the vulnerability of childhood, operates as a constitutive metaphor in *Common Sense*.[59] Paine forced his reader back on "the intimacy contracted in infancy" but always with a twist.[60] For if the truest reader was still at least symbolically the child of an European, the act of reading was calculated to resolve the dependency of that child in an acceptance of adult responsibility, and that new accountability could mean only one thing in context: parenting in a logically independent America.

Rhetorically, every theme held in common the erasure of a previous history. A government without kings, the timeless sanction of nature, the cruelty of forebears, the separate nuclear family, the innocent child—none of the images in question welcomed a return to the past. Of course, Paine was temperamentally suited and historically poised for just such a rejection. The successful immigrant kept only those elements of the past that were of immediate use to the present, calmly dismissing even his own former self. As he would later describe the attitude of 1776:

> Our style and manner of thinking have undergone a revolution more extraordinary than the political revolution of the country. We see with other eyes, we hear with other ears; and think with other thoughts, than those we formerly used. We can look back on our own prejudices, as if they had been the prejudices of other people.[61]

It is impossible to underestimate the psychological importance of "seeing with other eyes" as a project in *Common Sense*. Without this ideological leap, without dismissing conventional history altogether, no revolution could have been accomplished by the colonial mind in America. Ordinary wisdom, realpolitik, and the undergirding philosophy of the times all confirmed colonial attachment, loyalty, and imperial design in 1776. The greatest pamphleteer from the English side of the controversy proves the point nicely. Just a year before *Common Sense,* in 1775, Samuel Johnson had torn all the arguments for independence to shreds, and he had managed the feat by keeping his own eyes carefully on received history. Johnson's most telling maneuver in

Taxation No Tyranny: an Answer to the Resolutions and Address of the American Congress separated natural law from the standard history of English rights. In Johnson's devastating account, either the Americans were "naked sons of Nature," in which case their particular historical claims upon the Crown as Englishmen became nonsense, or, in claiming English rights, they accepted the time-bound legal obligations that went with those rights, including the premises of taxation. Assertions to the contrary were "airy boasts of malevolence"; to claim them meant either "interested faction" or, in a more withering thrust, "honest stupidity."[62]

The sting in Johnson's words was unavoidable unless the recipient learned "to see with other eyes," "hear with other ears," and "think with other thoughts." To answer *Taxation No Tyranny* and other writings like it, a very different conception of basic issues had to be found, and Paine showed his recognition of the problem with a series of opening instructions in *Common Sense*. Through "preliminaries to settle with the reader," he demanded that the latter "generously enlarge his views beyond the present day"; nothing less than the removal of all "prepossession" was required, a stipulation that clearly asked for more than the stock suspension of "prejudice."[63] These "preliminaries" reach for another level of aesthetic coherence. They show that Paine understood better than anyone else in America that "style and manner of thinking" might dictate the difficult shift from loyalty to rebellion.

Three constitutive or controlling metaphors dominate the writing of *Common Sense*. The first, already encountered, is "childhood," with the accompanying idea of maturation. The second and third involve more elemental abstractions, ones that allow Paine to manipulate the parameters of childhood for political effect. The second metaphor emphasizes "time present," and it emerges most frequently in Paine's reiterated use of the temporal adverb "now." The third dwells on the virtue that can be assigned to "simplicity." These stylistic devices ride the surfaces of Paine's prose, but they reinforce each other at deeper levels and in much more subtle ways.

Taken together, the metaphors in question enact a dramatic coordination of status, context, and aesthetic form in the overall narrative of *Common Sense*. Youthfulness (status) becomes dramatic in the myriad urgencies of "now" (context), and that basic drama, in turn, is sharpened in a redaction of the plain, the new, the common, the innocent, the fundamental, the direct, the simple, the peremptory—an aesthetic form that dominates both style and substance. Separately, the metaphors are devices on the page. Jointly, they produce "a strategy of intimacy" or identification between author and reader, a near prerequisite for communication in the print medium of a rapidly evolving democratic culture.[64]

The essential dynamic at work can be found in a single sentence. Deploring the failure of "repeated petitioning" for peace with England, Paine fastens his reader with a simple imperative: "Wherefore since nothing but blows will do, for God's sake, let us come to a final separation, and not leave the next generation to be cutting throats, under the violated unmeaning names of parent and child." Political negotiation, he continues, has become "too weighty and intricate," and further attempts "will in a few years be looked upon as folly and childishness," literally a regression in adult thinking.[65] Timeliness, simplicity, and proper domestic nurture all require separation. Anything else, anything but the stark urgency of physical retaliation— "nothing but blows will do"—ruptures the American family, leaving it to cope with "the violated unmeaning names of parent and child." A proper conception of the parent's role commands action now by reading the future in the name of the still innocent child. "In order to discover the line of our duty," Paine writes, "we should take our children in our hand, and fix our station a few years farther into life; that eminence will present a prospect, which a few present fears and prejudices conceal from our sight."[66]

Insistence on the present moment in *Common Sense* compels interest and drama by demanding that the reader make a choice immediately. Paine, in fact, reserves a special wrath for "men of passive tempers" and anyone else who hesitates through "ill-judged deliberation."[67] To grant the urgency in Paine's claims is to enter a sequence. If "now is the seed-time of continental union," it follows that "Britain, now being an open enemy, extinguishes every other name and title." The proposition that "Reconciliation is *now* a fallacious dream" translates easily into "reconciliation *now* is a dangerous doctrine," into "it is *now* the interest of America to provide for herself," into "We ought not now to be debating whether we shall be independent or not."[68] Each successive formulation binds the reader to a firmer acceptance of separation "now." Thus, "The present winter is worth an age if rightly employed" becomes "the present time is preferable to all others," becomes "the *present time* is the *true time*," becomes "The present time, likewise, is that peculiar time which never happens to a nation but once." In this hectoring fashion, Paine turns the reader's choices into group decisions. We read "to find out the *very* time," but we soon learn "the *time hath found us*."[69]

The vital importance of time present also contains an open threat for the reader. If history begins "now," then the reader of the moment is responsible for it. "'Tis not the concern of a day, a year, or an age;" Paine asserts, "posterity are virtually involved in the contest, and will be more or less affected, even to the end of time, by the proceedings now."[70] This definition of history through current events has fundamental psychological consequences. Although the past is dead, a sentient future watches over the living present. In effect, the future becomes a censorious audience of the present, and any American who tries to wait out the crisis of 1776 will figure as an enemy in this impending view of history. "Should a thought so fatal and unmanly possess the colonies in the present contest," Paine admonishes, "the name of ancestors will be remembered by future generations with detestation."[71]

The rhetorical creativity of *Common Sense* becomes apparent in the rich and varied tones of these threats. When all of history appears at risk, all of its registers can be brought to bear in a cautionary tale. Typically, in making a shift from "the present state" to "the present ability" of America, Paine inserts a remarkable gloss on present inability. Those readers who cannot act against England become the soldiers who crucified Christ. "Ye that oppose independence now," Paine intones, "ye know not what ye do."[72] Earlier colonials would have found blasphemy in this appropriation of the voice of Jesus, and today the association seems bizarre, but eighteenth-century Americans were steeped in a Bible culture even as they were concurrently obsessed with their place on the cutting edge of the Enlightenment. Caught up in secular–religious associations, they were neither surprised nor intimidated to find their independence presented as part of God's plan. Few Americans in 1776 questioned a comparable parallel in *Common Sense:* "The Reformation was preceded by the discovery of America, as if the Almighty graciously meant to open a sanctuary to the persecuted in future years."[73]

"As if"? Paine knew that a country of radical reform Protestants would be willing to pay a price for acknowledgment of its centrality in history; also that this price, willingly paid, might carry many of his readers beyond the raging debate over colonies versus nation. *Common Sense* cleverly manipulates the political dispute without running afoul of religious or philosophical differences. There is a warning for every ear in the following passage:

> Ye that tell us of harmony and reconciliation, can ye restore to us the time that is past? Can you give to prostitution its former innocence? Neither can you reconcile Britain and America. . . . There are injuries which nature cannot forgive; she would cease to be nature if she did. As well can the lover forgive the ravisher of his mistress, as the continent forgive the murderers of Britain. The Almighty hath implanted in us these unextinguishable feelings for good and wise purposes. They are the guardians of his image in our hearts.[74]

The Almighty of this text is both more and less than the angry, inscrutable God of Puritan theology.[75] Paine retains the emotion but reverses the flow of anger and, hence, the direction of revealed design. Without losing sight of divine wrath altogether, he concentrates on a justifiable, collective anger in the human world (also figured as "popular rage"[76]). History and nature are the mediate forms of Paine's deity, and they dictate a coherent or continental resentment in response to British abuses. Those abuses anger everyone because, as Paine's questions indicate, they violate everything, the domestic sphere as well as historical time: "can the lover forgive the ravisher of his mistress?" intensifies "can ye restore us to the time that is past?"

Orthodox colonial readers could still reach their Calvinist God through Paine's construct but just as available were a Quaker God (an image in the human heart), a deistic God (at work in nature's design), and a Scottish moral-sense God (instilling inextinguishable feelings for good and wise purposes). The Supreme Being remains scrupulously vague in the pages of *Common Sense*. No denominational flags fly, and Paine's inner conception grows out of one basic, reiterated, external premise, "above all things the free exercise of religion."[77] This elemental trait guarantees the acceptability of Paine's multifaceted deity. Simplicity of design invites alternative approaches to the divine, allowing each worshiper to fill in the relevant blanks.

This virtue in simplicity is Paine's third constitutive metaphor, and it shapes his writing in decisive and volatile ways. "I offer nothing more than simple facts, plain arguments, and common sense," Paine avers.[78] The claim is a disarmingly rudimentary one, deliberately so in its thematic and rhetorical thrusts, but despite the disavowal ("I offer nothing more"), it contains an underlying complexity of purpose and effect that is all the harder to grasp in a text that turns complexity into the symbol of evil. Stylistically, Paine's insistence on simplicity is as unambiguous as it is daring for the time. Eighteenth-century pamphleteering thrived on self-conscious erudition with constant asides to previous thinkers and a profusion of references to other works. Paine, by way of contrast, gives just three short sentences in fifty pages to the words of other writers (choosing to recognize only Milton and Dragonetti), and he alludes to just one other book in all of *Common Sense,* the Bible.[79]

As Paine's avoidance of other sources implies, his use of "the plain style" has as much to do with ideology as it does with diction. *Common Sense* eschews arch circumlocutions, latinates, elevated tones, and sophisticated nuances. The alternatives are common language, easy alliteration, balanced phraseology, and verbal antitheses in short, memorable sentences.[80] The rationale for these choices is apparent: closer association with the common people. Paine believed that anyone who understood basic English should comprehend his argument and, in one of his optimistic jumps, that the goal of writing was to make everyone eager to do so. When his opponents complained of a "vulgar style," they had this appeal to the lowest common denominator in mind, and their pejorative use changed the meaning of the term. For Paine, "vulgar" meant "common," "of the people." For his opponents, it suggested that which was boorish or debased.[81]

We are on the brink of a great ideological divide with Paine's seemingly guileless but actually manipulative simplicity in style. Writing to enlist universal involvement in politics frightened Paine's contemporaries. It led a figure like John Adams to deplore *Common Sense* as "so democratical, without any restraint or even an Attempt at any Equilibrium or Counterpoise, that it must produce confusion and every Evil Work." The debate between Paine and Adams raised a fundamental philosophical question. Would general participation in government introduce greater clarity or only confusion in the body politic? Answers to this query could only be conjectural in 1776. Adams published his own pamphlet, *Thoughts on Government,* in quick response to *Common Sense,* and he wrote to ensure that government be left "to a few of the most wise and good."[82]

Years later, knowing that he had lost the battle over participatory democracy, Adams vented his frustrations in a splenetic summary:

> I know not whether any man in the world has had more influence on its inhabitants or affairs for the last thirty years than Tom Paine. There can be no severer satyr on the age. For such a mongrel between pig and puppy, begotten by a wild boar on a bitch wolf, never before in any age of the world was suffered by the poltroonery of mankind to run through such a career of mischief. Call it then the Age of Paine.[83]

How promiscuous should the role of the people be in a people's government? Despite his vituperative rage, Adams saw clearly that the spontaneous vitality of the mongrel came from below. The monstrous lineage that he ascribed to Paine evoked the grotesque, but his fusion of wildness, youth, and transgressive procreation contained an admission. Paine's writings were the catalyst for something new in the world.

Common Sense fosters "the Age of Paine" by insisting on an alliance between common expression and the common in politics. Americans in 1776 were alarmed and many were confused by a world that seemed to be changing out from under them.[84] Paine cut through that alarm and confusion for anyone who would reduce the world to common principle. There is, he claimed, "a principle in nature which no art can overturn." Yes, "our eyes may be dazzled with show, or our ears deceived by sound," "prejudice may warp our wills, or interest darken our understanding," but everything becomes clear again when we return to a primary source: "the simple voice of nature and reason." And what did nature have to tell Americans in their mounting political crisis? In a formula that encompasses every argument in *Common Sense,* nature advises "the more simple any thing is, the less liable it is to be disordered."[85]

If you imbibe the plain style, you are susceptible to every subsequent declaration of "plain truth."[86] In a remarkable series of rhetorical strokes, Paine uses "the simple voice of nature and reason" to reverse the familiar and the strange in Anglo-American culture. He replaces the comfort of the historically commonplace with what would be a blatant oxymoron except for his management of the unfolding reading process. The willing reader must accept a new familiarity, everyday reason, from a friendly and colloquial but progressively importunate narrator: "I offer nothing more than simple facts, plain arguments, and common sense".[87] The qualification, "nothing more," represents a stock exercise in humility, but it also strips away a whole series of other intellectual dimensions and defenses. Conventional associations of continuing loyalty to England turn into complicating disorders; the originally more frightening prospects of treason and separation become, instead, the easy manifestations of a simpler order.

The force of this transformation can only be fully appreciated in the movement of Paine's narrative. *Common Sense* opens with the plainest version of social contract theory imaginable: "let us suppose a small number of persons settled in some sequestered part of the earth, unconnected with the rest, they will represent the first peopling of any country." This group, "four or five united," raise "a tolerable dwelling in the midst of a wilderness." The necessity of cooperation among them operates "like a gravitating power," and its influence moves "our newly arrived emigrants into society, the reciprocal blessing of which, would supercede, and render the obligations of law and government unnecessary while they remained perfectly just to each other." For an undetermined period of time, "the first difficulties of emigration" keep this "colony" together "in a common cause," but soon the complexity of their undertaking undermines "their duty and attachment to each other," and government, "the badge of lost innocence," must be accepted as "a necessary evil" and "punisher." It is also telling that this first attempt at government includes everyone. "In this first parliament every man, by natural right will have a seat."[88]

In the technical literary sense, Paine has written a parable. The extended metaphor of an original and happy social simplicity awakens Americans to the moral of their own imaginary founding; everyone is involved but with *the least* government.[89] The story works at several levels. Most obviously, its phraseology evokes a presumed narrative about new world beginnings. Americans in 1776 would have recognized their own forebears in these "newly arrived emigrants" who settle in a "sequestered part of the earth," who build homes "in the midst of a wilderness," and who overcome "the difficulties of emigration" to form a "colony." But Paine also uses these recognitions to create a philosophical counter-narrative to Samuel Johnson's sharp division between natural law and the history of English common law. *Common Sense* demonstrates that "natural right" and English legality ("this first parliament") met in colonial origins and that, in coming together, they created an original and unique felicity in early America.

Like other parables, this one compels additional reflection through a concluding twist of the metaphor. The appearance of political complexity, figured also as original sin, pollutes the happy origins of the social contract in America, and the reader must muse over both the religious analogy and the historical contrast. An available simplicity in society, which "promotes our happiness positively by uniting our affections," must be balanced against a tangled and unhappy political present, in which Americans feel disenfranchised. And the cause of all of this confusion and unhappiness? "The constitution of England is so exceedingly complex, that the nation may suffer for years together without being able to discover in which part the fault lies."[90]

Paine employs the bifurcation between happy origins and the present crisis to introduce his long dissection of the British constitution and monarchical government; both are historically debased and intricate sources of evil. Not surprisingly, these first two historical sections of the pamphlet conclude with a rhetorical question that is its own answer. "Why is the constitution of England sickly," Paine wonders, "but because monarchy hath poisoned the republic, the crown hath engrossed the commons?" Again, it is the complication of the combination that is important. Constitutional divisions and monarchical brutality compound each other; together, they portend a spreading corruption that must be stopped. Rhetorically, Paine has moved more than halfway to his central premise: "reconciliation and ruin are nearly related."[91]

"RECONCILIATION OR INDEPENDENCE?" screams the headlined final version of the recurring inquiry. The narrator has replied many times by this stage of the argument, but his last answer provides an aesthetic resolution beyond politics. The shift is from Europe to America and from the complexity and sin of history to the simplicity and virtue of nature as the controlling frame of reference. Paine is blunt about the importance of this philosophical change in perspective. Only "he who takes nature for his guide" can hope to see the crisis of 1776 with sufficient clarity to reach intellectual certainty. Through nature, the reader enters a more systematic and mediate universe, one that will sustain *"the answer without doubt."* To express his appreciation of this certainty in design, Paine gives his own version of the answer in geometric terms. "INDEPENDENCE" forms *"a SINGLE SIMPLE LINE, contained within ourselves,"* leaving *"reconciliation, a matter exceedingly perplexed and complicated."*[92] Indeed, reconciliation has become so perplexing and complicated that it cannot even be rendered in a discernible geometric form. Only independence can be made visible in meaningful action. Proving the point in his peroration, Paine beseeches all Americans to "unite in drawing a line, which, like an act of oblivion, shall bury in forgetfulness every former dissension."[93]

There are problems with Paine's strategy of virtue in simplicity, and some of them are implied when his simile of separation requires "an act of oblivion." To the extent that independence dictates the removal of previous intellectual affinities, it can leave the reader of *Common Sense* feeling terribly alone.[94] In an unguarded moment of the opening parable, Paine reveals that "the strength of one man is so unequal to his wants, and his mind so unfitted for perpetual solitude, that he is soon obliged to seek assistance and relief of another, who in his turn requires the same."[95] This identified human craving for social relief and comfort does not necessarily welcome a revolution. Paine's separating Americans can achieve the enlarged view of their national situation only by divesting themselves of all of the previous connections, loyalties, and thoughts on which their colonial society has been based. Then, too, Paine's alternative of continental attachment is painfully abstract, anti-local, non-experiential, even artificial in 1776. To become newly sufficient unto themselves, Paine's first readers must turn away from everything they know and face the void.

The final component in Paine's argument involves his manipulation of these fears. American forebodings must be turned into something more empowering, and Paine's solution contains a singular conversion. In *Common Sense*, anxious thought becomes righteous feeling. Anger provides the cohesive social force that mere misgivings cannot. Methodologically, the reader is asked to "examine the passions and feelings of mankind," always remembering that this exercise will require an explanation "by those feelings and affections which nature justifies." To perform this examination in the colonial context—to "bring the doctrine of reconciliation to the touchstone of nature"— means to arouse hatred instead of love. Paine is quite clear on the point: "'never can true reconcilement grow where wounds of deadly hate have pierced so deep.'"[96]

Anger supplies the emotional force to bring Americans together in a formative act of self-recognition. "Men read by way of revenge," Paine declares.[97] *Common Sense* is that reading. It fuels itself with images of blood, ashes, suffering, cruelty, corruption, monstrosity, hellishness, and villainy. When critics of *Common Sense* called its author "furious," Paine welcomed the accusation. "There are men, too," he responded, "who have not virtue enough to be angry."[98] This conjunction of anger and simplicity, under the rubric of virtue, was hardly accidental. Among other things, it supplied the perfect counter to a Loyalist rhetoric that asked Americans to rest in the familiar calm of complex colonial associations.[99]

Paine used the combination of anger and simplicity as a funneling device. Of all of the emotions, anger is the most difficult to control, and Paine's triumph in this regard is the great master stroke in his rhetorical plan. His "uncanny ability to articulate the emotions of the mob" allowed him to objectify colonial unrest as patriotism.[100] Only Paine really harnessed these forces in 1776. He alone, of all the writers of the Revolution, fathomed the depths of "popular rage" in America, and he plied that resentment to construct a vital identification between narrator and reader. It is this perception, more than any other, that carries *Common Sense* from story toward spellbinding myth.

A distinction must be drawn between the anger of colonial Americans in 1776 and their ability to express that anger in formal prose. Modern scholarship on the Revolution has puzzled over this paradox: pre-Revolutionary Americans were more fearful and angry than their circumstances warranted, but their "literature of revolution" appeared more decorous and less angry than English literary productions of the same period. *Common Sense* represented the exception that proves the rule. Written by a transplanted Englishman who brought his "daring impudence" with him, it rejected the "everyday, business-like sanity" of most colonial writings on politics.[101]

Anger, as such, surfaces most visibly in the frequency of popular uprisings throughout colonial America. Mob behavior was an intrinsic part of colonial life as well as an extra-legal arm in important communal decisions. At different moments, rioting paralyzed each of the major colonial cities, and violent uprisings in the countryside periodically destroyed property and brought government to a halt—sometimes pitting whole regions against each other, as in the Paxton riots of western Pennsylvania in 1763.[102] Moreover, mob violence increased exponentially after 1765, the year in which rioting throughout the colonies nullified the Stamp Act, and recognition of this change has led historians to assign "mass violence a dominant role at every significant turning point of the events leading up to the War for Independence."[103]

Even so, there is little commentary about mob behavior in the formal literature of the period, and when it does appear it is to maintain restraints upon that behavior. The second most popular propaganda piece of the Revolutionary era, John Dickinson's *Letters from a Farmer in Pennsylvania* in 1768, offers a good case in point. Dickinson began his long pamphlet by distinguishing between "inflammatory measures," which he "detests," and "a firm, modest exertion of a free spirit," which alone gave the proper tone to public protest. "The cause of liberty," he wrote, "is a cause of too much dignity, to be sullied by turbulence and tumult." On the face of it, unrest in America was almost as great a concern in colonial pamphleteering as British intransigence.[104] Rhetorical restraint and elevation were not just ploys to demonstrate rationality and accountability while petitioning the king; they were essential strategies for keeping the lower orders in line.

The many differences between Dickinson and Paine as pamphleteers flowed from as many historical factors, but the rhetorical contrast in their writing styles came down to an agenda of calm restraint against a program of deliberate emotional excess, cautionary balance versus fervent assertion. Psychologically, Paine was closer to the mob than Dickinson ever could be, and he knew how to manipulate its spiritual proclivities.[105] The artistry of *Common Sense,* like the animus of the mob, builds solidarity out of hatred. Paine engages his readers by promising them a final metamorphosis from anger to "the hearty hand of friendship," setting aside the question of whether rabble-rousing can ever achieve such a transformation.[106]

But if the ultimate price of fanning hatred remains unplumbed in *Common Sense,* the rhetorical payoff was great in 1776. Paine's substitution of assertion and excess for Dickinsonian prudence and reserve worked in his favor. Held back for years by the restraining influence and decorum of leaders like Dickinson and Adams, radical segments of the reading public welcomed the release of psychic energy that *Common Sense* offered.[107] Paine managed this release by discarding the historical colonial self-image of decorous self-restraint and by replacing it with an abstract process of reasoning that made anger compelling. His chain of postulates ran like this: anger is the natural and appropriate emotional reaction to an intensifying pattern of British tyranny; it is politically necessary to express this natural and appropriate feeling; communal health (often expressed as "manliness") also depends upon it; therefore, anger is the legitimate precursor of virtuous civic action.

This chain of logic is reinforced by a parallel sequence of identifications that either saves or damns the reader, depending on that reader's reaction to *Common Sense*. The psychological movement of the narrative is from general outrage over British attacks, to an explicit anger against the person of the king, to a demonstration that such anger must foster an irreconcilable hatred against the mother country, to the conclusion that individuals who remain loyal to England must share the reception of that hatred as traitors "against the natural rights of all Mankind."[108] This final level of hatred knows no real limits. It encompasses "all those who espouse the doctrine of reconciliation," but it also extends to "moderate men, who think better of the European world than it deserves." Anyone who remains unreceptive to immediate independence should be despised. In saying so, Paine espouses what will later become a central recognition in crowd theory: you are either for the mob or it is against you.[109]

The most impressive dimension in this spiral of hatred is the rhetorical administration of its growth. Paine begins simply enough by claiming "the Power of feeling" against those who have attacked America. Feeling, in this sense, moves in one continuum from a distaste for kingliness, to anger at the British monarchy, to "an universal hatred" of George the Third. Paine understood—as his colonial counterparts did not—that it would be easier to loathe an identifiable person, King George, than any abstract collectivity, whether of Parliament, the ministry, or the people of England. As he puts this realization, "it is scarcely worth our while to fight against a contemptible ministry only."[110] Significantly, there is a second and far nastier continuum of abhorrence in *Common Sense*. Paine reserves his ultimate vituperation for the unworthy American. It is not enough to expose those "who are not to be trusted" or even "prejudiced men who will not see." Paine, at the outset, says "I would carefully avoid giving unnecessary offense." By the end, however, the American who sympathizes with England in any way has devolved into something less than human. This American has fallen farther than even "the royal brute of Great Britain." He has "sunk himself beneath the rank of animals" and must "contemptibly crawl through the world like a worm."[111]

It would be hard to imagine a more devastating loneliness than the state Paine reserves for his American opponents. What natural rights, if any, remain to those placed below even a sub-human category, "beneath the rank of animals"? Since the closest emotion to anger is revenge, Paine is unstinting in his exercise of it.[112] There will be no forgiveness for those who dare to deviate from the republican norm. Paine's parting shot at any "Tories" who remain in America takes the form of a threat. If they fail to support a republican form of government, they should expect to lose the security that has previously "protected them from popular rage." Paine is vehemently part of that rage. As he has already noted, "there is no punishment which that man will not deserve, be he who, or what, or where he will."[113]

The anger in these words is important because it is responsible for a political solidarity that would otherwise be lacking. After all, the corollary to Paine's isolation of unworthy Americans is an unsettling one: "Independence is the only BOND that can tye and keep us together."[114] The *only* bond? But if so, why should it work? Why should the untested prospect of independence guarantee the political fabric of a vast and heterogeneous continental republic? How are the separate liberties of each and every citizen going to accomplish "the glorious union of all things" that Paine so confidently predicts for the American strand?[115]

Realizing that there are no philosophical or political solutions to such questions, Paine responds on a series of distinct rhetorical levels. First, he creates a cohesive or corporate American self out of first-person, plural, pronominal forms. The ever-present "we" of *Common Sense* comprises neither colonies, nor voting citizens, nor leaderships of any kind. This ubiquitous "we" is literally everyone—every reading self who has been arranged by the acceptance of Paine's language into a collective but equal audience capable of receiving and (through identification) of giving speech.

Both the collective and the egalitarian flavors of this American audience are calculated effects. Collectivity carries the presumption of truth within it. "Could the straggling thoughts of individuals be collected," writes Paine, "they would frequently form materials for wise and able men to improve to useful matter."[116] Equality, in turn, provides a comparable safeguard; it joins "the equal rights of nature" and benevolent social origins ("all men being originally equal") with plans for the new government ("a large and equal representation"). Equality and collectivity thus become the sources of all social agreement. "Where there are no distinctions there can be no superiority, perfect equality affords no temptation," Paine observes in claiming that equal states will always retain "a spirit of good order."[117] "Perfect equality" in the union of states is, in this sense, the political equivalent of the rhetorical "we" in *Common Sense*.

But Paine's language holds another meaning and a second rhetorical device for bringing separate Americans together. The absence of hierarchy in "perfect equality" marks an intended audience, the mob. Paine uses anger, the natural emotion of the mob, to urge the people as mob to express the general will of a republican citizenry. Noting that "the mind of the multitude is left at random," he writes to give it direction through the act of independence, and his facilitating tool is the "unexampled concurrence of sentiment" in an angry people. There are two steps in this process: the admittedly temporary emotion of the people must be recognized and celebrated; but next, the people's anger must be harnessed to the more permanent political end of independence.[118]

Common Sense then identifies three ways for gaining that independence: "by the legal voice of the people in Congress; by a military power; or by a mob." Paine's hope for an amalgamation of these compelling forces leads to his greatest expressions of urgency. He begs for immediate action because he believes that Congress, the soldiery, and the mob have a rare opportunity to act as one in 1776. In this moment, and perhaps in no other, "our soldiers are citizens, and the multitude a body of reasonable men." Poignantly, this moment also provides the context for Paine's most famous claim, "we have it in our power to begin the world over again."[119]

Popular acceptance of this appeal emanates from the mob's discovery of its own assigned purpose and dignity. After a decade of pamphleteering on the rationality of moderate opposition, Paine's different, free-wheeling endorsement of the people's emotions converts the mob from shameful by-product into a legitimate vehicle of colonial identity and cultural salvation. This shift, while superficial, is not without its subtleties. The mob responds initially to the narrator's buoyant inclusiveness ("we have it in our power"), but it remains engaged through an intricate arrangement of psychological ingredients. There is real acumen in Paine's comprehension of these ingredients and a master's craft in his applications.

Contemporary theories of crowd psychology suggest that the mob feeds on five qualities: it wants to grow, it seeks equality within itself, it loves density, it needs direction, and its most conspicuous activity lies in its destructiveness.[120] The rhetoric of *Common Sense* plays itself out along these axes: first, in its attacks on monarchy and its call to arms, which seek to destroy all linkage with Britain, next in its language of equality, then in its plans for solidarity or density through union, and last in its explicit insistence upon the continental growth of the republic.[121]

After strengthening the character of the mob in this manner, Paine cunningly leaves it with a preordained choice, one that will either confirm it or rob it of all identity. The mob can either declare for independence, with the life-giving violence that this will require of it, or it can hesitate, dwindle, and forever forfeit independence, leaving itself "continually haunted with the thoughts of its necessity."[122] That the mob easily imbibes the careful structures that we have identified— hatred of authority, outrage against wronged innocence, sympathy for domestic distress, identification with simplicity of design, and the acceptance of natural reason over historical experience—is a given. More arresting are the hidden patterns of deep threat that guarantee these investments. In the end, neither the thoughtful individual nor the emotionally driven mob have choices to make if they are to survive on anything like their own terms as willing readers. The wrath that Paine has raised has been primed to turn inward if it fails to reach designated external targets.

The potential viciousness in this trajectory gives one more proof of Paine's rhetorical power in 1776; his language convinced an unprecedented number of Americans to accept his arguments on his terms, and the result was a revolution against colonial rule. But seeing this rhetoric for what it is, in all of its angry impetuses and accusatory denouement, makes *Common Sense* a disquieting text in national formations. Only a zealous convert can ignore the ugly impulses in Paine's pamphlet. The unleashing and manipulation of group hatreds do not make for a pretty sight, and the success of *Common Sense* depends upon them. What is to be done with such levels of hatred, and how susceptible do present Americans remain to their influence? These questions are especially relevant for a people that can no longer embrace the intellectual safety valve of natural reason—the source that made common sense such a comfort for Paine and his first readers.

〜

If the angers of *Common Sense* are recognized for what they have become, national angers, they can be arranged and perhaps even curbed to serve a modern understanding. Nationalism in general thrives on two basic emotions, feelings of satisfaction raised by fulfillment and feelings of anger provoked by violation.[123] Paine is the first modern writer to grapple knowingly with these contrasting impulses in a revolutionary-minded state. What is more, his inspired exploitation of these satisfactions and angers contains the beginnings of a solution to the problems he has raised.

In modern theory, nations are not so much natural creations as they are invented constructs; nationalisms in such an understanding are not intrinsic ideas but cultural artifacts best recognized in the way language is used. National communities, in consequence, are known less by fixed or concrete conceptions and more by the flexible mode in which they are imagined.[124] In most cultures an ethnocentric view of the nation as a natural, prepolitical entity made up of the folk with an inherited form of life competes with a more modern, more cosmopolitan conception of the nation as a legal entity made up of citizens with constitutionally defined rights.[125] Tom Paine, as an eighteenth-century figure steeped in natural law, would not have agreed with these assessments, but ironically, he began to make them conceivable for others when he articulated a design for the American nation in 1776. *Common Sense* marks the divide between the two understandings of the nation as folk entity and legal entity. It privileges the first in the notion of an originally happy society without government, but it constructs the latter. For it is only through the nation as legal entity that republicanism receives a guarantee of its operations, and Paine is dedicated first and foremost to a republican ideal based on law.

The narrator of *Common Sense* assumes that everything will collapse without the swift implementation of a republic of laws. When he argues that "the Continental belt is too loosely buckled," he means that America is "Without law" and must rectify the situation immediately.[126] As Paine would later write of 1776, "we had no other law than a kind of moderated passion; no other civil power than an honest mob." He also saw that if these conditions had been allowed to continue "this continent would have been plunged into irrecoverable confusion." The situation is saved, in his understanding, by the introduction of republican institutions for "a regular people," but it is Paine's admission of an alternative danger that should catch our attention. Without law, he warns, no passion stays moderate, and no mob remains honest.[127]

Paine clearly believes in the control that republican institutions will engender. Under their influence, the mob somehow turns itself into "a regular people." The underlying theoretical basis of this transmutation is never fully articulated in *Common Sense*; as its author was the first to admit, he merely "threw out a few thoughts . . . for I only presume to offer hints, not plans."[128] Nonetheless, even if there is no mature plan, there is definitely a process in the "few thoughts" that are given.[129] Paine offers a story to register the transition from the mob to a regular people, and that story characteristically contains a multitude of complexities within the simplest of narratives. For all of these reasons, it is worth quoting in full:

> But where says some is the King of America? I'll tell you Friend, he reigns above, and doth not make havock of mankind like the Royal [Brute] of Britain. Yet that we may not appear to be defective even in earthly honors, let a day be solemnly set apart for proclaiming the charter; let it be brought forth placed on the divine law, the word of God; let a crown be placed thereon, by which the world may know, that so far as we approve of monarchy, that in America THE LAW IS KING. For as in absolute government the King is law, so in free countries the law ought to be King; and there ought to be no other. But lest any ill use should afterwards arise, let the crown at the conclusion of the ceremony be demolished, and scattered among the people whose right it is.[130]

The calculated indirections in this curious tale blend Paine's rhetorical methods with his political solutions. There can be no better concluding demonstration of his appeal as a writer, and the story itself gives an uncanny glimpse of the future, the republic as modern nation state. Many of the standard rhetorical devices of *Common Sense* are pres-

ent in this passage: exhortation, repetition, hyperbole, inversion, ana-
phora (using the same word at the beginning of successive clauses),
hypophora (asking questions and immediately answering them), and,
of course, frequent hectoring of the obedient reader ("I'll tell you
friend"). Also familiar, thematically, are the conflations of divine and
secular frames of reference, the contrasts between England and America, the parallel distinction between monarchical and republican
forms of government, the display of villainy ("the Royal Brute"), the
avowals of freedom found ("so in free countries"), and the casual assumption of an enormous, expectant audience ("by which the world
may know"). And yet the story that Paine gives here is so much
greater in the telling than the sum of its parts and devices might indicate.

Although a king is killed and metaphorically cannibalized in this
passage, the violence involved has been stylized. Neither blood nor
anguish ripples the surfaces of what has been "demolished." All
"havock" has been relegated to the other side. God reigns more be-
nevolently in America because unmediated by intervening kings. The
people, like any pious tribe left to its own social devices, seek that benevolence by courting divine favor through "earthly honors." Above
all, there is a saving sense of ceremony that is half biblical saga (a
crown is placed on "the word of God") and half colonial politics
("proclaiming the charter"). Here Paine uses the decorum of ritual to
subsume revolutionary angers. A day has been "solemnly set aside" to
make the law king, and the people are justified and dignified in their
actions by partaking of that authority, which is then "scattered" in
their midst. The obvious parallel is to the Christian sacrament of communion in a parataxis that points toward civil religion in the modern
nation state.[131]

More is at stake for the citizen than meets the eye in this ceremony of legal proclamation. Ritual in general promotes participation
over contest. It welcomes performers instead of designating winners
against losers, and it tries to bring everyone into the fold through an
exercise in consent. To participate is to belong, and the participant
usually engages with cooperation in mind.[132] There is little room for
anger in such a ceremony, particularly when it assumes the form of a
national celebration. The other or twin emotion of national sentiment—not anger from violation but satisfaction in fulfillment—tends
to rule in this situation. So when Paine follows the configuration of
ritual in his fanciful version of national ceremony, it represents an im-

portant variation. *Common Sense* is a text given over largely to American resentments, but anger suddenly becomes unseemly in this one ceremonial context, "solemnly set apart." The final scattering of a symbolic crown enacts a legal shift in empowerment and understanding rather than another act of rage. It is carefully designed to avoid further "ill use."

A whimsical, even jocular, celebration of the law as king may seem no more than that. Even a profound day "set apart" is but one day, and Paine's rather offhand account of national ceremony reads a little like a minimalist's attempt to quell the furies that he has aroused. Even so, if there is a saving difference, it lies in the controlling prescriptive language of the passage: "so in free countries the law ought to be King; and there ought to be no other." A national readership is being told that appropriate action should always take place through a recognition and acceptance of law, and the many deferrals in this aspiration do not make it any less real or compelling. Here, in effect, is an early rendition of the modern rule of law. In Paine's understanding, given in the last two sections of *Common Sense,* the process of law represents the stabilizing backbone for every other communal virtue in an advanced society, including free elections, a constitutional convention, an annual Congress, the security of property, the efficient use of bountiful resources, a strong navy, the growth of commerce, and the management of a national debt.

This rule of law is modern because it is accepted by all rather than imposed from above. Law always contains an element of imposition, but the modern rule of law, by definition, turns hierarchical intrusiveness into a penetrating force at work on every level of society, thus providing a structure accessible to the ruled as well as the ruler. As both typological superstructure and social infrastructure, this rule of law merges with the underlying basis of all productive relations. It becomes an unavoidable consideration for all concerned, whether in thought or in action. Rulers must turn to the logic of the rule of law to understand their own behavior; the ruled learn to keep power within constitutional limits and to insist on its applications. For everyone, the language of the rule of law stands for a cultural achievement of universal significance.[133]

Tom Paine brings all of these elements to bear in *Common Sense.* He then welds the aspiration of the rule of law to the act of revolution. Using a typically reductionist tactic, he announces that "independency means no more, than, whether we shall make our own laws." The quiet corollary to noisy independence is legality. As Paine tells his newly forming national readership, independence must be brought about by "the legal voice of the people in Congress"; only in this manner can "we have every opportunity and every encouragement before us, to form the noblest, purest constitution on the face of the earth."[134] *Common Sense* insists that a legal revolution will cap the angers that made independence possible. The crown of law will be scattered among the people, "whose right it is," and the exercise of that right will restore calm.

The optimism in such language functions as an intrinsic necessity in a rule of law. A people have to believe in the logic and the criteria of the law for it to work. The language and acts of the law must establish an expectation of justice within a receptive community.[135] Paine aims all of the solidarity that he has created in *Common Sense* in this direction. He is the first to predict that 'the noblest, purest constitution on the face of the earth" will be made on a continental scale. Independence is the first step in such a legal framework. "We shall then see our object," Paine concludes in his last paragraph, "and our ears will be legally shut against the schemes of an intriguing, as well as a cruel enemy."[136] Seeing the object clearly stages an overriding enlightenment norm, the restoration of calm through proper sight. No other sense is allowed to disrupt this primal and prescriptive clarity of light. With their ears "legally shut against . . . a cruel enemy," Paine's readers use the law positively to channel their understanding. To the extent that they see clearly, they exchange the shouts of the mob for the more measured voice of a people.

The peculiar juxtaposition of aroused anger and lawgiving calm means that *Common Sense* resists a simple reading. The pamphlet is there for the revolutionary mind; it is also there for the transcendent lawgiver. But rhetorically the writer has turned the combination into a vital sequence, and this affirmation is the key to a national text worth permanent scrutiny. Over and over again, Paine insists that a procedurally minded republic will find the forms that it needs in his pages. A knowing people must use those forms to participate intelligently in their own governance. These words and others like them come out of crisis but succeed in the solution rendered. They reach for the common reader as useful citizen. They say *Common Sense* is a source book for a deserving people—if, or when, things go badly wrong.

CHAPTER FOUR

Becoming American

Nothing conveys the utter fluidity in Revolutionary American culture more dramatically than the concept of treason. Treason, as John Locke made clear, represented the most heinous crime that anyone could commit in the Anglo-American world of the eighteenth century, and any individual so identified as a traitor deserved to be treated as "the common Enemy and Pest of Mankind."[1] Despite the general spread of the Enlightenment in the eighteenth century, treason remained a medieval crime. Punishment for the offense continued to rely on the most appalling and rigid of ancient forms—forms that in themselves reached back to primitive rituals. As late as 1769, within the orderly narrative pace of Blackstone's *Commentaries on the Laws of England*, encompassing reason gave way to something else, something "solemn and terrible" where treason was concerned, namely:

> 1. That the offender be drawn to the gallows, and not be carried or walk; though usually a sledge or hurdle is allowed, to preserve the offender from the extreme torment of being dragged on the ground or pavement. 2. That he be hanged by the neck, and then cut down alive. 3. That his entrails be taken out, and burned while he is yet alive. 4. That his head be cut off. 5. That his body be divided into four parts. 6. That his head and quarters be at the King's disposal.

Official punishment did not end even in death. Attainder, forfeiture, and corruption of blood in the traitor's line—all part of a judgment of treason—generated "future incapacities of inheritance even to the twentieth generation."[2]

Both the gravity of the offense and the corresponding horror in punishment took on added significance and ubiquity in Revolutionary America.[3] Every American faced the accusation one way or another in 1776. Since the act of becoming an American required rebellion, the language of community and the specific charge of treason doubled back and forth as mutually reinforcing or differentiating terms; it was a dangerous subject that depended on the outcome of the Revolution. When Benjamin Franklin supposedly told the other members of the Second Continental Congress that "we must, indeed, all hang together, or most assuredly, we shall all hang separately," he was reminding them of their universal treason in the eyes of the British Empire.[4] The warning was part of a cultural refrain, one that described the essence of being American in early republican society.

The cry of treason was particularly volatile in the act of national formations, and it arose as much from emotion as from reason but with a nugget of irreducible truth at its foundation. If early republicans remained confused about charges of treason and if they promiscuously leveled such charges against each other, finding hidden enemies at home and abroad, they did so because of their certainty that treason *had* been committed. The terms of the Revolutionary struggle decreed this much. Tom Paine in *Common Sense* cautioned against a state of affairs in which "there is no such thing as treason; wherefore every one thinks himself at liberty to act as he pleases."[5] Nonetheless, and even with treason frequently voiced as a concept, the ultimate question remained to be answered. *Who* had committed treason in British America? There existed just one person that every member of the English-speaking world could safely call a traitor. That person was Benedict Arnold.

So much attention, in fact, was given to Benedict Arnold and his act of treason that he can be used as a benchmark for a larger discussion of the fragility and general uncertainty of American aspirations and identity in the Revolutionary moment. George Washington, always stoical in the face of adversity, divulged the nature of that fragility in the instant of discovering Arnold's conspiracy. "Arnold has betrayed us!" he cried out impulsively to Alexander Hamilton and the Marquis de Lafayette on that traumatic afternoon of September 24, 1780, "Whom can we trust now?"[6] Lafayette confirmed both Washington's

reaction and the general atmosphere of the army in his own account
of the event. "Gloom and distrust seemed to pervade every mind, and
I have never seen General Washington so affected by any circumstance."[7] Arnold escaped, but his British contact, Major John André,
was captured, tried as a spy, and executed in an event that upset the
Revolutionary army in another way. No other episode of the Revolutionary War produced such a broad series of intense emotional responses among wartime participants as this one, and no other received such frequent and dramatic treatment after the event.[8] Why did
the Arnold conspiracy so capture and continue to hold the imagination of its own and later times? How are we to explain the strange
conflict of emotions that the event produced? Where does the image
of Arnold fit within the uncertain determinations of loyalty and appropriate patriotic behavior in 1780? What do the crafted solutions
to the problem of Arnold's treason tell us about the early republic that
he betrayed?

The surfaces in that betrayal can be summarized quickly.[9] In the fall
of 1780, Benedict Arnold, a major general and a legitimate war hero
in three earlier campaigns of the American army (Quebec, Valcour,
and Saratoga) contrived to betray the critical fortress and arsenal of
West Point into British hands in exchange for substantial monetary rewards, the promise of a later pension, immediate commanding rank
in the British Army of North America, and a per capita bounty for
captured Americans, including possibly General Washington himself.
Negotiations between Arnold and high-ranking British officers extended across two years, starting in 1778, and Arnold as commander
of American troops in Philadelphia first had to maneuver with Washington to obtain command of West Point, gateway to the Hudson
River and the line of forts along it. The conspiracy depended on the
belief of Sir Henry Clinton, then commander of British forces, that the
capture of West Point would split American forces north and south in
a decisive fashion. "Had it succeeded," Clinton later wrote, "all agree
it would have ended the rebellion."[10] Minimally, the capture of West
Point would have given control of the Hudson River to the British
navy and its banks to the British army at what was already the lowest
ebb in Revolutionary fortunes. The American army had suffered even
worse in the winter of 1780 than it had two years before at Valley
Forge. Disasters in the southern theater—the surrender of Charleston
to the British in May, in which more Americans were captured than in
any other action of the war, and the defeat of the army at Camden in

August—left Americans groaning under the reality of unending war with many of them wavering and doubting the patriotic cause.[11]

The times were ripe for betrayal. If historians now question General Clinton's strategy, no less a participant than General Lafayette conceded that all might have been "consequently lost." A confidant of Washington, Lafayette wrote that West Point would have fallen but for "an almost incredible combination of accidents" that beset the conspirators: "the plot," he concluded, "was within an ace of succeeding."[12] It failed because Major André was caught out of uniform behind American lines on September 23, 1780, with incriminating documents in his possession about the defenses of West Point—documents in Arnold's own hand. The two conspirators had met in secret rendezvous to insure Arnold's resolve. Even then, Washington inferred that André would have eluded final capture but for "an unaccountable deprivation of presence of mind in a man of first abilities."[13] Arnold, for his part, escaped to the British side by a hairsbreadth when he received word of André's capture.

The situation touched the vulnerabilities and the needs of a still-fragile American identity in very specific terms. Together, André and Arnold summarized a much larger American predicament. Alexander Hamilton, Washington's aide-de-camp and a close player in the event (he nearly captured Arnold and spent much time with the captured André), saw better than he knew when he wrote of André, "[T]here was, in truth, no way of saving him. Arnold, or he, must have been the victim: the former was out of our power."[14] Benedict Arnold was indeed beyond the power of Revolutionary America to determine or control. Safe within enemy lines, he immediately became the ungraspable phantom of an ideological nightmare. But to understand just how complicated a role he was to play in Revolutionary understandings, we must first return to the vexed history of loyalty as identity in British America. We get nowhere in understanding the period unless we first acknowledge how many quantum changes in thought were required of Americans in a very short period of time.

From the moment that a rhetoric of opposition even implied the separate possibility of revolution, treason took shape as the impossible problem in Anglo-American exchange. Already in 1721, Jeremiah Dummer, in *A Defence of the New-England Charters,* could, in one breath, insist on a response to the "Unnatural insult" in British denial of American rights and, in the next, regret as ludicrous all thought of unlawful resistance. "[I]t would not be more absurd," he wrote, "to place two of his Majesty's Beef-Eaters to watch an Infant in the Cradle, that it don't rise and cuts its Fathers Throat, then to guard these weak infant Colonies, to prevent their shaking off the *British* Yoke."[15] And yet Dummer's metaphors belied the surface of their meanings, and these discrepancies explain why John Adams could later refer to *A Defence of the New-England Charters* as the handbook of the Revolution.[16] To the extent that British rule figured as a "yoke," it implied the possibility and perhaps even the necessity of being thrown off. An infant cannot commit parricide, but, later and often enough, children do revolt against their parents. By 1750, Jonathan Mayhew's sermon, *A Discourse Concerning Unlimited Submission and Nonresistance to the Higher Powers* turned these contradictions into a dialectic where Americans could simultaneously "learn to be *free* and to be *loyal*."[17]

In the ensuing continuum of radical pamphleteering, rebellion remained the most abominable of crimes. An endless flow of questions about the true nature of loyalty sought to evade the stigma of treason when protest proved necessary. Assurances of loyalty competed on every page with discussions of a legitimate right of resistance. In part, the very horror of treason dictated the need for a separate possibility. When Locke argued that "all resisting of *Princes* is not rebellion," his words were useful, but he also wrote that "natural rights could never justify treason."[18] Most Americans accepted that their right of resistance existed only in the loyalty that secured their continuing prerogatives as English subjects. To properly resist encroachment by authority was to celebrate those prerogatives rooted in common law and English custom from time out of memory. To rebel, to the contrary, signified a break from the British Empire with all of its privileges; it meant the abdication and desertion of hard-won rights rather than the lawful exercise of them.

The chasm between legitimate resistance and outrageous rebellion explains Patrick Henry's famous exchange with other legislative members of the Virginia House of Burgesses in the crisis of 1775. When Henry proclaimed that "Caesar had his Brutus, Charles the First his Cromwell, and George the Third—," his sequence prompted interrupting cries of "TREASON!" in the House. "And George the Third," countered Henry above the din, "may profit by their example—if this be treason, make the most of it."[19] The exchange, at least on Henry's part, took a deliberately contrapuntal form. The juxtaposition of perceived connotations (a cautionary note for his king versus the implied threat of revolt) intensified both possibilities by "making the most" of opposition. Henry cleverly left his incensed auditors on the side of constructive resistance through his delayed presumption of advice to authority, but they, in hearing something else in his words and in their shouts of "TREASON!," had shattered every available decorum and legitimate limit to opposition. So unacceptable were the consequences that Henry, in the seldom quoted aftermath, had to apologize immediately for the overall effect, saying "that if he had affronted the Speaker, or the house, he was ready to ask pardon, and he would show his loyalty to his majesty King George the Third at the expense of the last drop of his blood."[20] Henry's words and the reaction to them in the House of Burgesses typified a continuing struggle to think the unthinkable in late eighteenth-century America. They also occurred at exactly the moment in time, 1775, when colonists began to refer to themselves as Americans more frequently than as Englishmen.[21]

The shift toward a separate identity took place in a spirit of opposition that resisted ultimate transgression. No eighteenth-century American at any point embraced the title of traitor. To do so would have meant rejection of the most basic communal premises of the time. Loyalty to one's sovereign was the same thing as duty to country. How could either be separated from the other without committing treason? In the most influential colonial writing of the 1760s, John Dickinson defined the acceptable parameters of American identity when he claimed that loyalty to the king and love of freedom had to be compatible qualities.[22] The craft in Revolutionary rhetoric came in maintaining that increasingly difficult combination. Early Americans struggled with the act of imagination that it required well into the republican era, and it left permanent marks on their thought.

Faced with the preconditions of loyalty and love of freedom as contradictory bases of identity, radical pamphleteers fashioned strategies that separated treason from the Revolutionary cause. In legal terms, protecting the people against arbitrary power ceased to be rebellion and became a natural right of defense.[23] In religious terms, using the motto that Franklin and Jefferson made famous, "Rebellion to Tyrants was Obedience to God."[24] As natural law justified opposition, so divine law brought resistance into the higher realm of a protected piety, but neither frame of reference welcomed the extreme or the name of treason, and accusations of treason continued to flourish on every side in Anglo-American politics. The end result was a reversal of implications that heightened the crime.

In effect, rebellion and loyalty changed places in the formation of national identity while treason remained the worst of crimes. By 1774, as the British navy closed the ports of Massachusetts, Nathaniel Niles, preaching in Newburyport, decided that anyone "who infringes on liberty rebels against good government, and ought to be treated as a rebel. It matters not what station he fills: he is a traitor."[25] In 1775, the Reverend John Cleaveland of Ipswich applied this logic more directly when he consigned Thomas Gage, governor of Massachusetts and commander of the British armies, straight to hell. As Cleaveland told Gage, "[Y]ou are not only a robber, a murderer, a usurper, but a wicked Rebel: A rebel against the authority of truth, law, equity, the English constitution of government, these colony states, and humanity itself."[26] While covering every base, Cleaveland and others were also relocating treason. "A line of distinction should be drawn," Paine argued in *Common Sense*, "between English soldiers taken in battle, and inhabitants of America taken in arms. The first are prisoners, but the latter traitors. The one forfeits his liberty, the other his head."[27] When loyalty and treason changed places, the price of the makeover was a magnification of each.

Several things follow from this tangled state of affairs. *First,* Americans were and always have remained curiously vulnerable, politically and psychologically, to charges of treason in their midst. As they have liked to level those charges at others, so they have been capable of obsessing about them as signs pointing toward their own troubled, originating identity. *Second,* even the briefest glance back over history shows that talk about treason began with religious as well as secular understandings. Scholars long have noted conflicting patterns between "the Age of Reason and the Age of Enthusiasm" in the formation of American character, and this "war between reason and emotion" has taken on special vehemence whenever loyalty and betrayal have been subjects of concern.[28] In the early republic, the odium and punishment attached to a traitor retained religious overtones while the assignation of treason belonged to the secular realm of law. Even today, the mix of these discourses remains an uneasy one. The first tortured shift from rebel into citizen, from colonial traitor into patriotic republican, required both innate reason and a leap of faith based on something other than evidence. *Third,* an effective new definition of treason with appropriate controls was an anxiously missed ingredient as the new nation formed. *Fourth,* even then, early republicans could see that any testing of the meaning of treason would have to take place in a courtroom but with intrusive lines of force involved from other cultural perspectives. If Benedict Arnold merits renewed attention, it is because his treason furthers discussion in each of these areas.

Rhetorically, the example of Benedict Arnold grew out of a compound negative. For while Arnold went unpunished for his treason and remained forever unrepentant about his actions, his British collaborator, Major John André, behaved beautifully within every decorum of the times and in a way that troubled his captors greatly as they executed him. Washington's army, if not Washington, was left wishing that its own inexorable machinery of military law might be stopped. "Never, perhaps, did any man suffer death with more justice, or deserve it less," Alexander Hamilton wrote of André.[29] As Washington's aide-de-camp, Hamilton knew everything about the proceedings against André, but he also observed that "every thing that is amiable in virtue, in fortitude, in delicate sentiment, and accomplished manners, pleads for him. . . . I reverenced his merit." "My feelings," he would later confess, "were never put to so severe a trial."[30] What the eighteenth century called sensibility or the power of sympathy came directly into play. "I became so deeply attached to Major André," wrote another important senior officer, "that I can remember no instance where my affections were so fully absorbed in any man. . . . All the spectators seemed to be overwhelmed by the affecting spectacle [of André's execution], and many were suffused in tears."[31] A presumably more objective medical examiner confirmed the accuracy of this description. "The spot," he wrote, "was consecrated by the tears of thousands."[32]

Why should seasoned leaders and hardened veterans of many military campaigns, men who had witnessed all of the horrors of battle, have been moved so profoundly by an enemy whose personal duplicity and ungentlemanly engagement in espionage had threatened their very existence? It was true that André died bravely, that his situation depicted "an ancient story of guilt, sacrifice, and betrayal," that as the head of British military intelligence in North America he fell tragically from a great height, and that his execution graphically symbolized a powerful conflict between two of the most compelling impulses of the day, sentiment versus authority—all arguments regularly presented to explain the outpouring of concern and emotion.[33] Even so, reactions were extreme then and have remained acute. More was obviously at work in the nature of American reactions.

The contrasts in André and Arnold went well beyond what either could bring alone to the situation and touched the vulnerabilities of a still-fragile American identity in very specific terms. Together but very much apart, the two conspirators summarized an early republican predicament. Was success—first in war but then in peace—going to be based on correct behavior and polished observances of decorum of the kind that the gentlemanly Major André demonstrated (he also drew, danced, and wrote with exquisite perfection), or would it depend on the raw but reckless energy and innovative imagination of *arrivistes*, men like Benedict Arnold, who had been Washington's greatest fighting general? And if the latter, what had gone wrong and when would it happen again? Correct conduct amounted to a preoccupation for new republicans in the chaos and uncertainty of the Revolutionary situation. It hurt everyone more than anyone could admit that an Englishman had behaved so well by all of the recognized standards of honor and virtue while his American counterpart outraged every sensibility and broke all of the rules. What did it say about the Revolutionary enterprise if only the former received punishment?

The perspective on André is the easiest to explain. Though English, André typified the danger to every wartime American of chance identification on the wrong side in the ever-shifting neutral territory of a bloody civil war—so much so that it would be the English officer André and not Nathan Hale, the American secret agent hanged by the British, who dominated the spy legend in early American literature. The two most successful early writers of American fiction, Washington Irving in *The Legend of Sleepy Hollow* (1819) and James Fenimore Cooper in *The Spy: A Tale of the Neutral Ground* (1821) as well as the leading playwright of the period, William Dunlap in *André: A Tragedy in Five Acts* (1798), all took up the subject. They fastened on André because of certain intangibles in the figure that carried beyond his obvious courage and intelligence. Significantly, Major

André failed not through lack of character but through too much of it. When captured, he could not make himself stoop to the level of low cunning that disguise required. Unwilling to compromise his honor and status as an officer and a gentleman, André allowed his military carriage and social bearing to reveal his true identity even before his own spontaneous and voluntary confession completed the act, a point that Cooper would emphasize in *The Spy*.[34]

Sincerity of character—a trait of colossal importance to Americans engaged in rebellion—and the assumption of honor that formed the foundation of that sincerity were the captured André's most apparent traits. Just as important was the way this sincerity and sense of honor overcame an apparent unseemliness. All of these traits dominated the first paragraphs of André's letter to Washington on the day of his capture:

> What I have as yet said concerning myself was in the justifiable attempt to be extricated; I am too little accustomed to duplicity to have succeeded.
>
> I beg your Excellency will be persuaded that no alteration in the temper of my mind, or apprehension for my safety, induces me to take a step of addressing you, but that it is to secure myself from an imputation of having assumed a mean character, for treacherous purposes or self-interest—as conduct incompatible with the principles that actuated me, as well as with my condition in life.[35]

André's use of the circumlocutions, abstractions, and arch delivery of the eighteenth-century epistolary style served several purposes here. It pushed all suggestions of meanness of character and self-interest onto Benedict Arnold, where Arnold's betrayed colleagues were only too happy to place all of the blame. As well, it cloaked André's reallocation of himself from conspirator into officer and gentleman through the saving principles of virtue, honor, candor, proper station, and personal disinterestedness. The reassignation of meanness and the "extrication" from a negative "imputation" played well in the America camp and for another reason. André's embarrassment over the charge of espionage paralleled Revolutionary Americans' comparable rhetorical problem in the charge of rebellion.

As gentlemen do not spy, so good citizens do not rebel. The rest of André's letter to Washington stressed the necessities that "betrayed" him into "the vile condition of an enemy in disguise." He wrote as one "involuntarily an impostor" and "to vindicate my fame" and "not to solicit security." Four of the last eight sentences in his letter fastened on the idea of honor. Their thrust sought to prove "that though unfortunate, I am branded with nothing dishonorable." The American officers in the Revolutionary army identified with this logic and with their captive because, at one level, his rhetoric was also theirs. A similar rhetorical pattern of conscious elevation above the fray "impels" the Declaration of Independence. Americans knew and identified with the measured calm, the reluctance in negative circumstance, the claim of betrayal, the need for a higher extrication. Above all, they identified with the mutual concern for world opinion and sacred honor.

Another affinity existed between Major André's proud sense of decorum and the controlling tones of the published proceedings of the Board of General Officers who adjudged him guilty of espionage and arranged for his execution. Trials that grip the communal imagination, as this one did, tend to formalize ideological paradoxes. The narratives about them attempt to resolve the predicament of conflict in a moment of decision by subsuming contending voices into that decision. Major André's measured calm and regret mixed with resignation were just what Washington, his assigned court of officers operating under military law, and the new federal government needed in a dangerous situation. Washington asked for "a careful examination . . . as speedily as possible." André's many acknowledgments of his own guilt and of perfect propriety during his examination by the court "evince that the proceedings against him were not guided by passion or resentment."[36] In the reimposition of decorum on everyone's part, all previous disruption and jeopardy could be relegated to the unpleasant past. The opportunity was lost on no one. Congress arranged for immediate general publication of the transcript of André's trial and designated a day of national thanksgiving to celebrate the country's narrow escape from the peril of the conspiracy.

The danger had been real and reached to the highest places. George Washington and, to a lesser extent, the federal government had to rectify impressions generated by the treason at West Point. The published transcript of the court of inquiry supplied the means. Washington's own reputation in a struggling army was by no means as secure as it would quickly become in victory, and he faced real criticism from several directions for his close association with Arnold. Washington had kept Arnold in command in Philadelphia despite evidence against Arnold of administrative and financial malfeasance; he had continued to sustain Arnold over repeated congressional objection; he had given Arnold command of West Point against his own better judgment; and he had allowed Arnold to slip away into the opposing camp, where, as an extremely able British general, the traitor would be a serious nuisance for the rest of the war. Washington needed answers that would minimize his own vulnerabilities and that would calm the nation's fears. The linkage between Arnold and André allowed him to reduce Arnold's character in the light of André's behavior at trial while also enabling him to cap the event through punishment of the discovered spy.

The military trial of André offered a substitution of type (André for Arnold) and of offense (espionage for treason) rather than a more slippery comparison of degree for the same crime. When one of his own officers, Lieutenant Colonel John Laurens, indulged in just such a comparison, imagining that "Arnold must undergo a punishment comparatively more severe [than André's] in the permanent, increasing torment of a mental hell," Washington would have none of it. "I am mistaken if, at *this* time 'Arnold is undergoing the torment of a mental Hell'," he observed brusquely in resisting the inference. "He [Arnold] wants feeling. From some traits of his character, which have lately come to my knowledge, he seems to have been so hackneyed in villainy, and so lost to all sense of honor and shame, that, while his faculties will enable him to continue his sordid pursuits, there will be no time for remorse."[37] Washington, of course, was angry, but his response raised another question. How could such a complete villain have escaped his own commander's detection and for so long? Major André supplied a special kind of surrogate for the unrepentant Arnold, and Washington's aide-de-camp Hamilton recognized the connection on the day of execution. "Poor André suffers to-day," Hamilton explained to his fiancée, "hard-hearted policy calls for a sacrifice. He must die."[38]

How André filled the role of a useful sacrifice can also be seen in the trial transcript. Two letters from Washington as commander in chief to Congress opened the court record, and they situated the desired narrative of André from start to finish. The first communication explained that the capture of André *enabled* the escape of Arnold, thereby reducing an obvious embarrassment; the second announced the execution of André as a foregone conclusion in formal closure of the only subject under investigation.

The transcript itself is a curious document worth closer examination. The proceedings of the court of inquiry occupy just five pages in a twenty-four page record, and half of these pages are given over to reiterated lists of the officers present; the court's formal reasoning and judgment require less than two hundred words.[39] The rest of the transcript is a composite of seventeen letters exchanged during the event: the earliest is a letter from André to Arnold proving the former's plan of disguise; three are from Washington to Congress and his judicial board of inquiry; two come from André to Washington; six involve formal exchanges between the heads of the two armies; four, and the longest, come from the pen of Benedict Arnold (three to Washington, one to Clinton); and one letter, the most affecting, is from André to his British commander, Sir Henry Clinton, absolving Clinton of all responsibility for André's fate. This dominance of the letter form in a legal document may seem strange to the modern eye, but it came naturally enough at the time. Like so many other writings of the period, the transcript of André's trial enacts "the epistolary moment" in Anglo-American literature.[40]

The generic impulse at work here should not surprise anyone, and neither should the creative options and the critical restraints that it dictated. Transcripts of trials are in general excellent artifacts for exploring the constructed form and the linguistic nuance of thought in moments of history. Recording the give-and-take of courtroom debate, they supply convincing explanations under the extreme pressure of winning a public argument, and the explanations themselves have to be couched in highly recognizable form in order to stimulate the all-important ingredients of belief and acceptance. A courtroom partakes of only those narratives of events that its audiences are already primed to receive. It needs all of the familiar ground that it can find to control the deviance under investigation and to legitimize its own solution to the problem at hand. Put another way, a courtroom transcript reveals the story that a community is willing to tell itself and in the form that best encourages reception. In this case, the generic form of the letter and the narratives that a series of letters encouraged were familiar to eighteenth-century readers steeped in epistolary genres. The transcript of Major André's trial, in reaching for that familiarity, leaves us with an important opportunity. How was the epistolary genre used here? In what ways did the properties of letter writing help to create meaning for anxious early republicans—early republicans who were facing treason not only in Benedict Arnold but potentially in a similar charge against themselves?

The generic dominance of the epistolary form encourages the formality of a predictable difference of views between André, Arnold, Washington, and the British commanders, Sir Henry Clinton and James Robertson, who contested American proceedings against Major André as a spy. At the same time, the genre governs the conflict in views by encapsulating them. The letters as artifacts convey an impression of reality or authenticity; these letters *were* written. The form and its constraints also allow for a similarity of diction and an understood quiescence of tone among gentleman of letters who agree on the form if not the content of their exchanges. The march of formal correspondence from page to page in the transcript dignifies the ceremonial proceedings against André and, by its very nature, presumes a conclusion—the conclusion "that Major André, Adjutant-General to the British army, ought to be considered a spy from the enemy, and that agreeable to the law and usage of nations, it is their [the court's] opinion he ought to suffer death."[41]

The means of that death, Washington's failure to see through Arnold, and the escape of the traitor remain controversial subjects, but here too, the epistolary narrative proves useful. Letter exchanges, which privilege the strict point of view and control of a writer to a specific addressee, allow for *"elliptical narration"* or the possibility of "nonnarrated events of which we see only the repercussions."[42] Not surprisingly, the problem of Arnold and his escape are "nonnarrated" here. In command of the letters they write, if not of the events they describe, all parties in the epistolary exchange of the transcript feel generically entitled to leave out or minimize embarrassing behavior, and each falls easily into a frequent mode of letter writing, self-justification.

The sequence of letters fulfills the needs of narrative in the same manner that similar patterns inform the epistolary novel. As in *The Coquette,* analyzed in Chapter 1, each separate voice, recognizable by situation within the whole, participates in a similarity of form and situation while addressing conflict. When the letters end, the story is presumed closed, and André is properly executed. In their polished punctiliousness, these aspects of the trail transcript also convey the sense of reintegration and balance that Washington and Congress desired. In keeping with other judicial decisions, the disruption of crime yields to the discursive reenactment of order through language. The words themselves help to signify to a governing elite—in this case, the Revolutionary army and, by extension, Congress—that it still governs.

One element resisted these integrative tendencies. The prisoner's cooperation in every procedural decorum underscored a discrepancy in the mode of his punishment, one that vexed every major external account of the trial and execution. André, "buoyed above the terror of death" on the day before his execution, wrote a second letter to Washington asking to be shot as a soldier and not hanged as a spy. "Sympathy towards a soldier," he pleaded, "will surely induce your Excellency and a military tribunal to adapt the mode of my death to the feelings of a man of honor." André added that he and Washington could hope to put all resentment behind them only "by being informed that I am not to die on a gibbet."[43] This letter boosts the epistolary form of the trial transcript into another realm, one that rarely failed to electrify eighteenth- and nineteenth-century audiences. We are suddenly in the presence of sentimental epistolary narration, where emotion is distilled and appreciated in the bridge of communication from writer to recipient and on to the later reader as vicarious participant. Not for the first time, Washington dealt with the situation by breaking the mold of narration. He utilized a very different strength in epistolary narration: the ability of the addressee to shape a writer's words through noncompliance.[44] Washington simply refused to respond in any way. There were limits, however, to his control of this aspect of the event. Every eyewitness description of the execution lingered over André's revulsion on first sighting the hangman's noose.[45]

The hanging of Major André by the stoical and apparently unmoved commander in chief of the Revolutionary army spawned a dilemma in the hagiographical tradition of George Washington. Alexander Hamilton, in full identification with André, did not hesitate to express his scorn on the spot:

I urged a compliance with André's request to be shot; and I do not think it would have had an ill effect: but some people are only sensible to motives of policy, and sometimes, from a narrow disposition, mistake it. When André's tale comes to be told, and present resentment is over; the refusing him the privilege of choosing the manner of his death will be branded with too much obstinacy.

He then gave his own version of "André's tale" to the *Pennsylvania Gazette,* but like so many inside narratives that are published, this one only increased the teller's own "present resentment." The need to "brand" Washington would lead Hamilton to break with his commander in chief soon after.[46]

Why *did* Washington resist André's request? From the first, the American leader held to the technical difference between spy and soldier. "I would not wish Mr. André to be treated with insult; but he does not appear to stand upon the footing of a common prisoner of war," observed Washington on the day after André's capture, "and therefore he is not entitled to the usual indulgences, which they receive."[47] Biographers have embellished the distinction by suggesting that any deviation from the prescribed method of punishment for espionage would have fueled additional British protest by suggesting an American inconsistency. Even so, the argument from policy does not reach the seeming cruelty or insensitivity of allowing André to remain uncertain until the moment of execution. Washington's only answer on the occasion came when André, expecting a firing squad, actually saw the gallows.[48]

Lost in these discussions is the intricate role of George Washington as commander in chief of the Revolutionary army in the act of discovering treason. As Cincinnatus, Washington stood for rigid Roman discipline as well as civic virtue, and that sense of discipline caused him to hand out brutal punishment at times. His general orders to the army commonly leveled the threat. As he told his troops, "an Army without Order, Regularity and Discipline, is no better than a Commission'd Mob," and he placed "fear of punishment" well above "natural bravery" and "hope of reward" in defining the effective soldier. Washington, the owner of slaves, knew the need to chastise insubordination all of his life. Floggings for relatively minor offenses, even to a hundred lashes with washings of salt and water in between, were permitted and conducted in the Revolutionary army.[49]

The Arnold treason had shaken a faltering American military to

its foundations—enough for the aloof, usually stern, and always unbending Washington to have found it an occasion for punishment of
the severest kind. Since the penalty for espionage, hanging, tallied
with the sentence of treason, the chance to convey a double lesson
in the execution of André would not have been lost on the disciplinarian. And behind the official need were subtler claims. The young
Washington laboriously wrote out 110 rules "of civility and decent
behavior in company and conversation" and learned to accept the
overriding importance of formal conduct. How to behave correctly
in the unprecedented crisis of the Revolution dominated the commander's concern for his officers and men, and much of the decorum
that he enforced on himself and others had to do with instilling basic
expectations in unexpected times.[50] In Washington's eyes, André was
well and properly hanged. The spy's peculiar contribution to the uncertainty of events doomed him to a certain and fixed death.

All cognizance of this disciplinarian would soon be sacrificed to
ideological formations in the new nation. The mythologized Washington who presides over the pantheon of the founders could not be left
to make the same assumptions about André as the commander of the
Revolutionary army.[51] In William Dunlap's play André: A Tragedy in
Five Acts, the figure of Washington agonizes openly until the "cruel
mockery" of a parallel British execution of an American officer eliminates all further need for hesitation. "My heart is torn in twain," cries
Dunlap's Washington in the moment of decision.[52] In Cooper's novel
The Spy, Washington even works secretly to free a falsely accused
British spy. Incognito and out of uniform in neutral territory, Cooper's
Washington could be convicted as a spy himself. The protagonist of
the novel, Harvey Birch, acts as a double agent hunted by all sides,
and it is this central character who delivers the lines that early republicans wanted to believe about the father of their country. "No-no-no,"
cries Birch, "Washington can see beyond the hollow views of pre-
tended patriots. . . . No-no-no, Washington would never say 'Lead
him to a gallows'." The Spy represents a bizarre response to those
who, in Cooper's words, "affected to believe this execution had sullied the fair character of Washington."[53] Meanwhile, the single most
popular contemporary work on the subject, The Ballad of Major
André, avoided the problem altogether by excising all mention of
Washington from the decision to hang André.[54]

These recontextualizations of Washington's handling of the trial of

André offer one more indication that the early republic was an imagined community—another proof, if one is needed, that the American experience may be distinctive in "the degree to which what is and what should be are identified one with the other."[55] Aspiration and reality challenge each other in patriotic rhetoric, and never more so than when the subject is treason. The conspiracy at West Point stimulated divergent acts of imagination from all concerned, and the gaps between encourage another look at the actual language of the event.

The trial transcript of Washington's board of inquiry told a story. It sought to establish the separate high-mindedness of the American army, acting "in such a manner upon the occasion as does them the highest honor, and proves them to be men of great virtue" while engaged in conflict with "the private and secret manner," the "feigned name," and the "disguised habit" of "a spy from the enemy."[56] In this narrative, decorum could notice and even sympathize with Major André across the formal divide of friend against enemy, but any such acknowledgment vanished when treason replaced espionage as the subject of interest. The transcript orchestrated a special need for an American ascendancy over everything *not* American in the situation, but that still left a difficulty in explaining the conspiracy.

Benedict Arnold was manifestly American, not *un*American, and he long had been a pivotal leader of those "men of great virtue" and "highest honor" in the American army. The celebration of an American ascendancy crumbled when Arnold came to mind—as indeed he did at every turn. It was clearly harder to place Arnold with satisfaction than André in both the moment and later literary representation. Joel Barlow, chaplain for the Third Massachusetts Brigade during the Revolution, supplies an ideal example of the problem as both a witness and a poet of the events in question. Like the other officers in the Revolution who saw the captured Major André, Barlow could not control his admiration ("a greater character of his age, is perhaps not alive"), and, again like them, his heart was "thrown into a flutter" by the horror of the execution. From the other side, Barlow's "flaming political sermon, occasioned by the treachery of Arnold" won him "great honor" within the army and an invitation to dine with General Washington, but Arnold would not stay down so easily. When the poet came to write his epic poem of the Revolution, Arnold would figure unavoidably and prominently as the hero of Saratoga even though treason "bade waves of dark oblivion round him roll."[57] Arnold would never disappear. Like the return of the repressed, he represented things that Americans did not want to face but could not ignore.

The substitution of André for Arnold in the formal investigation of the conspiracy and thus in the trial transcript mirrored the larger evasion of treason as an intellectual subject in Revolutionary America. What, the question remained, could be done with or about Benedict Arnold? No one could either forget him or apparently stop thinking about him. Not only did Arnold's betrayal excite "a uniquely intense obsession among Revolutionaries," the continuing vehemence and duration of that reaction also made the man "one of the most widely remembered Americans of the era." Even today, every American learns the name "Benedict Arnold." As the *New-Jersey Journal* would explain the emerging phenomenon a year after the treason, "the streets of every city and village in the United States, for many months, rung with the crimes of General Arnold."[58]

With the exposure of the conspiracy, the shift in propaganda terms was immediate, extreme, and lasting. Arnold the Revolutionary hero of Quebec and Saratoga instantly became "the most loathed name in American history." In a conventional eighteenth-century appreciation of character, absolute integrity in Arnold had acceded to the utter lack thereof.[59] And yet all of the vituperation heaped on Arnold—and the amount was incalculable—did not really come to grips with the observable facts about him, and neither did Washington's court of inquiry. Arnold's own letters published in the trial transcript substantiated the truth and scope of his treachery, but no part of the transcript ever mentioned the word *treason*. The continuing early republican fixation on Arnold sought to categorize him, but it never paused at any level to consider what actually drove him.

Arnold tellingly used his own access to the trial proceedings of Major André to resist the notion of any metamorphosis in himself. From the safety of a British sloop of war in the Hudson—some thought it aptly named *The Vulture*—he claimed a consistent rectitude and warned against mistaken acts of vengeance. "I have ever acted from a principle of love to my country, since the commencement of the present unhappy contest between Great Britain and the Colonies," Arnold wrote Washington, "the same principle of love to my country actuates my present conduct." Patiently, he reiterated the point in subsequent letters to Washington, each of which found its place in the trial transcript: "my attachment to the true interest of my country is invariable. . . . I am actuated by the *same principle* which has ever been the governing rule of my conduct in this unhappy contest."[60] Arnold, in fact, so convinced himself of his own invariable consistency and, by extension, of still operating principles of normalcy that he actually petitioned the United States for back pay after he defected![61]

This claim of consistency was exactly what early republicans could never accept. Neither Revolutionary nor post-Revolutionary thought could grant Arnold the uniformity of character that he claimed except through an assumption of unmitigated knavery. Rhetorically, there could be no middle ground for the traitor. Either Arnold had been a complete villain from the start or in 1780 he had undergone a remarkable transformation into one. The undiscovered villain made early republican patriots look foolish and gullible, but was it any easier to assume "two Arnolds," first the patriot and then the traitor? The extent of the problem can be seen in a ludicrous solution still employed today. The betrayed Revolutionaries boasted that if they captured Arnold, they would hang him but remove the leg that had been wounded in the battle of Saratoga for appropriate burial with military honors for its service to the country.[62] Today, half in jest but also in iconographic earnestness, a monument on the battlefield at Saratoga depicts the removed leg of Benedict Arnold as the only worthy American thing about him. The Saratoga dismemberment, a grotesque memorial, extends the joke, but it also contributes to an enduring symbolism about treason—a symbolism in which monstrosity, disfigurement, distortion, and irrational projection remain defining ingredients.

The desire to belittle and dismiss Arnold has already been glimpsed in Washington's description of Arnold as incapable of remorse and lost to all sense of honor and shame. But dismissal, however satisfying, foreclosed real explanation. Even if the patriotic projection of wickedness could be taken as truth, its rhetorical vehemence precluded rational avenues of clarification. Arnold, in consequence, devolved into an absent presence rather than a real person. He was and remains the unexplained mystery in Revolutionary history. The righteousness in Revolutionary condemnations gave him a static dimension. He was evil incarnate—so incarnate that further elucidation seemed unnecessary. Everywhere in public demonstrations, Arnold appeared as either the devil himself or the devil's disciple. He was "vile, treacherous, and leagued with Satan."[63] These rhetorical reductions were at some level deliberate. No one really wanted to ponder Arnold's authentic complexity. Scrutiny of the real Arnold was too unsettling, and it contained a cultural threat of fundamental proportions.

Another aspect of Arnold's claim of consistency helps to explain some of the obsessive alarm over him. He *was* without remorse. Where André sadly confessed that he was "too little accustomed to duplicity to have succeeded," Arnold stipulated a heart "conscious of its own rectitude." He refused to compromise his understanding of events in any way. Far from it. Instead, Arnold carried his belligerence in correspondence to eventual threats of retaliation in the name of "every tie of duty and honor." To those ties he annexed "heaven and earth to witness," not hesitating to place himself and his situation on the same level as Washington's own sense of honor and love of justice.[64]

Both the obdurate spirit and the skill of appropriation in Arnold were arresting. There was absolutely no concession or contrition, nor even an admission of failure in Arnold's language. He used the epistolary form to affect the surfaces of the sincere gentleman in his exchanges, presuming to be the exemplary character created in his communications—much like Lovelace in Samuel Richardson's *Clarissa*. The figure behind the language formed a remarkable type for the stock but capacious villain. Here was the embodiment of Tom Paine's greatest fear expressed four years before in *Common Sense*. Arnold stood for the proposition that "there is no such thing as treason."[65] His greatest claim, the license to disobey, caused further alarm by being so ideologically based.

Arnold found his own consistency in a Revolutionary American discrepancy. The self-confidence in his stance relied on culture-wide slippage in conceptions of loyalty. If the original colonial Englishman's devotion to king and country resonated between the personal and the abstract, the act of rebellion of republican citizens in 1776 diffused that emotion in the greater generality of country. The eighteenth-century duty to one's king was a concrete, fixed obligation that brooked little equivocation or room for disobedience. Some of that

standard—no one could say exactly how much—had been changed
by the more intangible concepts of honor and virtue, the hallmarks
of enlightened republican participation, and favorite terms in Washington's control of the American army. Emerging nationalism would
soon substitute a new emotional power, but in 1780 the Enlightenment code of honor and virtue reached for universal recognition and
depended as much on the exaltation of reason as on mass appeals to
the emotions or communal solidarity.

Whatever the strength of their appeal, honor and virtue were more
nebulous signposts for guiding political action than obedience to
one's king, and they allowed for a more flexible range in interpreting
personal behavior, particularly with the external code of the gentleman operating through a series of linguistic conventions that easily
confused determinations of character. Benedict Arnold showed how
quickly these terms could be turned back against their source in an atmosphere where the newly confederated states had few ideological
props and limited authority for preventing reconceptions. The anger
of rebellion in 1776 had unleashed an emotional permissiveness in de-
ciding the question of allegiances. Arnold, rebellious by nature, cap-
italized on its possibilities from the very beginning, and there was no
easy intellectual answer to his challenge when his rebellion took the
form of his own definition of honor. Arnold had been consistent in a
certain way; he had always been more *against* than *for*.

The result in the transcript of Major André's trial can be seen in a
strange imbalance between Washington and Arnold. Arnold's epistolary aggressiveness provoked only passivity from the commander in
chief of the American army. There are no letters from Washington to
Arnold in the transcript. Commentators on the conspiracy have regularly celebrated this restraint as part of Washington's perfect ascendancy over the treacherous subaltern Arnold.[66] But without questioning the cultural hegemony of these accounts, we can still find a more
problematic historicity in the primary records. Trial transcripts in-
scribe proximate actions, and, in their spontaneous generation, they
stand on their own as political and literary texts. Viewed in this manner, the transcript relation of Washington and Arnold in the André
case takes a curious turn. In the contrapuntal epistolary exchanges,
Washington's much noted decision not to answer Major André on the
form of his execution has obscured a far more subtle resolution to *ignore* Arnold on the whole subject of treason. Letters connect, either

by bridging or exacerbating differences, but a repeated failure to respond at all on the part of an addressee, as in this case, creates a narrative void.

Arnold's dogged persistence in writing without receiving responses across a number of letters makes the absence of all rebuttal from Washington especially interesting. Even André received an answer of sorts to his requests within the machinery of trial procedures, and it was duly noted in the transcript. "The practice and usage of war were against his request for a firing squad," runs the last line of the transcript, "and made the indulgence he solicited, circumstanced as he was, inadmissible."[67] Arnold, on the other hand, was left with nothing, without closure or circumstance of any kind, and his marginalization should be understood against a contrasting centrality. Not the subject of André's trial, Arnold was still pivotal to it. He contributed more words to the transcript of proceedings than any other single figure, including Washington. Nonetheless, within the workings of the epistolary tradition, he represents one hand trying to clap. He is without meaningful contact.

This relative disenfranchisement within the trial record is important because Arnold was a formidable rhetorical adversary. He, more than any other figure involved, reached for the creative modes of sentimental narrative in recognition of the power that they contained for persuading others to do something against their reason. Fearing, for example, that his wife and co-conspirator, Peggy Shippen Arnold, might suffer when he left her behind in the American camp, he took the first opportunity to steep the situation in as much emotion as possible, insisting to Washington that "she is as good and as innocent as an angel, and is incapable of doing wrong."[68] Most later commentators assume that Peggy Shippen Arnold, a leading and sophisticated social light in Philadelphia during the British occupation of that city and a personal friend of John André at that time, knew of Arnold's plans, and they suggest that her ensuing hysterics in Washington's presence immediately after her husband's narrow escape were part of a calculated and successful plan of evasion. Successful it was. Hamilton, who was also present, wrote to his fiancée that Peggy Arnold's "sufferings were so eloquent, that I wished myself her brother, to have a right to become her defender."[69] Washington, against all of the facts, allowed Arnold's sentimental narrative to stand when he automatically accepted Mrs. Arnold's presumed innocence and allowed her

to re-join her husband. Like so many of his negative fictional counterparts in the gentlemanly tradition of the epistolary novel, Arnold
knew how to hide behind the linguistic conventions.

Washington's silence seems at once fortuitous and planned. How
do we know that Arnold is such a criminal from a transcript that
never mentions his crime? The generic answer in epistolarity lies in
Washington's leverage as the first internal reader of Arnold's letters.
His prior reading controls the subsequent interpretations of external
readers, those early republicans who perused the letters only through
the transcript. Washington's refusal to respond to Arnold left two alternatives for those external readers: either the commander in chief
had been unthinkably rude in correspondence or Arnold was beneath
contempt. Silence in Washington also hid a significant inconvenience.
The justifiable aloofness allowed military rank against a failed subordinate masked the commander's obvious embarrassment in having to
confront his own creature, the trusted major general.

There were, however, deeper purposes in Washington's restraint.
The theory of give-and-take in trial advocacy gives each participant a
place in the ceremony of the trial (whether as defendant, witness,
or officer of the court). Each is allowed—as well as held to—the status
of an absolute level of truthfulness and assumed honor within the
process. The worst defendant still gets the dignity of official standing. Washington's decision to ignore Arnold stripped the latter of all
standing and left him utterly without caste. If in Revolutionary America the costs of betrayal were no longer personalized in the address
and punishment that a king could visit on a subject, they were beginning to take on another dimension within the more abstract republican ritual of patriotic dismissal. Washington's silence banished Arnold from the realm of honor and virtue that the commander of the
army symbolized. The abstractions of republican identity opened a
new register. In the trial transcript of André, Arnold entered upon a
hapless role that would follow him through history: he became the
permanent prodigal who could never be forgiven by the father of his
country.

This strategy of moral exile made it much easier to forget that Benedict Arnold had been an intrinsic component in Revolutionary success
and not an aberration or discrepancy. Still, and at bottom, there remained a contradiction to be faced in the act and claimed consistency
of the traitor. Arnold had been more than an individual hero. He had

been part of the fighting heart of Washington's army, "a genius at leading men" and arguably its greatest combat general.[70] The trajectory of Arnold's career—from a dissolute apothecary's apprentice in Norwich, Connecticut to the exalted station of major general in the Revolutionary army—can be read as one long, turbulent, and successful battle against civil authority. Combativeness and social mobility explained him. Made for crisis when he was not creating one, Arnold thrived on the disruption of rebellion, and he brought a powerful and useful characterological anger to every enterprise in it. The Revolution could not succeed without his type in place, and Washington had recognized the need by cannily guiding Arnold's rapid promotions through tangled military and political channels.

The career of Arnold presents a fascinating problem when taken as a whole. Governing Arnold's anger within the Revolution's new routinization of authority proved difficult even for Washington to manage, and the task was complicated by an unarticulated economic side of the picture. Of a respected but downwardly mobile Connecticut family, Arnold lived beyond his means and could never rest within the occasional prosperity that he achieved. He lacked the stable base and social standing to operate under the terms of disinterested service that Washington and the republican ideal expected. Ironically, success only enhanced Arnold's financial problems by increasing his status and corresponding need for costly display. Given social expectations, this problem was not entirely of his own making. Arnold's position as a major general required a certain visibility of him that was not without expense. Embezzlement charges and other accusations followed him everywhere, but again Arnold was hardly alone. Profiteering, graft, and fraud "pervaded the supply of the army throughout the war."[71] Characteristically, though, Arnold carried these matters to an extreme. His requests for money defined his military career almost as much as his capacity to take risks, and these traits combined in the act of betrayal.

Arnold and his growing predicament in the Revolutionary army were unusual only in the last step of treason that immediately came to define him. Until then, he was one of many "new men" struggling for place and importance in the flux of Revolutionary times. These new men always represented a potential threat in the eyes of leaders who were themselves more socially established but only newly entrenched as figures of authority. If the new men challenged incipient republican institutions in the same way that they were expected to challenge the British, if they moved further along the political continuum with their own more radical understanding, the Revolution would fail from another direction. Instead of facing the threat from abroad, the Revolution would fall apart from below. Benedict Arnold was the tip of an iceberg always feared and suddenly present. The invective unleashed against him had the added purpose of erasing the complicated and more threatening circumstance of the actual man.

Patriotic tirades lifted Benedict Arnold into the separate sphere of the lonely traitor, where the dangerous energy and resentments of all other Revolutionaries could be held in place by the contrary example. The negative contrast in Arnold's solitary treason dignified the presumed power of reason and virtue as controls in every other location. When Washington cut off Arnold in the trial transcript, relegating him to narrative limbo, he made it all the easier for others to reconfigure the traitor as the symbol and cause of every other republican ill.

The purpose of invective against treason is never to understand the culprit. Insight or reflection in such a context creates a positive danger; it invites potential sympathy for the betrayer and, worse, the prospect of further betrayal by revealing the path a traitor has taken. As the one figure in the Revolution that every English subject and American citizen (whether Tory or Whig, republican or loyalist) could identify as a traitor to their cause, Benedict Arnold became the lightning rod for all negative commentary. Inevitably, as well, reactions to him tell us more about the sources than the subject. Some of the earliest interpretations of Arnold were almost calculatedly perverse. General "Mad" Anthony Wayne, not settling for the truism "that honour and true virtue were strangers to [Arnold's] soul," argued against all evidence that "[Arnold] never possessed genuine fortitude or personal bravery."[72] Benjamin Franklin termed Arnold a "miserable bargainer." "Judas sold one man, Arnold 3,000,000," Franklin wrote Lafayette. "Judas got for his one man 30 pieces of silver, Arnold not halfpenny a head."[73] These and other accounts of Arnold are really about each observer's own closest value system. First Wayne, the soldier, and then Franklin, the entrepreneur, found what each most abhorred in his own world: cowardice and a bad bargain. Arnold very quickly came to represent everything that was wrong in the world.

Why Americans thought the way they did in this first major, highly publicized confrontation with treason is as relevant as what they thought. Colonel Alexander Scammell, who read the death sentence at Major André's execution and who described André as "perhaps the most accomplished officer of the age," had much to ponder when it came to the necessary converse in Arnold. His description of the army's reaction to Arnold illustrated a crucial dynamic at work in the culture at large:

> we were all astonished each peeping at his neighbor to see if any treason was hanging about him; nay, we even descended to a critical examination of ourselves. This surprise soon settled down into a fixed detestation and abhorrence of Arnold, which can receive no addition. His treason has unmasked him the veriest villain of centuries past and set him in true colors.[74]

In this passage, an isolating anxiety quickly alleviates itself in the name of a new collective aversion. Just as important is the conclusive nature of the second emotion the instant it has been fully conceived. The "abhorrence of Arnold" is immediately "settled down," "fixed", and "set"; it "can receive no addition." The redundancy in such a short passage works to eliminate all further need for reflection. Repetitive insistence on a new and absolutely permanent position supplies the means for recovering a solidarity lost in the actual contemplation of treason ("we even descended to a critical examination of ourselves"). Note, again, the convenience in making the traitor—not treason—the locus of attention.

The realization of awfulness in treason led to an explosion in the accepted scope of the Arnold conspiracy rather than an analysis of it. Could Arnold really be, in Colonel Scammell's words, "the veriest villain of centuries past"? Already on September 30, 1780, an editorial from *The Pennsylvania Packet* assumed that Arnold's corruption "exceeds all description." It found "such a scene of baseness and prostitution of office and character, as it is hoped the new world cannot parallel."[75] The submerged fear in this statement is nonetheless palpable. Would the new world lose its way and turn into a replica of the old through corruption and the loss of virtue?

The safer intellectual alternative was to present Arnold as a special aberration, and the language that served best in this regard turned on the most ancient image of evil. Arnold took on the dimensions of a monster that could not be descr.bed in normal terms. And like so many other rhetorical strategies applied to Arnold, the visualization of monstrosity drew attention away from the bewildering act and toward the ready figure of the traitor—from the continuing possibility of conspiracy to the fallen Arnold. "I took up my pen with an intent to shew a reflective glass, wherein you might at one view behold your actions," ran a direct address to Arnold from *The Pennsylvania Packet*, "but soon found such a horrid ugly deformity in the outlines of your picture, that I was frightened at the sight, so the mirrour dropped and broke to pieces! each of this discovered you to be a gigantick overgrown monster, of such a variety of shapes, all over ulcerated, that it is in vain to attempt to describe them."[76] The ability to engage in such hyperbolic censure eliminated the need for further explanation. Outrage curbed apprehension by accepting distortion as the handiest and most relevant norm for approaching the traitor. The writer in *The Pennsylvania Packet*, like so many others, literally refused to look at Arnold for what he might have been.

The language of deformity, monstrosity, and distortion served another rhetorical purpose. Arnold's unthinkable actions nonetheless required thought in response. The grotesque allowed that thought to take place on another level where familiar explanations could hold the traitor and his treason more firmly in place. How had Arnold managed to "astonish the people of America"? *The Pennsylvania Gazette* found that he had "improved on the blackest treachery and the most consummate impudence, in a manner that would cause the infernals [to] blush, were they to be charged with it."[77] More seriously but also typically, Colonel Scammell in camp at West Point found himself caught between very different explanations. Was the proper focus "actual transgressions" or "original sin"?[78]

A thoroughly secular individual, Arnold the traitor grew more meaningful and less puzzling in the spiritual domain. Starting with General Nathaniel Greene's general orders to the army on the day after Arnold escaped, early republicans left the ultimate discovery and explanation of the conspiracy in divine hands. Greene's formal words helped to create a convention of the times: "happily this treason has been timely discover'd, to prevent the fatal misfortune [of a deadly wound]—The providential train of Circumstances which lead to it, affords the most convincing proof, that the Liberties of America, is the object of Divine protection."[79] Similar claims soon found their way to every leader's lips. "The remarkable interposition of Providence to frustrate the diabolical conspiracy, will inspire every virtuous American with sincere gratitude to the great Arbiter of all events;" Governor William Livingston of New Jersey assured Washington, "we were, by the peculiar guardianship of Heaven, rescued from the very brink of destruction." Just as Judas had been an unwitting pawn in the hand of God, so Benedict Arnold, with whom Judas was often compared, could best be seen as a necessary tool in revealing God's plan to a worthy people. The narrow escape from Arnold's treachery had been a singular occurrence with a larger purpose. Few events in the Revolution would match it in evoking expressions, assurances, and celebrations of a providential hand at work. To make the connection was even a test of one's own virtue. No matter what "the modern wits" thought, Abigail Adams wrote of Arnold's exposure, "the virtuous mind will look up and acknowledge the great First Cause."[80]

But providential explanations, however satisfying in the moment, could substitute for secular interpretation only so far and for so long. The proper place for such an interpretation, admittedly as *obiter dictum* or a collateral opinion, had been in the trial transcript or court proceeding against Major André. Alternatively, Arnold might have been tried *in absentia*, but it didn't happen in either situation. Early republicans were still too tied to their colonial roots. They weren't ready to take on the concept of treason either as a formal intellectual exercise or as a social structure for delineating cultural accord. Better by far in 1780 to explain Benedict Arnold away, especially since the subject itself was an irresistible one. Not for the last time, in what remains an Achilles heel of American culture, the trauma of treason encouraged emotional appeals rather than clarifying investigation. All too frequently in the nation's subsequent history, these appeals have depended upon reflexive conflations in which the republic of laws meets the Bible culture.

The Federal Convention of 1787 would see the need for clarification. Montesquieu had argued that "if the crime of high treason be indeterminate, this alone is sufficient to make the government degenerate into arbitrary power."[81] The framers clearly agreed with this favorite postulate of the Enlightenment; there could be no safety in government without a careful and circumscribed legal definition of treason. As a measure of their concern, the framers wrote down just such a definition and made it the one crime to receive a separate section in the new and wholly secular Federal Constitution. Article three, section three states in part, "Treason against the United States shall consist only in levying war against them, or in adhering to their enemies, giving them aid and comfort. No person shall be convicted of treason unless on the testimony of two witnesses to the same overt act, or on confession in open court." These words are deliberately restrictive, sobering, and limiting.[32] They also define Benedict Arnold perfectly as one who adhered to the enemy and then levied war against his country. A meaningful test of it, and against a subtler figure, would not come until 1807, when another Revolutionary hero, Aaron Burr, would face the charge directly in a federal court with Chief Justice John Marshall presiding.

The similarities in the cultural treatment of Benedict Arnold and Aaron Burr across a quarter of a century are striking. Burr would encounter the threat of treason charges in very different circumstances than Arnold, but his trial inspired a similar round of demonizing commentary on the figure of the traitor. Soldier, leading lawyer, vice-president under Thomas Jefferson, western adventurer, and the gentleman duelist who killed Alexander Hamilton, Burr, like Arnold, played a thoroughly secular role in the early republic, but he was also the grandson of Jonathan Edwards, and his relation to the great revivalist stimulated powerful theological lines of force around him.[83] Early republicans and their antebellum successors were never shy about converting those religious lines into political and historical explanation. When they found Aaron Burr technically innocent of treason in court, they still regarded him as the satanic figure in the American garden. Virtually every subsequent nineteenth-century account followed prosecuting attorney William Wirt's insistence that America and Aaron Burr were, respectively, "the state of Eden when the serpent entered its bowers."[84]

Thereafter, and in many re-articulations, the subject of treason has continued to accommodate a religious strain of explanation—a strain that gives meaning to an otherwise incoherent though time-honored narrative of monstrosity. The invective that it invokes always looks for more than crime. It swims in the primal fears of first origins and on the reflexive hope that God will continue to "shed his grace on thee." Treason in America is where crimes against community turn into sins against humanity, where cultural fears mix explosively with cultural angers and with atavistic identifications, where the ritual of the courtroom reinforces a national faith as much as it offers a legal explanation, and where the continuing ideological severance of Benedict Arnold's patriotic leg from his traitorous self bespeaks a continuing disjuncture in every consideration of the theme.

CHAPTER FIVE

The Forgotten Publius

As drafters of eighty of eighty-five of *The Federalist* papers, Alexander Hamilton and James Madison rightly receive credit for the first sustained achievement in American political philosophy, but whatever its justifications, this focus has robbed "the third Publius" of his authorial due. John Jay, the best known of the triumvirate in 1787, is that "forgotten Publius," one often cast in the role of figurehead for the more creative energies and strategies of his younger colleagues.[1] Nothing could be further from the truth of events. Contemporaries saw and spoke of Jay's pivotal position during the ratification of the Constitution. Describing the early Federalists, John Adams thought Jay "of more importance than any of the rest, indeed of almost as much weight as all the rest."[2]

Observers have also understood that Jay's separate pamphlet, *An Address to the People of the State of New York*, gave the country its single most influential exposition on ratification, and every student of the period acknowledges that Jay secured New York's doubtful passage of the Constitution during the state convention held in Poughkeepsie. His contemporaries, including George Washington, attached major significance to the pamphlet written in the spring of 1788, urging its wider publication. Jay then personally engineered a narrow victory from almost certain defeat for the Constitution in New York in the following summer. His diplomacy, tenacity in debate, and careful use of language on amendment after amendment in the embroiled New York Convention were essential in slowly turning the tide from an original membership that, on June 17th, numbered forty-six anti-Federalists and just nineteen Federalists to the final "unconditional" vote in favor of ratification by thirty to twenty-seven with seven abstentions on July 26th.[3] Nevertheless, and despite all of its recognitions, this secondary focus on Jay the successful politician has obscured the writer's achievement almost as much as the dismissals and neglect of "the forgotten Publius." For while the skillful diplomacy of the officeholder and diplomat may *signal* his qualities of leadership, recognition of these facets does not begin to explain the peculiar nature of Jay's intellectual ascendancy in 1787.

What does explain that intellectual ascendancy? The question is worth answering in detail because it raises an issue of importance beyond the complexity of a particular founder's achievement. Jay succeeds first and foremost as a writer who has mastered the major political genres of his day—the pamphlet, the official document, and the epistolary exchange. His expertise and experience as a government figure naturally guided and even required these writings, but more than political astuteness and expertise guided the pen that persuaded his peers. What is creativity? In Jay's case, it meant the ability to establish a general mood in those around him. In deft combinations of philosophical import and literary form, he fired off countless letters to other early republican leaders to go with official commentary and essays as he developed what can only be called a communal touch. The ambiance of his writings managed to capture and then hold the imagination of the age. There is a buried quality in this achievement and in much of the best early republican writing left to us. Out of the agonized concerns of the worried man at his desk came a tonal assurance on the page that Americans of the time desperately needed.

As foreign secretary or secretary of state of the national government working under the handicaps of the Articles of Confederation, Jay saw the problems of the weak union before his contemporaries. He experienced those problems firsthand and analyzed them for others in probing, confidential accounts. Deploring "the feeble state of our federal government" in 1785, he deflected official requests that he could not handle by observing, "the chain which holds us together will be too feeble to bear much opposition or exertion." His primary goal from the beginning was a stronger union, and, as the official in charge of the impact of his nation on international relations, he quickly imagined a more holistic state of affairs: "It is my first wish to see the United States assume and merit the character of one great nation, whose territory is divided into countries and townships for the like purposes."[4]

Over the next two years, 1786 and 1787, while coping daily with the deteriorating Confederation, Jay worked out the details of what a "great nation" of divided countries might look like and how it might act. To George Washington, he warned that "some crisis, some revolution" was fast approaching, though he carefully reassured the already pessimistic Washington that Americans would still become "a great and respectable people." To prove it and to answer Washington's gloomy responses, he sketched in his own solution, a proper separation of constitutional powers in a more vigorous central government.[5] With John Adams, he exchanged detailed notes on the weaknesses of the Confederation, concurred "perfectly in sentiment" about the necessity and nature of change, praised Adams' own written efforts about reform (the first volume of Adams' *Defence of the Constitutions*), and, finally, with one eye on his own scrupulously preserved written records, predicted that "posterity will read the history of our last four years with much regret."[6] To Thomas Jefferson, he wrote often of the defects in the Confederation, confiding that the Constitution itself was "fundamentally wrong," and chafing under his own "awkward situation" as foreign secretary ("so very much to be done and enabled to do very little").[7]

Each of these complaints had both a negative and a positive dimension—so much so that prudent integration of them in correspondence left the writer with a profound sense of just how to articulate what was truly possible in the late 1780s. Those powers of articulation were not lost on others. John Jay, perhaps more than any other correspondent, helped to convince the reluctant George Washington to attend the Federal Convention in Philadelphia. Among other things, he gave Washington the terminology he needed to express and then overcome his fears about the potential failure and outright illegality of the Convention. While grudgingly ready to attend the Convention, Washington worried as late as March of 1787, just two months before the framers would convene, that it might be "premature." "In strict propriety," he wrote Jay, "a Convention so holden may not be legal." His own attendance was "inconvenient" and "perhaps improper." Would the military hero, so justly celebrated for his voluntary retirement from public life, ruin his reputation by joining an "illegal" junta in search of greater central power? Jay, for his part, had already worked hard, using the discourse of civic virtue, to get Washington to see the logical necessity of his participation. His letters said so outright; they also justified a political exertion beyond mere prudence, and they supplied the saving argument that the Convention itself would be legitimate if "deducible from the only source of just authority—*the People*." Jay's role did not end there. He was close enough to Washington that he could dare to continue his advice *during* the confidential deliberations of the Convention.[8]

Elsewhere, Jay's letters to federal leaders were filled with explicit and encouraging terms "for enlarging and invigorating" the government with corresponding plans "to assimilate the States, and to promote one of the first wishes of my heart, viz., to see the people of America become one nation in every respect."[9] To peruse the same letters today is to discover a telling mixture. Jay's official frustrations as foreign secretary emerge explosively in correspondence, but they yield quickly in every case to calmer, more theoretical argumentation in response to the recognized problems of the collapsing Confederation ("the inefficacy of our government becomes daily more and more apparent").[10] The result, in embryonic form, is the series of positive claims that Jay will soon use to support the Constitution of 1787 in *The Federalist* and his pivotal pamphlet, *An Address to the People of the State of New York*. The letters from 1785 to 1787 provide a proving ground for the emerging master stylist. They demonstrate that Jay was intellectually and rhetorically better prepared than most of his peers for the unprecedented national government that would appear so suddenly from out of the secret deliberations in Philadelphia, and they explain how Jay, as Publius, could equal Hamilton and Madison without sitting with them in the Constitutional Convention.

The stylist owed much of his power to his ability to meld influences in a seamless web of implication. Enlightenment ideology, eighteenth-century legal thought, American religious expression, the Revolutionary pamphlet tradition, and the civic discourse of Whig politics all came together in Jay's acceptance of an obligation to *write out* his knowledge of the American situation. Writerly obligations ran deep in Jay's correspondence. During the Federal Convention, Jay and John Adams wrote of preserving their letters for "an accurate account" to "future historians," of the necessity of regular publication "to remove prejudices and correct errors" in the body politic, of the responsibility of dedicating their pens to public service, of the duty of writing well, and of their determination to serve as "under-labourers" or "under-workmen" for the effort of the Convention.[11] But to understand this combination of influences *within* the spirit of obligation that Jay accepted, we must first recover a lost distinction: the crucial placement of Jay's admittedly limited contribution to *The Federalist*. Not enough has been made of that placement. The so-called "third Publius" wrote first, at the beginning of the collaboration, and four of his papers must be considered with this fact in mind.

A strict comparison of beginnings in *The Federalist* tells a singular story. If Alexander Hamilton established the overall purposes and agenda of Publius in "Federalist No. 1" on October 27, 1787, it was John Jay who set the underlying tone of their collaboration across the next four papers in the early weeks of November. "Federalist No. 2," "Federalist No. 3," "Federalist No. 4," and "Federalist No. 5" were entirely Jay's efforts. Properly read, they offer a subtle but compelling "aesthetics of ratification"—so compelling that his co-authors and, after them, the country quickly accepted its premises. Indeed, we have so thoroughly imbibed Jay's ideas that we have lost track of the originality that he brought to his writing as Publius in the Fall of 1787.

The similarities and continuities that critics like to trace between "Federalist No. 1," written by Hamilton, and the four papers that follow, written by Jay, *do* indicate a close collaboration, but they tend to disguise serious tonal differences, all of which point to the nature of Jay's personal contribution and originality. We can begin our examination of those differences by remembering that the statesman-like voice of "Federalist No. 1" does not represent Alexander Hamilton's first effort in defense of the new Constitution. In the summer of 1787, the feisty Hamilton initiated a series of vitriolic newspaper exchanges with anti-Federalists in New York, charging Governor George Clinton with treachery and anti-constitutional sentiments and calling for his impeachment. The subsequent furor extended into September and as far as Virginia, where it led to a private rebuke from Hamilton's former commander in the field, the same man who had just presided over Hamilton anew in the Federal Convention. Ratification, George Washington told his former aide, "calls loudly for unanimity"; he saw no reason why "Gentlemen of talent and character should disagree in their sentiment for promoting the public good."[12]

"Federalist No. 1" can be viewed as just such a dutiful attempt to achieve unanimity when it calls for "a judicious estimate of our true interests, unperplexed and unbiased by considerations not connected with the public good." Supporting this general interpretation are the writer's "lesson of moderation," his "contemplation of a sound and well-informed judgment," his reach for "an enlarged view of the subject," and his promise to keep all private motives and emotions deep within "the depository" of his own breast. Even so, Hamilton could not quite accept the force of the strategy that he knew he should follow. "Federalist No. 1" returns again and again to the themes of "ambition, avarice, personal animosity, party opposition, and many other motives not more laudable than these." "A torrent of angry and malignant passions will be let loose," Hamilton warns, and he gives whole paragraphs to a catalogue of the "obvious interest," "perverted ambition," "honest errors of mind," and "preconceived jealousies and fears" that dominate the "classes" of men who oppose the Constitution.[13]

Hamilton's opening essay thrives on querulous possibilities that lurk just beneath the surface, and he refers to them as already "whispered in private circles." The neoclassical balances and calming rhythms of "Federalist No. 1" have a contrasting obsession: "opposite parties" may control debate with "the loudness of their declamations and the bitterness of their invectives." Consensus remains an official goal, but disagreement is the writer's real subject of interest as he broods over "the most formidable of the obstacles which the new Constitution will have to encounter." Hamilton raises the public good only to suggest that others will never join in that lofty goal ("this is a thing more ardently to be wished than seriously to be expected"). This first Publius is also filled with Hamiltonian self-righteousness. "The consciousness of good intentions disdains ambiguity," he announces in summary of his own character, even as he promises to give "a satisfactory answer" to every objection that his opponents can possibly raise. No writer could have appeared more certain of his own convictions nor more contemptuous of the opinions of others.[14]

John Jay, by way of contrast, understood that greater flexibility might be necessary to secure a union of divergent parts. To be sure, "Federalist No. 2" takes up the announced themes of "Federalist No. 1" and in much the same language, but it brings those themes from darkness and conflict into the light, where harmony can reign. The tone of this second essay is also quite different. "No. 1" challenges the reader to the point where you dare not disagree with Publius on pain of attack; "No. 2" welcomes you into a gratifying joint enterprise. The many enemies of "No. 1" remain visible, but they are now mere shadows of their formerly dominating selves ("politicians," "some men," "certain characters"). More important, these malcontents no longer have the power to block "that sedate and candid consideration" required by the new Constitution. As before, many Americans may be "deceived and deluded," but this new Publius, looking back over the positive record of the Revolution, remembers something else. As he puts it, "the great majority of the people reasoned and decided judiciously; and happy they are in reflecting that they did so."[15]

There is good reason for the new optimism of "Federalist No. 2." John Jay wields a far more positive theme than Hamilton in his own assessment of "the values and blessings of union." He has relied on Hamilton's previous treatment, the *necessity* of union, but he has transformed that negative into an astounding painting of America, nothing less than a fully unified visual history of the new world ("Providence has been pleased to give this one connected country to one united people"). It is the craft behind that image, rather than its historical accuracy, that concerns us here. How does Publius render the image with such conviction and so compellingly? Certainly Jay saw the same problems that Hamilton had already discussed. "Federalist No. 2" revives the negatives of "Federalist No. 1," alluding back to "the foregoing paper" and its pessimistic language ("more to be wished than expected").[16] But what seemed to anger Hamilton and to drag him down into negative spirals of acrimony lifted Jay to new levels of accommodation and mediation. At issue is an aesthetics of ratification in Jay's writing and his awareness of that better strategy.

Aesthetics, placed in this political context, signifies the capacity to convey a political goal in an artistic manner by joining meaning to beauty in a way that also suggests a unifying simplicity of appreciation and control. For Jay, the trope of union supplied just that combination of beauty, aspiration, simplicity, and conviction. Consider, for example, the following passage from "Federalist No. 2":

> It has often given me pleasure to observe, that independent America was not composed of detached and distant territories, but that one connected, fertile, wide-spreading country was the portion of our western sons of liberty. Providence has in a particular manner blessed it with

a variety of soils and productions, and watered it with innumerable streams, for the delight and accommodation of its inhabitants. A succession of navigable waters form a kind of chain round its borders, as if to bind it together; while the most noble rivers in the world, running at convenient distances, present them with highways for the easy communication of friendly aids, and the mutual transportation and exchange of their various commodities.[17]

Who would not wish to share this vision and, in sharing, not want to become a citizen of the country described in it? Jay's Publius has managed to conflate politics (the Revolution figures in the phrases "independent America" and "western sons of liberty"), nature ("one connected, fertile, wide-spreading country,"), divinity ("Providence has in a particular manner blessed"), the economics of prosperity ("the mutual transportation and exchange of their various commodities"), and, not least, an individual capacity for perception of the beautiful whole ("it has often given me pleasure to observe"). The constitutive metaphor in the passage is linkage—of all kinds, on all levels, and in every direction—as part of an irresistible picture of union without loose ends. We have the direct and calculated obverse of Jay's poignant fears from 1785, when, as foreign secretary, "the chain which holds us together" had been "too feeble" to count for direction and assertion, much less for identity.[18]

The simplicity of the device should not mask Jay's adroit celebration of union nor the complex ideological goals that those devices tried to satisfy. Three premises, each with its own aesthetic basis in Enlightenment thought, dominated Jay's writings on the ratification of the new Constitution.[19] First, he saw that "the safe and easy path of union" would bring automatic coherence, prosperity, peace, and harmony to America because, in a phrase that Jay liked to repeat, "the safety of the whole is the interest of the whole." Once seen, that harmonious whole would always be easier to appreciate and understand than the appearance of any lesser unit or division. The idea of greater peace and prosperity in a more comprehensive union is the controlling theme of "Federalist No. 2" through "Federalist No. 5." The aesthetic aspects of this emphasis also appear strongly in "Federalist No. 64," where Jay writes "in proportion as the United States assume a national form and national character, so will the good of the whole be more and more an object of attention."[20]

Jay, an ardent Christian, understood that his many positive evocations of union made use of important homologies between religious and secular thought. "Visible union" was a source of general cultural yearning; it had been one of the great rallying cries of revivalism in America since the Great Awakening.² At the same time, the process of actually *seeing* union bespoke an eighteenth-century secular episte-mology. Like other Enlightenment thinkers, Jay assumed that the far-ther one could see, the clearer the order and unity of the universe would become. By analogy, this ordering of the universe allowed cor-responding possibilities for composition and purification in viewing the rapidly developing American nation. "Union" was both the sym-bol and the design that allowed an observer to extract greatness from a suddenly meaningful if still mysterious continental horizon. And, as Jay's descriptions made clear, that greatness deserved to be called a thing of beauty. "Federalist No. 2" notes that because "Providence has been pleased to give this one connected country to one united peo-ple," the people themselves have been filled with "a strong sense of the value and blessings of union." This feeling of union enables them to speak with "one voice" in any emergency.²² The same characteris-tics in *An Address to the People of the State of New York* lead to the further conclusion that "the people at large always mean well." They have considered the union "the most essential of human means" and have "almost worshipped it with as much fervor as pagans in distress implored the protection of their tutelar deities."²³

A second aesthetic premise of union carried the optimism of com-prehensiveness of place to the individual level. Jay assumed that a true citizen would exhibit the peace and prosperity of a better union through ever greater expressions of personal contentment, accommo-dation, equanimity, and fraternal affection. To make the connection clear, he played upon twin tenets of the eighteenth century: namely, reason always found a discoverable linkage in the order of things, and recognition of "the great chain of being" fostered personal tranquility as well as intellectual appreciation and control. Writers of the period, Jay included, often tried to imply these values as personal merits; they would bring a certain serenity of tone to bear on their favorite themes of an inclusive and comprehensive view. "Federalist No. 2," in the passage just quoted, supplies an obvious case in point. Jay is certain that "the great majority of the people reasoned and decided judi-ciously" and that they would continue to do so through "their univer-sal and uniform attachment to the cause of the Union." His favorite examples of the calm citizen come naturally from those to whom he assigns the largest view, namely, the membership of the Federal Convention itself.[24]

In a third aesthetic claim, Jay argued that a free people would overcome all of the evils that threatened them and that, in a sub-premise of frequent note in *The Federalist,* the people would do so by naming and following good leaders in forging a proper design of government. Turning again to the optimism of the Enlightenment, Jay assumed that evil was a temporary form of disorder rather than an innate and active expression of irrepressible malice or chaos. By eliminating evil, he could think of an ideal union that would be as beautiful as it was effective in the recognitions that it entailed. Citizens would *see* the light. With error removed, they would come together naturally in an appreciation of design that would eliminate misunderstanding in the realization of previously impossible levels of harmony and good will.

The best single expression of this idea comes in *An Address to the People of the State of New York,* where Jay writes "while reason retains her rule, while men are as ready to receive as to give advice, and as willing to be convinced themselves as to convince others, there are few political evils from which a free and enlightened people cannot deliver themselves." We are not far, in these phrases, from a form of secular millennialism. In fact, "Federalist No. 3" has already explained how "the best men in the country" would necessarily rise to manage "an efficient national government" and that they would do so with greater "moderation and candor" than at any point heretofore. "Federalist No. 4" reiterates the same point, and "Federalist No. 5" supplies a vision of union in which the people are "'joined in affection' and free from all apprehension and different 'interests.'" The explicit contrast is always to an idea of division and faction, in which the people are soon filled with envy and jealousy against each other.[25] The parallels between "enlightenment" and salvation on the one hand, "interests" and sin on the other, are easily drawn.

Whatever the artifice in the crafting of these premises, it is impossible to doubt Jay's sincerity in propagating them.[26] Somewhat more than Madison and certainly more than Hamilton, Jay accepted the Enlightenment norm that knowledge would build in a free marketplace of ideas. It would build from the particular to the general, from connection to community, from the local to the national. Success depended on an intrinsic human characteristic, "a desire of making par-

tial and personal objects bend to general union and common good."
If Americans heeded that desire, they would exchange "passion" for
"the fruits of reason." They would eliminate all suspicion and resentment, as the framers in Philadelphia had done before them, and they
would ratify the Constitution.[27]

The power of the aesthetic appeal in union can be seen in the palpable ugliness of Jay's projected alternatives. Each of his premises
contained a forlorn contrast. If a more perfect union meant general
prosperity, peace, equanimity, and contentment, the existing confederation threatened economic collapse, factionalism, political dissolution, war, and then chaos. Because the better idea of union would always be present, each negative had to be understood through the
themes of decay and ruin. Jay's highly visual control of these possibilities was powerful and direct—literally farsighted. As unity bespoke
beauty and pleasant vistas, so ruin and decay promised ugliness, political entrapment, and local chaos or absence of form. Not surprisingly,
Jay's negative corollaries in personal relations were anger, myopia,
conflict, and a spiraling downward course of social evils without end.
"Federalist No. 5" sketches the prospect of "discord, jealousy, and
mutual injuries."[28] *An Address to the People of the State of New York*
then takes up the theme in detail. The people could be seen to be losing their virtue in "the universal rage and pursuit of private gain."
"You must have observed," Jay warns his readers, "that the same
temper and equanimity which prevailed among the people on former occasions no longer exist." Sadly, "indiscreet and offensive acrimony" have developed, and they mean "that pernicious heats and an-
imosities have been kindled, and spread their flames far and wide
among us." This trajectory is painted as more than an alarming one.
The "seeds of discord and danger" have started to "take root in
America" and "will soon poison our gardens and our fields," and as
that happens "new Cromwells" begin to appear.[29]

Jay outlined the negative possibilities in sorrow rather than in
Hamiltonian anger, a tendency that confirmed vital aesthetic priorities. "'FAREWELL!'" Publius laments in the face of ruin at the end of
"Federalist No. 2," "'A LONG FAREWELL TO ALL MY GREATNESS.'"
These mournful tones are cleverly heightened by a contextual recognition. Ruin, if it comes, will come by the early republic's own self-de-
structive hand. Jay's farewell to greatness reaches back to the words
of Shakespeare's Cardinal Wolsey, who dolefully realizes that he has

brought about his own downfall. Looking to Europe at the end of "Federalist No. 4," Jay moans again, "what a poor, pitiful figure will America make in their eyes!"[30] When the beautiful has been lost or disfigured, it is to be pitied and not chided. Predictably, the same spirit of regret also colors the later pamphlet, *An Address to the People of the State of New York*. As "the old Confederation" finally collapses in Jay's negative scenario of coming events, the writer grieves in staged, theatrical terms. "'To your tents, O Israel!'" he cries, "Then every band of union would be severed. Then every State would be a little nation . . . against its former friends. Then farewell to fraternal affection."[31]

These tones were curiously disarming ones and difficult to counter or answer in 1787 and 1788. Jay wrote to encase his opponents, the so-called anti-Federalists, in a narrow but highly visible chamber of localism, self-interest, darkness, and imputed ignorance. Any failure of the union became, in his terminology, a sad betrayal of generations past and future; every objection to the new Constitution, an implicitly unpatriotic gesture. Just as his own equanimity in the prospect of future greatness bespoke a sense of the whole, so the voiced complaints of others evoked partiality and a lost cohesion. Jay used these distinctions to relegate his opponents to one of four categories of lesser knowledge: either they "obeyed the dictates of personal interest," or they held "a mistaken estimate of consequences," or they fell under "the undue influence of former attachments," or, worst of all, they possessed "ambition aimed at objects which did not correspond with the public good."[32] Regardless, they were all mistaken, and yet the evident lack of rancor or vituperation in Jay's descriptions of them kept him somehow above the fray, safely within a disinterested view, well away from the need to distinguish between narrow political categories.

All of these opponents could be lumped together for the ratification debates precisely because, in Jay's view, they had ignored the same cardinal principle. They had lost sight of the possibilities in meaningful design. They had forgotten that the harmony, prosperity, and greatness of America depended on its sense of union. What is more, Jay's calculated images of them were designed to convey that failing over and over again.[33] How, it might be asked, was an anti-Federalist to express relevant objections without violating Jay's rigid sense of decorum? "Let us therefore, as much as possible," Jay urged, "repress and compose that irritation in our minds which too warm disputes about it [the new Constitution] may have excited." The demeanor that he called for instead was "serene self-possession and presence of mind." But what if one truly disagreed with the Constitution under consideration? How did one express one's displeasure with "serene self-possession"?[34] To protest overtly was to place oneself under the tar of his brush. To so much as qualify the language of the new Constitution implied that the complainer could do better than the enlightened framers. Jay's writings ruthlessly closed off every line of resistance. His pamphlet in the spring of 1788 began and ended with his insistence that the people free themselves of every "conflict of arguments." The central argument of the essay denied all possibility of a better plan.[35]

No genius, John Jay came close to that mark in his understanding and imaginative use of place during the ratification debates. He was just close enough to the Confederation as foreign secretary, to insist on its failure without being challenged; just far enough from the Federal Convention (a supporter but not a member) to extol its work without embarrassment. After all, Alexander Hamilton and James Madison were somewhat constrained in their praise of the Constitution as members of the Federal Convention. Not the least evidence of Jay's own authority in the moment was his mastery of their vocabulary even though he had not spent four months in Philadelphia forging its terms. Underneath these tactical considerations came the all-important understanding of the professional man as writer. In 1787 Jay was complete master of the intellectual role of lawyer-statesman in a way that only John Adams and Thomas Jefferson could also claim, and these peers were abroad in ambassadorial roles that kept them out of the give-and-take of formal debate. Depending on Jay as foreign secretary for much of their information as well as technical instructions, Adams and Jefferson were his subordinates in their roles as envoys to England and France.

Two characteristics of Jay's ascendancy deserve particular elaboration. A lawyer's lawyer before entering government service during the Revolution, he knew better than others how to join the particular skills of legal practice to the more exalted role of lawgiver. As the first made Jay a tough adversary in debate, so the latter supplied rare eloquence and a platform for rising above debate on his own terms. Jay plied the two sides of this lawyerly divide with such skill that we no longer see the effort in the rhetorical shifts that it required. Everything came together in a writer who had learned to dispute while simultaneously denying the right of disputation as an acceptable form of exchange.

The lawyer in Jay understood and accepted the tactic that every advocate employs to win a case: you must give the central question of your argument in a way that dictates the answer you want to receive from the court.[36] Jay, first as Publius and then as an independent pamphleteer, always used this tactic to place his opponents at a rhetorical disadvantage. "Federalist No. 2," in demanding "a very comprehensive, as well as a very serious, view," begins with the question "whether it would conduce more to the interest of the people of America that they should, to all general purposes, be one nation, under one federal government, or that they should divide themselves into separate confederacies, and give to the head of each the same kind of powers which they are advised to place in one national government."[37] No one, of course, argued for a series of separate confederacies in 1787, and so none of Jay's opponents could be expected to espouse the alternative that Jay gave them here. Instead, Jay used the question to occupy all of the middle ground between positions. By turning division as the outcome to be expected from a weak confederation into his rhetorical reality, he turned his opponents into betrayers of the *existing* union as well as the foes of a stronger one.

"Federalist No. 3" through "Federalist No. 5" work in a similar fashion. Each asks the question "whether so many *just* causes of war are likely to be given by *United America* as by *disunited* America."[38] Never mind that no serious adversary in the debates of 1787 identified with the cause of disunion or disputed the need for a united America of the kind that the existing Confederation allowed! Publius forces the starker contrast by skipping, once more, to the implication that the Confederation will lead to disunion. Even so, it is not until the very end of "Federalist No. 4" that we get the logical conclusion of this argument. "[H]ow soon," wonders Publius at this point, "would dear-bought experience proclaim that when a people or family so divide, it never fails to be against themselves."[39] Pages before, his readers have been forced to choose prematurely between union under the new Constitution or disunion without it.

An Address to the People of the State of New York takes the advocate's strategy of steering the question to new heights of control. Caught up himself in the actual embroilment of ratification during the spring of 1788, Jay turns every fear and doubt over the new arrangement back on the anti-Federalists by asking three questions in succession. Warning first that each answer has "future consequence to America" and that "we must be highly responsible both here and hereafter," he asks "whether it is probable that a better plan can be obtained [at this point]." "Whether, if attainable, it is likely to be in season." And finally, "what would be our situation if, after rejecting this, all our efforts to obtain a better should prove fruitless." The importance of the interrogative mode in Jay's style of argumentation is visually apparent in this context. The format of the pamphlet sets off each question, and each is designed to force its recipient back on the austere choice of being totally for or totally against the new Constitution.[40] The writer who could insist five months before on the most meticulous and deliberate of considerations, now finds a deteriorating situation that requires a quick decision. Noting "our present humiliating condition," Jay doubts "whether we ought to give further opportunities to discord to alienate the hearts of our citizens from one another, and thereby encourage new Cromwells to bold exploits."[41]

The shrill tones in such prose are real enough, but they are softened and even answered by the other side of the lawyerly image that Jay held of himself, that of the lawgiver who drafted the state constitution of New York in 1776. Notably, this second side of John Jay shared a sacred mission. Lawyers supervised "the art of government" in the early republic and thought of themselves as the sole protectors of an evolving Anglo-Saxon heritage in the common law. They were central actors with a universal mandate: only intellectual heroes could take on the whole of human history to prove that a lawful people could live in civic virtue. They saw themselves fighting to legitimize, for the first time ever, the hope that individual societies might establish governments through their own acts of reflection and choice, and their professional understanding had provided them with the means.[42]

This image of the lawgiver relied on the Enlightenment's catalogue of the four degrees of "sovereign honor": *conditores imperiorum,* or founders of states, then *legislatores,* or lawgivers as "second founders," then *liberatores,* the heroes who save their countries from tyranny, and, finally, *propagatores,* those leaders who enlarge or protect a country's territory.[43] Jay and other leading lawyer-statesmen of his generation could claim membership in all four categories. From their perspective, they already had saved their country from tyranny and founded a republic in the Revolution. Now, in 1787, they sought to use fundamental law in the further creation of an expanded and unprecedented continental republic.

The confidence that Jay extracted from his own sense of place in this vision of country translated into tonal assurances in the writer. The vision alone reduced his opponents to pygmies. But Jay, as always, preferred to concentrate on the positive side of the issue, and the solution he offered was as simple and pleasing as it was visible. Taking the Federal Convention as his touchstone, he gave the American people an image of the lawgiver for guiding their own subsequent actions. One could not find the turbulent exchanges and other difficulties of the actual Convention in Jay's one-sentence summary of the framers from "Federalist No. 2":

> In the mild season of peace, with minds unoccupied by other subjects, they passed many months in cool, uninterrupted, and daily consultation; and finally, without being awed by power, or influenced by any passions except love for their country, they presented and recommended to the people the plan produced by their joint and very unanimous councils.[44]

But one *could* recognize the image of the classical or Solonic lawmaker, rendered in collective form to meet the ideological needs of a democratic people.

A democratic Solon may sound like a contradiction in terms. In fact, awareness of that problem may explain why the authors of *The Federalist* chose Publius over Solon as their *nom de plume*.[45] Plutarch, in a section of his *Lives* that leading early republicans would have known almost by heart, contrasts Solon and Publius as lawgivers. Publius gave everything to the Roman people, destroying even his own house when they became jealous of its seeming beauty and ostentation, while the more aloof Solon gave the Athenian people only that law that they were capable of receiving and spoke of them collectively as "one empty fool."[46] That said, Jay clearly wanted both identifications. On the one hand, his framers appeared aloof, cool, even detached and self-sufficient, and they dispensed their Constitution out of a private, uninterrupted consultation among themselves. On the other hand, they had won "the confidence of the people" through their status as selected representatives, through their demonstrable "patriotism, virtue, and wisdom" (already tested in the Revolution), and through the all-important unanimity of their results. Collective in name, they were as one in their result, and they did everything with but one passion, "love for their country."[47]

It is this last quality that Jay emphasizes most in rhetorical presentation. Although the people may be incapable of duplicating the actual wisdom of the framers, they can honor that wisdom by ratifying the result of it, the Constitution. First, however, and to accomplish this much, they must learn to share the temperament that brought the framers to write the Constitution. In *An Address to the People of the State of New York*, Jay goes to great lengths to describe this saving temperament at work. That the framers reconciled "clashing opinions" to "unite with such singular and almost perfect unanimity" is a credit to their "temper" as much as their "talents." They represent, in sum, the perfect predisposition of the Enlightenment. "Neither wedded to favorite systems of their own, nor influenced by popular ones abroad, the members were *more desirous to receive light from,* than to impress their private sentiments on, *one another.*" Jay wants to prove to his readers that the framers were unselfish, enlightened thinkers who brought a "spirit of candour, of calm inquiry, of mutual accommodation, and mutual respect" to their proceedings and who solved every difficulty through "that same happy disposition to unite and conciliate."[48]

The most colossal statement in Jay's ratification writings follows directly from the presumed cultural power of this happy disposition to unite and conciliate. Rampant factionalism notwithstanding in 1788, Jay hopes that the people will exhibit the same "serene self-possession and presence of mind" that he has found in the Convention, for if they do, the result will also be the same. He minces no words here: "if the community at large had the same lights and reasons before them they would, if equally candid and uninfluenced, be equally unanimous."[49] So great is the power of enlightened reason and understanding that true candor will always yield the same result. Neither Hamilton nor Madison could match such optimism, and even for Jay, there remained the problem of implementation.

How does one duplicate the mutual accommodation of the framers without the wisdom and experience on which it is based? How can feeling replace intellect as a source of unanimity in the people? Looking again to the framers, Jay as Publius answers these questions with the one passion that can blot out all further passion and conflict: love of country. "Federalist No. 2" finds a "universal and uniform attachment to the cause of the Union" and claims that "the people have always thought right on this subject." Only through such an attachment, it argues vehemently, could they have convened the Federal Convention "as with one voice."[50]

This spirit of attachment clearly belongs to the realm of feeling as much as thought; Jay refers to "uniform attachment" as "similar sentiments." "This country and this people seem to have been made for each other," explains Publius, "and it appears as if it was the design of Providence, that an inheritance so proper and convenient for a band of brethren, united to each other by the strongest ties, should never be split into a number of unsocial, jealous, and alien sovereignties."[51] The issue once again comes down to the subject's capacity to see far enough while ignoring distractions. But where is that discipline to come from when the vision of an entire people is at stake? Americans, "a band of brethren," must take a comprehensive view if they are to sense "the design," if they are to discover how they are "united to each other by the strongest ties," if they are to "feel" their union. Above all, they must see themselves and each other *on* the land and *with* its leaders.

The lens for such a viewing is necessarily telescopic with attention to horizons that others can only intuit with unaided sight. Love of country and the spirit of accommodation that it brings enables the larger view. The two set scenes in "Federalist No. 2" say as much. They depict, first, the fertile and connected wide-spreading country of continental union and, second, the unified Convention. Both scenes cry "union!," but it is their close association, one with the other, that must guide the people "to that sedate and candid consideration which the magnitude and importance of the subject demand." These evocative descriptions, perhaps the greatest in all of *The Federalist* papers, demand a series of necessary transferences.

Here is the aesthetics of ratification at work. The framers see and then calmly decide to strengthen the design of the American nation. The people, in turn, already sense their own unity through the land. ("We have uniformly been one people," intones Publius.) Now, however, they have the added good fortune to behold the serene demeanor and the unanimity that the framers' knowledge and consultation have produced as lawgivers. The people must copy the framers' attitude and actions through their recognition and acceptance of scenes that are at once political and natural, timely and ordained, complex and decidedly simple. They can participate in and encourage the order of things by ratifying the Constitution. Do the people have a choice after reading *The Federalist?* It is the craft of John Jay in 1787 that any other decision contains an implicit admission of blindness. To say "I don't see what you have seen" leaves the speaker with a divided America in ruins and chaos.

A wealthy cosmopolite of two leading New York families (the Van Cortlandts as well as the Jays) and marrying into another (the Livingstons), the urbane, college-educated John Jay was an atypical Revolutionary and a desk-bound intellectual more than a leader of men. Yet other early republicans sought him out, gave him high responsibility, and listened to him with special care. The man of affairs never sought office and yet held more of them—almost always with reluctance—than any of his peers. Jay was at various times a commissioner of boundary disputes between the colonies and then the states, a member of the New York Assembly, the official drafter of the New York state constitution, a member of both the first and second Continental Congress and its president in 1778, head of a secret Revolutionary spy ring, a colonel in his state militia, chief justice of New York, minister plenipotentiary to Spain, an official commissioner in the peace negotiations with Great Britain, foreign secretary, first chief justice of the United States, special envoy to England, and governor of New York for two terms. So central was he to national understandings that many thought of him as the logical successor to George Washington as president. The same man was aloof, unbending, reclusive, and something of a hypochondriac throughout his eighty-four years of life. It can be said that the times found him—though with one crucial exception.

The characteristic that separated Jay beyond others, that won him such confidence, and that made up for other deficiencies was his ability as a writer. Moreover, to explain the nature of that ability is to catch a vital characteristic in the troubled turn from dependent colonies into independent states. From the beginning of their association in the Continental Congress, John Adams saw what others would soon learn. Jay, he wrote in 1774, was "a Man of Wit, well-informed, a good Speaker, and an elegant writer."[52] We have seen his power over others, including George Washington, but what made him that way? What made this usually quiet man so persuasive? The aloof patrician managed to touch the hearts and minds around him with regularity and special power. Something, as well, allowed this unbending man to bend when others talked and wrote. In political disagreement, "Jay was invariably agreeable and conciliatory to his opponents and was universally trusted."[53]

An important clue can be found in the heated debates over the ratification of the Federal Constitution by the New York Convention in the summer of 1788. Jay was a master at pointing out areas of agreement with his adversaries. In debate, he did not so much give ground as set the tone for where acknowledgment and consent must take place. Anti-Federalists in the Convention had attacked the Constitution line by line in the week before when Jay rose for the first time on June 23rd. Alexander Hamilton had spoken in defense of the Constitution before him, alluding darkly to "doubtful surmises" that blocked "the evidence of truth." Less exacerbated and exacerbating than Hamilton, Jay took an entirely different tack. He quietly urged the anti-Federalists to convince him of the danger that could lead him to withhold his own acquiescence to the Constitution, and, in urging, he also asked them to move beyond mere debate. "We not did come here to carry points," he reminded the Convention at large. "If the gentlemen will convince me I am wrong, I will submit. *It is from this reciprocal interchange of ideas that the truth must come out.*"[54] Others might say as much, but Jay's worst enemies conceded that this speaker earnestly believed what he said.

As cunning as Thomas Jefferson in manipulating language, Jay, not coincidentally, sounded a lot like him in paradoxically assuming an absolute truth through the interaction of knowledge. The curious juxtaposition made both men master stylists. Jay, like Jefferson, accepted a psychology of thought processes from Enlightenment sources that enabled reason to win out over the emotions if given an articulate chance. Basic to this belief was a dual premise: the moral sense was an intrinsic, rational faculty in everyone and its operations could bring the problem of self-interest under control by stimulating a larger view of the good in mutual success. Providence had formed the human faculties "subservient to the necessities, convenience, and happiness of a rational system."[55] For Jay, the rational system of the Constitution supplied these necessities, convenience, and prospective happiness at the social level, and it therefore would tally with the same qualities in a rational person. It was the writer's job to draw the connection by appealing to the better self in everyone.

Jay wrote in such a way that you would have to be disappointed in either yourself or the world to differ with him. It was a rare knack born of language, tone, and the nature of the man. In Jay's instance, as the opening to *An Address to the People of the State of New York* indicated, an attractive optimism ("the people at large always mean well") within the pessimism of the moment ("there are times and seasons when *general evils* spread general alarm") lent urgency as well as sincerity, appeal, and eloquence to his words. The conclusion of *An Address* is similar. "Let us all be mindful that the cause of freedom depends on the use we make of the singular opportunities we enjoy of governing ourselves wisely," Jay wrote.[56] Forget ratification for the moment and consider the import of the words by themselves. There are singular opportunities, ones that do not come again, when common happiness is possible. The deceptively simple prerequisites for attainment are joint wisdom about institutional arrangements, collective mindfulness in the fragility of freedom, and mutual recognition of the opportunity. The key in each case is the knowledge of the people working together. The stakes are so high for Jay that there can be no excuse when the right words are not found or poorly communicated. Here, in the indefatigable search for the right words in a claim of community, is the essence of what drives early republican writing to its heights.

CHAPTER SIX

Finding Rome in America

The role of classical antiquity in the formation of American culture has been a subject of serious disagreement. Were references to the classics during the national founding—particularly to the history, institutions, and personalities of the Roman republic—determinative of thought or merely illustrative of opinions already formed and, therefore, indicative of a superficial influence at best?[1] In more methodological terms, should the whole question of influence be subsumed, perhaps even forgotten, by approaching reference to antiquity through how it actually functioned in early American culture?[2] And is there any middle course in these debates? Can we join the search for influence to the facts of actual use while also moving beyond the original points of contention? Fortunately, the frequency of resort to antiquity by early republicans provides an ample testing ground.

A functional approach wants to know "*who* was making use of Antiquity in any and every particular way." It searches for "a profile of those identified as having referred to Antiquity at a given time and place, joined to an estimate of their audience."[3] A merely illustrative resort to classical times can be a useful source when subjected to this more modest test. Although reliance may indeed have been superficial, many early republican quests for identity turned to classical frames of reference, often with considerable internecine debate over the nature of the reliance. The accuracy of those debates can always be questioned and exposed. Functional analysis tries instead to work with the admittedly imitative and parochial nature of classical study in eighteenth-century America. If early republican intellectuals brought nothing new or original except themselves to their study of the classics, their selective applications of classical works give some indication of the difficulties that they could and could not face. Moreover, their manipulation of what they knew reveals a great deal about their cultural and political needs.[4]

A celebrated use of Latin in 1776 should clarify some of these initial premises. When Benjamin Franklin, John Adams, and Thomas Jefferson, as a committee of the Continental Congress, suggested the motto *E Pluribus Unum* in their efforts to create an official seal for the new United States, they could have thought of Virgil's *Moretum;* after all, the other two Latin phrases on the eventual seal, *Annuit Coeptis* and *Novus Ordo Seclorum,* were definitely from Virgil. Or they could have considered another classical source of the phrase, Horace's *Second Book of Epistles.* The actual words may also have come to them first from an epigraph on the title page of *The Gentlemen's Magazine,* an English publication that circulated widely in the American colonies after 1731, or possibly even from "Essay Number 143" in *The Spectator* of Richard Steele and Joseph Addison, another English periodical that achieved lasting popularity in America.[5]

Whatever the source, the question of a classical impact was almost certainly multifaceted and refracted in this incident of national formation, and Congressional usage smacked more of appropriation than influence. None of the constitutive metaphors associated with the motto in the original texts—the making of a salad in Virgil, a proverb about plucking thorns in Horace and *The Spectator,* a bouquet of flowers in *The Gentleman's Magazine*—touched "the spirit of 1776." Congress, in accepting the motto, was not attracted by the beauties of Virgil or of Horace but by the isolated interpretation of high-sounding words that could be re-cast for the purposes of their patriotic mission. Utilitarian at best, the isolation in interpretation and the need for re-casting still point to a larger problem.

The capacities of Franklin, Adams, and Jefferson, extraordinary by any standard, were surely equal to the task before them. Nonetheless, the same founders who needed only a few days to write out the Declaration of Independence could not agree on a corresponding design for a national seal after six weeks of deliberation. "Some six years would pass before a design emblematic of the new Republic would finally be settled upon."[6] There were grave uncertainties about direction linguistically, institutionally, and politically in 1776, but the earliest republicans seem to have experienced even more direct intellectual difficulty in visualizing the outward show of their project. None of the trappings of modern European authority held any appeal, and many of them—a crown, official robes, a scepter, most official seals—would have been dangerous intrusions on the Revolutionary mission. At the same time, the need for highly visible, legitimizing symbols of authority was correspondingly great, and the symbolism of classical republicanism offered a ready source.

But if the source was obvious, it was also troubling. The early republican appropriators of classical symbols and terminology had to worry about what each sign meant and might come to mean, particularly in light of the failures of the Greek and Roman republics. What should be used from these sources? How should it be used? How would use be taken by a modern Revolutionary people? These were serious questions without real answers in the unprecedented situation and political flux of 1776. *E Pluribus Unum* may have tripped easily enough from educated tongues in the Anglo-American world of the eighteenth century, but it was another matter altogether to turn the phrase into an official article of faith for a whole people, very few of whom knew Latin.

More than two centuries after the fact, it is not easy to ascertain exactly what *E Pluribus Unum* meant in the first days of the American Revolution. At one level, "from many, one" conveyed the hope of a successful alliance among separate colonies as they embarked on a war to secure their declared independence from Great Britain. The Americans were fighting the greatest military power in the world. If they were to have any chance at all, it was crucial that the many different and separate voices of rebellion sound as one. At another level, when proposed on August 20, 1776, the phrase drew attention to a continuing multiplicity among thirteen distinct units; it signified the artificiality involved in combination. Like the salad or bouquet of flowers before it, the new motto implied a synthetic orchestration, one that was in some sense unnatural and that had to be arranged to succeed. For while the reverse proposition, "one" leading to "many," existed everywhere in the touchstone of nature and could be seen there in the regular and pervasive processes of procreation and evolution, the seeming contradiction of "the many" leading to "one"

appeared only in the social realms of human aspiration. Early republican efforts to depict that aspiration, a mysterious union out of separate parts, reached for symbolic support, but visual representation
remained problematic. Like the tripartite Godhead of Christian iconography, the new union required an act of faith to be viewed correctly. Its proponents needed all of the figurative help they could get
or manufacture for the new union to be seen at home and abroad.

Ideological sleight of hand over the classical tradition was a useful
tool in this regard. Consider for a moment the other two Latin slogans on the ratified Seal of the United States. *Annuit Coeptis,* translated as "God favors our undertakings," suggested a sense of collective destiny and assurance not found in the source. In Virgil's *Aeneid,*
the original phrase took the form of a personal plea from the fledgling
warrior Ascanius, the son of Aeneas in his first battle: *Jupiter omni-
potens audacibus annue coeptis,* or in English, "all powerful Jupiter
[please] favor my daring undertakings." Early republicans transformed this call for help into an assertion of providential favor by
changing the first person imperative subjunctive in "annue" into the
third person active transitive, "annuit": the result was an allusion to
"the many signal interpositions of providence in favor of the American cause." Similarly, *Novus Ordo Seclorum,* trumpeted in Revolutionary circles and after as "the new order of the ages" held a more
cyclical and limited historical significance in its first manifestation,
Virgil's *Fourth Eclogue.* The poet initially wrote "*magnus ab integro
saeclorum nascitur ordo*" or "the great *sequence* of the ages *starts
afresh,*" also translated as "a mighty order of ages is born *anew*" or
"the great series of ages *begins anew.*"[7]

Classical reference was useful, but it had to be made to serve. Some
discrepancies in form and translation flourished through ignorance;
more occurred through the calculated ambivalence that early republicans brought to their appropriation of the classical tradition and
through a corresponding desire to improve upon it. Thus, and despite
the aura of learned assurance that Latin quotation projected, early republican usage remained tentative. Greece and Rome were examples.
They were not models to be followed. The Revolutionaries of 1776
confidently spoke of a fundamental difference from the past in their
"new world." They wanted their history to be distinct; they expected
it to grow in a new and glorious fashion instead of repeating the past
in endless cycles of rise and fall.

Where did "the many leading to one" manifest itself in the earliest moments of the republic? In practical terms, the declaration of congruence appeared in the cooperation of Congressmen from different states as they conducted the official business of the new United States of America. The very word "congress," from *congressus,* denoted "a coming together." The motto, in consequence, read as a claim about the standard of conduct needed, but in 1776 no official basis or tradition for that level of cooperation existed. The new states, still the former colonies in many ways, continued to squabble fiercely over border disputes, voting rights, trading requirements, and the financial subsidy of the new confederacy. Not until 1781 did the Articles of Confederation receive formal ratification, and its members often fell short of both the spirit and the letter of its provisions.

The predicament of visualizing this emergent but highly uncertain union troubled early republicans. Enlightenment thought, so central to American Revolutionary impulses, assumed the dominance of visual metaphors in theories of understanding. Even in victory, however, the most prevalent and constitutive metaphor, the presumed spread of light, did not convert easily into an agreed upon structural order or presence in the still forming political experiment. The opening line of the national anthem presented the problem as a consuming question as late as 1814 when first uttered; the words themselves—"Oh say can you see?"—were a lively type for an artificially created nation on the edge of a still unknown and contested continent.[8] Thereafter, the rapidly changing nature of the nation and the widespread fear of incongruity in a *continental* republic continued to complicate the problem of perspective.[9] Early republicans struggled with a collective understanding of their union throughout "a crucible of confusion and conflict." After all, "almost every state and every major political faction and interest group attempted, at one time or other between 1790 and 1860, to weaken the power of the national government or to break up the Union directly."[10] In facing these problems, the founders understood that they had to create sight where the possibility was lacking. Adept in the use of words and political theory, they were unavoidably clumsier when turning to the images that might symbolize the structure of their connection.[11]

A knowledge of the classics, funneled through an eighteenth-century understanding, gave one answer to the problem of perception. Just as *E Pluribus Unum* voiced a linguistic yearning for cohesion in search of embodiment, so the history of antiquity, and particularly the history of the Roman Republic, furnished pictures for ordering reality. That history could be used, but it remained a two-edged sword that cut two ways, and it needed to be used with care. Everyone feared the rise of a Caesar.[12] "It is impossible," wrote Alexander Hamilton as Publius, "to read the history of the petty republics of Greece and Italy without feeling sensations of horror and disgust." His colleague, James Madison, also warned against "a blind veneration for antiquity" in an American Revolution that had "no parallel in the annals of human society." Still, there remained the problem of actually seeing the "new and noble course."[13] To the extent that history could be a guide, the leaders of the Revolutionary generation, including the appropriately named Publius, turned to classical antiquity and the lessons of Rome to understand the dangers and the potential of the republican form of government.[14] Whether in ignorance or calculation, they did not hesitate to make that history their own, and the story of their manipulations remains a largely untold one.

Identifications with Republican Rome could be especially powerful because, as John Adams told Benjamin Rush, "the period in the history of the world the best understood is that of Rome from the time of Marius to the death of Cicero. . . . There we see the true character of the times and the passions of all the actors on the stage." The period in question, roughly 129 to 43 B.C., spanned what is generally called "The Fall of the Republic," during which the creation of client armies led to alliances between Roman military leaders and political factions, and then to civil wars and the gradual destruction of existing governmental institutions. Revolutionary Americans were haunted by the possibility of a repetition in their own times. History supplied a uniformly sobering lesson. Studying Conyers Middleton's *The History of the Life of Marcus Tullius Cicero* (1741), Adams remarked "I seem to read the history of all ages and nations in every page, and especially the history of our own country for forty years past. Change the names and every anecdote will be applicable to us."[15]

Many of the parallels drawn from antiquity were undeniably superficial. The writers of the Declaration of Independence and, later, of the Constitution loosely referred to each other and themselves as Draco and Solon from Athens; Lycurgus from Sparta; or Romulus, Numa, and Tullius Hostilius from Rome.[16] The martyred generals of the Revolution, Richard Montgomery at Quebec and Joseph Warren at Bunker Hill, promptly became Marcus Atilius Regulus, the Roman general who voluntarily returned as a prisoner on furlough to Carthage and certain death in the third century B.C.[17] Most famously, when Washington voluntarily resigned from the Revolutionary army, relinquishing all thought of further power, he took the name everywhere of the American Cincinnatus.[18] The victories of America at Saratoga and Yorktown figured the birth of a new and better Roman Republic.[19]

These associations and others like them took flight in the American imagination no matter how superficial in origin. Would the resignation of Washington have reached such universality as a gesture without the reiterated comparison, acknowledged by all, to Cincinnatus, who also had relinquished power voluntarily? Would the classical associations assigned to the martyred Joseph Warren have been as powerful but for the fact that Warren had appeared dressed in "Ciceronian Toga" earlier in the year while delivering an oration commemorating the "Bloody Tragedy" of the Boston Massacre? Would American authors of national documents have won the same celebrity without the Enlightenment reiteration of the classical emphasis on *conditores imperiorum* and *perpetui principes,* founders of states and first lawgivers?[20] Classical reference heightened certain American events by helping them to attain the status of timeless tableaux in republican culture.

Parallels to antiquity put a stamp of legitimacy on the new historical moments. Indeed, visual representations of these events have tended to define the Revolution for Americans ever since. The painter John Trumbull chose exactly the scenes just noted for his own history of the Revolution: *The Death of General Warren at the Battle of Bunker's Hill, June 17, 1775* (1786), *The Death of General Montgomery in the Attack on Quebec, December 31, 1775* (1786), *The Declaration of Independence, Philadelphia, July 4, 1776* (1786–1820), *The Resignation of General Washington* (1824–28), together with *The Surrender of General Burgoyne at Saratoga, New York, October 16, 1777* (ca. 1816), and *The Surrender of Lord Cornwallis at Yorktown* (1787–1828). Versions of the last four paintings have become national icons. They hang in the rotunda of the national Capitol and tend to be reproduced in standard histories of the Revolution.[21]

Because an observer sees only what can first be understood, classical knowledge provided a symbolics for seeing in an unprecedented situation. The greatest difficulty for early republicans came not in finding heroes but in seeing themselves clearly and in learning how to behave as citizens instead of subjects. In the rapid change of events and attitudes, every major observer, no matter how acute, had to agree at some point with John Adams' admission to Jefferson in 1812. "There is something in this country too deep for me to sound," he wrote. Even Jefferson, who took a more positive view of matters than Adams, spoke of an uncertain because unfinished picture that was literally hard to see. "Never was a finer canvas presented to work on than our countrymen," he told Adams, writing about "the age of experiments in government." "*We have seen no instance of this,*" he added significantly, "since the days of the Roman republic."[22] In the new rhetoric of "we, the people," Americans needed to regard themselves and their public responsibilities in a different way. What that meant in practice was again a function of "the many becoming one" but this time at an even more amorphous level of perception. After 1781, when Congress extended its own motto to the entire nation, the words *E Pluribus Unum* had to find incarnation in ceremonies of the people assembled or acting together, an idea legitimized by the Federal Convention of 1787 and extolled in the ratification process of the Constitution.[23]

The new language of the people heightened the dilemma as well as the stakes in how the people themselves might be seen. To be sure, early republicans all agreed that "the people" constituted the only legitimate foundation of government, but a growing democratic intensity wrapped every further question in deepening controversy. The Revolution itself would quickly divide over the role of the people. Describing the split into separate parties in the 1790s, Federalist against Republican, Jefferson, looking back, could not resist citing antiquity to prove that "every one takes his side in favor of the many, or of the few." "Whether the power of the people, or that of the ['aristocrats'] should prevail," he explained to John Adams, "were questions which kept the states of Greece and Rome in eternal convulsions."[24] Adams, in turn, could agree with the classical example without accepting its application to his republican present, a frequent source of debate in most resorts to the classical tradition. Privileging the people also left the problem of their proper role unanswered. Every early republican leader recognized a dangerous continuum from the people to faction, to the crowd, and finally into the mob; it was a danger already endured in the riots of the Revolution and not to be repeated.[25]

How were the people to exercise their power in legitimate concert? When were they to act? How were they to engage in the activity of safely recognizing and participating in the continuing fact of consent with each other? Where were they to express their dissent when dissent was needed? Could elections alone handle all of these problems and, if so, how many people and under what circumstances should be allowed to vote?

American answers to such questions turned frequently on eighteenth-century notions of observed classical decorum. Charles Lee put the matter graphically when he wrote in 1782 that "the splendid picture" painted by Greek and Roman historians and orators enabled young Americans to find "liberty in a republican garb."[26] John Adams hinted at the same thing in pronouncing the figures of classical Rome to be the most visible actors ever to appear on the stage of history. These comments on costume and scene were more than metaphors in a theatrical age. They helped to explain the elaborate staging of oratory and patriotic performance in early republican culture.

The pairing of the intellectual legacy of antiquity with eighteenth-century notions of spectacle or show gave added vitality to each. Exactly how the two frames of reference were to inform each other becomes clear in two other comments by John Adams. In the first, from 1786, Adams argued:

> The History of Greece should be to our countrymen what is called in many families on the Continent, a *boudoir*, an octagonal apartment in a house, with a full-length mirror on every side, and another in the ceiling . . . where, in whatever direction they [ladies and gentlemen out of humour] turn their eyes, they see their own faces and figures multiplied without end. By thus beholding their own beautiful persons, and seeing, at the same time, the deformity brought upon them by their anger, they may recover their tempers and their charms together.[27]

In the second, from 1805, he explained how "'The Scenery of the Business'" often outstripped substance in public life: "The scenery has often if not commonly in all the business of human life, at least of public life, more effect than the characters of the dramatis personae or the ingenuity of the plot," he wrote Benjamin Rush. "Recollect within your own times. What but the scenery did this? or that? or the other? Was there ever a *coup de théâtre* that had so great an effect as Jefferson's penmanship of the Declaration of Independence?"[28]

Both statements recognized the peculiar value of visual representation, particularly of tableaux, as a compelling and even controlling source of comprehension. As the first indicated the method to be used, so the second called that method by its proper name, artifice. The fixed or arranged scene lent a vitality to perception that would clarify when properly used, and the need for clarification was paramount in controlling behavior and in contributing to the ceremony of public life. The goal was to bring as much light from as many different angles as possible to bear upon parallels between the present day and the best moments of antiquity. The beauty, proportion, and truth of the original classical scene, properly understood, would translate into the present; it would conquer "the deformity" and "anger" of the present, restoring every observer who was willing to look to a larger understanding.

To see as much as possible meant simultaneously to perceive and to become whole and thereby calm. Anger, by way of contrast, bespoke a lack of perspective and forced deformity on both subject and object. Within these tenets, Adams believed that the greatest available source of light for the recognition of truth in human affairs was the history of the classical republics. As he told Lafayette in 1782 while tracing "all the best things in civil life," "Athens and Rome have done more honour to our species than all the rest."[29] The light of classical history could be used to guide early republicans away from their own quarrels and toward a proper sense of political equanimity in republican harmony. Demonstrations of classical composure in public ceremony would also dampen the potential explosiveness of the people without, however, undermining their active virtue.

Adams possessed a strong rather than an original mind; he is useful in this context precisely because he had such a good grasp of the conventional thinking of his time. The timeliness of his enthusiasm is a reminder that the Revolution in America coincided with a vital Enlightenment interest in antiquity through the excavations of ruins that began at Herculaneum in 1709 and Pompeii in 1748. Throughout the eighteenth century, a new disciplined mode of seeing in the birth of modern archeology and the beginnings of a modern history of art gave special vigor to the themes of ancient civilization in works like Montesquieu's *Considérations sur les Causes de la Grandeur des Romains et de leur Décadence* (1734), Edward Gibbon's *Decline and Fall of the Roman Empire* (1776–1788), and Adam Ferguson's *History of the Progress and Termination of the Roman Republic* (1783). Channeling much of this excitement was the seminal work of the German philosophe Johann Joachim Winckelmann, whose search for idealized beauty in classical forms controlled the perception of antiquity for the rest of the century.[30]

Strategically placed as a special consultant to the Vatican and the curator of Cardinal Alessandro Albani's famous collection of classical artifacts in Rome, Winckelmann insisted in his history of ancient art, *Geschichte der Kunst des Altertums* (1764), that the ancients had achieved an ultimate beauty through noble simplicity and quiet grandeur and that modern art should imitate them through the availability of classical sculpture. Not coloring but contour and archeological accuracy provided the truest sources of a stripped-down beauty in Winckelmann's understanding of art. The modern artist, in following these strictures, was to take the legends and forms of antiquity as primary subjects and to "make every picture a school of virtue".[31] The combination of aesthetic concern and moral obligation gave an important license to every user: the main objective in the search for proper form encouraged reduction of the complexities in antiquity into simplicities for immediate and effective use.

The subsequent, if indirect, application of these premises in America transcended mere art. Most early republicans knew nothing of Winckelmann directly and only something of his Anglo-American popularizer, Joshua Reynolds.[32] They imbibed their ideas on the relation of art, politics, and the classics secondhand through republican theory and through a derivative source, the eighteenth-century American school of historical painting, the panoramic canvases of Benjamin West, John Singleton Copley, Charles Willson Peale, and Gilbert Stuart. Arriving first in Rome in 1760, West studied under Winckelmann and Winckelmann's protégé, the painter Raphael Mengs, and the result in West and his followers was a series of paintings on classical historical subjects that became the most popular art works of the age. The intellectual affinities involved were more or less everywhere in Anglo-American culture before 1776, but the Revolution would take singular advantage of them. The appeal of the orientation both before

and after independence can hardly be overemphasized. West did not
pursue classical subjects so much as they found him. Winckelmann
and Mengs instantly persuaded the already inclined West of the validity and importance of their own focus on antiquity and of their techniques in rendering that subject. After studying in Rome, West moved
on to London in 1763, where he instructed Copley, Peale, and Stuart
in the same techniques and "exerted unparalleled influence on the development of American art for over half a century, from the mid
1760's until his death in 1820."[33]

The immediacy of impact together with the overwhelming and lasting popularity of West's work indicate more than influence. West's
sudden prominence was part of a larger refraction in the history of
ideas, part of the conjunction of classical ideals, republican principles, empathic historical imagination, and Enlightenment aspirations
in eighteenth-century thought. The specific conceptual solutions of
Winckelmann were perfect for later republican use and exhibition.
West's capacity to give those solutions the clearest representational
form would become an instrumental aid as well as a source of national pride. In a typical celebration of the painter, Joel Barlow's post-
Revolutionary epic poem on the rise of America, *The Columbiad*,
would give significant space to West for the way he "calls to life each
patriot." The enthusiastic poet would even add an eight-page note
cataloguing all of West's paintings and their locations to help his readers find them.[34] These affinities between West's pre-Revolutionary art
and later Revolutionary and post-Revolutionary use must be understood carefully. West's paintings did not turn him into a closet republican in Europe in the middle 1760s, but like many other American intellectuals of the age, he was eager to receive classical Roman themes,
usually with a republican emphasis, and his facility in converting the
classical ideal into extremely popular art suggests a functional need in
West and his admirers for what will subsequently be called "neoclassi-
cism."[35]

How did a colonial American in 1760 learn to reach so expressively
and boldly for solutions that he barely understood? West, arriving in
Europe at twenty-one, was caught between colonial and cosmopolitan needs but made both work for him. He was at once a prodigy
painting in Rome and the son of a Quaker innkeeper from the back
country of Pennsylvania. The combinations that made him successful
would also serve a new republican elite when it entered its own period

of rapid transition a decade later. The idealization of classical form met the colonial artist's parochial search for order, control, and recognizable virtue even as it satisfied very different European standards of accuracy, refinement, and style. The proof can be seen in two of West's most famous renditions of classical scenes: *Agrippina Landing at Brundisium with the Ashes of Germanicus,* begun in 1766 and completed in 1768 for Robert Drummond, Archbishop of York, and *The Departure of Regulus,* painted for and at the suggestion of George III during 1767.

In both cases, West took classical events of frequent reference in eighteenth-century discourse and distilled them into pictorial representations of ideas that would take center stage in the conflict and eventual rupture of relations in the Anglo-American world. Germanicus, military hero and adopted son of the emperor Tiberius, died under mysterious circumstances, possibly from poison but certainly involving political treachery, in 19 A.D. His funeral and the public outpouring of grief, in Tacitus' reading of the event, represented the final loss of hope in restoring the republic. Germanicus "had the idea of comprehending in a restored era of freedom the Roman people under equal laws." Agrippina, in courageously bringing her husband's ashes to Rome, typified what little remained of "the glory of the country."[36] Marcus Atilius Regulus, a more shadowy figure from the earlier Punic Wars, played, if anything, a sharper cameo role in epic understanding. On parole from captivity in Carthage in 255 B.C. for the purpose of negotiating peace terms and an exchange of prisoners, Regulus urged the Senate to decline the Carthaginians' terms and then, to keep his word, returned voluntarily to suffer certain death by torture. In the poet Horace's famous account, "far-seeing Regulus" pushed "through crowds/ Of grieving friends, exile and glory-bound./ And yet he knew what the barbarian torturer/ Had ready for him."[37] Benjamin West painted the poignant moment of Regulus' final departure from family and friends in Rome.

The two paintings captured the declension of political virtue through, on the one hand, the display of Regulus's utter selflessness in the name of patriotic service to the republic of Rome and, on the other, recognition of the loss of all civic virtue in later imperial Rome when the untimely death of Germanicus, perhaps through murder at the hands of political rivals, led to "one universal groan." As such, these two works depicted the highest aspirations and worst fears in the debate just beginning over the location of virtue and corruption in Anglo-American culture. Heroic sacrifice for one's country was a compelling theme everywhere in the emerging nationalism of the eighteenth century, and it quickly became an obsession in Revolutionary America.[38]

A more subtle thematic similarity is perhaps of even greater interest and lasting import. Panoramic in intent and scope, containing more than seventy figures each with the suggestion of thousands beyond, both *Agrippina Landing at Brundisium with the Ashes of Germanicus* and *The Departure of Regulus* took moments of maximal cultural distress. How, a collected populace must ask itself in each instance, should it behave? As Tacitus described the arrival of Agrippina, "every place which commanded the most distant prospect were filled with crowds of mourners, who incessantly asked one another, whether, when she landed, they were to receive her in silence or with some utterance of emotion. They were not agreed on what befitted the occasion." Horace, too, in his ode on Regulus, described "the wavering Senate" and the conflict of feelings among kinsmen and the people as they tried to hold the hero back.[39] These painted scenes captured a burning question asked both from above and below in Revolutionary America. How were the people supposed to conduct themselves?[40]

One key to the immediate popularity of West's work lay in his handling of this presumed volatility in the people. Despite their common theme of popular disruption, neither painting allowed an overt display of passion. Instead, in keeping with the generally held aesthetic premise that passion distorted form, West distilled all emotion into a beholding sorrow that was profound rather than egregious. "If you mean to preserve the most perfect beauty in its most perfect state," Joshua Reynolds explained, in describing the eighteenth-century goal in art, "you cannot express the passions, all of which produce distortion and deformity, more or less, in the most beautiful faces."[41] True, indistinct figures gesticulate from a distant rampart in *Agrippina with the Ashes of Germanicus,* and, true again, the wife of the departing hero has fainted in *The Departure of Regulus,* but nothing disturbs the pervading sense of unified melancholy in either scene, and even this emotion appears contained by a more positive sense of veneration flowing toward the central figure from all directions. Agrippina and Regulus were so useful in an eighteenth-century perspective because they held every eye through their noble comportment, courage, and utter self-possession.

The crowd, though it appeared under enormous strain in West's paintings, accepted its own cue accordingly, occupying the position of formal witness and fulfilling several functions in that process. Aesthetically, the crowd met the artistic imperatives of graceful accommodation and reflective beauty required of all subordinate parts in a composition; it sustained the central subject without detracting from any part. As political representation, it responded to a powerful generalized need for realized decorum in Anglo-American culture during a period of extensive popular unrest in America and of unusual acrimony and political drift in England.[42] As historical paintings in the tradition of the *exemplum virtutis,* where representation sought to induce behavior by illustrating virtuous conduct, *Agrippina with the Ashes of Germanicus* and *The Departure of Regulus* spoke to both leaders and led. The meritorious stances of the superior figure found their corollaries in the popular recognition of virtue in control and in cohesive submission to it. Interestingly, and in both cases, vaguely military, political, and religious figures continue to perform their tasks while the people mourn. West used light not only to accent his central figures but also to touch these relatively public personages, giving them subtle badges of authority and importance.

The reception of West's paintings as moral tableaux flowed from a powerful form of cultural wish-fulfillment. In the most forceful modern analysis of the mob in action, Elias Canetti has noted that "the destructiveness of the crowd is often mentioned as its most conspicuous quality," and he explains how enclosure or containment, "The Crowd as a Ring," affords an important antidote to its potential for violence.[43] West's vast historical paintings, and after them those of John Singleton Copley and John Trumbull, operated in much this way. The crowds in *Agrippina with the Ashes of Germanicus* and *The Departure of Regulus* were painted so as to appear quadruply ringed. First, and most crucially, they were held to the center of concern by their recognition of a superior and unforgettable figure in their midst, and that figure, in the instant of performance, functioned as a mesmerizing source of emulation. "Be calm amidst seemingly impossible burdens," this first ring of implication announced. Then, in aspects of each painting not previously mentioned, the central figures took additional meaning from surrounding architectural structures of sublime simplicity and majesty. From the top of these high structures in the distance, extended crowds yielded a third confinement by turning the entire scene into an arena or amphitheater. Finally, the frame of the painting held everything in place, refusing addition or further development.

The absence of a sophisticated artistic tradition notwithstanding, early republican culture would duplicate in ceremony this tableau of the ringed crowd by translating the notion of picture into oratorical performance. Public speakers in the "Golden Age of American Oratory," roughly from the 1760s to the 1850s, instinctively adapted the devices of control and enclosure to their own needs.[44] Their acknowledged task was to create an "aesthetics of cohesion" wherein speaker and audience could reenact the promise and reality of the republican experiment. Fisher Ames and John Quincy Adams were the theorists of this tradition; a generation later Henry Clay, John C. Calhoun, and Daniel Webster were its greatest practitioners.[45]

Fisher Ames, who spoke first on these matters, specifically raised the parallel of Germanicus in his own most sustained comment on the proper relation of leader to led, virtue to emulation. "We weep, as the Romans did over the ashes of Germanicus," he spoke and wrote in eulogy of Alexander Hamilton. Hamilton, like Germanicus, had fallen under the hand of his political enemies, in this case Aaron Burr. Consciously or unconsciously, Ames reinvoked the theme of Benjamin West's painting when he argued that the best judge of the controversial Hamilton would be "the body of the people, who cannot feel a spirit of rivalship towards those whom they see elevated by nature and education so far above their heads." His own gauge for the fallen leader of the Federalists also reached to the past. Hamilton personified "the best Romans in their best days." The higher dynamic that controlled here was of leader to follower and, by extension, of speaker to audience. "The most substantial glory of a country," concluded Ames, "is in its virtuous great men; its prosperity will depend on its docility to learn from their example."[46] Naturally, the place for the people to demonstrate their "docility to learn" came in the public forum, where speakers could direct them in the lessons of republicanism. The people's assigned role was to listen.

American oratory transformed the tableau of the classical ideal into tableau vivant, the living speaker as performer before a knowing audience. Ames, the most eloquent rhetorician in New England at the beginning of the nineteenth century, was particularly useful in noting the transition. His use of classical analogies bordered on the compulsive, and through those analogies, he explained the symbiotic relation between speaker and audience in republican culture. An embattled and increasingly embittered Federalist, he found Epaminondas in Washington, Demosthenes and Cicero in Hamilton, and, alas, Philip of Macedonia and Caesar in Thomas Jefferson. Article after article traced the collapse of Greece and Rome afresh in American experience.[47] "Here let Americans read their own history," ran the shrill claim in parallel after parallel. "Is Virginia to be our Rome?" gasped Ames in horror over the growing string of presidents from that state. Baltimore emerged as Antium and Philadelphia as Capua, and both appeared ready to bow "their proud necks to a new Roman yoke."[48]

The felt immediacy and despair in such passages, together with the wildly inventive character of his correspondences, made Ames the master in a political invective of classical reference. More interesting, however, was the way the same qualities carried him beyond identifications and toward an underlying theory of behavior and cultural accomplishment. The ancients excelled through their belief in the public "assembled in person." "It was enough to inspire the poet's enthusiasm," explained Ames, "to know beforehand that his nation would partake it." Reception took place not in the "cold perusal" of a mere reading. No, "all Greece, assembled by its deputies beheld the contests of wit and valor," and there the poet actually "*saw* his work become the instructor of the wise, the companion of the brave and the great."[49] The reciprocities in performance were the keys to this thesis and to Ames' hopes for America. He and others, most notably John Quincy Adams, transmitted the implications of performance from painting and poetry to oratory, where the bond between performing speaker and listening audience became the whole aim of language.

The most useful classical figure in this act of transmission from literature to politics was invariably Cicero.[50] The lectures that John Quincy Adams gave between 1806 and 1809 as Harvard's first Boylston Professor of Rhetoric allowed him to think of himself as "the principal founder" of popular oratory in America, and Cicero figured more prominently in them than any other historical character. Every warning against Caesarism in America, and this warning was endlessly reiterated from both pulpit and political platform, implied Cicero, "the voice of Rome," as the ultimate messenger. Adams found the ideal perfection of an embodied speaker in this source.[51]

Cicero, Adams told his students, applied to eloquence the same conception and pursuit of beauty that the sculptor brought to marble. Cicero's works, but also Cicero himself, formed "a delineation of the talent" in speaking. Again, the emphasis was on the nature of visibility in voice. Always, in the case of Cicero, "the orator is a portrait of the speaker." For Cicero, "it appears to have been the study of his whole life to form an idea of a perfect orator, and of exhibiting his image to the world." The image was crucial because "what a speaker should be" created "the idealized image of a speaker." Americans who read carefully could at least glimpse the image through "the mind of Cicero." So integral was this source of absolute form and proportion that to be *without* Cicero was to suffer disfigurement in oneself. "To live without having Cicero and a Tacitus at hand," wrote Adams in his diary, "seems to me as if it was a privation of one of my limbs."[52]

These opinions had almost nothing to do with the historical realities of Rome in the first century B.C., but their expression in the early nineteenth century indicated a great deal about American self-perception. Alexis de Tocqueville, traveling in the country in 1831, summarized the peculiarly American perspective on classical texts through an American observer: "[these texts] have some special merits, admirably calculated to counterbalance our peculiar defects. They are a prop on the side on which we are in most danger of falling."[53]

The perceived defects and dangers in America were linked and threefold: demagoguery, popular unrest, and eventual dissolution. It was the task of the orator to answer each by preserving liberty, order, and connection in American culture. Only the truly eloquent speaker, wrote John Quincy Adams, could hope at once "to appall the heart of the tyrant upon his throne, and to control the wayward dispositions of the people," while also acting as "the instrument, whose operation can affect the acts of all our corporate bodies; of towns, cities, counties, states, and of the whole confederated empire." This was the challenge that Adams sent his students and fellow citizens. They had to learn how to wield "those unresisted powers, which mould the mind of man to the will of the speaker, and yield the guidance of a nation to the dominion of the voice."[54]

Everything about these statements emphasized the crucial role and reciprocities of public performance. As the will of the speaker "moulded" an audience through "the dominion of the voice," so that audience would demonstrate its patriotic acceptance by submitting to the proper speaker's "guidance." In this fashion, speaker and audience acknowledged in each other the fact of their common or unified nationhood. Mere words alone could never elicit such a powerful demonstration. In Daniel Webster's explanation, "true eloquence, indeed, does not consist in speech. . . . Words and phrases may be marshaled in every way, but they cannot compass it. It must exist in the man, in the subject, and in the occasion."[55] The successful speaker had to unify or "compass" an audience by learning to represent the subject at hand in the ceremony of speaking. Webster understood better than any other orator in antebellum America the need for a visible standard to which an audience of American citizens might react. As he told one large gathering, Americans should "study to be what they behold."[56]

Throughout the early republic, the spectacle in performance—especially in the resonance between a speaker and a unified and, therefore, visible listening audience—was never far from the imagination or from the goal of American oratory. Were accompanying references to antiquity "props on the side," as de Tocqueville called them, or vital manifestations in the crafted synergy between orator and audience? Where prop verges on manifestation is a difficult distinction to draw, but the line between them can be seen more clearly in one last resort to the technique and works of Benjamin West. The painter strove to convey an absolute accuracy in the classical artifacts of his historical scenes, and this desire for faithful imitation soon became a requirement in early republican usages.

West modeled the background of *Agrippina with the Ashes of Germanicus* on the Diocletian palace at Spalato by using the drawings of the building published by Robert Adams shortly before the picture was painted, and he also copied the entire central cluster of people in the painting (Agrippina, her children, and attendants) from a procession of the imperial family on the *Ara Pacis Augustae*, erected in Rome by Agrippina's grandfather in 14 B.C. or just a few decades before the death of Germanicus.[57] For West and the early republicans who came after him, accuracy in detail was the quintessence of historical tableaux, even though such a frozen accuracy was totally de-contextualized. The main figures in West's painting appeared in frieze-like permanence, central objects for the surrounding mourners to hold and gaze upon forever in the moment of recognition. By setting off his main figures as hallowed objects within the painting, West also created the curious effect of connecting the surrounding mourners in spirit to the eighteenth-century viewer of the painting. Tableau encouraged identification across time through empathetic similitude.

The same inclinations, the desire to highlight the precise classical object, also dominated public architecture in the early republic and for some of the same reasons. Once again, the perfection of a central object could be manipulated to reduce the implications of the chaos around it. Early republican leaders insisted almost with one voice that their official buildings follow classical models, and they made it a foregone conclusion that Washington, D.C., the planned capital, would be a domed and colonnaded city. Leading founders like Washington and Jefferson were uncharacteristically rigid and vocal on this point, insisting that public buildings take a classical form. It was under Washington's explicit instructions that Pierre Charles L'Enfant transformed the City Hall in New York, first capital of the new republic, into Federal Hall for Congress with a dramatic shift from the Palladio-like sixteenth-century style favored by English architectural enthusiasts into a more classical structure with larger windows and the addition of panels of relief sculpture, Tuscan piers, and Roman Doric columns. Jefferson's corresponding designs in the 1780s for the Virginia statehouse were inspired by his regard for the temple form of the classical past and particularly for the temple he had seen in Nimes, which he considered a product of Republican Rome.[58]

The ideal, in Thomas Jefferson's description of the plans for Washington from 1791, would be "the adoption of some one of the models to antiquity which have had the approbation of thousands of years." When the new Capitol building in Washington supplied an initial step, he observed that the country was receiving "the first temple dedicated to the sovereignty of the people, embellishing with Athenian taste the course of a nation looking far beyond the range of Athenian destinies."[59] Jefferson's explanation resolved a troubling discrepancy. What could it mean to build Greek temples without the belief system that produced the originals? Jefferson and the other leaders of his generation, "looking beyond the range of Athenian destinies," clearly assumed that a secular faith in republican destiny could substitute for the religious beliefs of antiquity in the name of a common republican ideal. Even so, the enormity of the step taken in adopting classical ar-

chitecture should not be overlooked. How government buildings dedicated to the people were supposed to look was an unprecedented
question in history when it was first raised in early republican culture.

The decision to answer the future so decisively out of the distant
past reflected an obsessive need to safeguard the present. Leaders like
Jefferson were ashamed of the colonial architecture of public buildings in America. They felt that the paltry nature of existing structures
contributed to a prevalent and dangerous contempt for government.[60]
Simple and elegant but obviously part of a static and often dysfunc-
tional classical theory of architecture, the first official buildings responded to this problem by seeking to instill veneration, decorum,
and propriety—the same sentiments found in West's mourners around
Agrippina.[61] These virtues enabled many otherwise critical Americans
to accept stagnation with equanimity. "How strange it is," observed
the leading New York intellectual Philip Hone in his diary, "that in all
the inventions of modern times architecture alone seems to admit of
no improvement—every departure from the classical models of antiquity in this science is a departure from grace and beauty."[62]

The element to concentrate on here is not so much the conservatizing frame of the classical tradition as it developed in America,
though that calculation should be made, but rather the facility with
which an eighteenth-century classicism lent itself on all sides to public
spectacle, to action distilled and rendered quiescent. Early republicans
chose not the turbulence and the pugnacity so rampant in an expanding Roman empire; they stressed the decorum, proportion, simplicity,
and aspiration in classical form, and they tried to inject these values
into their own imperfect sense of public life. In this way, Benjamin
West's paintings were highly symptomatic of that part of antiquity
that would find its way into American ceremonial practice. For, as in
West's paintings, American imitation of classic architecture sought to
authenticate a human source of fascination. In the early republic that
human figure was the timely speaker who could also cross over and
personify the guiding spirit of antiquity. It was in this context that
John Quincy Adams could point so confidently to "the peculiar utility
of [oratory], in the situation of this country."[63]

The classics helped early republicans to see themselves in the ceremony or act of speaking to each other, where the ceremony itself was
driven by the quest for a moment of mutual recognition. Daniel Webster illustrated the phenomenon perfectly and in its most theatrical

posture, that of the tableau vivant. He also exemplified the multiple ironies in a selective appropriation of antiquity or *classica americana*. An indifferent scholar, Webster could laughingly edit away classical references, once killing in William Henry Harrison's inaugural address "seventeen Roman pro-consuls as dead as smelts." But he claimed the study of ancient literature "especially for public action," and, as the acknowledged Cicero of his culture, he stood for "decorum reigned supreme." He carefully described his great rival John C. Calhoun as "Scipio Africanus South Caroliniensis" and "a Senator of Rome, while Rome survived." Solemn courtesies, the sobriquets were also serious assertions. They turned Webster himself into *ultimus romanorum,* and that exalted designation reached beyond momentary politics to shape both his thought and action.[64]

Webster on the speaker's platform assumed that figurative role, symbolically the last of the Romans. Customarily dressed in the colors of the Revolution, blue and buff, and intoning over and over again that "Adams and Jefferson are no more," or addressing Lafayette, or holding up "the bright model of Washington," he tried to turn himself into the final incarnation of each past moment that he described. Pictorially, he represented "that one great link, connecting us with former times."[65] He became John Adams in person, borrowing Adams' voice for the great debate over independence as "our colossus on the floor." He even became the monument at Bunker Hill, "a memorial of the last, and a monitor to the present and to all succeeding generations." Webster's invariable theme was connection with the past. Pausing long for effect, in another one of those moments of living tableau, he actually turned to the Bunker Hill Monument and repeated the conceit ten times in a paragraph: "it is itself the orator of this occasion. . . . The powerful speaker stands motionless before us . . . it looks, it speaks, it acts, to the full comprehension of every American mind."[66] The impossible personification always seemed to work for Webster. Long after his own dismissal of the man, Ralph Waldo Emerson would still argue that "Webster is very good America" and a presence "such as one cannot hope to see again in a century."[67]

These associations made sense only in the context of the classical tradition in America. No one today would think of Webster's speeches as a sufficient history of the country as his contemporaries did. The claim arose and took hold because it mirrored the highest goal of the classical textual orientation in Webster's time. Cicero's works were also said to encompass the history of his country; mastery of them, "the standard of moral and intellectual worth, for all human kind." By itself, Cicero's *De Officiis* provided "the manual of every republican" and "the pocket and pillow companion of every man desiring to discipline his heart to the love and the practice of every virtue."[68]

To aspire to a position of leadership in the early republic required at least some familiarity with a range of classical sources. Exposed by an older colleague for his failure to recognize passages from Horace, the young James Kent in 1786 immediately sought to amend matters in a quest for "solid happiness and honor" that would eventually make him chancellor of New York. "I said nothing, but was stung with shame and mortification," he confessed. "I purchased immediately Horace and Virgil . . . and formed my resolution, promptly and decidedly, to recover the lost languages."[69]

ॐ

But what did such a recovery of what had been lost actually mean? We grasp the extraordinary emphasis given to classical orientations by early republicans only by first understanding that their ideological needs led them to lift both words and interpretation out of context in a search for functional equivalents. Their own new and urgent context privileged "a declamatory literature" in performance, where the ceremony of speaking and listening enabled the mass of Americans to see themselves and, hence, their unprecedented union through the windows of a thoroughly imagined classical understanding.[70] Cicero from antiquity and Webster from the American republic became the archetypes of transmission in this process because their lives and works formed visible models against the created backdrop of classical reference, whether of architecture or pictorial representation. Their oratory, in turn, offered solutions to a consuming problem. In an extended simile, where Roman citizens were said to swarm like bees in a honeycomb as proof of the social virtues in humanity, Cicero celebrated speech over mere thought; only the former, he claimed, "extends its benefits to those with whom we are united by the bonds of society."[71] The simile was more than apt. The making of honey, just like the giving of speeches, represented an innate capacity that produced something of higher value beyond the maker or even the combination of makers. Here, if anywhere, was the original political aesthetic of *E Pluribus Unum,* the many coming together and cooperating as one to create a separate worth out of combination.

Psychologically, more has been at stake for Americans in this process of recovery than the seemingly quaint reliance of their ancestors on a classical frame of reference might indicate. The emphasis on antiquity flourished for another reason that would filter down in a variety of forms to every later generation. In effect, early republican evocations of "the integrated civilization of antiquity" created thought patterns central to the culture ever since.[72] The patterns themselves can best be described through a technical division in terms: restorative nostalgia versus reflective nostalgia. Nostalgia, a late seventeenth-century conception, signifies a longing to return home, and it pointedly came into being with the rise of nationalistic understandings. Restorative nostalgia stresses the actual attempt to return; reflective nostalgia, the yearning process behind it. Both aspects flow from the need to seek comfort out of dislocation, but the latter, with its emphasis on yearning, operates not so much through the hope of return as through a hold on the past that allows familiarity in the bewildering present.[73] As critics have noted, nostalgia of this reflective kind operates prospectively as well as retrospectively, looking forward in its desire to disconnect the past in the service of the present. It stresses the need for connection between the individual and the group, and it invariably summons the imagination to temper memory and knowledge.[74]

There is a distinction to be drawn here between the first seventeenth-century manifestations of nostalgia in America, namely the Puritan desire to restore the primitive church of Christ in the new world, and the eighteenth-century brand of reflective nostalgia that early republicans conceived in their use of antiquity while breaking away from England. The former, impossible except through an act of faith, was qualitatively different from the selective and largely secular applications of the latter. As Puritanism searched for religious truth in its thirst for an orthodoxy found only in the past, so the *classica americana* was largely political in its conscious manipulation of troubling pagan sources, and yet the two were immediately tied together in an American civil religion, and they have been utterly intertwined and have continued to function in American understandings ever since.

The conflation of Christian and pagan frames of reference was a deliberate one on the part of those who brought the classical tradition into the highest formulations of national identity. The calculated impositions of the Latin mottoes in the Seal of the United States—*E Pluribus Unum, Annuit Coeptis, Novus Ordo Seclorum*—placed both secular and religious impulses in full play, one with the other, and they did so even though the intellectual capacity to separate those impulses may never have been greater than in the Revolutionary moment and in the organizers of the national seal. At no point in the country's history has its national leadership been more deliberately aloof from religious affiliation and thought than in the early days of the republic, one more reason perhaps why classical sources were such an attraction to them and why their specific interest in the pagan republic overshadowed curiosity about the later Christianity of Imperial Rome.

The obvious success of the founders should not blind us to a long-range price in their contrivances. Reflective use of the classical past proved twice as effective when linked to the restorative inclinations of Reform Protestantism, and early republicans clearly needed some hold, however artificial, on what went before to keep the turbulence of national beginnings from overwhelming them, but the conflated use of two very different, sought-after versions of the past has had some unexpected results. Together they created an intrinsic but basically confused nostalgic bent in American understandings.

Nostalgia, in the end, is a historical emotion in which past, present, and future are arranged to provide comfort. If the selective classical tradition in early America served well in this regard, the pattern of thought it invoked was not an altogether healthy one for the insight it provided on current events. Moreover, the continued disruption of rapid change with its threatening sense of dislocation in virtually every succeeding period has strengthened collective reliance on nostalgia as a defense mechanism. Yearning for an earlier and better time against all of the evidence now ranks as one of the central explanatory impulses in the culture. In consequence, the confusion between belief and manipulation of a usable past has grown exponentially.

Nostalgia distorts reality by carrying its willing victim from studied particulars to pleasurable vagaries. It condenses history into a perpetual and portable present.[75] To what extent does an American integrity depend upon an accurate knowledge of its past? Any answer to this question must contend with painful realizations. Today, a memory born of nostalgic recognitions leaves most Americans conceptually bound by "the way we never were."[76] Republicans today take the imitated architecture of their public buildings and the appropriated terminology of the ancients for granted on their own presentist terms. And yet, despite vast increases in the available objective knowledge

of antiquity, they have lost all interest in classical history. The last
two centuries have brought a curious twist to *classica americana*.
Only the pattern of distortion in the workings of nostalgia remain
the same. Americans can now find ancient Rome more easily and accurately than ever before and any time they want to. It is their own
past, twisted out of shape in the playground of cultural memory, that
eludes them.

CHAPTER SEVEN

Gabriel's Rebellion

The many successes of the early republic have shaped understanding of the period. It could hardly have been otherwise within the conventional record of achievement. The list of accomplishments is long: the completed Revolution itself, constitutional legitimation, accepted political routinization, the swift settlement of vexed interstate boundary disputes, the fortuitous acquisition of western lands, the effective incorporation of territories into the system of statehood, the realization of continental scope, the gradual democratization of the republican polity, the avoidance of foreign entanglements, the emergence of an accepted party system for handling major differences, broad acceptance of religious toleration, widespread economic prosperity, and enormous growth in a diverse population willing to call itself American—to name only the traditional candidates. These successes are justly celebrated because they were never certainties, but they also control perception through the orientation of national formations. The country's failures, in some cases the obverse of a success just noted, are more obscure and inevitably more difficult to grasp.

The truism that history is determined by victors at the expense of those who have been displaced or defeated certainly applies here.[1] It applies, however, in ideologically constrained terms in the presumed trajectory of the American experiment with its promise of "liberty and justice for all."[2] Recent historians have devoted time and energy to restoring the lived actuality of those who were left behind in the promise of the new nation—those who were either unjustly defeated, or silenced, or removed, or enslaved in republican culture. Unfortunately, the relative paucity of surviving records has complicated the task immensely. Discrimination on the part of the dominant culture is clear enough, but the reality of those discriminated against remains relatively obscure. What can be recovered with historical integrity from the largely inadequate evidence of lives restricted, disenfranchised, removed, and destroyed? Which tools are best suited for a recovery that can only be partial under the best of circumstances? Where does the limited act of recovery in itself fit into further explanation or revision of our understanding of the period? What does the repression of failure continue to signify in a country so oriented to the story of its own success?

This chapter seeks the beginning of answers to such questions through the study of Gabriel's rebellion, an unsuccessful slave insurrection that took place outside of Richmond, Virginia in the summer of 1800. Don E. Fehrenbacher's brief but convenient summary in *The Slaveholding Republic* gives the few facts on which all sources agree:

> A large number of armed slaves, led by a tall young black named Gabriel, began to assemble near Richmond with the intention of marching on the city. But a heavy rainstorm forced them to disperse, and the conspiracy collapsed as troops called out by Governor James Monroe began arresting the ringleaders. Although no white person had been harmed, at least twenty-six slaves were hanged.[3]

How many slaves and free blacks were actually involved in the conspiracy, whether or not the rebellion would have succeeded but for the unforeseen storm that blocked timely access to Richmond on the night before the insurrection, what led a flourishing artisan (a valued and successful blacksmith like Gabriel Prosser) to risk all as a rebel leader, which minds created an elaborate organization with a disciplined army within the conspiracy—these and other details are matters of conjecture. It is clear, however, that the conspiracy was fairly widespread, that it was ruthlessly repressed, that the punishment doled out to its imputed leaders through the forced testimony of co-conspirators was severe, and that three founders of the Republic—Thomas Jefferson, James Madison, and James Monroe—played a crucial role in determining those punishments. It is equally certain that Virginia and other southern states quickly took official measures to prevent a recurrence in the same moment that all public discussion was abruptly terminated.

These facts and their limitations render Gabriel's rebellion an ideal choice for considering the problems and rewards in attempting to recover a repressed history. Like any other act of recovery, this one must also try to avoid an obvious pitfall: namely, the imposition of current values on an early republican frame of reference. If the attempt is still worth making despite the danger, it is because the repression of unpleasant events colors the nature of success in history. Gabriel's rebellion raised vital questions about the terms of achievement in the early republic. No one involved either in fomenting or punishing the rebellion could avoid renewed reflection on the meaning of the Revolution. What did the assumption that "all men are created equal" actually mean? Where was the promise of the Revolution supposed to end? Who could make the claim to be an "American" with the prospect of freedom that the claim entailed? The rebellion turned an abstract nightmare into a concrete reality. Where, early republicans had to ask themselves, would the contradiction between a successful republic and a thriving slave economy take them?

Gabriel's rebellion is worth attention for another reason. The ideological crux of the rebellion comes to us through the trial of the captured rebels in the special slave court of oyer and terminer of Henrico County, Virginia. Courtroom trials are unusual in the dynamic that they bring to the one-sided nature of ruling elites dealing with disenfranchised groupings. The adversarial nature of the legal process requires even the most marginalized defendant to *speak,* and the substance of that speech must not only be *heard,* it must also be *written down* as part of a court record or transcript for still others to hear. The result is a *compelled narrative,* one in which even the most disadvantaged figure in a confrontation is encouraged to offer an alternative point of view. In a courtroom the minimal standards involved in the rule of law forces a level of consideration that communities can more easily ignore or evade in every other context of engagement.

The alternative point of view presented in the Henrico County slave court of 1800 forms the center of this inquiry. Placed on trial for his life but also under scrutiny as a defective piece of property, an unnamed slave responded to the charge of having to explain his own part in Gabriel's rebellion with the following comment:

I have nothing more to offer than what General Washington would have had to offer, had he been taken by the British and put to trial by them. I have adventured my life in endeavouring to obtain the liberty of my countrymen, and am a willing sacrifice to their cause: and I beg, as a favour, that I may be immediately led to execution. I know that you have pre-determined to shed my blood, why then all this mockery of a trial?[4]

This statement vividly accentuates the contradictions between republican ideology and slavery. As such, it represents an intolerable response to the Virginia squirearchy that placed the speaker on trial, and, like so many aspects of Gabriel's rebellion, it was immediately suppressed in consequence. Ironically, the same statement absolutely typifies current interest in the rebellion, and in most cases, it is all that a twenty-first century reader will hear about the event. This anomaly—the former dismissal of language in the light of current magnification—epitomizes the problems in a meaningful act of recovery; it also tells us something about the nature of repression in a rule of law.

The historical fact of repression in 1800 and after is clear on a variety of levels. A figure like James Monroe, governor of Virginia at the time and later fifth president of the United States, would subsequently refuse to discuss the slave rebellion trials with anyone. Pressed toward the end of his life, he admitted only that "several of the conspirators were hanged," a figure well short of the twenty-six official executions bearing his signature in 1800. Nor do Monroe's words correspond with earlier ones. Chilling private letters between Monroe as governor and Thomas Jefferson as presidential nominee in 1800 reveal the founders of one revolution squelching another and discussing among themselves "whether mercy or severity is the better policy in this case." Their main uncertainty came in a telling question: "when to arrest the hand of the Executioner." In discussing policy, Monroe as governor described with some satisfaction how he "made a display of our force and measures of defence with the view to intimidate those people." Jefferson, in response, agreed to the need for "some severities." He also showed his alarm, wondering aloud "whether these people can ever be permitted to go at large among us with safety."[5] More elaborate restrictions on the movement of blacks in Virginia would swiftly follow. Repression also included mobs and roving bands of white vigilantes that terrorized blacks in the aftermath of the rebellion.

Politically, legally, and intellectually, repression took a variety of forms: the scourging of slaves who refused to confess or bear false witness in the trials of Gabriel and his fellow conspirators, the creation of a police force, greater restrictions on the movements of blacks, new limits on vocational opportunities, more pointed laws against the literacy of slaves, added stipulations against the rights of free blacks, and more vigorous enforcement of existing statutes against assembly by blacks and against miscegenation.[6] The step from formal repression to intellectual forgetfulness was also a short one. The rebellion, which led immediately to more negative treatment of slaves everywhere in America, remained largely submerged in the national consciousness until the civil rights movement of the twentieth century. As late as 1974, Daniel Sisson's monumental study, *The American Revolution of 1800,* failed to mention the insurrection, even though the unrest between Federalists and Republicans in the election of that same year contributed to the slave rebellion and even though Sisson's leading protagonists were heavily involved in both events.[7]

The points to remember, for present purposes, are that repression outlives its original context and that it returns to haunt the consciousness that created it. Admittedly, the connection between social repression and a psychological dynamic of explanation is a problematic one, but carefully used, it provides useful tools in a methodology of recovery. The classic theoretical parallel between the psychological state of an individual and a civilization appears in *Civilization and Its Discontents,* where its decidedly legal formulation is useful in the current trial context. Sigmund Freud draws on the parallel to explain social development from its inception in "justice" as "the decisive step" and "first requisite of civilization" to its logical conclusion or "final outcome" in "a rule of law." In this process, civilization is both the ultimate source of salvation and the fountain of all individual frustration and, as such, it creates a veritable force field of repression, "an irremediable antagonism between the demands of instinct and the restrictions of civilization." In another analogy, this one between the "Eternal City" of Rome and the human mind, Freud provides the key to recovering these patterns of repression by maintaining that nothing perishes in mental life: "everything is somehow preserved and . . . in suitable circumstances . . . it can once more be brought to light."[8] Elsewhere, this return of the repressed takes the form of the uncanny, something secretly familiar that has undergone repression and then returned to consciousness all of a sudden in sometimes frightening and recurring patterns.[9]

Alternatively, the repressed can be thought of in sociological and anthropological terms. Mary Douglas writes convincingly about how "institutions create shadowed places in which nothing can be seen and no questions asked." The result is a kind of "structural amnesia." The social scientist unravels these structures by learning "the processes of public memory," by examining "the storage system for the social order," by asking "what are the impossible thoughts?," and by discovering the principles of institutional coherence that allow repressed thoughts to escape oblivion, though usually in distorted form.[10] Just as repression must be viewed as a multifaceted phenomenon, so a variety of disciplines are relevant in the explanation of it.

The actual pattern of repression in the trial comment under investigation can be seen in the nature of its transmission. The primary utterance of the speaking slave in the Henrico County slave court is at least thrice removed from us today. The unnamed defendant may have used the exact, highly sophisticated words ascribed to him in court, but they do not appear in any of the relevant trial transcripts of 1800. What is the evidence that something like these words were actually uttered there? The typical slave trial of the period relied on a turncoat who, in seeking a pardon or a reduced sentence, informed on fellow conspirators, and the trials in Henrico County were no exception. The convicting testimonies of the two main informers, themselves conspirators, indicated that as many as several hundred slaves might have been actively involved in the conspiracy and that they were led by literate artisans versed in the revolutionary rhetoric of their time. Gabriel, a successful black blacksmith who could read and write, planned to march on Richmond under the banner "death or liberty," a conscious inversion of Patrick Henry's famous rallying call, "give me liberty or give me death." Furthermore, he was fighting "for his Country" as well as for black freedom when he divided his followers into a series of military units.[11] Quite obviously, the ability and the temperament to deliver such a statement existed among the leading conspirators.

Even so, the printed words that survive are not the slave defendant's but those of an English Quaker traveling in American in 1804, and they could have been written in their present form as late as 1811.

Robert Sutcliff, a commercial traveler on business near Richmond, recorded his own conversation with an unnamed Virginia lawyer who, in turn, claimed to have heard the words spoken at the trial, "by one of them being asked, what he had to say to the court in his defence."[12] The actual words depend, then, on a double transmission with several interstices in between, and they belonged for a considerable period of time, four years in fact, to an oral tradition of the Virginia aristocracy that suppressed the rebellion—an oral tradition that only a sympathetic foreigner dared to record and publish. Is it a remarkable or a commonplace effect or an irrelevancy that this refracted and partially repressed transmission left the slave who spoke at trial as eloquent as possible? The historian faces so many contingencies that almost any response might be defended.

In any case, the eloquence as artifact is clearly accessible and deserves careful attention. One of the hidden virtues in the statement resides in its concision. Brevity in a recollected statement suits the memory of an oral tradition as well as the needs of the casual journalist in transcription, but the higher value of concision also flows from the honed or refined language of repetition. How many times did the unnamed member of the Virginia gentry hear and repeat the story among his peers in the four years before he encountered Robert Sutcliff? No one can say, but if there were originally excess words, they have been removed, and we are left with the most concise statement against slavery in America of its time. Every word taken from— or applied to—this doomed slave's mouth counts.

The best of the Virginia planter class understood its own dilemma over slavery and could express it with power and conviction. As early as 1767, Arthur Lee warned Virginia that it lived on "the very brink of ruin" from slave rebellion. "On us, or on our posterity," he wrote in the *Virginia Gazette*, "the inevitable blow must, one day, fall." In Lee's view, the "Bondage of the Africans" superseded every relative moral consideration. "There cannot be in nature, there is not in all history, an instance in which every right of men is more flagrantly violated."[13] Thomas Jefferson's more famous cry of despair over the possibility of a slave rebellion came in 1787 in *Notes on the State of Virginia:* "I tremble for my country when I reflect that God is just: that his justice cannot sleep for ever. . . . The Almighty has no attribute which can take sides with us in such a contest." Later, in 1797 and 1820, he would return to the subject with feelings of "terror." "[I]f something is not done, & soon done," he wrote in reference to the potential rebelliousness of Virginia's slaves, "we shall be the murderers of our own children [for] the revolutionary storm, now sweeping the globe, will be upon us." And again: "we have the wolf by the ears, and we can neither hold him, nor safely let him go."[14] But while such statements are trenchant and informed by a rhetoric of revolution, they were shaped by a fear of its implications rather than the "spirit of '76" that early republicans liked to claim for themselves, and both men also wrote in part to resist their own logic.

The words of the slave defendant survived because they coincided in 1800 with a controlling institutional "principle of coherence."[15] Early republican culture insisted on the right to rebel against tyranny in the name of liberty. In the one moment of required speech at trial, the moment when the defendant must respond to formal accusation, the Gabriel conspirator used that principle to give the best conceivable answer available to him from the field of ideological concerns established twenty-five years before in the Revolution. "I have adventured my life in endeavouring to obtain the liberty of my countrymen," he told the court. Having failed to achieve liberty, he was prepared, as Patrick Henry claimed to be, for death: "I beg, as a favour, that I may be immediately led to execution." This request, part of the exemplary courage of the true revolutionary, gained great rhetorical fortification from the formal circumstance in which it was uttered. The legal platform of the trial and the slave defendant's response in procedural context magnified his words and turned them into a colossal statement within and about the American republic of laws.

The five judges in the Henrico County courtroom had no choice but to agree with the defendant before them on the abstract level of ideology. Indeed, for their own inconsistency, they would have needed only to glance at the state seal that they used regularly to ratify their judgments. The Virginians of 1776 devised that seal to depict "VIRTUS, the genius of the commonwealth . . . treading on TYRANNY, represented by a man prostrate, a crown fallen from his head, a broken chain in his left hand, and scourge in his right." Affixed to it was the state motto: "*sic semper tyrannis,* or "thus always to tyrants."[16] Stripped of all place in the Revolution, American slaves supplied a negative example in the imagery and language of colonial rebellion. They appeared as the disembodied presence in their masters' litanies against the dangers of enslavement—literal reminders of the prospect of liberty in chains.

Slaves were the nightmare presence behind a white quest for independence, and the speaker in the Henrico County courtroom of 1800 appeared as the repressed reality in that nightmare come to life. Figuratively, the chains on his body were meant to be broken.

These judges would also have understood that vital underpinnings in their own discipline, natural law, sided with the defendant and against them. When they asked him what "he had to say to the court in his defence," his words echoed the reigning theorist of Anglo-American culture, John Locke. In *An Essay Concerning the True Original, Extent, and End of Civil Government,* the condition of slavery was defined as "nothing else but the *State of War continued.*" In Locke's understanding, a slave retained the right to resist "whenever he finds the hardship of his Slavery outweigh the value of his life." The defendant in the Henrico County courthouse took that position. He preferred to die rather than remain a slave and said so. That was the price of fighting for his freedom. "I know that you have predetermined to shed my blood," he reminded his judges. Power and not law held him in place, "Absolute, Arbitrary Power" constituting the greatest evil in Locke's social contract as well as the definition of tyranny in the organized political state.[17]

Nonetheless, the same five judges condemned the defendant and at least twenty-five others like him to death, and they proceeded easily and quickly. They convicted and sentenced, reaching the required unanimous decision in a slave court for capital punishment in under an hour for most of the cases brought before them on charges of conspiracy and insurrection. In what connotation, then, can it be said that the answering words of the doomed slave were peculiarly troubling—so troubling as to be carefully retained within "the processes of public memory"? Why, in fact, *were* the slave defendant's words retained in the manner that has been described? One answer lies in the return of the repressed in an official court of law. The defendant's voiced analogy to a black George Washington fulfilled rather precisely one definition of the uncanny. Here, in keeping with that formulation, was the sudden appearance of something familiar but not known and, therefore, terrifying—something repressed that came to the light in a recognizable but threatening, because alienated, form.[18]

How the uncanny manifests itself depends on what has been repressed, and the two Southern jeremiads on slavery already noted help to provide that insight. As leaders of the Virginia slavocracy, Arthur Lee and Thomas Jefferson agreed that "freedom is unquestionably the birth-right of all mankind." They also acknowledged that the dissemination of knowledge through the Enlightenment, an inevitable phenomenon in their frame of thought, meant that their slaves would evince an ever-growing capacity to seize that right. Both writers recognized the implications of injustice, morally and practically, so what could possibly have prevented their logical acceptance of emancipation? They responded with racist constructs against what Lee termed, in one of several distancing devices, "those unfortunate and detestable people." To the extent that American slaves were "unfortunate" or, in Jefferson's understanding, "inferior," they could be seen to lack the capacity to act for their own freedom, and if they were also "detestable," then their moral right to freedom could be qualified emotionally as well. Jefferson had to admit "liberties are of the gift of God," but he found "physical and moral" differences between the races that might also be from God or at least "fixed in nature," which meant that "their inferiority is not the effect merely of their condition of life." Blacks were either "originally a distinct race, or made distinct by time and circumstance," and both explanations consigned them to fewer rights *at least for the moment*.[19]

Since timing and capacity were everything in an Enlightenment understanding of the spread of knowledge, the comfort zone for repression in the slavocracy took the form of "not yet." Not coincidentally, as blacks demonstrated unmistakable capacities for freedom, the racist theories of delay received more vehement formulation from Southern writers. Their underlying goal was always to stretch out the timing for when a legitimate revolution might take place and thus to make rebellion in the moment an abnormal act. In the words of one such apologist for slavery, "to turn [the Negro] loose in the manhood of his passions, but in the infancy of his uninstructed reason, would be to raise up a creature [Frankenstein's monster] resembling the splendid fiction of recent romance."[20] Accordingly, when a black person actually appeared to demand the equality under law that republican ideology promised, that person could only be seen in twisted or unnatural form.

The black George Washington in the Henrico Country courthouse stood against these evasions and for the proposition that already in that moment, in 1800, he was the equal, morally and physically, of the best of his masters. He was at once an ideological claimant as speaker and a twisted representation in the sight of his horrified listeners—a representation, as thoroughly capacious rebel, that they could neither forget nor accept. The combination made him forever memorable while robbing him of his name and all personal context in history. We know only that he stood before his judges in chains, that he spoke in continuing defiance, and that his anonymity has made him every slave who ever protested that condition. The words that survive to us are worth a closer look.

When the slave defendant announces that he has "nothing more to offer than what General Washington would have had to offer, had he been taken by the British and put to trial by them," he is a Virginian speaking to Virginians about another Virginian at a moment when Washington, who died at Mount Vernon less than a year before the trial, has entered a complex process of transfiguration. His claim is so forthright as to be virtually unique for its time. For while there are white variations on the theme of a minority founding father, they tend to be uneasy ones that mediate the notion of violence through virtue and social success. The energetic entrepreneur Venture Smith, in the slave narrative of 1798 that we examined in Chapter 1, becomes "a Franklin and a Washington, in a state of nature" in the eyes of his white editor, but only after he has been safely "broken by hardships and infirmities of age." Later, the black harpooner Queequeg, in *Moby-Dick,* is "George Washington cannibalistically developed," but again, the description casts its subject in repose, as "a bosom friend," rather than in one of Queequeg's many moments of prowess or physical power. Each representation, in its own way, works to defuse the logic of rebellion.[21]

The same figuration in the martial capacity, defiance, and fact of rebellion gives rise to intolerable thoughts in the Henrico County courthouse. "The accused have exhibited a spirit, which, if it becomes general, must deluge the Southern country in blood," runs the account of one frightened observer. "They manifested a sense of their rights, and contempt of danger, and a thirst for revenge which portend the most unhappy consequences."[22] The hope for a black Washington and its corollary, the fear of a black Washington, meet unavoidably in the logic of rebellion, and the politics of both emotions reside in the comment before us. Any deconstruction of the iconography around the figure of Washington must recall that the comment in question is a multilayered text. The uncanny resides in the gaps of a compelled narrative that contains, at once, the repressed voice of a speaking slave, the reiterated oral tale of an apprehensive Virginia lawyer, the receptive recapitulation of a Quaker Englishman, every reader's own reactions, and the critic's realization of the aspirations and limitations in all four. There are, as well, three facets of the Washington figure embedded in the comment: martial glory, service to country, and the Virginia planter as slave owner.

The speaking slave reminds us first that military power defines Washington's personal success. We would certainly think less of the Revolutionary soldier if he had been beaten and captured in the 1770s and then hanged as one of many disappointed rebels in a still-thriving British Empire. The conditional perfect verb form—"what General Washington *would have had* to offer"—catches this implication nicely. Meanwhile, the reference to rank—"General" rather than "George" Washington—emphasizes the rebellious activist over subsequent and more benign images of the later national leader as constitutional framer and first president. Significantly, the aspect of the slave rebellion that bothers the judges most in Henrico County comes in testimony that the leading conspirators have formed a military organization and assigned to themselves official military rank. Gabriel is elected general and his direct subordinates are colonels and captains in a revolutionary army that observers believed would have taken Richmond except for a violent rainstorm that delayed the conspiracy just long enough for the plot to be exposed.[23] Asked what he has to say, the speaking slave does not hesitate. He deliberately draws attention to these parallels.

George Washington's military career figures in one other fashion. The leader of the American Revolutionary army was a stern disciplinarian who flogged his soldiers much in the way that he scourged slaves at Mount Vernon. He once wrote that neither bravery nor hope of reward but "fear of punishment" distinguished the real soldier from others, and in 1776 he quickly demonstrated that he would "punish every kind of neglect, or mis-behavior," whether in offices or men. Big and physically very powerful, he brought a forceful presence to the position of commander in chief, and his rare bursts of anger intimidated those closest to him, filling them with dread and alarm.[24] Even in casual social interaction with his peers, Washington aroused feelings of awe akin to fear. Thomas Jefferson once observed that Washington possessed a temper "naturally high-toned" and that when "it broke its bounds, he was most tremendous in his wrath."[25] The Virginia elite in the Henrico Country slave court would have known this side of Washington firsthand. For them, a black Washington carried connotations of a personally severe ascendancy lost to a modern appreciation.

The second and more familiar facet of Washington's import for early republicans, that of the selfless father of his country, also receives a twist in the defendant's response at trial. When the speaker, oral transmitter, and journalist jointly reveal that the defendant has "adventured . . . to obtain the liberty of my countrymen," the first-person possessive attached to the word "countrymen" anticipates a separate nation. The defendant at trial appears as the father of *another* country, one that implicitly raises a new but familiar dimension. A "willing sacrifice to their [his countrymen's] cause," the defendant who has "adventured" will not be called an outlaw. He is, rather, a visionary seeker after justice with the social ramifications and status that a fresh founding of black freedom entails. Disinterested service, the eighteenth-century ideal of public virtue intrinsic to Washington's reputation, remains intact in the slave about to be executed.

The remaining facet of Washington's public persona is even more illuminating when caught in the prism of the trial process. If there is one area where Washington appeared to fall squarely on the side of the judges in Henrico County, it would surely have been in the daily life of the Virginia planter as slave owner, but that presumption had already crumbled on December 14, 1799, the date of Washington's death. For while the rest of the country mourned the man "first in the hearts of his countrymen," his neighbors would have been reeling with the news that he had emancipated his slave force in his last will and testament. In the end, Washington deserted the slavocracy of Virginia in order to vindicate and secure his republican reputation, writing in his own hand, "Upon the decease [of] my wife, it is my Will and desire th[at] all the Slaves which I hold in [my] *own right,* shall receive their free[dom]." The form of the devise gave the emancipation provision special prominence; the provision appeared on the first page in just the fourth paragraph of a document of more than five thousand words, preceding all other bequests with the exception of those to Martha Washington, "my dearly loved wife."[26] Given one chance to speak in the Henrico County courthouse nine months later, a rebelling slave could well have realized that what Genera. Washington finally "had to offer" was nothing less than the liberty of his countrymen.

There was a last reason for suppressing the slave's comment in 1800. The confidence with which the unknown speaker wields his arguments is a matter of record. Although the Virginia lawyer gives no description in transmitting the speech, he was impressed at the time by the "manly tone of voice" of the responding defendant.[27] This degree of confidence follows naturally from the strength of the speaker's arguments, but it also leads that speaker to another level of rhetorical performance in the courtroom. Knowing what he knows, the defendant can reject the authority of a court that holds his body but not his mind. Asked a question, he asks one of his own in return: "[W]hy then all this mockery of a trial?" We can close the analysis of his statement by trying to answer that question for him.

Courts, even very oppressive or totalitarian courts, feel compelled to leave an orderly record of their proceedings. They need to believe in that order, and they count on the responsiveness of all concerned to accomplish these ends for them. Trials, in this sense, are both contests and rituals, with the technical distinction that these terms invoke. In Claude Lévi-Strauss's formulation, contests or games have "a *disjunctive* effect; they end in the establishment of a difference between individual players and teams." The reference of difference is to winners against losers, an inescapable by-product in courtroom decisions. "Ritual, on the other hand, is the exact inverse: it *conjoins,* for it brings about a union (one might even say communion in this context) or in any case an organic relation between two initially separated groups."[28] The contest in a trial decides winners and losers (a foregone conclusion in the case before the slave court in Henrico County), and it extracts punishment and sometimes revenge. Ritual, by way of contrast, bespeaks a more strategic, if vaguer, notion of participation, one in which notions of resolution, closure, publication, acquiescence, the status quo ante, and recognition play themselves out in the consensual forms that define a republic of laws.

The judges in Henrico County instinctively need the minimal cooperation of question and answer from the defendants before them, but they do not get it in this case, and the alternative response given— "why then all this mockery?"—is unacceptable to their ears. Without primal concurrence, they cannot assure themselves that they *do* govern by law instead of force; nor can they convince the governed that they are fairly governed. Procedurally, these judges are left with naked power in the place of consensual, validating process. In the words of Mary Douglas:

> [I]nstitutions survive by harnessing all information processes to the task of establishing themselves. The instituted community blocks personal curiosity, organizes public memory, and heroically imposes certainty on uncertainty. In marking its own boundaries it affects all lower-level thinking, so that persons realize their own identities and classify each other through community affiliation.[29]

Courtrooms as institutions that require reciprocity are vulnerable to mockery when they face the tasks of imposing boundaries and establishing themselves, something that they must do in every trial in order to justify their decisions before the community affiliation that they serve. The elaborate give-and-take of legal procedures, a symbol of underlying cooperation by all involved, leaves numerous opportunities for breakdown, and the antagonistic participant, one who also has courage, can achieve a profound level of disruption by violating the fragile decorum and sense of ritual in the sequence of question and answer. Severe disruption also means that there can be no agreement, no imposed certainty, over *what has happened* and over *what should be done about it,* the aims of compelled narrative in every courtroom.

The defendant in the Henrico courthouse has the fortitude to resist the information, the certainties, and, most of all, the frame of thought that the existing legal structure and the power elite would impose on him as his ticket for admission to the ritual of trial performance. His voice mocks that ritual, destroying its delicately complicit rhythms and leaving in place mutually recognized ideological contradictions between a judge and a defendant who are also master and slave. The speaker is soon silenced, but the implied thoroughness of courtroom narrative signifies that his voice will be heard again when the contradictions involved in his case and treatment become culturally intolerable.

There is, however, a larger methodological complication in making such an assertion. The high level of noncooperation in the slave defendant flashes a warning signal across time. He does not want to belong to the conventional success that is destroying him. Who, in consequence, can be said to speak for this slave defendant? What is the critic's responsibility in attempting to do so? The danger of imposing current values in sympathy with a position that only becomes historically recognized long after the fact is very real here, and that danger only grows with the realization that "the intellectual is complicit in the persistent constitution of Other as the Self's shadow." The speaker in the Henrico courtroom uses the language and the values of his oppressors, but he is even more interested in declaring himself unalterably "other" to their concerns by maintaining his own separate place through solidarity with his differentiated "countrymen." That separate place can never be fully fathomed. The doomed slave's statement, taken as a whole, forces the recognition of "a radical textual practice of differences." It reduces interpretation to "the *mechanics* of the constitution" of his situation and away from "invocations of the *authenticity.*"[30] We cannot know the defiant rebel's mind, only his influence upon and under circumstance.

These observations reinvoke and complicate the question of the original inquiry. What, it must be asked again, can be recovered with integrity from the inadequate record of an obliterated past that nonetheless remains with us? The inquiry itself has narrowed the question through a process of investigation: what remains of use and importance when a relevant claim is actively repressed in a republic of laws? The simple answer would seem to be that the claim always returns, but on what terms and whose terms? In the rugged exchanges of courtroom advocacy, a relevant story that is effectively told, like that of the slave defendant, belongs to the republic of laws for ready use. Ideologically, it remains available to everyone as a cautionary tale and conceivable resource in further decision making. However, when such a claim is actively repressed in a legal forum dedicated to thoroughness and fairness, it belongs instead to the agent of the repressed.

The notion of owning a story in these terms may sound disturbing. To be sure, casual references using this kind of expression abound. Phrases taking the possessive form—"it is your story to tell" or "your story deserves to be heard"—appear in daily conversation, and storytellers copyright their work all the time. But certain historical stories—particularly stories of rampant discrimination that have destroyed whole groupings in the national polity—carry implicit prerogatives and burdens when institutional authority, by suppressing them, have kept them from contributing their weight to communal understandings. In failing to tell these stories, legal authority in particular loses control of them on its own terms.[31] Perhaps in consequence, modern black legal scholars have found both a prerogative and a burden in speaking about the failures of the law in personal or confessional mode because they believe that the repressed past has left America "unsafe." Writing the subsequent story of discrimination is simultaneously therapy and hard duty, part of the need to recover and represent those "who never really have been heard from."[32]

The price of repression in a republic of laws can be very high. Urged to speak when captured as the leader of the rebellion of 1800, Gabriel apparently refused to do so. In the words of Governor James Monroe: "It appeared he [Gabriel] had promised a full confession, but on his arrival here he declined making it. From what he said to me, he seemed to have made up his mind to die, and to have resolved to say but little on the subject of the conspiracy."[33] The factual accuracy of Monroe's account does not reach its ultimate implications. What could "a full confession" have meant for a charismatic leader whose followers, the rank and file of a new revolutionary army, had voted "to give him the voice for General."[34] Gabriel obviously had much to say but only to those compatriots who had earned the formal right to receive his message. His silence reaffirms the declared separation of the black Washington in the Henrico County slave court, but it does more. It literalizes a void that could not be crossed then and that still cannot be bridged today. Discussion stops with the "différend," the inaccessibility of one mode of discourse in dispute with another.[35]

Who then speaks for the eighteenth-century Gabriel today? This last question has been a subject of implicit debate in the literary criticism of modern times. In the continuum of publication around a trial, imaginative literature provides the zone where the repressed can lurk with special freedom. To use Freud's own words, the uncanny in literature "is a much more fertile province than the uncanny in real life."[36] It should, in consequence, surprise no one that the greatest national story of a slave insurrection skirts the issue of speech altogether. Writing in 1855, Herman Melville sets Benito Cereno in 1799, the time period of the Gabriel rebellion, but his story never enters the mind of the arch-conspirator, Babo, who, like Gabriel, refuses to speak when captured. Instead, Melville provides an endless series of external misreadings of the rebel leader alongside a deliberately defective official transcript of his later trial. All narration in Benito Cereno is manifestly unreliable. Readers know that Babo is the "plotter from first to last" and the "helm and keel of the revolt," but they ponder these matters only through the executed slave's severed head, "that hive of subtlety," and through the deposed captain of the slave ship, the traumatized Benito Cereno, who is completely consumed and finally undone by continuing dread of "The negro."[37]

The difference in the most visible twentieth-century novelization of a slave rebellion is striking. William Styron's *The Confessions of Nat Turner,* from 1966, has been controversial precisely because the author presumes to enter and understand the mind of Nat Turner, the historical leader of a slave rebellion in Southampton, Virginia, in 1831.[38] Many critics have deplored this perceived impertinence, claiming that "Nat Turner still awaits a literary interpreter worthy of his sacrifice," and the ensuing search for the real Nat Turner has become something of an academic cottage industry.[39] Clearly, there is no easy return of the repressed. But if the uncanny comes to light through anger and anxiety, nevertheless it comes. "Time is not a river. Time is a pendulum," Arna Bontemps asserts in his own novel based on the Southampton rebellion, *Black Thunder.*[40]

Translating into the terms of this inquiry, a story wrongly refused by the law will return in a republic of laws as cultural narrative and, often enough, as renewed legal event. The law does not get beyond what it has not worked through. The pendulum swings back because the culture has made an ideological commitment to social justice and because the expectation of justice causes injustice to loom large. The point is most aptly put by Nathaniel Hawthorne in *The House of the Seven Gables.* "What is there so ponderous in evil," he asks there concerning the law, "that a thumb's bigness of it should outweigh the mass of things not evil, which were heaped into the other scale! This scale and balance system is a favorite one with people of Judge Pyncheon's brotherhood."[41]

Who ultimately can speak for Gabriel? When all is said and done, Gabriel speaks for himself, but through the two conflicting levels of majority and minority understandings. The obscure eighteenth-century blacksmith who fought and died for his freedom remains a prototype and example of revolutionary aspiration. Somewhere at this very moment, another rebel, perhaps the leader of a street gang or a rapper from the ignored underclass of any one of a number of urban ghettoes, is preparing to seek justice, and Gabriel will be an inspiration. There already has been some preparation for this eventuality. In the peroration of *Soul on Ice,* written in prison, Eldridge Cleaver seeks to speak with "the new voice," "the voice of the Black Man," away from the "obsequious whine of a cringing slave," away from the "unctuous supplications of the sleek Black Bourgeoisie," away from even the "bullying bellow of the rude Free Slave." To do so he actively invokes the spirits of black rebels past: Touissaint L'Ouverture, Gabriel Prosser, Nat Turner, and Denmark Vesey. They are part of a larger promise: "we shall have our manhood. We shall have it or the earth will be leveled by our attempts to gain it."[42]

Gabriel also continues to speak through the dominant culture's own realization of racial unrest. Glimpses of injustice, past and present, have forced Americans to contemplate the present danger of racial cataclysm. Typifying this state of mind in a description of the actual uprising of blacks against whites in *Benito Cereno,* Melville writes that "past, present, and future seemed one."[43] Here, fears that are tied to a repressed past but realized in the present have brought an utter collapse in time categories, and there is a larger message. Injustice in a republic of laws always finds the present tense.

Paying closer attention to the full continuum of publication around the trials of Gabriel and his fellow conspirators offers the chance to bring these conflicting understandings of hero versus nemesis into a socially productive tension with each other. Rereading the all-too-brief trial records of these slave defendants represents an act of partial recovery. Methodologically, it divulges the complexity in hauling a major event out of the deep shadows into which it was calculatedly plunged by an early republican elite. Philosophically, it yields insight into the vexed interplay of race and revolution in early America and into previously unrealized levels of slave engagement in those issues.

A final psychological dimension applies more directly to the republic of laws that the early republic aspired to create. Better understanding of the trials and executions of forgotten slave conspirators may help the country to face its repressed fears without panic—without the collapse of the future into a bitter past. Gabriel himself seems to have had some hope for that better future. In the conflicting testimony against the doomed but silent leader at trial, one slave witness offers a startling prospect. Gabriel meant to take Richmond by force, but what then? Even the refracting testimony of an informer cannot hide the optimism that follows.

At least for a moment in 1800, looking back to the successful Revolution a quarter of a century before, Gabriel seems to have given the lie to the racist nightmares of black rebellion and to have overcome the injustice of his situation. "If the white people agreed to their freedom," the rebel leader is said to have observed, in encouraging his slave recruits about his plans for conquered Richmond, "they would then hoist a white flag, and he would dine and drink with the merchants of the city on the day when it should be agreed to." There is real poignancy as well as a lesson in this appeal. When he asks others "to join him in fighting for his country," Gabriel may well have had all Americans in mind.[44]

CHAPTER EIGHT

Jefferson at Monticello

Thomas Jefferson's lifelong obsession with Monticello helps to explain both the nature of his thought and the mysteries of the man.
Owner, architect, and construction manager all in one, he began in
1768 but repeatedly tore apart his own handiwork, rebuilding compulsively across half a century before leaving the house unfinished at
his death in 1826. Throughout, Jefferson's declared love for the tranquility of home warred with his compulsive desire to tinker with its
terms, and he saw the contradiction clearly enough to acknowledge it,
once referring to the presumed grandeur of Monticello as living in a
brick kiln. "Architecture is my delight," he confessed, "and putting
up and pulling down, one of my favorite pursuits."[1] There is a puzzle
to be read in these conflicted efforts and the house they produced.
"Architecture as a spatial creation is the outer garment of a secretive
and vital system; it is a nonverbal manifestation of a preconscious
condition."[2] If so, the presumed link between outer and inner frames
of reference would seem to be especially significant in an architect
who so self-consciously and laboriously turned his private home into
a public symbol of his time and place.

The many roles of the public man—politician, scholar, inventor,
lawyer, farmer, and slave owner—meant that Jefferson built for many
different purposes and, not least, with a national audience in mind.
The symbol of the ideally constructed house was a vital one for a new
nation absorbed in problems of self-definition, and the relative insuf-

ficiencies of early American society encouraged its participants to emphasize the house as the basic unit of meaning over larger elements in
the social fabric.[3] This heightened symbolism of the house applied
with special force in the aristocratic South. The Virginia planter class
to which Jefferson belonged used the manor or plantation house to
enact the social code of hospitality that it lived by and as a controlling
metaphor for enforcing caste and hierarchy in a slave culture.[4] Town
life, as Jefferson made clear in *Notes on the State of Virginia*, was virtually nonexistent; the basis of communal identity was indeed the
manor house, and Jefferson was peculiarly receptive to the symbolism
involved. He worried about the absence of important buildings and
architectural sophistication in American society; these absences, he
argued, undermined social authority as well as republican principle.[5]

The commitment to build a house that would be more than a house
left Jefferson with several obvious difficulties. Unified symbols do not
easily emerge from the messiness of everyday life, and early Americans were fond of reminding themselves that "a house divided against
itself cannot stand."[6] Monticello could not help but be such a divided
house. Literally a monumental extravagance, it arose out of a slave
economy that the architect-owner hated, and it simultaneously bespoke the debtor status of a planter class that needed forced labor to
support its lavish lifestyle. Monticello also staged a more personal
struggle: the public figure entertained frequently but still insisted on
his own privacy in conflicting patterns of hospitality and architectonic
withdrawal. Guests at Monticello typically found the openness of its
design to be of little avail; a series of carefully locked doors cut up the
interior floor plan, thwarting access to the best rooms for everyone
except their host. No one but Jefferson had access to his private quarters and the renowned library.[7]

But even if Monticello can be seen as a house divided against itself,
we must not overlook the forgotten unities that made Monticello a
potent symbol, then and now. Jefferson displayed enormous ingenuity
within the functional integrity available to him. He brought unique
form as well as beauty to a brick mansion of thirty-five rooms—
a mansion built not on a riverbank, where most plantation houses
stood for reasons of commerce, but, improbably and inefficiently,
on the top of a mountain, where access was hard and construction
twice as difficult. Not the least of Jefferson's difficulties in building
Monticello on a mountain was the problem of finding water, so neces-

sary for his essential building material, brick.[8] Inevitably, the tensions involved attract the modern observer, but in regarding these tensions, we should consider first the purposes that presumed discrepancies might have served in their own time. Jefferson built his house on a mountain because he wanted to see farther and because he wanted to be seen clearly in the mind's eye. Monticello, in this sense, was explicitly a house of the Enlightenment, and to understand it requires recognition of the ideology that gave its builder tools of construction as relevant as any hammer or trowel.

The attempt to see Monticello as a house of the Enlightenment should be especially rewarding if just because critics have ignored the underlying complexity of Enlightenment thought in early republican culture and because Thomas Jefferson epitomized that frame of reference. Lost, in particular, is the originating philosophical notion of *the process* of Enlightenment, of *seeking* knowledge, as opposed to the more superficial affirmations about knowledge *attained* that historians tend to stress in revealing the rhetorical excesses of the philosophe tradition.[9] Immanuel Kant's injunction in "An Answer to the Question: 'What is Enlightenment?'" took the form of the command *"Sapere aude!"*: "dare to know!" or "have courage to use your *own* understanding!"[10] Properly understood, this command helps to explain what is perhaps the greatest puzzle of Jefferson's house. Why did Monticello remain unfinished while the mansions of other leaders in the Virginia pantheon—leaders as busy as Jefferson—were routinely completed?

To begin to answer that question and the more complicated issue of Jefferson's achievement, we will examine ten relevant aspects of Monticello here: three elements in the physical structure of the building, four aspects of what might be called the process of living there, and three moments of Jeffersonian observation from the vantage that Monticello allowed. Taken together, all ten factors raise the question of "seeing" or point of view, the angle of refraction that seeing takes and the meaning that it allows. Through point of view, we can hope to approach "the posted presence of the watcher," Jefferson himself.[11] Sight, after all, was the constitutive metaphor of the Enlightenment. Jefferson relied heavily on the metaphor but with a nuanced understanding of problems in epistemology that he is rarely given credit for having considered. One can, in fact, go further. Jefferson's understanding of Enlightenment epistemology turned perceived discrepancies into something far more important, a philosophy to live *by* and

in. Monticello and the building of it represent the architectural proof
of that philosophy.

The three physical or structural elements of Monticello to be considered have been chosen because they link serious problems with abiding interests in Jefferson the architect. They are, in ascending order of
conceptual difficulty, the inner staircases of Monticello, Jefferson's almost fetishistic interest in clocks, and the most dominant feature of
the finished house, the spectacular dome room. There are, to be sure,
many other features that might be considered for investigation, but
these three elements contain mysteries that bring us closer to the purposes and idiosyncrasies of the secretive Jefferson, and each element
opens into a larger explanation of the house.

Anyone who has climbed either of the two inner staircases of
Monticello immediately understands the problem in the first element.
The stairs are narrow, dark, steep, and twisting—dangerous to life
and limb. Critics have agreed in calling them "the most serious design
flaw in the building." One ingenious explanation assumes that the
democratic Jefferson, resenting the grand staircase as the scene of "an
elaborate ritual of rank," decided to reduce this "spirit of aristocracy" to the utilitarian function of clambering up and down.[12] Jefferson gave a simpler explanation: "great staircases . . . are expensive
and occupy a space which would make a good room in every story."[13]

But neither the rejection of rank nor the question of expense provides a convincing argument for the apparent deficiency. Monticello
projects a primal sense of hierarchy from the tip of its dome to the
undercellar of its hidden slave quarters, and the painstaking care and
expense that Jefferson gave to other areas of design belies the explanation of cost. The separate question of space, raised by Jefferson
himself, opens in two directions. Jefferson would double the size of
his dwelling between the first and second plans for Monticello, but he
was knowingly building in the second instance for a much larger en-
tourage of collateral dependents, grandchildren, and house guests,
and the constraints of the first plan left him with intrinsic design restrictions. Numbers alone had to daunt the architect. Family in the
house varied from year to year, but a dozen regular occupants was
routine, and there were usually more, with a constant flow of guests.
Along with Jefferson's own two children, there were at various times

his two widowed sisters, the six children of one of them, and later, his daughter Martha's eleven children. That said, and however different the second Monticello is in design and conception from the first, it nonetheless builds within the understanding of the first—a reminder that knowledge is always cumulative in a Jeffersonian understanding. In any case, the problem of space did not lead to other space-saving decisions of note.

A more important consideration for minimal staircasing seems to have been Jefferson's recognition that he already had built a natural staircase. True, the Palladian design of Monticello dictated the model of a single story, but while this issue began in the question of European and classical influences, it did not end there. Jefferson, on top of his mountain, was already as high as he needed to be, and he knew who he was there and what it could mean. He called it "the new Rowanty," his own Olympus or mountain of the world.[14] This mountain site, as many have noted, was a massive inconvenience for economic reasons, but it fulfilled as no other location could the Enlightenment imperative of seeing as far as possible and in every direction. Monticello is a virtual glass house with vistas to all points of the compass from the open expanse of its first floor. Windows are everywhere, a priority that its builder maintained despite serious difficulties in maintenance and heating.

Jefferson was well ahead of his time in the attention that he gave to light in architecture. He pushed to its structural limits the "Italian" rule of his day that windows should represent at least one-third of wall space in a dwelling, and, as we know from historical accounts, he followed the sun from room to room in the course of a day, even scheduling meal times so that dinners could always be served by daylight. The desired plane of sight at Monticello is always horizontal and outward and on a pivoting rather than a vertical or inward-looking axis. This controlling perspective of Jefferson's, seeing around and down at the world, was heavily reinforced by aesthetic considerations—considerations that, for all of their spirit of adventure architecturally, were conventions of the spread of Enlightenment as Jefferson had come to understand it. Of course, from an entirely different perspective, architecture must also allow for the mundane in daily life. We have the factual information that Jefferson rarely moved above the first floor at Monticello. Perhaps alone among the regular inhabitants, he didn't need a decent staircase!

Clocks, the second structural element under consideration, are everywhere at Monticello, and they play on another convention of the age—the clockwork universe and the notion of mechanism that it expressed. Time is invariably an ambivalent construct within the mortal condition. The Enlightenment tried to think of time as flowing with the growth of reason and understanding in an improving universe. "The general spread of the light of science," Jefferson claimed, two weeks before his death, "has already laid open to every view the palpable truth, that the mass of mankind has not been born with saddles on their backs, nor a favored few booted and spurred, ready to ride them legitimately, by the grace of God."[15] A form of secular salvation in human progress powered such thinking, a parallel to millennialism but a millennialism lacking the idea of personal salvation. Jefferson looked only to the conjunction of human history and science for help. In the moment that death touched him most closely, the loss of his wife, Jefferson chose a pagan reference for comfort. Martha Wayles Jefferson's tombstone inscription reads that she was "torn from him," and it invokes in Greek the passage from *The Iliad* that reads "Nay, if even in the House of Hades men forget their dead, yet will I even there remember my dear comrade."[16] As for himself, he took pride in a fatalistic stoicism on the point. "I assure you," he wrote John Adams as early as 1816, "I am ripe for leaving all, this year, this day, this hour." By 1823 he could even think of quietly welcoming an end in which "the friendly hand of death shall rid us of all at once."[17]

When placed against the assumption of human progress, this cosmic fatalism meant that every minute had to count as long as one was in the land of the living. Jefferson made it an absolute duty to subordinate time to the accumulation of knowledge. Idleness was the great sin in his secular theology, and time represented both a measure and a disruption to be reckoned with at every moment. "If at any moment, my dear, you catch yourself in idleness," Jefferson once wrote his daughter, "start from it as you would from the precipice of a gulf." The most industrious of men, he believed "the idle are the only wretched," and he acted on the premise.[18] Edmund Bacon, a plantation overseer with direct and frequent access to his employer day and night, found him inactive just twice in twelve years; once with a toothache and once with a migraine attack.[19] Late in life Jefferson boasted, in a comment scarcely credible in another, that the sun had not caught him in bed in fifty years. A special clock at the foot of his alcove bed, just six feet from the resting head, chimed the hour and half hour. Jefferson would rise the moment he distinguished its hands from the darkness.[20]

Chiming clocks dominate every major room at Monticello, led by the great Chinese gong clock in the front hall, specially ordered in 1792. The workings of this clock also form the celebrated cannonball mechanism, where a second face of the clock tells the days as the weights in question fall through openings cut for that purpose in the hall floor. The gong, in the emphatic tolling of the hours, sounds "like a washtub has been banged."[21] The half-moon window on the west portico or front entrance is also marked in the ambiguous form of a clock or rising sun—a sun that can also be understood to be setting. Meanwhile, the special alcove bed clock in the master bedroom, designed by the French clockmaker Chantrot to Jefferson's careful specifications in 1791, duplicates its owner's favorite symbol of death: the neoclassical obelisk cast here in black marble.[22] The point is not that Jefferson was preoccupied with death but rather with the twofold possibility in time: use and waste. He knew and accepted that time would cut across his plans as surely as the mechanism of the hall clock required an unsightly hole in his floor. Vigilance was both the price and the reward of intelligence.

The third structural device worth considering has to do with the renowned neoclassical dome of Monticello, the first of its kind in America, designed entirely by Jefferson and built at exorbitant expense starting in 1800. The salient feature of the dome room is its utter impracticality. All scholars of Monticello agree on this point. Unheated, lacking a proper staircase for easy access to it, the dome room would have been too cold in winter and too hot in summer. Casual speculation that Jefferson meant for it to be a billiard room but then changed his mind because of a law against it seems pointless against the facts that no such law has been found and that Jefferson disliked gaming of all sorts. In the words of one critic, the dome room is "Monticello's appendix—a useless architectural appendage."[25] Jefferson, the master of efficiency and utility, asked nothing of this room except that it be there. Its significance lay entirely in its aesthetic merit—a consideration that needs to be understood beyond the superficial equation of Jefferson's acceptance of Palladian influences in general and of French examples in particular. Commentary that stops with references to Jefferson's appreciation of domed buildings while in Paris (including the

Hôtel de Salm, the Hôtel de Langeac, and the Halle aux Bleds) misses
a vital concern. The real issue to be faced here is quite different and, in
the end, much more significant. Jefferson's dome is physical proof that
a major structural item and, therefore, knowledge itself can have a
purely aesthetic function in his philosophy.

The redoubled implication of Jeffersonian aesthetics lies in the need
to be seen even as one sees. Monticello was both a platform for seeing
and the spectacle that was seen. The dome in particular—Jefferson
liked to call it his "sky-room"—was the reflection or mirror of the
man, the symbolic head that could be seen and that also proclaimed
the circularity of perspective (the ability of the seer to pivot on an axis
that encompassed the entire world). Here, too, the emphasis was on
light. The dome and its corollary in Jefferson's architecture, the octagonal room, stand for the further privileging of light over darkness.
Both allow greater receptivity to natural light over the four-cornered
or rectangular room. But there was also a darker underlying purpose.
Just as the gothic novel in representing the house as a head invariably
projects a state of mind through architecture, so the overshadowing
mass of Jefferson's unique and deliberately monumental dome supplied the quality of mind that every slave plantation required and that
Jefferson brought nearly to mania: the possibility—indeed the necessity—of surveillance.

Over and over again in his correspondence, Jefferson noted the impossibility of accomplishing anything on his house unless he was present and presiding over every detail, one reason for its slow progress
during the years that he was a public servant in Paris, Philadelphia,
and Washington, D.C. These complaints can be traced to the irre-
placeable expertise of the perfectionist builder as architect, but they
had more to do with the unwillingness of slave labor to perform on its
own. Slaves apparently worked only if they were constantly watched
at Monticello, and Jefferson complained frequently about the problem.[24] Even today, the small pavilion that rests on the retaining wall
just above the garden terraces at Monticello, a room where Jefferson
worked in the afternoon, vividly conveys this notion of surveillance.

Jefferson's dome represented the logical extension of surveillance,
carrying the physical fact of being watched to the level of psychological perception. As the visible center of Monticello's slave economy,
the dome introduced into that community the panoptic effect of control analyzed at some length in Michel Foucault's *Discipline and Pun-*

ish.[25] Here, literalized in architectural form, was an overriding connection, that of master and mansion. Poised in space, the dome also formed an externally oriented, logical continuum from master, to overseer, to house servant, to field hand. Anyone within its purview would have felt watched. The beauty of that form—what the philosopher Gaston Bachelard has called "the phenomenology of roundness"—signified geometrical perfection, completeness, and inclusiveness.[26] Above and duplicating the essence of the mountain itself, the dome held those beneath it enthralled and, in this context, also captivated. A slave positioned underneath all of that beauty and power could have practical alternatives in mind but no aesthetic answer. The only options would have been cooperation and acceptance or escape, and to escape meant more than the risk of being caught by the unseen eye in the dome; it meant leaving the most beautiful man-made thing the observer had ever seen or could imagine.

Jefferson, to be sure, would not have expressed matters in these terms, but there was an eighteenth-century vocabulary to help him toward just such an understanding. He certainly believed in the aesthetic power of architecture as a form of social control. As he told his house joiner James Oldham, "a single example of chaste architecture may guide the taste of the city."[27] "Palladio is the Bible," explained Jefferson in ranking his architects, and it was Andreas Palladio who ordered that the ideal house be made an organic, holistic extension of its owner, "suitable to the quality of him that is to dwell in it," but also a demonstration of social harmony in both, where "parts correspond to the whole and to each other."[28]

How such an extension of ownership worked for a planter with slaves in eighteenth-century Virginia had many nuances but a single controlling principle. The definition of the eighteenth-century gentleman to which Jefferson adhered suggested a configuration of concentric circles, leading from private, to domestic, to vocational, to communal and then public life.[29] Jefferson's primal signature in architecture, the octagonal room, was an extension of the dome motif through his house, and it eloquently registered the controlling idea in concentricity—a privacy or mystery or authority at the center that radiates toward the mastery of surrounding spheres.

All three of these structural elements taken together—stairs, clocks, and dome—suggest priorities in an aesthetics of seeing. Jefferson used his house to act out a complicated dynamic of vision, spectacle, mirrored reciprocity, intellectual vigilance, social surveillance, and the perception of beauty where grace in form is also a conscious exercise of power. Sometimes that dynamic involved a series of balances; at other times a qualified displacement; at still others, a deliberate conflation in which the desired result tricked the observer by relying on a distorted sense of placement in the eye of the perceiver.

The underlying bases of these strategies can be seen in four aspects of life at Monticello and, since each aspect contains a conundrum or riddle, they are best expressed in the form of questions. *First,* how could an Enlightenment intellectual who valued accuracy in sight as the first order of knowledge engage so readily in artifice for visual effect? Reducing two stories to the visual appearance of one story through window combinations, hiding the slave quarters or dependencies underneath the structure of his house, creating false balustrades and railings to conceal imperfections in the roof and dome all afford unsettling examples here. Some of the practical consequences are worth enumerating. The double or stacked windows connecting the first and second stories leave very inefficient or low windows in the darkened second story of an architect who worshipped light. The removal of slave quarters and other dependencies to a lower level rather than the standard plantation practice of more visible but scattered and usually shabby outbuildings created problems in plantation management. Jefferson's false balustrades, unworkable on his slanting roof in any case, led in places to balustrades that actually cut into the moldings of window frames.

Second, in this listing of riddles, why didn't Jefferson's compulsive insistence upon record keeping and minute accountability in financial matters help him to minimize the economic ruin that his records showed was coming? "How could a man who recorded every penny he earned or spent, who kept accounts as rigorously as a banker," the critics ask, "allow himself to slip so deeply into debt?"[30] *Third,* what of the secrecy and occasional reclusiveness of the private life up against Jefferson's insistence upon an active social arrangement of continuous hospitality? *Fourth,* what are we to make of the unfinished nature of Monticello, a building that Jefferson put up and tore down repeatedly between 1768 and 1826? This last charge can also be leveled another way. Visitors to Monticello reveal that Jefferson allowed parts of the building to fall into utter disrepair and even into an unkempt state as he continued to labor on new parts and the completion of his plans. Why?

These questions all have major dimensions, but a common key to each puzzle is the intellectual *process* of Enlightenment, which, in turn, explains some of the peculiar combinations in the aesthetics of seeing just noted. Jefferson could falsify elements in the structure of his house and could hide his slave quarters and even his servants within the daily routine of the house because he believed in form as a saving reality. In order to see farthest, one must eliminate that which disturbs form in immediate proximity. Looking in a comparable way for the order in Nature, Ralph Waldo Emerson would come to much the same idea when he told his readers to keep their eyes on the horizon and away from close or secondary desires.[31] Jefferson removed slavery from the vision, if not the reality, of his plan because he assumed slavery would pass from view in subsequent American history. Emancipation was one of the "great objects I have in view," Jefferson wrote in 1785, and through life he believed that "the hour of emancipation is advancing, in the march of time it will come."[32] Meanwhile, the sight of it disturbed the truth that one was trying to promote.

The same construct of willed disregard applies to the plantation economics that held Jefferson and many another Virginia aristocrat in permanent debt. Even as he noted every account, Jefferson always expected his farming enterprise to fail on its own terms. He loathed the tobacco economy that was his main staple. "It is," he wrote, "a culture productive of infinite wretchedness," and he expected Maryland and Virginia "to abandon the raising tobacco altogether" in the near future.[33] Building for time and distance, the architect-owner of Monticello stripped slavery and tobacco from his sight as much as possible. The higher vision of a more timeless truth held the planner, as another Enlightenment figure who visited Jefferson in 1782, the Marquis de Chastellux, intuited. "For no object had escaped Mr. Jefferson," wrote Chastellux, "and it seemed as if from his youth he had placed his mind as he had done his house, on an elevated situation from which he might contemplate the universe."[34]

Another side of Jefferson, the Virginia gentleman, understood perfectly well that slavery and tobacco were essential realities in the practical order of his world. Both were cornerstones of the hospitality that he encouraged—even though his constant reception of guests went against every intellectual impulse in his being and even though his elaborate treatment of visitors plunged him ever deeper into the indebtedness that would destroy his estate. But something more than duty was at stake in such entertainment. In support of the obligation of hospitality was another level of meaning: the idea of spectacle.

Spectacle defined the successful planter within aristocratic Virginian society. Thus, when Martha Jefferson Randolph, the long-suffering hostess of Monticello, finally complained to her father against the stream of visitors that filled her daily life, Jefferson responded in just these terms. Spectacle, after all, was the reverse side of vision in eighteenth-century culture. "The manner and usages of our country," Jefferson wrote, "are laws we cannot repeal." To revolt against them "would undo the whole labor of our lives." These words, coming from the great Revolutionary innovator, sound curiously passive until we note "the pleasing side," which Jefferson also recorded. As he told his daughter, "these visits are evidences of the general esteem which we have been . . . all our lives trying to merit."[35]

The visits were "evidences" because they supplied connection between the inner and outer life. Whether in the form of minute plantation records, which collectively established an understanding of larger enterprise, or in the social opinion of the visiting community, which assured the aristocrat of his sense of place, the builder of Monticello was absolutely invested in "evidences" as thinker, farmer, architect, and political leader. His obsession with accumulating facts, which existed at every level of investigation, was another gauge of this temperament. The philosopher in the man assumed that all of the facts would some day add up, if not in his own time, then for others when the proper amount and coordination of information were in place. Knowledge was cumulative in an organic sense, one reason why Monticello, to remain state of the art, had to change with each incremental piece of understanding. In "daring to know," the architect of the Enlightenment also dared to change the structures that held him back, and there was something wonderful in this stance. Jefferson never seems to have given in to the mere passiveness in living.

The house of the Enlightenment was never about ease, leisure, and comfort; it was about the constant struggle to improve one's understanding and to demonstrate that understanding to a candid world. New coats of paint and the mundane notion of repair had little to do with the spirit behind that demonstration. Restoration was not exactly immaterial to aesthetic appeal—beauty must always be young and vital—but for the increasingly embattled Jefferson, running out of time and money, upkeep did not begin to approach the fascination with design and form that drove him. Monticello was not a house that could be finished on the terms that its architect set for himself. Only today, as a retrospection, is Monticello a finished work, and there is some reason to believe that its original owner might query its current value as a static or fixed museum piece. Jefferson would have had a constant flow of suggestions for its continuing improvement, and he would have searched compulsively through science for the internal measures that would have kept its conveniences up-to-date.

Three moments of observation by Jefferson can illustrate aspects of what we have been calling an eighteenth-century Enlightenment aesthetics of seeing. They are, in order: the famous description of "looming" in *Notes on the State of Virginia*, published in 1787 but written at least three years before, the placement of Monticello in Jefferson's equally famous dialogue of the head and the heart in his letter to Maria Cosway from 1786, and, less noted but perhaps even more telling, the Reverend Henry C. Thweatt's description of a conversation with Jefferson at Monticello during a storm that they watched together in 1826, the last year of Jefferson's life.[36] All three passages commend the unique perspective that Monticello offered for purposes of observation, and all three suggest a special value in elevation as the truest platform for the process of human understanding, but there are also differences between them that show what Monticello finally came to mean for its complicated owner.

The description of "looming," when, in Jefferson's words, "distant objects appear larger, in opposition to the general law of vision, by which they are diminished," comes after many pages of precise observations in *Notes on the State of Virginia,* and it serves the purpose of suggesting how easily observation can be deceived when it is not driven by scientific method and an accurate sense of "philosophy." Jefferson's focus is another mountain, which he knows to be forty miles distant, and about the way "it assumes at times the most whimsical shapes, and all these perhaps successively in the same morning." Method appears in Jefferson's repeated measurements of the weight, moisture, and heat of the atmosphere during the process of looming.

And yet the writer admits that no measurement has made any real difference. "Refraction will not account for this metamorphosis," he concludes, but neither does he leave the investigation there.

The rest of the passage limits the degree of error that others have brought to "the whimsical shapes" of looming, and the removal of error becomes in itself a vital contribution to enlightened science, where superstition and ignorance have previously reigned. Jefferson offers no positive hypothesis where scientific explanation "by none of its laws, as yet developed" can support him. All of his integrity rests in the qualification ("as yet developed"). He observes for others who will follow, and he never doubts but that new laws, when developed, will render Nature mediate on this point and every other. As the structure of his knowledge is there for others to build upon, so the example of Monticello is a structure for others to measure themselves against. Not surprisingly, many of the compromises at Monticello are about the elimination or at least the displacement of discovered error.

The description of Monticello offered to Maria Cosway is of a very different and yet eerily similar character. The language is far more effusive, but once again "the workhouse of nature" is the subject, and Jefferson's stress is once again upon repeated observation and the calm that it produces. "With what majesty do we there ride above the storms!" exalts Jefferson. This passage comes in one of those rare moments in the embattled dialogue between the head and the heart, where the two combatants agree absolutely. From Monticello can be seen "subjects worthy of immortality," and it is instructive that Maria Cosway, a painter and sketch artist, can achieve immortality herself by elucidating them, a process that can "make them, & thereby ourselves known to all ages." The monumental dome of Monticello, its own elucidation, is another sketch by another artist, and it too is about imposing form beyond the immediate press of time. The axis of sight is automatically improved by the capacity "to look down into" the workhouse of nature.

The last passage, that of the Reverend Thweatt, takes on the press of time more directly. Nature arrives with force in this scene instead of waiting to be observed. This time we are subjected to the very storm that we were permitted to ride above in majestic calm during the letter to Maria Cosway. Jefferson and his guests sit, in Thweatt's description, in "a room walled on every side but one by glass," and they wait for the storm to hit. When it does:

this scene of indescribable terror continued near . . . an hour during the silence of death [that] pervaded the room. Not a word had been spoken . . . during the whole. At length as the storm subsided . . . I ventured to ask Mr. Jefferson if it was not often unpleasant to him . . . to be thus exposed to such violent & terrible storms . . . and if during the present one he had not felt a good alarm—that for my part I had never before during my life been more frightened. . . . With his usual placid & soft, tone of voice he answered, "I was not in the least alarmed my son but silently enjoyed the solemn grandeur & awful sublimity of the scene. I have witnessed many such here & elsewhere and always on like occasions endeavor as best I can to realize the presence, power & majesty of the almighty Being."

The theme of this little story is, of course, Jefferson's singular equanimity amidst the consternation of others, but the narrative also tells us something about the process of seeing and what it meant to the master of Monticello.

Jefferson has been a witness "here & elsewhere" many times before, and his equanimity is of the hard-won variety in which all terrors have been faced and rendered describable. Within months of his own "silence of death," this figure is perpetually ready. Meanwhile, he has secured his own privacy within the circle of publicity around him ("not a word had been spoken during the whole"). At one level, the passage is a conventional early nineteenth-century description of the sublime. At another, it is an appropriately subtle manifestation of what has been called "the dialectics of outside and inside."[37] Forty years before, the man now in the eye of the storm had written "all my wishes end, where I hope my days will end, at Monticello," and he speaks now, knowing that it is one of the wishes that he has been granted.[38]

Jefferson possesses the most vivid and irreducible sense of place in this final scene. Every other figure is an intruder as he alone "silently enjoys" the perspective that he has both achieved and built. He sits in a room where "presence" overcomes the silence of death, where "power" lies in the match of inner calm to outward turmoil, and where "majesty" appears in the position and availability of every conceivable window. Architect, owner, and philosopher are one and the same in this scene, and their joint equanimity is all the greater when we recognize that Jefferson fully understood that his house and maybe even his nation were crumbling around him in 1826. Such equanimity can come only from many different sources at once, but one source stands out as we reach a last time for the indefatigable, adventuring architect of Monticello. The goal, whether one is caught in the storm or allowed to ride above it, is always the same. Faced with the ultimate challenge of meaning, Jefferson relies on a special kind and definition of effort. What he tells Henry Thweatt has been his perpetual measure, resource, and comfort through life: "[I always] endeavor as best I can."

CHAPTER NINE

Charity in the City of Brotherly Love

Legal commentators call the *Girard* will case, argued before the Supreme Court in 1844, the source of modern charity law in the United States, and historians generally agree that Joseph Story's concluding decision gave "a large forward step in encouraging the whole field of philanthropy that would be significant throughout the next century."[1] For rather different reasons, *Girard* was a major cultural event of the 1840s, one of sufficient constitutive power to help define a decade and the direction of years beyond. "Few cases," Charles Warren has argued, "ever more keenly interested the general public or brought it more closely in contact with the [Supreme] Court."[2]

Several levels of implication overlap in such statements. As court decision, *Girard* represents one of those junctures in the creation of a communal norm. It demonstrates how legal notions of philanthropy have contributed to national character. As a cultural event coming out of a major city, Philadelphia, the case helps to identify the murky dividing line between the early republic and antebellum America, a troubled period of "heart-freezing change." Starting in the 1820s, political unrest, cycles of boom and bust, and rapid technological change made "instability the natural condition of American life," and *Girard* made leading intellectuals talk about it.[3] Court decision and cultural event come together in a third level of implication that is harder to grasp. The trial as a formal decision made out of messier event ensures a double perspective on the "making" of history. It supplies a complicated dialectic in cultural analysis, one that enables a critic "to brush history against the grain."[4]

The peculiar power of the courtroom dialectic depends upon an innate double function in American trial procedures: the advocacy system simultaneously enacts as it resolves conflict. Famous trials like *Girard* magnify differences and thereby formalize paradoxes in cultural understanding. By capturing the imagination, they become barometers for gauging ideological aspirations, tensions, and contradictions. Exhaustive recording mechanisms render that gauge a fine one. The many compelled narratives in a famous trial articulate the predicament of unresolved conflict while the ongoing process in court seeks to settle or at least contain conflict in a moment of judgment. *Girard* was both intellectual catalyst and cultural ceremony in the American republic of laws. Its parts, the tools of conflict, competed with the momentum of the whole toward collective understanding and acceptance. To study *Girard* is to see the way in which the competitions of event and interpretation, part and whole, yield particular patterns of historicity or meaning.

Forms of giving suggest something about a culture. Sudden shifts in those forms reveal even more. *Girard* is important because it underlines a startling anomaly in the history of the American law of charities. Communal charity flourished in the colonial period. Courts and assemblies went out of their way to remove obstacles in the way of bequests as communities tried to take care of their own in more or less formal ways. Pragmatic social needs and the intentions of donors frequently outweighed legal stricture, and the colonies grew famous for stressing the liberal side of English charity law.[5] In time, this permissive doctrine fed the assumption—now general among Americans—that a powerful and innate generosity adhered to national communal character. The philanthropic impulse became one of "the distinguishing marks of the American way."[5] But this impulse, if central, was strangely absent from the American courtroom of the 1820s and 1830s.

Beginning in the supposed Era of Good Feeling and extending into the Jacksonian era, American judges rejected the permissive policies that had originated in colonial communal practice and applied the narrowest construction of available law to deny philanthropic bequests. The leading case was *Philadelphia Baptist Association v. Hart's Executors* in 1819, toward the end of the early republican period. In his *Hart* decision, Chief Justice John Marshall struck down a philanthropic bequest on the technical ground that the power to enforce a charitable trust depended on the Elizabethan Statute of Charitable Uses of 1601, which no longer applied in Virginia. The courts of first Virginia and Maryland and then New York and Pennsylvania soon carried the restrictive principles of the *Hart* decision into general use through the 1820s and 1830s. The *Girard* case of 1844, in effect, reversed the *Hart* decision, reestablishing the earlier permissive charity doctrine as the dominant tradition in American jurisprudence but with a new twist.[7]

What caused the shift toward a restrictive charity policy in the early republic? Part of the answer surely lies in those aspects of the American personality that run counter to the assumed generosity just mentioned. "[T]here is something about philanthropy," Robert Bremner has noted in his history of the subject, "that seems to go against the democratic grain." The leveling processes of the Revolution, along with growing value placed on individualism (self-help in social advancement), complicated the hierarchical dynamic in all of charity, the giving from rich to poor.[8] Scholars also have suggested that disestablishment and the doctrine separating church and state caused early republicans to curb religious societies by limiting their access to charitable donations and bequests. Charities "symbolized advancing clerical power in society" and needed to be controlled, much as English law had controlled ecclesiastical ownership of land through mortmain or "dead hand" statutes against the charitable conveyance of property to the church. Early republicans, the argument continues, feared that the "dead hand" of self-perpetuating, ecclesiastical charitable trusts might capture and monopolize the wealth of the country and that, therefore, they should be restrained.[9]

The problem with these explanations is that they appear less convincing when placed against actual events. The danger of hierarchical or anti-democratic tendencies in charitable giving could hardly have been a paramount consideration for the conservative Federalist judges who decided *Philadelphia Baptist v. Hart's Executors*. Admitting that the Supreme Court blocked a charitable trust to a religious organization in *Hart*, why should figures like John Marshall and Joseph Story have worried overly about the separation of church and state in 1819

and not before? Why should the same figures have feared an ecclesiastical monopoly of property at the very moment when America was
doubling and tripling in size through vast wilderness tracts to the
West? Mortmain statutes may have been necessary to restrain a mon-
olithic established church in the crowded, land-poor British Isles or
even to reassure Revolutionary Americans who feared the prospect of
British bishops in the new world, but how did these issues translate
forty years later in 1819 to a thinly populated but rapidly expanding
continental republic served by dozens of competing religious sects?

The value of the trial as cultural indicator lies in its specificity and
enracinement (literally, its rootedness). *Philadelphia Baptist v. Hart's
Executors* forces a distinction between 1819 and generalized arguments that apply more readily to 1776. Like all court cases, it brought
the authority of the past to bear upon a challenge of the moment,
thereby tempering traditional language and thought with a new sense
of concreteness and urgency. Joseph Story, who silently concurred
with Marshall in the *Hart* decision, did worry in conventional terms
about religion and property in an unsigned appendix attached to the
case report. Not satisfied with just the report, he then, rather disinge-
nuously, praised his own anonymous assertions in an article of the
North American Review.[10] Appendix and article together show how
easily the language of English law could be lifted from its original
context for new purposes.

Story calls here for mortmain statutes or laws that restrict charitable conveyance "with a view to prevent undue influence and imposition upon pious and feeble minds, in their last moments, and to check
that unhappy propensity which sometimes is found to exist under a
bigoted enthusiasm, the desire to gain fame as a religious devotee and
benefactor, at the expense of the natural claims of blood and parental
duty to children." Fear about property then follows. "We are in some
danger," adds Story, "of having our most valuable estates locked up in
mortmain, and our surplus wealth pass away in specious or mistaken
charities, founded upon visionary or useless schemes, to the impover-
ishment of friends, and the injury of the poor and deserving of our
own countrymen." The solution offered, once again, is "to check
improper donations procured by fanatical or other delusions," and
Story urges it as a matter of "immediate and pressing importance."

At issue in such language is not the separation of church and state, a
doctrine firmly established more than a generation before, but rather
Joseph Story's deep fear of the waves of revivalism that flooded Amer-

ican culture in the first half of the nineteenth century. His opponent was not the organized church or even a series of churches but, in his words, the "enthusiasms" of the "religious devotee," the visionary and the fanatic. Story stands on one side of the great divide in nineteenth-century sensibilities between evangelical assertion and legal understanding.[11] There was no more implacable enemy of revivalism in 1819 than the conservative leaders of the American bar.

Story's fears about property are a little harder to explain because they have more to do with the changing conception of property than with the actual language of scarcity and take-over that he once again borrowed from his readings in English legal history. By 1819, the year of the *Hart* decision, real property, land, was losing its central political significance in national life. Universal manhood suffrage ended the property qualification for voting, and the negative implications of this shift filled the private correspondence of Story and his colleague James Kent, Chancellor of New York, with gloomy predictions of "popular clamours" and an "American elective monarchy."[12] Kent, in formal debate during the New York constitutional convention of 1821, summarized the thinking of both men: "The tendency of universal suffrage is to jeopardize the rights of property and the principles of liberty. There is a constant tendency in human society . . . there is a constant tendency in the poor to covet and to share the plunder of the rich; in the debtor to relax or avoid the obligations of contract; in the majority to tyrannize over the minority, and trample down their rights."[13]

Kent, Story, and other conservative judges of the period like Henry Saint-George Tucker of Virginia feared for property because they sensed something changing out from under them. Morton Horwitz has described this process as "dethroning landed property from the supreme position it had occupied in the Eighteenth-century world view; and ultimately, in transforming real estate into just another cash commodity." More recently, J. G. A. Pocock has demonstrated how the shift from a static land-use concept of property toward a dynamic market orientation could threaten personality itself. Property, for Story, Kent, and the founders before them, supplied the foundation for independence, virtue, and citizenship. The figure who possessed these qualities, "the individual as classical political being," to use Pocock's terms, was "rendered uncertain and dissolved into fantasy, other-directedness, and anomie by the corruptions of the new com-

mercial politics." The early republican "as Roman patriot, self-de-
fined in his sphere of civic action," had stood above but now seemed
to be falling before "the individual in the society of private investors
and professional rulers."[14]

Only with the divide between sacrificing citizen and economic actor
in mind can one appreciate the later early republican's near obsession
with regular inheritance, what Story called "the natural claims of
blood and parental duty to children." These claims of automatic descent ran directly against the artificial conveyance of the charitable
trust at a time when Americans felt increasingly isolated and alone
with the passage of the Revolutionary generation. The enormous ceremonial response to Lafayette's return to America in the 1820s represented a widespread attempt to reconstitute a former sense of sacred
community against the commercial forces of breakdown.[15] Alexis de
Tocqueville saw this growing spirit of isolation working itself into
new emotional and economic patterns. Democratic men and women
in a changing world had to "acquire the habit of always considering
themselves as standing alone." By the 1830s, these patterns could be
thought of as the beginnings of an "imperial self," but in the 1820s
the brute fact of loss still dominated.[16]

Profound loss is answerable only by an act of linkage and recovery.
Americans still needed to belong to the world that they were losing as
the Era of Good Feeling and the last presidencies of the founding generation came to an end. Not surprisingly, the controlling metaphor for
place in a shifting world was the act of inheritance, the continuing legacy of an American Revolutionary heritage. When Daniel Webster in
his Plymouth Rock Oration of 1820 sought to reassure his audience,
he turned primarily to this metaphor. Webster's goal in this bicenten-
nial celebration of the Pilgrims' landing, literally Founders' Day, was
to transform "mere isolated beings without relation to the past or the
future" into citizens "closely compacted on all sides with others" as
"links in the great chain of being." Five pages of the Plymouth Oration were given over to a detailed analysis of "the laws which regulate
the descent and transmission of property" in America, England, and
France. The conveyance of land represented the most vital connection
between past, present, and future, and Webster easily drew his audience into this process of transmission.[17]

Orator and audience at Plymouth Rock performed a mutual public exercise in self-esteem through which the property of all Ameri-

cans was conveyed from one generation to the next. Those gathered were to leave "some proof that we have endeavored to transmit the great inheritance unimpaired." This exercise was necessary not just because republican principles must be conveyed anew but also because those in attendance, the generations *after* the Revolutionary founders, needed to feel that "we are not altogether unworthy of our origins." "We are in the line of conveyance," Webster announced, after showing that republican institutions, like property, must be "transmitted, as well as enjoyed." "We would leave for the consideration of those who shall then occupy our place, some proof," he concluded, and the reiterated phrase "some proof" formed a peroration in which tangible evidence was needed. In the end, everything came together in a common moment of feeling to be shared by those who would rise in "long succession, to fill the places which we now fill."[18]

The extraordinary power and tenacity of formal inheritance as a controlling, legitimating symbol in antebellum America can be seen as well in the major fiction of the period. From James Fenimore Cooper's *The Pioneers* (1823) to Nathaniel Hawthorne's *The House of the Seven Gables* (1851), youthful protagonists first appear as forces for unorthodox change. They rail against existing property distributions only to be subsumed over time in proper and regular inheritances that provide plot resolution. Cooper and Hawthorne intrude with lengthy general discussions of the rise and fall of families amidst the uncertain economic conditions of the early republic. Old wealth gives way to new in a never-ending process that inheritance reinforces and controls.

In Cooper's words, those who depend exclusively upon hereditary wealth descend, while those who are forced to rely upon their own powers rise. "In this republican country, amid the fluctuating waves of our social life, somebody is always at the drowning point," adds Hawthorne in his own description of the Pyncheon family now at its lowest ebb. Both novels present sets of families that meet on the rise and fall. Inheritance operates as a regularizing force, a source of definition, moderation, and distribution within rapidly accelerating cycles of wealth and poverty or between, in Hawthorne's terms, marble and mud. Proper descent supplies the minimal rules of order that prevent the competitive game of prosperity from degenerating into social warfare and chaos. And just as inheritance is an intrinsic force in these novels, so offers of charity appear a weak afterthought or even as shams in the working out of communal conflict and the claims of injustice.

Both authors go out of their way to illustrate the minimal and ambiguous role of charity as a corrective force in American culture. The aged Indian John's apotheosis in death as the mighty Mohican warrior Chingachgook at the end of *The Pioneers* begins with his firm rejection of Elizabeth Temple's misplaced beneficence ("John's hand can make baskets no more—he wants no shirt."). Hawthorne's sarcasm over Hepzibah Pyncheon's transformation from "the patrician lady . . . into the plebeian woman" depends upon a similar disparagement of charity; Hepzibah must learn to join "the rest of the world" in "fighting out its battle with one kind of necessity or another."[19] Both novels, and countless other works of fiction from the period, contain much that reflects the Supreme Court's restrictive attitude in *Philadelphia Baptist v. Hart's Executors*.

All of the factors mentioned—a democracy's ambivalence regarding philanthropy, concern about the impact of revivalism, uneasiness over the "dead hand" of the charitable trust, loose fears about property changes, and an abiding need for patterns of regular inheritance—helped to account for a restrictive charity policy in the 1820s, the last days of the early republic, but what explains the Supreme Court's sudden reversion back to a more permissive construction of charitable uses in 1844? Most of the problems of the 1820s remained problems in the 1840s, and some had grown worse. Moreover, Joseph Story had become more pessimistic about solutions to those problems by 1844. Why does a conservative figure like Story completely reverse his own previous stance, and what does the precise nature of that reversal mean for a modern conception and practice of charity? Answers to these questions turn upon the *Girard* will case as an unfolding legal event and larger ceremony in republican culture. The same answers also suggest the shift toward an American modernity.

Even a brief description reveals a powerful symbol system at work within the trial process.[20] At his death without direct heir in 1831, the Philadelphia merchant and banker Stephen Girard had amassed the largest single fortune the new world had ever seen. An elaborate will made some provision for relatives, but the great bulk of the Girard estate (worth the then stupendous sum of $7 million) went to the city of Philadelphia in trust to establish a school or college for poor, white, orphan boys. Detailed instructions on the location, size, nature, and administration of the college included the express stipulation that no minister or ecclesiastic of any sort should ever be allowed on the premises. "I do not mean to cast any reflection upon any sect or person, whatsoever," Girard explained in his trust agreement, "but as there is such a multitude of sects, and such a diversity of opinion amongst them, I desire to keep the tender minds of the orphans . . . free from the excitement which clashing doctrines and sectarian controversy are so apt to produce."

Girard's disenfranchised collateral heirs attacked the will on three grounds, claiming that the city of Philadelphia could not legally take the devise, that the trust itself was too vague and uncertain to be enforced, and, finally, that Girard's exclusion of ecclesiastics negated the whole concept of a charitable trust because it was at odds with the Christian religion, which had been declared an integral part of Pennsylvania's common law. The first two arguments were well within the spirit if not the letter of the Supreme Court's earlier decision in *Philadelphia Baptist v. Hart's Executors.*

When the case reached the Supreme Court in 1844, Horace Binney, the acknowledged leader of the Philadelphia bar, represented his city against Daniel Webster who appeared for the heirs as plaintiffs. Oral argument before the Court extended across ten full days, drew packed crowds from Washington society, and received extensive coverage from the national press. *The New York Herald* found "a grand illustration of a conflict between mind and mind, and the final surrender of the powers of self-interest to the majestic decision of the law." The many fashionably dressed women in attendance, sitting near and even alongside the jurists, appeared as so many "vernal flowers springing up amid the crevices of immovable and everlasting rocks." "In fact," concluded the *Herald,* "it looks more like a ballroom sometimes . . . this mixture of men and women, law and politeness, ogling and flirtation, bowing and curtseying, going on in the highest tribunal in America. Yet it all works well."[21] Working well in this instance meant a complete victory for Horace Binney and the City of Philadelphia. Joseph Story's opinion for a unanimous court upheld the validity of the Girard will on all counts. Though distinguishing *Girard* from *Philadelphia Baptist v. Hart's Executors,* Story actually overruled the earlier decision.

Not least in the power and eventual course of this trial was the ghost of Stephen Girard.[22] Girard's lack of immediate heirs, his partial provision for remaining family members, the immense size of his fortune, which transcended every range of conceivable individual need, and his careful, detailed specifications on the proposed college all made it easier for the court to entertain the public character of his bequest. So did memories of the man. Girard was an important transitional figure from early republic culture to the fluctuating norms of antebellum society. His coldly practical and ruthlessly financial approach to life made him the economic symbol of the new order. Arriving in Philadelphia at its highest moment, June of 1776, Girard made money instead of politics. And yet the wealthy merchant and manipulative banker could and did turn selfless citizen in moments of crisis. The cynical, even misanthropic Girard risked his life in volunteering and then organizing medical relief for Philadelphia during the appalling yellow fever epidemic of 1793. Later, his crucial financial support of the federal government during the War of 1812 required a considerable gamble in personal resources. His career straddled the ideal of virtue and the new commerce just enough to make Girard a thoroughly familiar figure along different lines of explanation. The fulfillment of his will by the Supreme Court played off of these useful combinations.

The trial itself reflected the changing nature of legal practice in America, and this, too, influenced the Court's decision. The battle of legal giants, Binney against Webster, acted out a contrast beyond mere argument, one that many noticed at the time. Binney's presentation for the city of Philadelphia contained an occasional flourish, but it reads today like a modern legal brief. On the other side, Webster's three-day performance was and is a nineteenth-century speech, evoking applause and even tears from its immediate audience but little from the bench that it hoped to persuade. These different approaches openly clashed in a high moment of courtroom ritual described by an observer in the audience:

> [Binney] had just begun, when Mr. Webster rose and apologized for not having obeyed the rule before [of furnishing opposing counsel who preceded in an argument with one's own concluding points and citations]. . . . Mr. Binney paused to hear him with his arms folded, and when [Webster] was done, smiled a sweet smile of indifference, and gently said, with a slight wave of his hand, that he "fully excused his learned brother for his delay of citation, for he would have no occasion

to touch a single point, or anything cited by him," and then unfolded
that masterly treatise on charitable uses, which his great argument deserves to be called a standard of authority now on the doctrines then in
debate. Mr. Webster was taken aback and staggered.

Binney well knew that his own exhaustive preparation put him on a
separate plane. If the assertion of "learned brother" bespoke customary decorum, there was ironic bite in those folded arms and subsequent waving off of the "staggered" Webster for "delay of citation."

The New York Herald, while regretting that "Mr. Binney went off
into a district of the law as dry as the African deserts," drew the same
conclusions about the contest. Binney's "pulverizing announcement"
was "like a huge screw, slowly turning round on its threads, but at last
coming down on the object to be squeezed with irresistible power."
The unusual modern image of inexorable machinery signaled something beyond the ordinary effusions of antebellum courtroom oratory.
The Herald also noticed the most immediate consequence of change:
"Mr. Webster looks on with undisguised dismay."[23]

The unexpected depth of Binney's professional knowledge marked
a major difference between the *Hart* decision in 1819 and the *Girard*
will case in 1844. John Marshall's original decision went off in part
on the Court's general ignorance of English chancery and common
law and on Marshall's related unwillingness, in his words, to trust
"principle concealed in a dark and remote antiquity."[24] Binney's brief
in *Girard* brought definitive light into that darkness through citation
after citation, all of which demonstrated a more permissive treatment
of charitable uses in Anglo-Saxon jurisprudence than previously realized. Suddenly, the whole debate over the applicability of the Elizabethan Statute of Charitable Uses to American jurisdictions became a
side issue; everyone now knew that many relevant cases predated the
statute of 1601. "That statute," Story now saw, "only created a new
jurisdiction; it created no new law."

Story shrewdly adopted Marshall's own metaphor of darkness and
light to overturn the former chief justice without seeming to do so.
New case law, in particular *Magill v. Brown* from the United States
Circuit of Pennsylvania in 1833, and the recent publication of old
common law and chancery reports, had thrown "very strong additional light" on charity law where all previously had been "in no
small degree shadowy, obscure, and flickering."[25] The Court, in other
words, was not reversing itself between *Hart* and *Girard* so much as it

was continuing to discover the true path of the law. Story merely followed where Marshall would have led if darkness had not prevented him.

Implicit in the same metaphor, however, was a new perspective on how the Court wielded law as an available tool. More light meant a different kind of knowledge. The Court of 1819 had relied more upon natural law and common sense to explain away the shrouded mysteries in English common law. Subsequent disclosure of those mysteries inevitably carried the Court toward a more technical dependence on man-made law, toward legal positivism. In the growing availability of case law and in his mastery of it, Binney not only won his case, he demonstrated that the days of the courtroom orator were numbered. Webster's mere eloquence missed the point now that decisions required detailed case law instead of general social principle and the best expression of opinion.

For all of these reasons, it is Webster that readers fail to understand today, not Binney or Story. In attempting to evade the revealed complexities of charity law, Webster concentrated instead on the religious issue. His three-day oration relied upon a single premise: that the Girard will, by excluding orthodox clergy and religious instruction, created a heathen trust in derogation of the Christian religion and, therefore, constituted no charity at all. "If charity denies its birth and parentage," he claimed, "if it turns infidel to the great doctrines of the Christian religion, if it turns unbeliever, it is no longer charity . . . for it separates itself from the fountain of its own creation." Having removed Stephen Girard from God, Webster quickly attached him to the one fallen member of the founders' pantheon, Thomas Paine, in an analysis that traced the will back to a radical deism: "it is *mere, sheer, low, ribald, vulgar deism and infidelity*," he thundered. "It opposes all that is in heaven, and all on earth that is worth being on earth. It destroys the connecting link between the creature and the Creator; it opposes that great system of universal benevolence and goodness that binds man to his Maker."[26]

Considerable method informed Webster's seemingly superficial emotionalism. The constitutive metaphor in his performance involved the notion of broken linkage with the ensuing isolation and chaos that such a break must mean. Over and over again, whether quoting scripture or praising the clergy or condemning infidelity, Webster preyed upon the primary fear of dwindling relation and lost ties that haunted the end of the early republic and helped to define antebellum America. "It destroys the connecting link," it "denies its birth and parentage," "it separates itself from the creation"—these phrases described the threat that Girard's will posed in the terms of a familiar anxiety. Ingeniously, Webster made much of the inherently ruptured status of those whom Girard would benefit. *"They are orphans,"* he intoned, in a litany of lost fathers, mothers, and spiritual instructors. "If they were only poor," he wished, "there might be somebody bound by ties of human affection to look after their spiritual welfare. But they have none." Specific parental loss easily came to signify generalized cultural isolation and privation.

All Americans gradually shared in this orphaning process when Webster showed how Christianity, as the central conserving principle of society, would fall if Girard's devise was allowed to stand. "What would become of all that now renders the social circle lovely and beloved?" he asked. "What would become of society itself? How could it exist?" Nothing would survive a charity that, in Webster's words, "tends to destroy the very foundation and framework of society." Finally, in his peroration, the master orator seized upon the inner nub of his listeners' fears. It was only through religion and an American faith in religion that the founders continued to address the nation. "The dead prove it as well as the living," Webster concluded. "The generation that are gone before speak to it, and pronounce it from the tomb. . . . All, all proclaim that Christianity . . . is the law of the land." As ever, the solutions to American fears depended upon a correct inheritance.[27]

Story and his colleagues on the bench bought little of such preaching. Story, in private, dismissed Webster's "address to the prejudices of the clergy," its "semi-theological character," and all of those "homilies of faith."[28] His decision in *Girard* circumvented Webster's projected fears. Christianity was indeed the law of the land or part of the common law of Pennsylvania, but freedom of religion protected it only from an open and malicious attack that annoyed believers or injured the public. The Court found no evidence that the bequest impugned or repudiated Christian doctrine as such.[29] Christianity, however significant in itself, was irrelevant to the legal issues at hand.

Story found himself with a golden opportunity in *Girard;* he was in the rare position of furthering charity without encouraging the sectarianism and revivalism that he feared. A letter home showed his awareness of that opportunity: "you know that I have ever been a sturdy defender of religious freedom of opinion, and I took no small pains to answer Mr. Webster's argument on this point, which went to cut down that freedom to a narrow range."[30] Webster would have tied charitable giving to Christian faith. *Girard* separated the creation of charitable trusts from all notion of a religious orthodoxy, safeguarding the possibility for every religious group and, by implication, for any other group that wished to contribute to a larger sense of social justice.

∾

For modern philanthropy, Story's decision meant the first step in a paradigmatic migration of terms of significant proportions. The overall effect of *Girard* was to shift the whole concept of beneficent giving toward a secular basis. Charity as a legal concept had never been defined at common law except through an enumerated list of appropriate ends under the Statute of Charitable Uses.[31] Thus, although the basis of charitable giving incontestably grew out of religious impulses, the law chose to stress the object of the bequest instead of the donor's intent. *Girard* cleverly made use of that stress to legitimate the secularized giving that Stephen Girard began and that so many other individuals, corporations, and other institutions would follow in the modern era. Webster's challenge, one that clergymen published across America in the 1840s, shows that it need not have been so. In *Girard*, Story and his colleagues on the Supreme Court removed Christianity as a potential restriction upon giving in American culture. Religious preferences might still stimulate, but henceforth they would neither define nor inhibit a donor's wishes at law.

If the other lasting implications of *Girard* are harder to summarize, they are perhaps even more important in coming to grips with the combination of issues that marks a major trial. Joseph Story, for one, worried more about these other implications. He handled the religious question with ease. It was the underlying emotional basis of Webster's appeal that bothered him more. The Supreme Court justice who listened to the *Girard* arguments in 1844 was a troubled man. He feared the breaking linkages and the potential collapse of the culture that Webster described for him, and his pessimism had grown with each passing year. Story became obsessed with what he called "the melancholy lessons of the past history of republics down to our own." Shortly after completing his *Girard* opinion, he wrote in despair to James Kent: "How can a Republic long continue when the People . . . refuse to listen to the counsels of Wisdom and Experience? . . . For myself, I do not believe in the practicability of maintaining our Republic against such fearful odds. The law is now and has long been our only strength but it is crumbling under us." [32]

The greatest formal expression of this despair came in a public address on "Literary Tendencies of the Times" in 1842 in which Story's language eerily prefigured Webster's own two years later in the *Girard* case. Condemning "the tendency to ultraism of all sorts, and in all directions," Story observed that "dreamy expectations" concerning the future, "rash men" in the public forum, "the importunate reformer," and a "reckless spirit of speculation" were destroying all reverence for the past and encouraging the "shipwreck of our best hopes . . . desolation and ruin on every side." Gone were the connections and linkages that had held America in place for half a century. "Is it not painfully true," asked Story, "that the spirit of the age has broken loose from the strong ties, which have hitherto bound society together by the mutual cohesions and attractions of habits, manners, institutions, and literature?" "No single generation of men," he warned, "can accomplish much of itself or for itself, which does not essentially rest upon what has been done before."[33]

Story, if anything, believed more vehemently than Webster that the conserving elements and important models in American society were failing in their designated functions, and his response in *Girard* must be read with this in mind. *Girard* offered a solution in prospect to the kinds of difficulties that he and Webster faced. Something beyond traditional institutions had to supply the continuity between increasingly separated generations of Americans, and that something was going to be corporate power. To the extent that Girard's collateral heirs sought to restrict those powers, they were trying "to introduce a doctrine inconsistent with sound principles and defeat instead of promoting the true policy of the state."

The *Girard* decision went to great lengths not just to find the necessary power to support Girard's bequest to the corporation of Philadelphia but to merge that power with the force of individual human rights. "It is now held," wrote Story, "that where the corporation has a legal capacity to take real or personal estate, there it may take and hold it upon trust, in the same manner and to the same extent as a private person may do." No language was ever more deliberate. As he told Kent later in their mutual jubilation over *Girard,* "I equally rejoice, that the Supreme Court has at last come to the conclusion, that a corporation is a citizen, an artificial citizen, I agree, but still a citizen."[34]

The corporation appeared a faceless monster in much of the democratic rhetoric of the period. Democrats, whether Jeffersonian or Jacksonian, vied bitterly with Federalists and then Whigs over the emerging role of such institutions. For the former, corporate power tainted where it did not directly contradict the true course of the people's republic. For the latter, the corporation provided "a rock-like legal foundation to save wealth, learning, and respectability from the shifting sands of public favor." To this struggle, a conservative judiciary brought "the evolution of legal doctrines that considered the corporation an inviolable contract" and "the clarification of equity doctrine and equity jurisdiction that permitted private persons to transfer property freely to corporations, and permitted the corporations themselves to deal with property with the full rights of legal personhood."[35]

Girard furnished the perfect case for implementing conservative judicial policy. As a devise for poor orphans in Philadelphia, the city of brotherly love, it contributed to the new institutional form without obviously exacerbating the political struggles involved. What better and safer way to increase corporate power than to humanize it in a trust for the benefit of the people themselves? In *Dartmouth College v. Woodward* in 1819, the Supreme Court already had held that the right of contract protected corporations from subsequent interference by the states. "The purpose of the decision," Lawrence Friedman has noted, "was to secure property interests, and to protect ownership and management rights from shifting, temporary winds of public opinion."[36] The *Girard* case gave that protected corporation all of the additional rights of a normal citizen. With these twin holdings, the corporation was well on its way to a commanding position in the American economy, where the Supreme Court would remain its staunchest defender for a century to come.

It would be a mistake to think of Story as furthering the evolution of corporate law as a simple articulation of vested interests. His role could be so overwhelming because he matched cultural aspirations and vested interests in a dynamic way. His substitution of citizen for corporation in the aftermath of *Girard* touched a profound need. The trope of the corporation as a person deserving protection in the same way that every citizen deserved protection supplied a creative alternative, a substitution for the sense of deference, hierarchy, linkage, and order that Webster and Story saw as lost. Neither should the potential of the corporation as "artificial citizen" be trivialized. Republican culture made use of the familiar concept to recognize and accept an efficient, trouble-free, but wholly new device for managing and distributing capital. The corporation as citizen not only protected property for those already in possession, it also personified the whole notion of ownership at the very moment when property seemed to be evaporating into a commercial commodity.

How much of this conceptual framework did Story himself foresee in the writing of the *Girard* opinion? He had thirty-four years to ponder his role as a judge of the highest court in the land, and, quite early in that tenure, in a definition of the responsibilities of jurisprudence, he outlined exactly what was expected of him and his generation. "It depends upon the present age," he wrote in 1821, "whether the national constitution shall descend to our children . . . to protect and unite the country; or whether, shorn of its strength, it shall become an idle mockery, and perish before the grave has closed upon the last of its illustrious founders."[37] The corporation, for Story, represented a new form of strength for a Constitution stripped of its patriotic creators. The founders may have fallen, but the corporation, a sort of everlasting big brother, promised to be perpetual.

A prominent case like *Girard* clearly lends itself to different lines of analysis. That is the value of every major trial as cultural barometer and also the essential problem in interpretation that each of them raises. In the trial at hand, the particulars of charity law, the changing nature of legal practice, the communal need for regular inheritance, the secularization of American thought, the reinforcement of corporate power, and the search for ideological confirmations are related but competing lines of analysis in the larger act of interpretation. What, in the end, is the importance of *Girard*? This question can only be answered by considering the dialectic of the trial as historical event and as legal decision. In methodological terms, interpretation requires an interdisciplinary rapprochement between history (event), law (court decision), and literature (texts joining event to decision).

The more one separates event from decision, the less important *Girard* becomes. John Quincy Adams' acidic summary at the time illustrates some of the dangers in treating the major trial as simple spectacle:

> [I] went into where the Supreme Court were in session, to see what had become of Stephen Girard's will, and the scramble of lawyers and collaterals for the fragments of his colossal and misshapen endowment of an infidel-charity school for orphan boys. Webster had just before closed his argument, for which, it is said, if he succeeds, he is to have fifty thousand dollars for his share of the plunder.[38]

Adams' comment is invaluable for what it suggests about the power of the moment—the "colossal" wealth involved, the ensuing "scramble" for lucre, the scandal in Girard's "misshapen" because "infidel-charity," and the antics of the great in Webster's "share of the plunder." These ephemera explain much of the contemporary appeal or why so many nineteenth-century Americans eagerly awaited "what had become of Stephen Girard's will," but these immediacies fail to reach the larger potential of *Girard* as intellectual gauge and cultural determinant.

From the other side, legal historians have concentrated on the applicability of the *Girard* will case as court decision. Recent studies of relevant case law reveal that charity law has developed mostly through state rather than federal jurisdictions and that a greater diversity than previously realized has characterized that development. What then is the practical scope of *Girard*, a federal court decision? The focus on case law privileges direct use, frequency of application, and jurisdictional integrity. Lacking in immediate applications by this standard, *Girard* seems less important than the original outcry over it indicated. It follows that the study of legal applications turns instead for the evolution of charity law to the many jurisdictions that have employed it in different ways.[39] And yet the actual relevance of *Girard* cannot be reached in this manner either.

Missing from the orientation of case law study is precisely that alternative sense of *Girard* as major event. In the American republic of laws, the platform of the Supreme Court and the impact of a major trial form a whole greater than the sum of their parts. *Girard* in 1844 immediately occupied center stage in a far more general debate on the role of charity in American culture—a debate that included a potentially troubling inconsistency over national self-perceptions. The ultimate importance of *Girard* consists in the way that it mediated in civic discourse between belief in an innate American generosity and belief in a self-sustaining American individualism.

The empowering example of Stephen Girard stimulated countless other wealthy donors, and the articulated policy of the case that bears his name ratified corporate, secular, and, above all, private patterns of giving. His example and the legal policy that followed therefrom merge in the idea that self-sustaining individuals will assume the burden as well as the direction of public charity in American society. *Girard* set the course for rich individuals to act as the private trustees of communal giving in what, by the end of the century, would be universally called "the gospel of wealth."[40]

Charitable impulses both reform and protect the status quo. They exact even as they reward, and they reflect structures of power as much as they identify needs and support cultural aspirations. Trials do the same. *Girard*, as perhaps the most visibly contested act of giving in American history, reveals a nation in the act of understanding its own process of change as both a people and a polity. An impressive conflation of private and public communal charity remedies from the early republic fades away in the antebellum period.[41] In its place appears a new pattern in which private decisions structure public endeavors. As others have argued, this control of public action by the private sector is one of the traits that distinguish the modern American experience from that of other western cultures.[42]

Stephen Girard left his enormous fortune to solve the social problem of his choice. He meant well and, characteristically, he did not leave either problems or solutions to others. His devise and the Supreme Court's ratification of it helped to create twin expectations in the increasingly commercial United States. Henceforth, the assumptions would be that other "fortunate" Americans would want to respond to the social problems of their choice in their own way, and that most such problems deserving of charitable attention would be solved by initiatives of this sort either by thoughtful individuals or the corporations in which they served. The hidden premise, not always articulated, was that communal well-being could trust to these arrangements and their private institutions to identify and correct the problems of society while government continued to limit itself to the role of public overseer. Americans live today with the impact of these assumptions. After *Girard*, for better or for worse, the individuals who were best off in American society would determine the problems and the needs most deserving of charitable attention in the community at large, and that orientation remains firmly in place as many social ills spin increasingly out of control at the beginning of the twenty-first century.

CHAPTER TEN

The Last Early Republican Text

What can it mean to call a novel like *The Last of The Mohicans* from 1826 the last early republican text? The question alone raises significant problems. *The Last of the Mohicans* belongs to the beginning, not the end, of James Fenimore Cooper's long career; it is just the sixth of thirty-two novels that Cooper would continue to write through mid-century. Why select a novel to represent an era in which intellectual texts, sermons, pamphlets, public documents, and almanacs were clearly more dominant? Then, too, why mark an era with a demonstrably false claim about disappearing Indians? For while it is true that some forty American novels appear on the theme of the vanishing Indian between 1824 and 1834, Native Americans don't vanish; they are killed or pushed aside and then ignored through Indian removal policies.[1] What importance can one attach to a designation of this kind anyway? How does it help interpretation to have *The Last of the Mohicans* mark the end of an era? Answers to such questions must also deal with recent attacks on the entire concept of periodization as "fatally reductive," "a facile totalization," and, at best, "an essentially problematic part of reading" to be avoided when possible.[2] Why undertake such risks?

There are, to begin, at least seven reasons for making the attempt, and they have the added advantage of reaching toward a general explanation of American culture. *First, The Last of the Mohicans* is a troubled and troubling book in 1826. It is simultaneously Cooper's most popular novel and his bloodiest, cruelest, darkest, most puzzling, and most controversial work. What does the dark appeal of the novel reveal about the nature of an American leadership? *Second*, as the most flexible and innovative genre of the period, the novel turns out to be a peculiarly relevant form for understanding early republican sensibilities. *Third*, Cooper himself is unusually representative of the urgencies of his time. A novelist of ideas, he was obsessed with dramatizing republican culture—more so, in fact, than any other imaginative writer of the age—and he portrays its problems with unusual courage. Where does this courage come from and what form does it take in the forgotten artist as early republican? *Fourth*, the vision of history in *The Last of the Mohicans* is so disturbing in its implications that it still threatens conventional conceptions of the nation. How then can the book have *remained* so popular with so many readers for so long? *Fifth*, there is no better work for examining the vexed but intrinsic relationship between catastrophic event and conceptions of history in American thought. *Sixth*, *The Last of the Mohicans* encourages inquiry into the way that Americans engage in the artifice of understanding history. *Seventh*, the novel is about the failures of its day—failures that American culture still contends with and that define it as much as its more familiar successes. In all of these ways, *The Last of the Mohicans* functions as a seminal text that each generation of readers should approach anew.

That *The Last of the Mohicans* is a vexed work is clear from the many heated debates over interpretation of the novel. Critics continue to argue over the essence of each major character, the many improbabilities that strain the plot, Cooper's views on race and gender, his use of history, the jumble of tragic and comic affects on almost every page, structural problems in the novel, Cooper's depiction of Native Americans, his generic idiosyncrasies, his control over his material, and even over the integrity of the author's design. Inevitably, these same critics rarely agree about the novelist's overall accomplishment. The book has been called an adventure story, a gothic tale, a romance, a historical novel, a comic epic, a mock heroic, a captivity narrative, an allegory, a love story, and a frontier myth.[3] Cooper himself has complicated each of these debates by mixing modes and by refusing to give answers to the philosophical issues that he raises. The first complication of mixed forms reflects a forgotten aesthetic in early republican

imaginative writing, but the second and more interesting, Cooper's refusal to answer ideological dilemmas that he has raised, is symptomatic of a new conception in thought—a conception that contains a direct challenge to conventions in early republican understanding.[4]

Cooper wrote against the grain in 1826, presenting more problems
than answers, and he expected to be misunderstood. The short initial
preface to the novel is full of admonition. It asks only serious readers
to proceed, warning all others "to abandon the design" at the outset.
Those who do persevere must exchange "the four walls of a comfort-
able drawing room" for "shocking" possibilities that might "disturb
their sleep."[5] *The Last of the Mohicans* tells a tale of origins in which
everything of value has already been lost in the woods. There is no relief in the telling, and its author knew as much when, shortly after fin-
ishing it, he abandoned America for seven years of travel in Europe.
Cooper deliberately dramatizes a predicament that his countrymen
have never wanted to face squarely. His book floats the proposition
that history might not be on one's side.

The preface even clarifies why misunderstandings will occur. Em-
phasizing the subtitle that he knew everyone would ignore, *A Narrative of 1757*, Cooper reminds us that his book "is exactly what it pro-
fesses to be in its title-page—a narrative," which is to say that it is not
"an imaginary and romantic picture of things which never had an
existence." *The Last of the Mohicans* depicts the collision between
messy historical fact and the presumed ordering of American destiny
from out of those facts (p. 1). What 1757 imparts to 1826 is Cooper's
real subject, and it is one in which he found alarming discrepancies.
Missing from the early republic were the principles that might clarify
the promise in American experience.[6] By 1834, giving way to despair
over his own search for those principles and preparing to "lay aside
the pen" in consequence, he confessed "I have felt a severe mortification that I am to break down on the question of distinctive American
thought."[7]

Both the presumption of philosophical importance and the despair in
this authorial stance can be traced to the second proposition listed
above: the novelist of the period wrote to preserve republican sensibilities. The affinities at work in this felt obligation are complicated. History emerged as "queen of the disciplines" in early nineteenth-century

thought because its proponents thought that to understand history was to change it. "The history of Mind and the history of Society" were "inextricably linked" with "the destiny of humankind at stake in that union." It followed that an accurate rendering of "a philosophic politics of freedom under law" would lead to communal well-being for all.[8] Of course, even the most optimistic historian had to admit that the dreary annals of politics supplied little support for this vision and that actual history obscured the theory. Enter the novel. The belief that philosophical ideas and social reality could cohere in a vision of progress granted implicit scope to the new genre of the novel because the latter gave "form to what happens to the idea in real life." The novel, as "the necessary epic form" for understanding nineteenth-century culture, allowed its readers to see more clearly what could only be intuited from random events. It accentuated possibilities without destroying a sense of reality.[9]

This essentially European formulation—Enlightenment belief in the human capacity to craft a better future out of the failed past—took on refracted urgency in the early republic. How could Americans use history to escape it? The overwhelming desire for a positive answer brought ideological pressure to bear on the genre of the historical novel. Early republicans knew that history by itself gave little encouragement to the prospect of a long-lasting republic, and many responded with "a kind of national hypochondria which professed to see fatal dangers" on all sides. They were convinced of "the essential fragility of civilization and of its liability to instantaneous and utter destruction."[10] It also seemed that the greater one's knowledge, the greater the alarm. John Adams, writing to Thomas Jefferson in 1812, saw the union as "a brittle China Vase," "a Palace of Glass" easily destroyed.[11] His son John Quincy Adams, who would be president when *The Last of the Mohicans* appeared, gave a more detailed explanation. "Although our complicated machine of two co-ordinate sovereignties has not yet fallen to pieces by its own weakness," he observed as secretary of state in 1822, "it exists in perpetual jeopardy."[12] Neither secular nor religious leaders placed much faith in a permanent republic, and the closest observers of the American scene thought that they already saw signs of decay. Political unrest and open conflict as well as economic and geographic instabilities contributed to the general assumption of frailty and approaching ruin.[13]

Fear within the desire for a long-lasting republic tugged at every American in 1826, and the duty of the responsible citizen was clear.

"We can win no laurels in a war for independence . . . their remains to us a great duty of defence and preservation." Daniel Webster observed, commemorating the Bunker Hill Monument in 1825. But if the duty was great, it was also a holding action that required an answer to the momentums in history. A year later, over the seemingly providential deaths of John Adams and Thomas Jefferson on July 4, 1826, Webster explained how preservation might work for a republican intellectual with the gift of imagination: "The tears which flow, and the honors that are paid when the founders of the republic die, give hope that the republic itself may be immortal."[14]

Webster's close friend Rufus Choate summarized the implications for a novelist like James Fenimore Cooper. The nation needed "a series of romantic compositions" that would "begin with the landing of the Pilgrims, and pass down to the war of Independence, from one epoch and one generation to another." Fiction provided the best vehicle for this project because it responded to the "deficiencies of history" and could "speak directly to the heart and affections and imagination of the whole people." Such writing "would reassemble, as it were, the people of America in one vast congregation," where the alleviation of primal fears would be the main agenda. "I cannot help suggesting," Choate concluded, "at the hazard of being thought whimsical, that a literature of such writings as these, embodying the romance of the whole revolutionary and anti-revolutionary history of the United States, might do *something* to perpetuate the Union itself."[15]

Cooper embraced the spirit of alarm and the duty of preservation voiced by his contemporaries. Neither the passion nor the accomplishment of his fiction can be understood without these twin goals in mind. As he put the national situation himself, "the points of main interest are, whether the present republican institutions of the country will endure, and whether the States will long continue to act as one people, or will submit to be divided into two or more confederacies."[16] A "break up" was most likely "in consequence of a false direction having been given to publick opinion," and Cooper expressed immediate concern. The saving truths of the Revolution were "gradually yielding to a new set of sophisms, more peculiar to the present order of things."[17]

These worries clarified the citizen's duty of defense and preservation, and they gave the writer a mission. The stresses on imagination, on authorial creativity, on the role of the hero in recalling a virtuous past, on the translation of history into fictional epic, on the novel as the ideal genre for conveying the realities in national identity, on the transforming power of literature through mass readerships—these postulates in nineteenth-century romanticism were also Cooper's, and he began by dutifully scanning colonial and revolutionary history in search of relevant material to these ends. He planned thirteen historical novels that would represent each colony on its way to statehood.[18]

Fortunately or unfortunately, something relatively unique for the times happened to Cooper along the way. A more nuanced observer than most of his contemporaries, he quickly recognized a dilemma in coping with Choate's "deficiencies of history." The closer he looked, the less he found of a virtuous past that might guide the nation. Instead of a shining touchstone for the present, the past of *The Last of the Mohicans* supplies a series of appalling cautionary tales. Philosophically, the present *becomes* the past, only more impoverished because of the mistakes made back then. Fearful for the republic, Cooper is courageous enough to see history for what it is, a series of contingencies made worse by blunder after blunder. His novel depicts the unknowing birth of a new nation through the failures that made it possible, and he allows the acute reader to share a larger realization; more failures, similar to those from before, were going to occur anytime and in any place.

The Last of the Mohicans uses the historical record of mistakes from 1757 to catalogue cultural fear in all of its ramifications. With a "scene of strife and bloodshed" in colonial affairs as his initial canvas, an omniscient narrator opens the story by connecting "unexpected disaster" and "a thousand fanciful and imagined dangers" to the sudden appearance of "more substantial evils." This accumulation of distress leads to increasingly visible patterns of cultural panic: "the magnifying influence of fear began to set at naught the calculations of reason" (pp. 12–13). In what follows, neither reasoned discourse nor straight shooting alters matters, even though there is plenty of both from Natty Bumppo, who is first fully realized as the frontier hero here in the second leatherstocking tale. Fear, always the dominant emotion, reigns until the very end of the novel, when apprehensions of defeat and failure are realized on every level. Cooper, in the words of one critic, "gives us not the rising glory of America but the universal tears of things," but the philosophy of his narrative promises even

worse than that.[19] The novelist relentlessly ties each positive to a negative. Manifestly, the rising glory of America already contains the
premise of tears. The tragic ending of *The Last of the Mohicans* reveals what will happen again and again in the momentary rise and
certain fall of civilizations.[20]

History in the end levels everything and everyone, and Cooper's interest in that problem leads him to construct *The Last of the Mohicans*
around the theme of catastrophe. Two catastrophes in particular
dominate the action, and they can be used to explain the complicated
relationship between structure and plot in the novel. The first major
calamity, which also supplies Cooper's subtitle, plays off of a real colonial event from August 10, 1757: the mass slaughter of defenseless
British soldiers and American civilians, including women and children, by Huron Indians when the British and Americans exited from
Fort William Henry on Lake George under a flag of truce during the
French and Indian War. Cooper makes this traumatic historical event
the centerpiece of his book. His main account of it falls exactly in the
middle of the seventeenth of thirty-three chapters, and, in the first edition of two volumes, his two gruesome descriptions of the massacre
end the first volume and open the second. A related decision, putting
the year 1757 in the subtitle (*A Narrative of 1757*), carefully height-
ens the conceptual importance of the event for those first readers in
1826, every one of whom would have immediately thought of "the
bloody and inhuman scene . . . conspicuous in the pages of colonial
history" known by "the merited title of 'The massacre of William
Henry'" (p. 180). One of two benchmarks in Anglo-American condemnations of Indian ways, the other being the scalping of Jane
McCrea in 1777, the massacre shaped early republican assumptions
about Native American culture.[21]

The second catastrophe in the novel, a fictional projection from the
first, revolves around the capture and attempted rescue of two half-
sisters, both daughters of British Colonel George Munro, the commander who surrenders Fort William Henry to his French counterpart, the Marquis de Montcalm. The frontier guide Natty Bumppo,
also known as Hawk-eye, and his Indian companions, Chingachgook
and Uncas, father and son and the last of the Mohicans, struggle to recover the sisters, Cora and Alice Munro, from their Huron captors,

the leader of whom, Magua, has sworn eternal vengeance against Colonel Munro for having Magua whipped over a minor infraction. Final catastrophe, a refashioned version of the death of Jane McCrea, arrives in the eventual murder of Cora Munro and of Uncas, last of the Mohicans, in his attempts to save her. Critics have noted convenience in the death of Cora, the dark heroine whose Creole mother figures her as ethnically black, while the completely white Alice is reserved for marriage to Colonel Munro's aristocratic subordinate, Major Duncan Heyward. Even so, neither his squeamishness over miscegenation, nor the racial construct of Euro-Indian relations, nor the constraints of class behavior—often discussed—hinder Cooper's deeper preoccupation with the role of disaster in designs of history.

The careful arrangement of the two catastrophes is particularly important because they work in sequence to rob the world of the novel of meaning. As the first catastrophe, the massacre of Fort William Henry, leads the author to remove his five male protagonists from the event in order to protect them from aspersions of cowardice and futility—a maneuver that is as awkward and artificial as it is unexplained—so the second, the murder of Cora and its consequences, destroys all sense of philosophical futurity. Cooper's heroes—Hawk-eye, Chingachgook, Uncas, and Heyward—are all left without meaningful progeny at novel's end. As Hawk-eye expresses this problem to Chingachgook, "I have no kin, and I may also say, like you, no people" (pp. 348–349). Children are regularly destroyed in *The Last of the Mohicans,* every parent is deprived of at least one child, and mothers die or are already dead. Every affirmation is tied and then lost in the complex character of Cora Munro.

Cooper's account of the massacre of Fort William Henry, while true to the historical sources known to him, reaches for heightened affect.[22] The descriptive powers of the novelist substantiate and then augment an already powerful negative response at large in early republican culture:

Death was every where, and in his most terrific and disgusting aspects. Resistance only served to inflame the murderers, who inflicted their furious blows long after their victims were beyond the power of their resentment. The flow of blood might be likened to the outbreaking of a torrent; and as the natives became heated and maddened by the sight, many among them even kneeled to the earth, and drank freely, exultingly, hellishly, of the crimson tide. (p. 181)

More is at stake in this description than slaughter and death. Just before the massacre, Cooper has described a world of contrasting beauty in which "all that pertained to nature was sweet, or simply grand; while those parts which depended on the temper and movement of man were lively and playful" (p. 150). The massacre changes nature itself. Three days after the actual massacre, Cooper returns to it:

> The sun had hid its warmth behind an impenetrable mass of vapour, and hundreds of human forms, which had blackened beneath the fierce heats of August, were stiffening in their deformity, before the blasts of a premature November. . . .
>
> . . . here and there, a dark green tuft rose in the midst of the desolation; the earliest fruits of a soil that had been fattened with human blood. The whole landscape, which, seen by a favouring light, and in a genial temperature, had been found so lovely, appeared now like some pictured allegory of life, in which objects were arranged in their harshest but truest colors, and without the relief of any shadowing.
>
> The solitary and arid blades of grass arose from the passing gusts fearfully perceptible; the bold and rocky mountains were too distinct in their barrenness, and the eye sought relief, in vain, by attempting to pierce the illimitable void of heaven. . . .
>
> [A few hungry ravens] gladly stooped at random to their hideous banquet. In short, it was the scene of wildness and desolation; and it appeared as if all who had profanely entered it, had been stricken, at a blow, by the relentless arm of death. (pp. 181–182)

Cooper's first view of nature in its bounty and sweetness may not have been exactly an apparition, but a deeper reality pertains to these blackened and increasingly indistinguishable bodies. Here is the more accurate "allegory of life." "The relentless arm of death" has come to all and paints life in its "harshest but truest colors." Notably, the word "harshest" is much easier to accept and apply in this description than "truest." What does it mean to say that the massacre presents life in its "truest colors"? To respond to this question is to explain why Cooper brings the Massacre of Fort William Henry out of the past of 1757, giving it new life sixty-nine years later in the present of 1826. Why, we must ask, has Cooper made this horrible event the linchpin of his novelistic concern?

The only good answer to these questions is a devastating one. The massacre is where "the God-forsakenness of the world reveals itself."[23] What does Cooper tell us through his description of the massacre? He tells us that heaven has become an "illimitable void," that the world in its "barrenness" is suddenly "fearfully perceptible," that uncaring nature feeds and grows on the banquet of human failure, that the human eye can expect no relief from either the recognition or the consequences of its insight. Philosophically speaking, one does not need a massacre to learn this lesson. Cooper makes the same essential point earlier in the novel through a famous set description of Glenn's Falls. The passage in question is often summoned to explain Cooper's understanding of the sublime, but it can be used just as usefully to convey the gravity of his pessimism. "[L]ook at the perversity of the water!," exclaims Hawk-eye, Cooper's keenest observer of the natural world, "It falls by no rule at all . . . as if, having broke loose from order, it would try its hand at everything." "And yet what does it amount to!," he concludes. "After the water has been suffered to have its will, for a time, like a headstrong man, it is gathered together by the hand that made it, and a few rods below you may see it all, flowing on steadily towards the sea" (p. 55). Nature, much like history, levels meaning and human distinction in the long view of things.

If the scene of massacre appears more important ideologically than studied contemplation of the waterfall, it is because the former renders an intolerable truth more terribly available and inescapable. A viewer may withdraw into the beauty and majesty of a waterfall, but there is no avenue of psychological retreat from the horror of the massacre. Cooper also fixes us to the sticking point through the structure of his presentation. Catastrophes take on historical definition only through survivors who must come to grips with what has happened; they convey the horror by making it known. Those who remain must somehow classify the event *within* life. As survivors, they are the keepers of history. A participant acts and falls under disaster; those who witness give it shape and meaning, and therein lies the genius in Cooper's doubled description of the massacre. The first description gives us the necessary action; the second, in which wolves will be heard munching on the dead, solidifies the reader's perception through the survivors' points of view.

Cooper handles this process of *naming* catastrophe through a catalogue. He objectifies his heroes into "the forms of five men" who arrive on the scene "an hour before the setting sun." Significantly, each form has a different reaction ("as different as the characters") to what it sees. Colonel Munro groans aloud, searching for his daughters among the dead; Duncan Heyward shudders in sympathy with his companion; Uncas steps lightly, "afraid to exhibit his feelings" except through "furtive glances at the mangled victims"; Chingachgook, already war-painted as the symbol of death, passes with "a steadiness of purpose" born of "inveterate practice"; Hawk-eye, bringing up the rear, responds in bitterness with thoughts of revenge. Still, and in every instance, Cooper gives us the form rather than the named character: "One, whose gray locks and furrowed lineaments, blending with a martial air," "The young man at his elbow," "The youth in front," "His red associate," and "the straggler" (p. 182).

The reader knows who these figures have to be from earlier descriptions, but Cooper insists on his abstract types for a reason; he uses the device to underline the logical range of reactions to catastrophe. We move from the agony of personal tragedy, to empathy with that tragic figure, to avoidance, to the stoicism of heartless experience, and on to thoughts of revenge. And yet a singularity of reaction encompasses all. For each type the question remains the same. Who or what can explain, much less justify, the loss of innocent life on such a massive and oppressive scale?

All of this is preparation. The ultimate presentation of catastrophe and its connection to history comes through Cooper's second calamity, and this one is manufactured entirely by the novelist. Why does Cooper murder Cora Munro? His dark heroine represents not only the hope of history but, more narrowly, the only articulated answer to the vicious circles of time and plot in *The Last of the Mohicans.* Critics who have argued that Cooper necessarily prefers the "light sister," Alice, to the "darker" Cora through the traditional patterns of epic romance have done author and novel a disservice. The first two Leatherstocking tales, *The Pioneers* and *The Last of the Mohicans,* privilege the so-called dark lady as the center of energy, attention, and dramatic value.[24] Cora, in the latter, is Cooper's pearl beyond price. He eliminates her at novel's end not in recognition of social decorum or racial prudishness, though one can find both in the novel, but in search of the same kind of philosophical truth that leads Shakespeare to eliminate Cordelia or Herman Melville to kill Billy Budd. Through the death of Cora, "Cooper shapes his plot to comment most tellingly on the America to come."[25]

Cora takes her name from the Latin *cor* or *cordis,* meaning "heart, mind, judgment," and *cordi esse* ("to be pleasing"). She is all of these things, and as such, she offers both the best judgment and literally the pumping heart of the novel in thematic and structural terms. The constitutive metaphor of *The Last of the Mohicans* is blood. The word appears at least ninety-five times: blood spilled, blood mixed, blood without a cross, blood relation, blood pollution, blood curses, blood curdled, blood rising, blood bursting, blood flowing freely, blood running in torrents, bloodthirstiness, and blood actually drunk.[26] Cora supplies the one positive frame of reference for the metaphor through her stunning complexion, which is "charged with the color of the rich blood, that seemed ready to burst its bounds" (p. 19). Her beauty, courage, and integrity attract all other characters, and she affords the one opportunity for cleansing the world of the novel of polluting hatred and racist constructs, both of which are figured repeatedly in blood. All action and emotional nuance circulate through her centrality to Cooper's captivity narrative and the ensuing failure to rescue her.[27]

Cooper leaves nothing to chance in his validation of Cora Munro. He renders his dark heroine worthy by contrasting her many virtues to the "infantile dependency" and consistent weakness of her blonde sister, Alice, who cries, panics, and faints away in every scene of crisis in the novel. Cooper highlights Cora's own reservoirs of courage, nobility, and resolve most clearly in chapter eleven. Here, in the one moment where Alice must make a decision, Cora has to wait "in painful suspense" to discover whether or not Alice is willing to make anything like the same sacrifice for her half-sister that Cora makes instantly and constantly throughout the novel for Alice (pp. 80, 108–110).

Cora's importance also transcends gender considerations. She emerges as the most compassionate and intellectually resourceful character in the book. A paragon of courage, sacrifice, and Christian faith, she alone refuses to judge others in racial terms (pp. 21, 53). She alone remains undisturbed when Hawk-eye and others react superstitiously to a wild cry in the night (pp. 59, 62). She alone devises the escape plan for Hawk-eye and his Indian companions from the cave at Glenn's Falls (p. 78). She alone acknowledges the unfair punishment by her father in whipping her nemesis, Magua, for the minor offense of drunkenness (pp. 103–104). She even asks "penitence and pardon" for Magua in christological terms as he prepares to torture her: "he . . . knows not what he does" (p. 108).

Cooper thinks so well of Cora Munro that he allows her the one philosophical affirmation of the novel. In the final confrontation between Anglo-American and Native American views in the Delaware camp, Cora stands forth, "a beauteous and breathing model of her sex," but she is considerably more than that. The model for everyone, she challenges "the evil of the world" on both sides. Those capable of seeing through that evil, she proclaims, "should know how to temper its calamities to the miserable" (p. 303). Moreover, the special significance that contemporary readers assigned to Cora's speech in 1827 can be seen in the Hudson River artist Thomas Cole's decision to portray it on a vast canvas as *Cora Kneeling at the Feet of Tamenund*, the single most famous illustration from the many painted of the leatherstocking tales. In Cole's two renditions of the same scene, Cora appears at the center of two vast circles, first, a darkened ring of watching Native Americans and, beyond, the surrounding mountains. She is kneeling and dwarfed but easily distinguished by her raised hands and brilliant white dress, the gesture of prayer and the color of hope.[28]

The dark lady, as many have noted, also embodies the sexual anxiety of miscegenation and the related fear of cultural assimilation at a time when both are becoming stricter taboos in America.[29] Mostly white but also black, Cora acts out these problems, caught between Uncas and Magua, the good and bad Indians. At the same time, she represents the possibility of joining all three races together in the promise of a strange but exciting vitality. As Tamenund, the Delaware chieftain, reasons with Cora when he leaves her to Magua in obedience to Indian law, "Girl, what wouldst thou! A great warrior takes thee to wife. Go—thy race will not end" (p. 313). Meanwhile, the attraction between Cora and Uncas, subtly apparent from the beginning, is celebrated in their final funeral (pp. 53, 56, 343). Neither figure can actively choose, and Cora's actual decision of death over life with Magua hardly betokens an American "ideal of self-determination."[30] Nonetheless, Cora always knows her own mind, and the world of the novel is impoverished, even bereft, without it.

Cooper engages in possibilities more than he declares certainties. He arranges his novel of ideas around paired opposites: not just the light lady and the dark lady, but also the good Indian against the bad (Uncas and Magua), the psalmist of revival religion against the worshipper of nature (David Gamut and Natty Bumppo), the gentleman warrior against the backwoods hunter (Duncan Heyward and Hawk-eye), the natural philosopher against his Native American counterpart (Hawk-eye and Chingachgook), and so on. Each member of a pairing gains moments of ascendancy within the contrast, a dynamic that begets ideological predicaments without resolution. At issue in these exchanges are the questions of social justice between Euro-Americans and Native Americans, racial stereotyping, and the misunderstandings that reduce the world of the novel to a scene of horror.

Creativity lies in the manipulation of "starkly opposed cultural types," as "elements of thought" in philosophical exchange.[31] Cooper never hesitates to give the seemingly negative side of a pairing the upper hand for ideological reasons. Magua, the villain of the novel, wins every debate over Native American rights and Euro-American intrusions upon them (pp. 102–103, 300–302); the ineffective Duncan Heyward nonetheless stops Hawk-eye from unnecessary killing (pp. 209–210); David Gamut, a comic figure, refutes Hawkeye's quest for vengeance (pp. 273–274). Hawk-eye, the most racist speaker in the book, still corrects Duncan Heyward's own tendencies in that direction, reminding everyone that stereotypes about Native Americans flow out of the injustice done to them: "you have driven their tribes from the seashore, and would now believe what their enemies say, that you may sleep at night upon an easy pillow" (p. 50). Readers who read closely find themselves forced beyond the conventional wisdom of their day. Cooper resists customary celebrations of republican virtue as a beacon to others.[32] His goal is not affirmation but reflection. *The Last of the Mohicans* is all about loss, and the deeper levels of that loss remain to be plumbed.

The one certainty in Cooper's clash of alternatives is declension for all concerned. No one is better off at novel's end. Cora Munro, in this sense, symbolizes the philosophical hopelessness of the novel. The mediating woman of many possibilities, she is at once the element that everyone fights over and the only value or asset available to help stop the fighting.[33] Twice in *The Last of the Mohicans*, all other White captives may go free if Cora accepts life with Magua, and in the second instance Magua rejects a king's ransom in order to hold her (pp. 108–110, 313–314). In the massacre of Fort William Henry, Magua carries off the passive, unresisting Alice only because he knows that the very active and more desirable Cora will follow (p. 178) and that her struggles would be too much for him. At Cora's funeral, in a deliberate irony on racist constructs, Indian maidens announce again her unmatched worth: "That she was of a blood purer and richer than the rest of her nation, any eye might have seen" (p. 343). Cooper makes it hard to quarrel with this assessment. Cora in death leaves only sorrow with cycling hatred and revenge in her wake. Nor is that all. The prominent keeper of these continuing cycles is a stunning one.

Hawk-eye, the paragon of the novel, is unmistakably the agent as well as the guiding spirit of hatred and death in *The Last of the Mohicans*. To fully comprehend this point it helps first to think of the changes in the character of Leatherstocking from novel to novel. Natty Bumppo in his first incarnation plays the role of an aged environmentalist who kills only for food in *The Pioneers* (1823). He turns into something of a pacifist in *The Prairie* (1827), and a romanticized Adamic hero in *The Pathfinder* (1840) and *The Deerslayer* (1841), but in *The Last of the Mohicans* from 1826 he is exactly what D. H. Lawrence has so famously called him: "hard, isolate, stoic, and a killer."[34] Hawk-eye, the very name denoting the focus of a predator, kills at least ten times in *The Last of the Mohicans*. He enjoys it, and he would kill more but for the intervention of others. His battle cry encapsulates his perspective: "Extarminate the varlets! no quarter to an accursed Mingo!" (p. 112).

The thinking man behind these actions is, if anything, a more chilling specimen. Hawk-eye longs for "the beauty" of war in a "secret love of desperate adventure . . . necessary to the enjoyment of his existence" (pp. 210, 228). "[I] have followed the trail of blood for weary miles," he boasts in extracting revenge (p. 183). His rifle "kill-deer," which his enemies know him by and which he proudly names the most dangerous weapon on the frontier, has killed a living body on every square mile in the territory (pp. 111, 205, 209, 314, 136). Here, too, killing reduces the killer. Like the savages he fights, Hawk-eye continues to slay after his victims are dead: "the honest, but implacable scout, made the circuit of the dead, into whose senseless bosoms he thrust his long knife, with as much coolness as though they had been so many brute carcasses" (p. 114). Like them as well, he has polluted the lake water with blood in a massacre that he has led (pp. 135–136). This Indian killer of *The Last of the Mohicans* lives by values that other renditions of the Leatherstocking character eschew. When, for example, Magua makes an offer that will save Cora— "Will the 'long rifle' give his life for the woman?"—the calculating

warrior responds. "No, no; I have not said so much as that," Hawk-
eye replies calmly, "drawing back, with suitable discretion." And the
reason is clear. "It would be an unequal exchange, to give a warrior, in
the prime of his age and usefulness, for the best woman on the frontiers" (p. 314). Cora *is* "the best woman on the frontiers" and more,
but Hawk-eye's fighting mentality undermines her value in this situation.

There is a simple but twofold philosophy behind these thoughts
and actions. On the one hand, Natty Bumppo blames providence.
He has been hardened because "blown upon by the Heavens in their
anger" (p. 208). On the other hand, he knows that humankind so
treated is responsible for its own mayhem and that it falls to its lowest
common denominator when threatened. "When men struggle for the
single life God has given them," Hawk-eye explains, "even their own
kind seem no more than the beasts of the wood" (p. 47). Appropriately enough, Natty becomes that beast of the wood in his final act of
killing. As he levels his rifle at Magua for the last time, he appears
"crouched like a beast about to take its spring." His only worry at
this moment is a telling one. Hawk-eye's trembling eagerness to kill is
the only thing that might spoil his always perfect aim (p. 338).

The story of *The Last of the Mohicans* is so awful in narrative detail and philosophical implication that no modern rendition has ever
dared to convey it as written. There have been at least ten films, three
plays, one opera, two television series, nine comic books, two ani-
mated cartoons, and two radio shows based on the story. To take only
the two best known, the first, a 1936 film by Philip Dunne, a star vehicle for Randolph Scott, stresses the capacity for noble sacrifice on the
part of the conventional frontier hero; the second, a more recent attempt to film the novel, claiming greater historical authenticity, is Michael Mann's *The Last of the Mohicans* from 1992, starring Daniel
Day-Lewis. Here, Natty Bumppo, now called Nathaniel, is a communal leader and proto-Revolutionary figure who kills only in self-de-
fense and to save Cora Munro (Madeleine Stowe), whom he loves and
successfully wins for himself. The themes of miscegenation and assimilation are safely dropped from the film, with Uncas reduced to more
of a supporting role. Alice Munro, still the light sister but modern-
ized, commits suicide to avoid the clutches of Magua. Just as conve-

niently, Duncan Heyward, now a malevolent figure who loves Cora instead of Alice, is killed by his rival, Nathaniel, but only to save Heyward from the pain that he is enduring from final torture at the stake. Those characters whom Cooper saves (Colonel Munro, Alice Munro, and Duncan Heyward), Mann destroys, and vice versa. Cooper kills Cora to make his largest point; Mann saves her for Hawkeye. Perhaps most incongruously of all, Magua, still the villain, seeks not revenge but his own share of the material wealth that he sees in British America.

Even Cooper withdraws from the sharper edges of his conception in the remaining leatherstocking tales. Not for the first time a writer seems to have created better than he knew or could tolerate for long. Yet the tale as written, despite a philosophical pessimism not generally found or accepted in American culture, is the one that most readers appreciate and remember. Why have so many booklovers so readily embraced a story with such negative ramifications?[35] Our preliminary answer has emphasized a recovery that welds the present of 1826 to the past of 1757 in quest of a meaningful future. Uncas, the most confident figure in the novel, puts this anxiety over futurity succinctly. "Our eyes are on the rising, and not towards the setting sun!" he exclaims as his true identity is revealed in the Delaware camp, "We know whence he comes, but we know not whither he goes" (p. 311). But these insights carry us only so far in gauging the continuing popularity of the novel.

To complete Cooper's act of recuperation, to capture the vitality and lasting resonance in his agonized uses of history, we must return to the half-knowing artist as early republican who was living on the edge of intellectual transitions. Caught between the requirements placed on the willing citizen and the very different needs of his novelistic craft, Cooper responded by yoking two very different perceptions of history to the artifice of making sense of his world. *The Last of the Mohicans* takes the puzzle of an evolving national history as its sub-theme, and it is not too much to suggest that Cooper's conflicting conceptions of that theme appealed, then and now, to very specific American hopes and fears.

The first conception of history that informs *The Last of the Mohicans* comes directly and conventionally from the early republican classical tradition. To the extent that Cooper wrote within this frame of reference, he thought of history as mediate. The essential premise, which he shared with most early republican intellectuals, presupposed that if you asked the right questions through historical inquiry you could prevent mistakes and improve upon the present. Belief in progress meant that history was full of answers. History itself was an ordered phenomenon and part of a larger design. Most early republicans took these assumptions on faith and used them to believe that history was—or wanted to be—on their side. They searched the past for direction, and used what they found to build an ideology of progressive republicanism. Moreover, the idea of a prefigured destiny, whether manifest or implicit, transposed all of their ideas directly into a national rhetoric where it remains to this day. In context, the positive answer that a Jeffersonian republican like Cooper could expect from observing history involved enlightened rule for the people by virtuous and informed governors. Had not history shown as much? Ideal leaders, exemplified in the generation of the founders, could provide good government and a free society for a virtuous people.

But where were those leaders in America in 1826? The founders were gone, and their replacements seemed lesser men. This concern about lost leaders dominates the novel. In *The Last of the Mohicans*, Cooper supplies an ideal leader (but only for a future that never comes) in Uncas, the youthful warrior as last of the Mohicans; his death presages the end of the Delaware nation. Uncas leads, however briefly, through the qualities of his noble character; it is not what he says that allows him to rule but rather who he is. Totally ineffective in speech in the great confrontation with his own Delaware people, Uncas manages only to antagonize the people who seek his real identity. His voice is indeed a powerful key. "What voice is at his ear!," exclaims the aged Delaware chieftain Tamenund in expression of a central republican wish. "Have the winters gone backward! Will summer come again to the children of the Lenape!" But Uncas's actual words lead him to the stake. He extricates himself only because of the awe-inspiring tattoo of the turtle on his chest in identification of his lineage as the one who "upholds the earth" from out of "the grandfather of nations." (p. 307–310).

By way of contrast, his foil and the man who kills him, Magua the Huron, represents a false leadership from below, the kind of ruler who persuades entirely through "eloquence and cunning' (p. 281). Cooper is endlessly explicit about Magua's "fatal and artful eloquence" and "his fame as an orator," an art that he has developed into a unique power by joining his own natural Native American elo-quence to the deceitful manifestations of English speech (pp. 102–103, 175, 249, 280–283, and 287). Symbol of the dangers apparent in demagogic oratory, Magua gains illicit control "by flattering the self-love of his auditors; a never-failing method of commanding atten-tion" (p. 282). He represents an emerging "democratic personality," and it is noteworthy that the Huron tribes he leads, the most demo-cratic of peoples in *The Last of the Mohicans,* lose all control and be-have the worst when their leader fails them.[36] Cooper's application to 1826 is an obvious one. Magua provides the textbook case of the demagogue corrupting a republic. He dupes the people by telling each faction what it wants to hear, gaining a momentary popularity until he becomes "in truth, their ruler." Once that happens, Cooper warns, "no monarch could be more despotic." By the end of the novel, Magua has swollen into something larger than life, "the Prince of Darkness, brooding on his own fancied wrongs, and plotting evil" (pp. 282–284).

The theme of ideal leadership as an ordering device for both the citizen and the writer can hardly be overstated.[37] Early republicans viewed history through personalities and recent history through their founders. The inevitability of the theme and the top-down perspective that it engendered appealed to the novelist for other reasons. Cooper was hardly alone in feeling that the bland quotidian of democratic life could never interest a readership. "There are no annals for the histo-rian;" he complained, "no follies (beyond the most vulgar and com-monplace) for the satirist; no manners for the dramatist; no obscure fictions for the writer of romance; no gross and hardy offences against decorum for the moralist; nor any of the rich artificial auxiliaries of poetry."[38] Only the founders in their national story could be counted on to hold the attention of large numbers. Cooper, by way of explana-tion, notes that an ordinary leather bucket at Mount Vernon lacks all "dignity" until it is noticed that "the words 'Geo. Washington' are legibly written on it in white paint"; then it becomes "distinct, iso-lated, and almost endowed with the attributes of the human form." So endowed, the bucket brings blood to the heart and tears to the eyes. Cooper always knew he needed that "white paint."[39]

Not surprisingly, then, the absence of good leaders creates most of the problems in *The Last of the Mohicans.* In proving "the imbecil-ity" and "fatal want of energy" in all colonial administrators, Cooper catalogues each individual's failures in painstaking detail (p. 12). The British General Daniel Webb "betrayed" the garrison at Fort William Henry on Lake George under Colonel George Munro by refusing to send reinforcements against the besieging French army under the Marquis de Montcalm (p. 164). Colonial Munro, for his part, has foolishly incurred the enmity of Montcalm's Huron allies by punishing their leader, Magua, for a minor offense (pp. 20–21,102–103), and his subordinate, Major Duncan Heyward, acts even more foolishly in the events that follow.[40] From the other side, the French Commander Montcalm is "deficient in that moral courage, without which no man can be truly great" when he fails to protect the surrendered garrison under its flag of truce and leaves defenseless men, women, and children to be slaughtered by his Indian allies (p. 180). Finally, Cooper's last major leader in the novel, the once-wise but now half-senile Delaware Sage Tamenund, makes decisions that destroy Cora and Uncas (pp. 312–317).

Even so, there is a measure in these kinds of failures; they belong to a history with answers. The Massacre of Fort William Henry and the murder of Cora Munro occur because of compound deficiencies in leadership. Catastrophe thereby enters the domain of reason. Any observer can see that mistakes have been made, that blame can be assigned, and that measures can be taken to prevent a recurrence. Conversely, just as poor leadership causes breakdown, so proper leadership produces right social conduct in the name of a larger order. The good citizen always knows how to behave in Cooper's fiction. Thus Natty Bumppo can ridicule the bumbling of the Virginia patrician Duncan Heyward while in the woods, but, when they are gathered together in the great Delaware council where everyone's fate is about to be decided, Cooper tells a different story. Here, the unlettered woodsman has "placed himself a little in the rear, with a deference to the superior rank of his companions" (p. 312). Decorum in the citizen reflects an order in history. Deep in the wilderness, Cooper's characters remain chess pieces on the game board of a polite society based on proper hierarchy, and the good players always accept their appropriate roles.

The problem, of course, is that disaster and decorum don't go together. Even as he perfects his choreography of social propriety and political station, the writer is forced toward a far more contingent conception of history. Sooner or later catastrophe on the scale of Cooper's interests swallows every available formality. The characters in *The Last of the Mohicans* have been tied to a level of disaster that their behavior and understanding cannot handle. When Cooper removes his heroes from the Massacre of Fort William Henry, literally lifting all of them out of the novel for that time, he admits that they are insufficient for the nature of the event. An unavoidable conclusion follows: it is not enough to look for Washingtons or even the absence of Washingtons to explain history. Certain occurrences cut across conventional understandings. Cooper never loses interest in the construct of the noble leader, but he learns as he writes that the value placed on personalities and individual influence is not enough to explain his art even to himself. Somewhere in the process of composition, the novel in his hands takes on philosophical dimensions of its own. Slowly but surely his monody on catastrophe brings him face to face with "the terror in history."[41]

The novelist, to his credit, doesn't flinch from the prospect. Instead, he takes his story to the very brink of lost meanings. He can do so because his narrative device of choice, allegory, gives form to chaos through a simulacrum or semblance. The Indian world of *The Last of the Mohicans* functions as a primary locus of concern (the fall of Indian civilization), triggering reflection on a secondary but much more threatening possibility (the potential collapse of republican culture).[42] Magua, as the demagogic orator who overthrows a democratic regime, supplies only the most obvious of many parallels designed to put early republicans on notice.

The Indian world of the novel destroys itself when it loses sight of previous harmonies and balances. These losses speak directly to national fears in 1826 about immigration and sectional strife. In Cooper's narrative, foreign intrusion and divergences in Indian languages have exacerbated tribal differences and magnified regional hatreds to the point where Indian confusedly strikes Indian as in the biblical fall of Babel.[43] Magua, the most effective Indian linguist, can barely pronounce the name of his chief enemy, Uncas, and the wholesale proliferation of names for each character leads to further confusion in communication (pp. 91, 287). Cooper means to show that no unifying leader can possibly succeed in a spiraling pattern of cultural disintegration. There are no solutions. The rationales that might end conflict become less and less clear as the fighting remnants destroy more and more of the fabric of their society. The Indians of *The Last of the*

Mohicans have lost the very world in which their reasons for shedding blood made sense.

The primary level in Cooper's allegory, this Indian story, is so useful because it provides a relatively safe cautionary tale for translation into republican concerns. By 1826, Euro- Americans, particularly in the Northeastern base of Cooper's readership, regarded the tragedy of Native American culture with a mixture of remembered trauma and indulgent sympathy. Cooper relies on this tepid level of engagement, but his skill lies in forcing his readers beyond it. *The Last of the Mohicans* succeeds so well because it converts a linear approach to the Indian problem into more troubling philosophical planes of investigation. Realizing that allegory works best by encouraging a play between levels, Cooper uses the strategy to create a vision in the crossovers between levels, and his key crossover comes predictably through the central pairing in the novel. He begins by making a white man and an Indian permanent companions with opposing characteristics. Hawk-eye is a killer with a point; Chingachgook, who has painted his body in "a terrific emblem of death," is instead a killing machine (p. 29). As the first represents the meaning of history, so the second stands for its chaos. Significantly, constant cooperation between these two characters only highlights the contrasts between them. The result is an intrinsic level of crossover between cultures and concepts, and Cooper makes sure that it is a crossover from which there is no escape.

The ultimate problem in history can best be seen in an episode that ends in unspeakable horror and guilt for all concerned (pp. 136–139). As Hawk-eye and his Mohican companions guide Duncan Heyward with Cora and Alice Munro through enemy lines toward Fort William Henry early in the novel, they are challenged by a French sentry on the edge of a dark pond (pp. 136–139). Duncan and Cora successfully fool "the young soldier," a friendly and sympathetic figure, "a gay, young boy," by addressing him in French. Cora, in particular, puts the youth off guard by entering into sophisticated banter, making him "her friend," and praising "the character of men of war" to get by him. Cooper the adventure novelist could have let matters rest there in terms of plot, but the man of ideas has deeper interests. This more profound side of Cooper wants to involve every social level in a tragic denouement. Accordingly, the unsuspecting sentry bursts into song— "long life to wine and love"—only to have his own life cut short in mid-verse by Chingachgook, who tomahawks and scalps him on the spot before dumping the dying man into water suddenly "awakened from the silence of creation."

The death of the sentry, conveyed through his horrendous groans, is a gratuitous one at every level of concern, and all of Cooper's white heroes and heroines are complicit in the murder when Chingachgook, "gliding out of the thicket" attaches "the reeking scalp of the unfortunate young Frenchman to his girdle." The darkened pond furnishes "a frightful memorial of the deed of blood they had just witnessed" and the group casts "furtive glances at its appalling dreariness." All form and decorum are meaningless in this moment. There can be no justification, only rapid movement away. "Enough!" cries Heyward, as Hawk-eye tries to explain. As much as possible of what has happened must be left behind. The rest is transit: "all that passing and gloomy scene," the now hideous pond, "melted in the darkness, and became blended with the mass of black objects in the rear of the travelers."

It is difficult to summarize Cooper's purposes here because they are so bleak. A different kind of historical recognition is clearly at work where "the inner most terms, the most deeply ingrained categories with which, and not about which, one thinks" have led to "a radical change" in the questions posed.[44] Cooper understands that something has gone seriously wrong. How to explain it is another matter. The perspective that he encourages in the episode of the French sentry is not far from Walter Benjamin's angel of history, where the face of a figure with outstretched wings is turned to the past as the wind of time propels him backward into the future. Instead of perceiving a chain of events or progress, the angel of history sees only "one single catastrophe which keeps piling wreckage upon wreckage and hurls it in front of his feet."[45] The melting darkness with the mass of black objects in the wake of travelers who go forward while looking behind them is where Cooper leaves us. The torment in his position is made clear by two facts brought out in dialogue. Chingachgook is the one character to feel no guilt in this situation, and, as Hawk-eye notes, his companion has done nothing wrong ("tis the gift and natur of an Indian"). In other words, either no one or everyone is to blame for what has happened, and either alternative is terrible.

Cooper continues to probe. He compounds this problem of meaning through the ongoing pairing of his two killers. Hawk-eye, who hits everything he aims at and always acts with strict honesty in mind, stands for the proposition that the true American is a straight shooter, and this perspective, based upon pride in his skills, allows him to find meaning on every trail that he follows.[46] Chingachgook, on the other hand, is named Big Serpent because he "understands the windings and turnings of human nature" better than others, and he finds only death and mutual destruction in his path (p. 57). What Chingachgook says at the beginning he still believes at the end. "I am on the hill-top," he tells Hawk-eye in his first appearance, "and must go down into the valley [of death]" (p. 33). The metaphor changes but not the speaker's meaning at the last: "I am a blazed pine, in a clearing of the pale-faces" (p. 349). Natty's protests against the philosophical pessimism of his companion are noticeably lame ones. "Every thing," he tries to answer, "depends on what scale you look at things" (p. 32).

Alas, no scale can ever help Chingachgook, and the ultimate scale confirms a more dreadful truth about the man who finally, poignantly, and ironically carries the eponymous title, last of the Mohicans. In the next cycle of history, already written by Cooper in *The Pioneers* (1823), the renowned warrior turns into a basket-weaving charity case. As Indian John in the early republic of the 1790s, Chingachgook becomes the drunken Indian that he previously despised in Magua.[47] If one is capable of empathizing with the degradation and meaning-less end of a noble life, the tragedy of Chingachgook is unbearable. Moreover, if his tragedy counters the adventure story of the white hunter as crack shot—and Cooper seems to have meant it that way—the counter never resolves itself into a saving balance. Whose reaction to the massacre of Fort William Henry do you prefer? Hawk-eye's belief in the meaning of history causes him to swear vengeance in what will terminate either in endless cycles of retaliation or extermination; the Big Serpent's acceptance of chaos leads instead to a blooded sto-icism that borders on indifference. Neither alternative is acceptable, and that too seems to have been part of Cooper's plan. Chingachgook gives the last lie to history as a story of developing human relations with three simple words that every living person must utter at some point in time, and yet the Big Serpent can claim these three words as no other. They are his last ones in the novel: "I am alone—" (p. 349).

There is nothing but ruin in such utter and uttered isolation. Like Nathaniel Hawthorne and Herman Melville after him, James Feni-more Cooper says "No! in thunder" and writes his book in "hellfire."[48] If we fail to see that, it is because we recognize neither the world that Cooper protests against nor the intellectual courage of a writer who challenges the now forgotten imaginative conventions of his day. The literature of the early republic features "the deep need of those who composed it to identify with greatness and permanence" as they tried "to escape time and history."[49] In response, *The Last of the Mohicans* deals in failure and evanescence, tying the reader inexorably to the moment. The novel stands for the proposition that there is no escape from history. Instead of nation building, Cooper proposes the disintegration of a culture. Instead of life and progeny, he gives us death and sterility. Instead of the winners in history, he offers a portrait of its losers. Everything he depicts suggests that Americans should think again about their changing situation.

The Last of the Mohicans stresses endings over beginnings, the burden of the past over the future glory of America. More than any other work of the period, it conveys that the earliness of the early republic is over, and that something else is taking its place. Cooper was just cognizant enough of what was passing to see it more clearly than others. Psychologically, his description of the irretrievable loneliness of a last Indian arouses vague but very powerful feelings of privation that Cooper's contemporaries clearly shared with him. In 1826 and after, Americans looked back to their founders with "deep feelings of loss and present deficiency." They grasped that the high drama and presumed virtue of the Revolution were no more, and that a world they admired had changed forever. Cooper's own comprehension of what had passed took the form of a cerebral sense of declension. He knew what others have only recently dared to say about the creation of the republic: "for a brief moment ideas and power, intellectualism and politics, came together—indeed, were one with each other—in a way never again duplicated in American history."[50] The universal appeal of *The Last of the Mohicans* lies in its manipulation of this sense of loss in historical context.

Not sequence but repetition drives this vision of history. Cooper places his early republican reader in a pre-republican moment where its leaders behave in dangerously similar fashion to the leaders of 1826. Each set of leaders threatens a golden age that has gone before: 1757 destroys the age of Native American integrity under the great Mohican Sagamores (p. 127); 1826 appears to be undercutting the spirit and virtue of the American Revolution. The pre-republican moment is filled with characters who will never appear again—not just the Mohican Indians but also the peerless Leatherstocking and Cora Munro—and the same is true of the Revolution. Those who have come after are lesser figures. Incompetence or worse has ruined something of infinite value in both golden eras.

There is, however, a silver lining. Cooper uses the lost pre-republican past and the fallen republican present to bracket the golden age of the Revolution, the moment in time that his readers accept as uniquely valid in communal understandings. The novel invokes that encapsulated moment briefly but in grandiose terms that require no further explanation. The British army is saved in 1757 "by the coolness and spirit of a Virginian boy, whose riper fame has since diffused itself, with the steady influence of moral truth, to the uttermost confines of Christendom" (p. 13). This historical interpolation offers a sop to the reader. As the Massacre of Fort William Henry forms the centerpiece of the novel, so George Washington's "well-merited reputation" and "steady influence" arrest, for an instant, the endless cycles of rise and fall.

Readers reach this momentary zone of safety through nostalgia. The term itself means homesickness—*algos* (pain) connected to *nostos* (home)—but it signifies a homesickness that feeds on return to a better time rather than familiar terrain. The wistful hope of the nostalgic person centers not so much on location as on status, not on home but on one's lost youth. Culturally, the same emotion involves the desire to repossess a moment or an age that is beyond reach.[51] The utility in nostalgia comes in a spirit of recollection that gives a certain shape to one's situation; it is something to hold on to. The danger, conversely, lies in the way that nostalgia foreshortens and simplifies the past in a convenient and therefore pleasant form of forgetting, making it better than it was. National ideologies in particular rely upon this process of collective amnesia. They encourage just enough memory to disarm complete recollection. By ignoring disturbing data—like the official removal of large numbers of Native Americans from their lands—an ideology of, say, "westward expansion" can substitute pleasurable vagaries for painful particulars.[52]

A nostalgia that forgets history eases the intellectual distress at the core of Cooper's novel by disguising its early republican roots. A reader who carries the romanticized Leatherstocking of the 1840s from *The Pathfinder* and *The Deerslayer* back into the Natty Bumppo of *The Last of the Mohicans* discovers a very different novel. The Hawk-eye of 1826 is garrulous to a fault, superstitious, illiterate, splenetic when crossed, occasionally comic, boastful, and eager to kill—all characteristics to be expected from an uneducated back-woodsman in a time of war. The very name Hawk-eye, which will come to signify natural wisdom and pantheistic insight in the later mythology of Leatherstocking, originally indicates a low vigilance and cunning against immediate enemies, "symptoms of habitual suspicion" in a dangerous world (p. 30). This angrier Hawk-eye is a problem as well as the straight-shooting solution in *The Last of the Mohicans*. By the same token, when Natty tells the grieving Chingachgook that "God has so placed us as to journey in the same path," an inflated view of the speaker obscures the actual path taken by these figures—a path of unmitigated blood on the part of twin killers. Nostalgia magnifies the two characters, turning them into a synecdoche for the whole. Their recognition of each other replaces social orientation and mitigates the political tragedy of Native American culture in the name of felt companionship.

The predicament of the novel lies here. Should one give in to an available nostalgia on the surface level of narration or turn instead to the more vital but infinitely more troublesome novel of the writer's historical concerns? Consider, once again, that Cooper asks for only the serious reader. *The Last of the Mohicans* is about how catastrophe comes despite the vigilance in common understandings. Hawk-eye functions within that catastrophe as the symbol of a culture in the process of losing itself. Like many great stories, this one tells a tale of failure, and the centrality of that failure leads many readers to look the other way. Ideologically, failure has no acceptable place in a national myth of self-made success. Americans identify success with worth, dislike the subject of failure, rarely want to hear about it, and easily carry their strategies of evasion to other levels of engagement by concentrating on *individual* achievement and demanding that failure be thought of on the same scale. The result is blindness to many forms of distress and particularly to those with general ramifications. No other prosperous western nation has exhibited such a singular inability to face its social problems or has done so little in such a land of plenty for the marginalized groups in its midst (the poor, the sick, the elderly, the homeless, the unemployed, the otherwise disadvantaged). The neglect involved is intrinsic to a general way of thought. Nations, like other institutions, "create shadowed places in which nothing can be seen and no questions asked."[53]

The Last of the Mohicans, with its many conveniently dead Indians and its high percentage of dead women, contains some of this structural amnesia, but it dares to reach into the shadowed places of early republican understandings, and it asks questions that few at the time were willing to consider. Cooper grapples with the unsolved problems of his day, and he courageously illustrates their intractability. The result is both timely and timeless, contextual yet universal. The questions asked in *The Last of the Mohicans* identify an era, but they also reach beyond in our continuing failure to answer. The racial prejudice, misogyny, violence, crime, and cultural injustice so apparent in the novel take other forms today, but the resemblance is clear and part of a continuum that resists solution in predictable ways.

It means something that Natty Bumppo, Cooper's hero of many rescues, fails in his most important attempt, the recovery of Cora Munro. This largest of failures dooms an assertion from the lost heroine that any culture could be proud to accept when it finally decides to address its problems. The defeated Cora speaks not for herself but for all others when she claims that leaders who have "seen the evil of the world, should know how to temper its calamities to the miserable" (p. 303). Cooper is rarely subtle in his literary effects, but he seizes upon a deeper reality, one still with us, by having her plea fall on deaf ears.

EPILOGUE

Early eighteenth-century intellectuals began to see that an understanding of the past might depend less on universal theories of social origins or on biblical interpretation than on one's knowledge of the peculiar texture of each past society. As Giambattista Vico, the first truly modern historian, famously put the matter in 1709, "every epoch is dominated by a 'spirit,' a genius of its own."[1] The Enlightenment seized upon this concept as "the standard-bearer of a new time," one in which the acceptance of change and constant newness would dominate thought and control the way questions would be asked about events into the present day. Here, in essence, was the turn to modernity in thought. The acceptance of constant newness, with the discovery that each historical moment had to be understood in the particularity of its own setting, led quickly to another realization, the concomitant awareness that the future was free to be shaped by new forms of human enterprise. The past no longer dominated the present in the name of a future that previous generations had thought to be predetermined by constants in human nature and scripture.[2]

The American Revolution took place in the springtime of these recognitions. In Thomas Paine's rallying words, "a new method of thinking hath arisen," "we have it in our power to begin the world over again."[3] Although they were not free of the past by any means, the creators of the American republic assumed that they possessed a spirit or genius entirely their own, and they proceeded with such confidence because the negative consequences in unending change were not yet fully apparent to them. They could be bold in transcending the world they had been born into because they could not yet see how their innovations in politics would recast the social order in which they and their progeny would live.[4] Indeed, many of the tangles in early republican thought can be read as anxiety over a dawning recognition: something had been started that could not be stopped in its initial trajectory of Revolutionary articulation, and no one knew where it would end.[5]

Full realization of the chasm between the vanished past and an unsettling present developed quickly. By 1830 Thomas Carlyle could summarize the philosophical difficulty by contrasting the regular sounding of the hourly clock against the hush of time. "[N]o hammer in the Horologe of Time peals through the universe when there is a change from Era to Era," he observed. "Men understand not what is among their hands."[6] Novelty made history mysterious, the past strange, and the present ephemeral, cloaking everything in the prospect of loss as it slipped through the fingers of the present. Viscerally gripped by change, the founders who lived long enough, together with the first inheritors of the Revolution, talked and wrote incessantly of their growing personal sense of loss. Since then, every later generation has increased its distance from the founding not just in time but in conception by granting the Revolutionary forebears their claim of a unique genius. Ironically, these celebrations of uniqueness have also made it harder to think of what might be retained. In American history the founders have become "a galaxy of leaders who were quite literally incomparable." They appear "a cluster of extraordinary men such as is rarely encountered in modern history." "No one, it seems, can look back without being overawed by the brilliance of their thought, the creativity of their politics, the sheer magnitude of their achievement."[7] Nevertheless and in looking back, these admirers always ask the same question with variations on the theme. What really made the founding generation that way? Where was the real source of their genius? How does the prevalent emphasis on personalities determine answers to these questions? Which parts of their legacy can be said to survive their unique powers of formulation?

Current historians have grappled with the possibilities. Were the architects of the nation such "uncommon men" because "they were intellectuals without being alienated and political leaders without being

obsessed with votes"? Did they "combine ideas and politics so effectively" as forerunners to the democracy that they themselves created—a democracy that, whatever its advantages, brought "a decline
in the intellectual quality of American political life and an eventual
separation between ideas and power"?[8] Or, is it more useful to think
of these "truly creative people" as fortunate provincials on the edge of
a dominant but corrupt Anglo-American empire? Were they able to
articulate the benefits of that empire without being hampered by its
conventionality? Is it possible that "remoteness from the metropoli-
tan world gave them a moral advantage in politics"? Could it be that
"provincialism, and the sense they derived from it of their own moral
stature, had nourished their political imagination"?[9] Reaching beyond personalities, others have approached the puzzle of the founding
through the emergence and presumed dominance of print culture,
which "elevated the values of generality over those of the personal"
and encouraged "the disinterested virtues of the public orientation"
over more locally invested speech. Or, more concretely, scholars have
stressed how "the extraordinarily rapid spread of printing presses"
made print culture and political culture "twins" in the early republic.[10] Still others argue for "the intimate association" between the
founding of the nation and "acts of voice."[11]

Within their many differences, all of these approaches share the
common belief that early republicans were driven by excitement over
the word. Americans revolutionized the very term "revolution"
in 1776. The traditional Aristotlean signification of "circulation"
through a fixed pattern of the forms of government (monarchy, aristocracy, democracy with their degenerate forms of tyranny, oligar-
chy, and mobocracy) disappeared, pushed aside by more dynamic and
open-ended conceptions of change, upheaval, and aspiration.[12] It was
in this sense that the United States of America could be thought of as
the first modern nation with new opportunities available in thought
and practice. Just as words more than swords created the Revolution, so they provided the structure of the republic and became shrill
weapons in the disagreements over its unfolding meaning. The point
always was to be *heard,* and here the puzzle over accomplishment
deepens. The users of these words displayed a sophistication that con-
tradicts the thesis of their provinciality and a rhetorical need to reach
all levels of social understanding that belies the claim of their undem-
ocratic detachment, though there were always vexed questions over

what democracy could mean. Then, too, the emotional pitch, power, and influence of their words, both in speech and writing, carried beyond the salient explanations of print culture and its supposedly disinterested mien. Disinterest is a claim rather than a fact in their language.

Reading the Early Republic maintains that it is possible to recover this foundational excitement over words. The language cannot be repossessed, but it can be understood through closer attention to its actual workings, better awareness of its formal arrangement, and greater appreciation of the audiences that found it meaningful. The mantra of the times—repeated at all levels and in all kinds of writing and speech from the earliest stirrings of the Enlightenment in America—is instructive in this regard. Every American shared an intellectual obligation in "promoting useful knowledge among the British Plantations of America." Benjamin Franklin said so as early as 1743 in forming the American Philosophical Society. William Livingston concurred in connecting "*the Strength and Diffusiveness of Public Spirit*" to "*the true Dignity and Glory, the Stability and internal Tranquility of every State*" in *The Independent Reflector* in 1753. For Thomas Jefferson, "the diffusion of knowledge among the people" was "by far" the most important priority of the 1780s. Only "a crusade against ignorance" could "fairly put into the hands of their own common sense" a people who were learning to master the rules of their own best interest. Twenty years later and from a different region, the writers of *The Monthly Anthology and Boston Review* continued to harp on the identical theme in article after article. The connection between the state of knowledge and the prosperity of the country was as intimate as it was vital. Whatever their politics or situation, early American writers acted on their belief in the connection by sharing "their high duty in fixing fundamental principles" in a new world "where great happiness is the portion of every one."[13]

Intermediate possibilities did not appeal in the early republican rhetoric of mission. The writer in each case chose starkly between barbarism in an undeveloped land and total felicity in the systematic spread of knowledge. The means of "diffusion," the word used over and over again for the spread of knowledge, was just as stark. Truth and light would replace ignorance and darkness at an ever-accelerating pace. Bold words indeed, but how was such a transformation going to take place, and even if it did, how was it to be sustained? Again

Jefferson spoke for the new age. As he explained in *A Bill for Establishing Religious Freedom* from 1779, "truth is great and will prevail if left to herself." In one of the most colossal statements of the period, he added "she [truth] is the proper and sufficient antagonist to error . . . errors ceasing to be dangerous when it is permitted freely to contradict them."[14] John Dickinson, seeking ratification of the Federal Constitution in 1788, carried Jefferson's point into a statement of particulars. "TRUTH becomes infinitely valuable . . . not as a matter of curious speculation, but of beneficial practice," he argued, "a spirit of inquiry is excited, information diffused, judgment strengthened." The tellers of truth had a collective burden of responsibility because so much was possible in the American people. The truth belonged to whoever would receive it, and every enlightened person wanted more of it. As such, it became "not only their *right,* but their *duty.*"[15]

Not just a personal right but a collective duty—the language of obligation explains why "diffusion of knowledge" in the early republic must be thought of in terms of reciprocities rather than as a linear or top-down manifestation. In order for an idea to be successful it had to enter the minds of a receptive people. Meaningful knowledge depended on how the people would absorb and then convey it themselves in peaceful expansion, prosperity, and support of the truth through their own articulation of republican principles. The words sent forth meant nothing unless they won the proper response from a duly informed and necessarily massive audience. Of course, this way of thinking also meant that the knowing writer held a tiger by the tail. The state of the new union depended absolutely on the demeanor and behavior of an increasingly active and demanding people. Even conservative Revolutionaries accepted that the people would rise in energy and take more control as their knowledge increased. John Adams described the eventual likelihood most graphically. "I believe this many-headed beast, the people, will some time or other, have wit enough to throw their riders," he wrote in 1785, "and if they should, they will put an end to an abundance of tricks, with which they are now curbed, bitted, whipped, and spurred."[16]

The ambivalence in Adams' terms bespoke the problem. Who or what would control "this many-headed beast, the people"? Who or what would ensure "wit enough" once the rider was thrown? Those leaders who wrote in the early republic saw themselves in a race against time. Words *were* exciting in their presumed efficacy and even more so in the urgency of making them effective at once. The people had to be educated before a merely licentious understanding of their power developed. Moreover, everyone saw that the people were already rambunctious. More democratic than most, Jefferson notoriously recognized that "a little rebellion now and then is a good thing," but it is forgotten that far more conservative members of his generation realized and accepted the same premise before Jefferson. John Jay, a leading Federalist in 1786, argued that "in free states, there must and ought to be a little ferment." Healthy republics required the people's energy. Jay wanted ferment because he feared "the vigour of a republic soon becomes lost in general relaxation."[17] The questions began over what constituted *a little* rebellion, *a little* ferment.

Real creativity in early republican literature lies in this troubled nexus. Leaders and led began to realize that you could not change the world without changing the way it was understood and approached on every level. From their side, the people imbibed diffusion of knowledge through a language of protest, and they were quick to use it in extending their democratic prerogatives. The radical implications of Revolutionary rhetoric were there to be read. Protest served the needs of every aspirant looking for advantage in the flux of early republican life. The whiskey tax of the 1790s, universally loathed in the western part of the states, caused self-created "democratic societies" to rise in protest and rebellion. The tax was not just unwise policy; it was "oppressive" to the people and "hostile to the liberties of this Country."[18] Organizations of all kinds assumed "the ability of the people to govern themselves," and they entered the same race against time, each from its own direction. Thus, for example, the American Tract Society distributed its evangelical pamphlets with a special urgency in the understanding that "it is not enough that a portion of the people, or even a majority, are enlightened . . . neglect of any part endangers the safety of the whole." Once again universal knowledge was the promised panacea against potential disaster. "We are embarked in a noble vessel," the founders of the Tract Society told themselves, "but the starting of a single plank, the shifting of the ballast, the parting of a shroud, may engulf us all."[19]

The pressure on language to solve or at least comprehend the precarious American situation came from every direction, and it tended to collapse the categories and balances in a classical republican understanding. The lowest common denominator in language, one that would reach all, was a mandatory ingredient; so was "friendly equality" as the surest guarantee in "the happiness of any state," and both helped to diminish the previously "immense distance between the rulers and the ruled." If the rhetoric of friendly equality sounded unnecessarily shrill or belligerent at times, it was because the stakes were so high. The republic was simultaneously fragile, even ephemeral, and yet on the verge of stupendous accomplishments that would change the rest of the world. "In the United States," avowed the American Bible Society in 1816, "we want nothing but concert to perform achievements astonishing to ourselves, dismaying to the adversaries of truth and piety, and most encouraging to every evangelical effort, on the surface of the globe."[20]

The brag and bounce in such declarations exposed another and deeper contradiction. Claims of diffusion, cohesion, and concert allowed others to protest more effectively. If you were outside of the unifying dispensations in Revolutionary success, you held to the original challenge in them, and no intellectual rejoinder from the commonality of American feeling could qualify your valid need. To be a slave in America meant to be "as desirous of freedom as any of you." To be a vanquished Native American leader in America showed where the ideology of liberty did not apply. "I would that I could make the red people as great as the conceptions of my own mind," Tecumseh mournfully told William Henry Harrison on his way to final defeat and death. To be a woman in America brought one face to face with the hypocrisies in Enlightenment thought. Did growth in knowledge confer worth on an individual? How was it, then, the Female Advocate of New Haven asked in 1801 that "the arrogant assumers of male merit" could assume "our sex arrived at its zenith of improvement, at the age of twenty-one" in the superficial show and accoutrement of physical beauty?[21]

There were no good answers to these reproaches when they were first raised. They signified rather that republican thought contained major implications that early republicans could not tolerate. The self-evidence of truth made certain truths unpalatable. Even so, the driving logic of republican thought in America meant that these and other claims of injustice would surface again and again until they were met in some way, a process that would take centuries and counting. Their persistence raises both timely and structural questions. When would these voices be heard within the democratic continuum? What did the continuing failure to hear them say about the framework of thought in a culture ideologically committed to the diffusion of knowledge and the spread of truth? Each question reveals a vulnerability in the makeup of national thought, and it may be here that the study of origins in a national language may be especially valuable.

The failure to hear a justified claim and the incongruity between ideological assertion and practical acceptance undercut meaning in the language that made the republic possible. Strangely, however, these failures did not destroy the cultural-wide efficacy or the inspirational significance of the language itself. Justified protest has remained remarkably vital in republican society. An example can help to explain the puzzle involved. Less than two weeks before he died at the age of eighty-three in 1826, Thomas Jefferson wrote that "all eyes are opened or opening to the rights of man." He also proclaimed "the palpable truth, that the mass of mankind has not been born with saddles on their backs, nor a favored few booted and spurred, ready to ride them legitimately."[22] How could the same man punish slaves on his own plantation and ruthlessly urge the execution of those who rebelled in 1800? How could he, as president in 1803, urge the intimidation of Native Americans in the Indiana territory by making them see "we have only to shut our hand to crush them"?[23]

The quick answer is that it was not the same man. The self-conscious architect of republican thought in 1826 is not the official of 1800 and 1803. The often noted hypocrisies in Jefferson are less important, in this context, than the already routinized patterns of thought that allowed him to write in both ways. Language in control of the early republic was always an assertion of practical power as well as a claim about how citizens should feel and act. Calculated discrepancies between the terms of rule and the language of cultural understanding were in place from the beginning. As we saw in the never-ending construction of Monticello, Jefferson lived in the possible of his moment while always hoping for and believing in a better future. Language was the key to that better future, and no early republican used it to better or more knowing effect in trying to narrow the apparent gaps between the exercise of power and the articulation of republican value. Nonetheless, the discrepancies were there, and they remain in the language of the modern nation-state. In fact, these discrepancies have grown greater as the distance between ruler and ruled also has grown.

Outrage over the ideological inconsistencies of a nation built on words has its place, but it is less useful in most instances than a careful understanding of where the incongruities between thought and practice lie so that they can be circumscribed and limited by common understanding. Republicanism stands for the proposition that there is a way for leadership to speak and act that can be held in place. The great mystery of American culture, first launched in the early republic, lies in the largely intangible and consensual means of enforcement. The collective expression of a society privileges certain ideas as well as a peculiar way of talking about them. Terms like "liberty," "virtue," "union," and even "republic" do not percolate regularly in contemporary American speech in the way that they did in early republican society, but the concepts themselves remain vital as long as a "crystallization of past experiences and situations retains an existential value, a function in the actual being of society." They work "as long as succeeding generations can hear their own experiences in the meaning of the words." Words can also change or lose their meaning; they either lie dormant, waiting for later use, or they die "when the functions and experiences in the actual life of society cease to be bound up with them."[24]

This book takes no stand on whether crucial words in the American past will remain vital to citizens of the twenty-first century or lose their significance, but it raises a series of questions through investigation. Can the language of the founding survive in anything like its original vitality without a closer understanding? Is it important that it do so? If it is unimportant, why do we refer back to it with such frequency? If instead the language remains important, how do we continue to secure it? The study of the past leaves room for both hope and fear on these questions but never indifference.

NOTES

INDEX

NOTES

Introduction

1. John Adams to Benjamin Rush, April 4, 1790, in Alexander Biddle, *Old Family Letters*, 2 vols. (Philadelphia: J. B. Lippincott Company, 1892), I: 55–56.

2. Pierre Bourdieu, *The Logic of Practice* (Cambridge: Polity Press, 1990), 56, and Bourdieu, *In Other Words: Essays Towards a Reflexive Sociology* (Stanford: Stanford University Press, 1990), pp. 11, 13, 190. See, as well, Michael Billig, *Banal Nationalism* (London: Sage Publications, 1995), p. 42.

3. John Adams to Benjamin Rush, April 18, 1790, in Charles Francis Adams, ed., *The Life and Works of John Adams*, 10 vols. (Boston: Little, Brown, 1850–1856), IX: 566.

4. David Lowenthal, *The Past is a Foreign Country* (Cambridge: Cambridge University Press, 1985), p. 215.

5. See Lewis P. Simpson, "Writing A Nation," *The Sewanee Review*, 106 (Summer 1998), 501; Robert A. Ferguson, "'We Hold These Truths': Strategies of Control in the Literature of the Founders," *Reconstructing American Literary History: Harvard English Studies 13*, ed. Sacvan Bercovitch (Cambridge: Harvard University Press, 1986), 1–28, and John C. Fitzpatrick, ed., *The Writings of George Washington from the Original Manuscript Sources, 1745–1799*, 39 vols. (Washington, D.C.: U.S. Government Printing Office, 1931–1944).

6. For the terms of criticism used in this paragraph, see I. A. Richards, "The Four Kinds of Meaning," *Practical Criticism: A Study of Literary Judgment* (New York: Harcourt, Brace, & World, 1929), pp. 175–176, and Reuben A. Brower, "The Sound Matters," *The Fields of Light: An Experiment in*

Critical Reading (New York: Oxford University Press, 1962), pp. 58–62. For an extended demonstration of the mixing of "generic ambiguities" and "the highly manipulable nature of republican language" in national beginnings, see Philip Gould, *Covenant and Republic: Historical Romance and the Politics of Puritanism* (Cambridge: Cambridge University Press, 1996), pp. 9–60.

7. I. A. Richards, *The Philosophy of Rhetoric* (1936; New York: Oxford University Press, 1965), pp. 3, 11.

8. For details, see Peter Shaw, *The Character of John Adams* (1976: rpt. New York: W. W. Norton, 1977), pp. 225–230, 240, and Frank Donavan, "The Vice-President," *The John Adams Papers* (New York: Dodd, Mead & Company, 1965), pp. 210–246. For other comments on the inability to recover the real truth of the Revolution, see JA to William Tudor, August 11, 1818; JA to Hezikiah Niles, January 14, 1818; and JA to Henry Niles, February 13, 1818, in Adams, ed., *The Life and Works of John Adams*, X: 343–345, 274, 282; and JA to TJ, July 30, 1815, TJ to JA, August 10, 1815, and JA to TJ August 24, 1815, in Lester J. Cappon, ed., *The Adams-Jefferson Letters: The Complete Correspondence Between Thomas Jefferson and Abigail and John Adams*, 2 vols. (Chapel Hill: The University of North Carolina Press, 1959), II: 451, 452, 455.

9. "Of Books" [II, 10], *The Complete Essays of Montaigne*, trans. Donald M. Frame (Stanford: Stanford University Press, 1958), p. 304.

10. For the "ideology of national character" at work, see David Waldstreicher, "National Characters," *In the Midst of Perpetual Fetes: The Making of American Nationalism, 1776–1820* (Chapel Hill: University of North Carolina Press, 1997), pp. 108–173.

11. See, in particular, Michael Kammen, *Season of Youth: The American Revolution and the Historical Imagination* (New York: Knopf, 1973), pp. 21, 163.

12. Mary Douglas, *How Institutions Think* (Syracuse: Syracuse University Press, 1986), pp. 63, 93, 35, 50.

13. I paraphrase here from Maurice Halbwachs, *On Collective Memory*, trans. Lewis A. Coser (Chicago: The University of Chicago Press, 1992), p. 51.

14. Kerwin Lee Klein, "On the Emergence of Memory in Historical Discourse," *Representations*, 69 (Winter 2000), 43.

15. JA to William Tudor, August 11, 1818; JA to Hezikiah Niles, January 14, 1818; and JA to Henry Niles, February 13, 1818, in Adams, ed., *The Life and Works of John Adams*, X: 343–345, 274, 282, and JA to TJ, May 18, 1817, Cappon, ed., *The Adams-Jefferson Letters*, II: 516.

16. See Harlow W. Sheidley, *Sectional Nationalism: Massachusetts Conservative Leaders and the Transformation of America, 1815–1836* (Boston: Northeastern University Press, 1998).

17. For the theoretical problems in periodization, see Lawrence Besserman, ed., *The Challenge of Periodization: Old Paradigms and New Perspectives* (New York: Garland Publishing, 1996), pp. xx–xxiv, 3–27.

18. Richards, *The Philosophy of Rhetoric*, pp. 11, 72–73.
19. William L. Hedges, "The Myth of the Republic and the Theory of American Literature," *Prospects* 4 (1974), 110; Hedges, "Toward a Theory of American Literature, 1765–1800," *Early American Literature*, 4 (1970), 7; and Andrew Delbanco, *William Ellery Channing: An Essay on the Liberal Spirit in America* (Cambridge: Harvard University Press, 1981), p. 62.
20. "Textualism" is the latest influential interpretive school in legal thought. Its primary theorist is Associate Justice of the United States Supreme Court, Antonin Scalia. See Antonin Scalia, *A Matter of Interpretation: Federal Courts and the Law* (Princeton: Princeton University Press, 1997), pp. 22–23. Scalia's essay explaining the theory of textualism is then criticized by a number of leading historians and legal scholars in the same volume, including Gordon S. Wood, Laurence H. Tribe, Mary Ann Glendon, and Ronald Dworkin.

1. The Earliness of the Early Republic

1. Alexis de Tocqueville, *Democracy in America,* trans. Phillips Bradley, 2 vols. (New York: Vintage Books, 1958), II: 105–106.
2. See David Lowenthal, *The Past is a Foreign Country* (Cambridge: Cambridge University Press, 1985), pp. 324–362, 383, 399–412.
3. See Daniel T. Rogers, *Contested Truths: Keywords in American Politics Since Independence* (New York: Basic Books, 1987).
4. I take the phrase from Lowenthal, *The Past is a Foreign Country.*
5. Samuel Sherwood, *The Church's Flight Into The Wilderness: An Address On The Times* [New York, 1776] in Ellis Sandoz, ed., *Political Sermons of the American Founding Era* (Indianapolis: Liberty Press, 1991), pp. 521–523.
6. *Report on Manufactures*, in Harold C. Syrett, ed., *The Papers of Alexander Hamilton*, 25 vols. to date (New York: Columbia University Press, 1961—), X: 251–258.
7. See Joseph Kett, "Youth in the Early Republic," *Rites of Passage: Adolescence in America 1790 to the Present* (New York: Basic Books, 1977), pp. 9–110.
8. For the quotation and the timing of child labor laws, see Viviana A. Zelizer, "Childhood," in *A Companion to American Thought*, eds. Richard Wightman Fox and James T. Kloppenberg (Oxford: Blackwell, 1995), pp. 115–116. For the gradual shift in the treatment of children in America, see Jay Fliegelman, *Prodigals and Pilgrims: The American Revolution against Patriarchal Authority, 1750–1800* (Cambridge: Cambridge University Press, 1982).
9. See Jean Starobinski, "The Idea of Nostalgia," *Diogenes: An International Review of Philosophy and Humanistic Studies*, 54 (Summer 1966), 83.
10. Perry Miller first divided "the life of the mind in America" into "The Evangelical Basis" and "The Legal Mentality," and the division remains useful

even though the two frameworks must be understood in symbiosis with each other. Miller, *The Life of the Mind in America from the Revolution to the Civil War* (New York: Harcourt, Brace & World, 1965), pp. 1, 97.

11. Sherwood, *The Church's Flight Into The Wilderness*, p. 526.

12. I paraphrase from John C. Miller's analysis of *The Report on Manufactures* in Miller, *Alexander Hamilton: Portrait in Paradox* (New York: Harper & Brothers, 1959), p. 285.

13. For Hamilton's expressed faith and his commitment to Christian values, see AH to James Hamilton, September 6, 1772; "Fragment on the French Revolution," [c.1796]; "Last Will And Testament of Alexander Hamilton" [July 9, 1804]; and AH to Elizabeth Hamilton, July 10, 1804, all contained in Richard B. Morris, ed., *Alexander Hamilton and the Founding of the Nation* (New York: The Dial Press, 1957), pp. 422–423, 569, 609, 610. "The scruples of a Christian" will keep Hamilton from aiming at Aaron Burr in the duel that will kill him. His two-paragraph Last Will and Testament takes the form of a prayer, refers to God four times, mentions "the eternal world" that will come after, and puts all of his trust in Providence.

14. Sherwood, *The Church's Flight Into The Wilderness*, pp. 523–524.

15. AH to Gouverneur Morris, February 27, 1802, in Morris, ed., *Alexander Hamilton and the Founding of the Nation*, p. 602.

16. See William L. Hedges, "Toward A Theory of American Literature, 1765–1800," *Early American Literature* 4 (1970), 10–14.

17. Hannah Webster Foster, *The Coquette; or, The History of Eliza Wharton; A Novel; Founded on Fact*, ed. Cathy N. Davidson (Oxford: Oxford University Press, 1986). Further references to the novel in the text are to this edition, first by roman numeral that identifies the letter in the epistolary novel where it appears and then by arabic number to the page in this edition.

18. For this standard feminist reading of the plot, see Cathy N. Davidson, *Revolution and the Word: The Rise of the Novel in America* (Oxford: Oxford University Press, 1986), pp. 143–149. Davidson also details the great popularity of the novel and its structural parallels to the death of Elizabeth Whitman.

19. Samuel Johnson, *A Dictionary of the English Language*, first edition, 2 vols. (London: W. Strahan, 1755).

20. See John Trumbull, *The Progress of Dulness* in *The Poetical Works*, 2 vols. (Hartford: Samuel G. Goodrich, 1820), II: 77–82, and Royall Tyler, *The Contrast, A Comedy; in Five Acts*, ed. James Benjamin Wilbur (Boston: Houghton Mifflin, 1920). For the coquette figure in these works, see Robert A. Ferguson, *Law and Letters in American Culture* (Cambridge: Harvard University Press, 1984), pp. 100–106, 115–119.

21. For how rapid change prevented easy comprehension and decision making with related feelings of dislocation in early republican culture, see Joyce Appleby, *Inheriting The Revolution: The First Generation of Americans* (Cambridge: Harvard University Press, 2000), pp. 1–55.

22. Appleby summarizes the predicament of refinement and gentility in a democratic culture, in *Inheriting the Revolution*, pp. 146, 150.

23. For these political divisions, see Stanley Elkins and Eric McKitrick, *The Age of Federalism* (Oxford: Oxford University Press, 1993). See in particular Chapters 7 and 10–15.

24. For the parallels between *The Coquette* and the politics of the late 1790s, see Julia A. Stern, *The Plight of Feeling: Sympathy and Dissent in the Early American Novel* (Chicago: The University of Chicago Press, 1997), pp. 82–112. See, as well, Linda Kerber, *Women of the Republic: Intellect and Ideology in Revolutionary America* (Chapel Hill: University of North Carolina Press, 1980), pp. 248–249; Carol Smith-Rosenberg, "Domesticating 'Virtue': Coquettes and Revolutionaries in Young America," in Elaine Scarry, ed., *Literature and the Body: Essays on Persons and Populations* (Baltimore: Johns Hopkins Press, 1988), pp. 169ff, and Jan Lewis, "The Republican Wife: Virtue and Seduction in the Early Republic," *William and Mary Quarterly*, 44 (October 1987), 689–721.

25. For a theoretical discussion of "epistolary mediation," see Janet Gurkin Altman, *Epistolarity: Approaches to a Form* (Columbus: Ohio State University Press, 1982), p. 13.

26. Major Sanford, describing his conquest of Eliza, quotes "stolen waters are sweet, and bread eaten in secret is sweet," but has forgotten the source, Proverbs 9:17 (LXV, 139).

27. See Laurel Thatcher Ulrich, *The Mid-Wife's Tale: The Life of Martha Ballard, Based on Her Diary, 1785–1812* (New York: Vintage Books, 1991), pp. 148–151.

28. Venture Smith [Broteer Furro], *A Narrative of the Life and Adventures of Venture, A Native of Africa, But Resident Above Sixty Years in the United States of America* (1798; rpt. Middletown, Conn.: J. S. Stewart, 1897). All further references to the *Narrative of Venture*, noted parenthetically by page number in the text, are to this edition.

29. For the generic features of the slave narrative in *Narrative of Venture* and information on the background of the text and its author, see Robert E. Desrochers, Jr., "'Not Fade Away': The Narrative of Venture Smith, an African American in the Early Republic," *The Journal of American History*, 84 (June, 1997), 40–66.

30. For civic virtue as a guide in republicanism, see J. G. A. Pocock, *The Machiavellian Moment: Florentine Political Thought and the Atlantic Republican Tradition* (Princeton: Princeton University Press, 1975) and *Virtue, Commerce, and History* (Cambridge: Cambridge University Press, 1985). For counterclaims on the greater importance of commerce in early republicanism, see Joyce Appleby, *Liberalism and Republicanism in the Historical Imagination* (Cambridge: Harvard University Press, 1992), and Isaac Kramnick, *Republicanism and Bourgeois Radicalism: Political Ideology in Late Eighteenth-Century England and America* (Ithaca: Cornell Univer-

sity Press, 1990). For a summary of these debates, see David Wooten, "Introduction: The Republican Tradition: From Commonwealth to Common Sense," in Wooten, ed., *Republicanism, Liberty, and Commercial Society, 1649–1776* (Stanford: Stanford University Press, 1994) pp. 15–18.

31. "Ecclesiastes Or, The Preacher," I: I-4. See, as well, R. B. Y. Scott, *The Anchor Bible: Proverbs, Ecclesiastes* (New York: Doubleday, 1965), pp. 191–211.

32. Herman Melville, *Moby-Dick or The Whale* [1851], The Northwestern-Newberry Edition (Evanston and Chicago: Northwestern University Press and the Newberry Library, 1988), p. 424.

33. Abigail Adams to John Adams, March 31, 1776; John Adams to Abigail Adams, April 14, 1776, in Charles Francis Adams, ed., *Familiar Letters of John Adams and His Wife, Abigail Adams, During the Revolution* (Boston: Houghton, Mifflin and Company, 1875), pp. 149, 155.

34. The Declaration of Independence claims the people's right "to assume among the powers of the earth, the separate and equal station to which the Laws of Nature and Nature's God entitle them." In 1896, the Supreme Court of the United States turned to that language in *Plessy v. Ferguson,* to propound "the separate but equal" doctrine in support of racial segregation. Not until *Brown v. Board of Education* reversed *Plessy,* in the second half of the twentieth century, is the separate but equal doctrine overthrown. See *Plessy v. Ferguson* 163 U.S. 537 (1896); *Brown v. Board of Education,* 347 U.S. 483 (1954); and Brook Thomas, ed., *Plessy v. Ferguson: A Brief History with Documents* (Boston: Bedford Books, 1997).

35. Charles Warren, *Jacobin and Junto or Early American Politics as Viewed in the Diary of Dr. Nathaniel Ames, 1758–1822* (Cambridge: Harvard University Press, 1931), p. 289.

36. Thomas Jefferson to Thomas Mann Randolph, November 16, 1792, in Julian P. Boyd, ed., *The Papers of Thomas Jefferson,* 30 vols. (Princeton: Princeton University Press, 1950–2003), XXIV: 623.

37. Ames' diary from July 5, 1808, quoted in Winfred E. A. Bernhard, *Fisher Ames: Federalist and Statesman 1758–1808* (Chapel Hill: The University of North Carolina Press, 1965), pp. 349–350. See, as well, John R. Howe, Jr., "Republican Thought and the Political Violence of the 1790s," *American Quarterly,* 19 (Summer, 1967), 147–165.

38. For the nature of such rhetoric, see Bernard Bailyn, *The Ideological Origins of the American Revolution* (Cambridge: Harvard University Press, 1967).

39. Alexander Pope, "Argument for the First Epistle," and "Epistle I, [Verses 231–232, 291–292]," *An Essay On Man or The First Book of Ethic Epistles* [1733], in Aubrey Williams, ed., Riverside edition, *Poetry and Prose of Alexander Pope* (Boston: Houghton Mifflin, 1969), pp. 122, 128, 130.

40. Benjamin Harrison Smith, *Remarks on Education: Illustrating the Close Connection Between Virtue and Wisdom, To Which is Annexed a System of Liberal Education* (Philadelphia: John Ormrod, 1798), in Noble E.

Cunningham, Jr., ed., *The Early Republic* (New York: Harper and Row, 1968), pp. 227–239, 236.

41. The argument about the nature of virtue in this paragraph and the next relies on Ruth H. Bloch, "The Gendered Meanings of Virtue in Revolutionary America," *Signs: Journal of Women in Culture and Society*, 13 (August, 1987), 36–58. See in particular pp. 38–41, 50.

42. For the contrasting philosophies and quotations between Nathaniel and Fisher Ames traced in this paragraph, see Warren, ed., *Jacobin and Junto*, pp. 30, 45, 12, 25, 59, 161, 99, 107, 158, 172, 158, and Seth Ames, *Works of Fisher Ames*, 2 vols. (1854; rpt and enlarged, Indianapolis: Liberty Press, 1983), I: 156, 131–134.

43. Quoted from Warren, ed., *Jacobin and Junto*, p. 293.

44. Ibid., pp. 286–287, 15.

45. Ibid., pp. 312–314.

46. Ibid., p. 290. For the lawyer's sudden control of early republican society and government, see Robert A. Ferguson, "In America the Law is King," *Law and Letters in American Culture* (Cambridge: Harvard University Press, 1984), pp. 11–33.

47. For the history of the reception of Jefferson's *First Inaugural* and the only book-length analysis of it, see Stephen Howard Browne, *Jefferson's Call for Nationhood: The First Inaugural Address* (College Station: Texas A & M University Press, 2003). My own analysis of Jefferson's address is indebted to Browne's scholarship on the subject.

48. *First Inaugural Address*, March 4, 1801; TJ to John Dickinson, March 6, 1801; TJ to Dr. Joseph Priestley, March 21, 1801; TJ to Elbridge Gerry, March 29, 1801 in Thomas Jefferson, *Writings: Autobiography, A Summary View of the Rights of British America, Notes on the State of Virginia, Public Papers, Addresses, Messages, and Replies, Miscellany, Letters*, ed. Merrill D. Peterson (New York: Library of America, 1984), p. 493, 1084–1086, 1088. All further references to the *First Inaugural*, noted parenthetically in the text, are to this collection of Jefferson's writings. Where possible, other references to Jefferson's writings will be to this convenient Library of America edition, noted as Jefferson, *Writings*.

49. Tom Watson, *The Life and Times of Thomas Jefferson* (New York: D. Appleton and Company, 1903), p. 398.

50. See, as well, TJ to Thomas Jefferson Randolph, November 24, 1808, in Jefferson, *Writings*, pp. 1195–1196.

51. TJ to John Bannister, Jr., October 15, 1785, and "The Autobiography," in Jefferson, *Writings*, pp. 839, 53; TJ to David Harding, April 20, 1824, in Adrienne Koch and William Peden, eds., *The Life and Selected Writings of Thomas Jefferson* (New York: Random House, 1944), p. 713.

52. Quoted in Claude G. Bowers, *Jefferson in Power: The Death Struggle of the Federalists* (Boston: Houghton Mifflin, 1964), pp. 54–55, and *Gazette of the United States*, April 15, 1801, p. 2.

53. "Query XIII," "Query XI," *Notes on the State of Virginia,* and *Autobiography* in Jefferson, *Writings,* pp. 246, 220, 38–44.

54. *A Summary View of the Rights of British America,* in Jefferson, *Writings,* p. 121.

55. Pierre Nora, "Between Memory and History: *Les Lieux de Mémoire,*" *Representations,* 26 (Spring 1989), 9–10.

56. Alexander Hamilton, "An Address to the Electors of the State of New-York [1801]," in Syrett, ed. *The Papers of Alexander Hamilton,* XXV: 365.

57. The most famous expression by Jefferson on the separation between church and state will come just months after the *First Inaugural,* in TJ to Nehemiah Dodge and Others, a Committee of the Danbury Baptist Association in the State of Connecticut, January 1, 1802, in Jefferson, *Writings,* p. 510. Jefferson here calls for "building a wall of separation between church and state" through the First Amendment, and the Supreme Court of the United States will confirm his wording and his logic in demanding an even more vigorous separation in the twentieth century. See *Everson v. Board of Education,* 330 U.S. 1, 15–16 (1947).

58. For the emergence of a civil religion in early republican society, see Robert N. Bellah, "Civil Religion in America," *Daedalus,* 96 (Winter, 1967), 1–21, and Bellah, *The Broken Covenant: American Civil Religion in a Time of Trial* (New York: Seabury Press, 1975).

59. See Daniel Boorstin, *The Lost World of Thomas Jefferson* (1948; rpt. Boston: Beacon Press, 1960), p. 203, 171, and Adrienne Koch, *The Philosophy of Thomas Jefferson* (New York: Columbia University Press, 1943), pp. 23–30. For Jefferson's own words in the quoted passages, see TJ to John Bannister, Jr., October 15, 1785; TJ to Peter Carr, August 10, 1787; TJ to François de Marbois, June 14, 1817; and TJ to Roger C. Weightman, June 24, 1826, in Jefferson, *Writings,* pp. 839, 901, 1410–1411, 1517.

60. TJ to François de Marbois, June 14, 1817, in Jefferson, *Writings,* pp. 1410–1411.

61. Gordon S. Wood, "The Democratizaton of Mind in the American Revolution," in *Leadership in the American Revolution: Library of Congress Symposia on the American Revolution* (Washington, D.C.: Library of Congress, 1976), p. 64.

62. Warren, ed., *Jacobin and Junto,* pp. 5–6.

63. See Quentin Skinner, "Meaning and Understanding in the History of Ideas," *History and Theory,* 8 (No. 1, 1969), 3, 42, 47–53.

64. "The Circus Animals' Desertion," in *The Collected Poems of W. B. Yeats,* definitive edition (New York: Macmillan Company, 1956), p. 336.

2. The Dialectic of Liberty

1. Baron De Montesquieu, *The Spirit of Laws,* trans. Thomas Nugent (1748; New York: Hafner Press, 1949), p. 149 [Bk.XI, No.2]; Richard Price, "Ob-

servations on the Nature of Civil Liberty, the Principles of Government, and the Justice and Policy of the War with America," *Hibernian Magazine,* 6 (1776), 77, reprinted in Price, *Two Tracts: Tract Two,* p. 5; Thomas Bernard, *An Appeal to the Public, Stating and Considering the Objections to the Quebec Bill* (London, 1774), p. 28.

2. Samuel Johnson, *A Dictionary of the English Language* (London: W. Strahan, 1755). For a catalogue of the uses of the term *liberty* in England and America, see John Phillip Reid, "A Word We Know," *The Concept of Liberty in the Age of the American Revolution* (Chicago: The University of Chicago Press, 1988), pp. 11–21.

3. William Wirt, *Sketches of the Life and Character of Patrick Henry* (1818; Philadelphia: Claxton, Remsen, and Haffelfinger, 1878), pp. 141–142, but see David A. McCants, "The Authenticity of William Wirt's Version Of Patrick Henry's 'Liberty Or Death' Speech," *The Virginia Magazine,* 87 (October 1979), 387–402, and Christopher Looby, *Voicing America: Language, Literary Form, and the Origins of the United States* (Chicago: University of Chicago Press, 1996), pp. 270–278.

4. Peter Oliver, *Origin and Progress of The American Rebellion: A Tory View* [1781], eds. Douglass Adair and John A. Schultz (Stanford: Stanford University Press, 1967), p. 41. For the ministerial role in rousing the colonists in the 1760s and after, see Alice M. Baldwin, *The New England Clergy and the American Revolution* (Durham: Duke University Press, 1928), Alan E. Heimert, *Religion and the American Mind: From the Great Awakening to the Revolution* (Cambridge: Harvard University Press, 1966), and Richard H. Brown, "Spreading the Word: Rural Clergymen and the Communication Network of 18th-Century New England," *Proceedings of the Massachusetts Historical Society,* 94 (1982), 1–14.

5. Abraham Lincoln, "Fragment on the Constitution and the Union" [c. January, 1861] in Roy Basler, ed., *The Collected Works of Abraham Lincoln,* 8 vols. (New Brunswick: Rutgers University Press, 1953), IV: 169.

6. "In 1740 America's leading intellectuals were clergymen and thought about theology; in 1790 they were statesmen and thought about politics." Edmund S. Morgan, "The American Revolution Considered as an Intellectual Movement," in Arthur M. Schlesinger, Jr., and Morton White, eds., *Paths of American Thought* (Boston: Houghton Mifflin, 1963), p. 11.

7. See Leonard W. Levy, *The Establishment Clause: Religion and the First Amendment* (New York: Macmillan Publishing Company, 1986), pp. x, 123–131, 180–182. See, as well, *Lemon v. Kurtzman,* 403 U.S. 602, 612–613 (1971).

8. Reported in Gideon Welles, *Diary of Gideon Welles, Secretary of the Navy Under Lincoln and Johnson,* 3 vols. (Boston: Houghton Mifflin, 1909–1911), II: 190. For Lincoln's heavy reliance on religious language and imagery as president, see Robert A. Ferguson, "Lincoln: An Epilogue," *Law and Letters in American Culture* (Cambridge: Harvard University Press, 1984),

pp. 305–317, and Dwight G. Anderson, *Abraham Lincoln: The Quest for Immortality* (New York: Alfred A. Knopf, 1982).

9. The assumption that early American thought is dominated by a combination of religious and legal frames of reference has been made previously by Perry Miller, *The Life of the Mind in America from the Revolution to the Civil War* (New York: Harcourt, Brace, and World, 1965) and by J. C. D. Clark, *The Language of Liberty 1660–1832: Political Discourse and Social Dynamics in the Anglo-American World* (Cambridge: Cambridge University Press, 1994), pp. 1–45, 296–372. The first to note the twin dominance of religion and law in American thought and action was Edmund Burke, who also called each impulse a "main cause" of a uniquely American attachment to liberty, in Burke, "On Moving His Resolutions for Conciliation with The Colonies, March 22, 1775," *The Works of the Right Honourable Edmund Burke*, 16 vols. (London: F. and C. Rivington, 1803), III: 52, 54–55.

10. See Miller, *The Life of the Mind in America*, pp. 2–155.

11. See Leonard W. Levy, "State Establishments of Religion," *The Establishment Clause: Religion and the First Amendment* (New York: Macmillan Publishing Company, 1986), pp. 25–62, and Michael W. McConnell, "The Origins and Historical Understanding of Free Exercise of Religion," *Harvard Law Review*, 103 (May 1990), 1436–1437. For the original power and later dwindling status of the clergy in Revolutionary America, see Emory Elliott, "The Dove And Serpent: The Clergy In The American Revolution," *American Quarterly*, 31 (Summer, 1979), 187–203, and Don Weber, *Rhetoric and History in Revolutionary New England* (New York: Oxford University Press, 1987), pp. 152–154.

12. For the centrality of a rhetoric against luxury in the Revolution and subsequent problems in applying that rhetoric to post-Revolutionary America, see Edmund S. Morgan, "The Puritan Ethic and the American Revolution," *The William and Mary Quarterly*, 3rd series, 24 (1967), 3–43.

13. John Adams, *A Dissertation on the Canon and Feudal Law* [1765], in Charles Francis Adams, ed., *The Works of John Adams* 10 vols. (Boston: Little, Brown, 1850–1856), III: 451–453, 462.

14. For "building a wall of separation between church and state," see Thomas Jefferson to the Baptist Association of Danbury, Connecticut, January 1, 1802, in *The Writings of Thomas Jefferson*, ed. Albert E. Bergh, 20 vols. (Washington, D.C., Thomas Jefferson Memorial Association, 1907), XVI: 281–282 and *Everson v. Board of Education*, 330 U.S. 1, 15–16 (1947), where the Supreme Court explicitly adopts and extends Jefferson's language and intent. See, as well, Robert A. Ferguson, *The American Enlightenment* (Cambridge: Harvard University Press, 1994), pp. 73–79.

15. See Max Farrand, ed., *The Records of the Federal Convention of 1787*, rev. ed., 4 vols. (New Haven: Yale University Press, 1966), I: 450–452. For the framers' decision to separate religion from the state, see Walter Berns, "Religion and the Founding Principle," in Robert H. Horwitz, ed., *The Moral*

Foundations of the American Republic, 2nd ed. (Charlottesville: University Press of Virginia, 1979), pp. 157–182.

16. For decisions by the Supreme Court of the United States that have construed the Establishment Clause of the First Amendment to limit severely government recognition of religion and to restrict religious expression in aspects of the public sphere, see *Lemon v. Kurtzman*, 403 U.S. 602 (1971) (forbidding "an excessive government entanglement with religion"); *County of Allegheny v. American Civil Liberties*, 492 U.S. 573 (1989) (holding unconstitutional a freestanding display of a nativity scene on the main staircase of a county courthouse); *Wallace v. Jaffree*, 472 U.S. 33 (1984) (forbidding a one-minute period of silence in public schools "for meditation or voluntary prayer"); and *Lee v. Weisman*, 505 U.S. 577 (1992) (forbidding the offering of prayers as part of an official school graduation ceremony).

17. *Committee for Public Education v. Nyquist*, 413 U.S. 756, 820 (1973).

18. Levy, *The Establishment Clause*, pp. 180–181. Philip B. Kurland, using a different section of Lewis Carroll's *Alice's Adventures in Wonderland* comes to the same conclusion about the Court's confusion and willful shifts in direction. See Kurland, "The Religion Clauses and the Burger Court," *Catholic University Law Review*, 34 (Fall 1984), 14.

19. See Jesse H. Choper, "A Century of Religious Freedom," *California Law Review*, 88 (December 2000), 1741, and McConnell, *Harvard Law Review*, 1410–1415.

20. *Michael A. Newdow v. U.S. Congress, United States of America*, United States Court of Appeals for the Ninth Circuit (June 26, 2002), No. 00–16423 (D.C. No. CV-00-00495-MLS/Pan). See, as well, *The New York Times*, June 27, 2002.

21. Adams, *A Dissertation on the Canon and the Feudal Law*, in Adams, ed., *The Works of John Adams*, III: 449, 462. In 1788, in his *Defence of the Constitutions of the United States of America*, Adams would confirm his ongoing attachment to natural law by proclaiming that "The United States of America have exhibited, perhaps, the first example of governments erected on the simple principles of nature." *Works*, IV: 292. For the legitimizing gestures of longevity, "time out of memory," lending credence to Anglo-American law, see J. G. A. Pocock, *The Ancient Constitution and the Feudal Law: A Study of English Historical Thought in the Seventeenth Century* (1957; rpt. New York: W. W. Norton, 1967), pp. 30–55, 232–233, 241, and Pocock, *The Machiavellian Moment: Florentine Political Thought and the Atlantic Republican Tradition* (Princeton: Princeton University Press, 1975), pp. 506–552.

22. See Nathan O. Hatch, *The Sacred Cause of Liberty: Republican Thought and the Millennium in Revolutionary New England* (New Haven: Yale University Press, 1977), and Donald G. Mathews, "The Second Great Awakening as an Organizing Process, 1780–1830," *American Quarterly*, 21 (Spring, 1969), 23–43.

23. See J. C. D. Clark, *The Language of Liberty*, pp. 44–45. Publishing rec-

ords in early America also support the notion of a switch in emphasis. See Charles Evans, "preface to vol. 3," in Evans, ed., *American Bibliography: A Chronological Dictionary of All Books, Pamphlets, and Periodical Publications Printed in the United States of America, 1639–1800* (Chicago: Blakely Press, 1905), III: vii.

24. See Hatch, *The Sacred Cause of Liberty,* pp. 15–20, and Barry Alan Shain, *The Myth of American Individualism: The Protestant Origins of American Political Thought* (Princeton: Princeton University Press, 1994), pp. 167–240.

25. For the most complete account of Samuel Spring's descent into the grave of George Whitefield with relevant primary sources, see Charles Royster, *A Revolutionary People at War: The Continental Army and American Character, 1775–1783* (Chapel Hill: University of North Carolina Press, 1979), pp. 23–24, 383. See, as well, J. T. Headley, *The Chaplains and Clergy of the Revolution* (New York: Charles Scribner, 1864), pp. 92–93. The earliest printed account of the incident may well have been by the loyalist minister, Samuel Peters, in "Genuine History of Gen. Arnold, by an old Acquaintance," *Political Magazine* [London], I (Nov.-Dec., 1780), 746, reprinted in Kenneth Walter Cameron, ed., *The Works of Samuel Peters of Hebron, Connecticut* (Hartford: Transcendental Books, 1967), p. 164.

26. See Hatch, *The Sacred Cause of Liberty,* pp. 74–79. Samuel Sherwood, in perhaps the most influential single sermon from 1776, would draw particular attention to "jesuitical emissaries, the tool of tyrannical power" in *The Church's Flight Into The Wilderness: An Address on the Times*, in Ellis Sandoz, ed., *Political Sermons of the American Founding Era* (Indianapolis: Liberty Press, 1991), p. 512. See, as well, Stephen J. Stein, "An Apocalyptic Rationale for the American Revolution," *Early American Literature,* 9 (Winter, 1975), 211–225, and John Adams to Thomas Jefferson, May 18, 1817, in Lester J. Cappon, ed., *The Adams-Jefferson Letters: The Complete Correspondence Between Thomas Jefferson and Abigail and John Adams,* 2 vols. (Chapel Hill: University of North Carolina Press, 1959), II: 515.

27. Samuel Adams, "Article Signed 'Valerius Poplicola'" [*Boston Gazette,* October 5, 1772], *The Writings of Samuel Adams,* ed. Harry Alonzo Cushing, 2 vols. (1906; New York: Octagon Books, Inc., 1968), II: 336.

28. Most Revolutionary pamphlets that treated the subject claimed that the Puritans' first priority in settlement was religious liberty and that this priority kindled other forms of liberty. The actual accounting in the text is paraphrased and quoted from John Adams, "*A Dissertation on the Canon and Feudal Law,*" Adams, ed., *The Works of John Adams,* III: 445–464.

29. J. Hector St. John de Crevecoeur, "Letter III: What Is An American?" *Letters from an American Farmer* [1782] (New York: E. P. Dutton, 1957), pp. 36, 47.

30. Jonathan Edwards, *Some Thoughts Concerning the Present Revival of Religion in New England,* in Peter N. Carroll, ed., *Religion and the Coming of the American Revolution* (Waltham, Mass.: Ginn-Baisdell, 1970), pp. 2–9.

31. Edwards, *An Humble Attempt to Promote Explicit Agreement and Visible Union of God's People, in Extraordinary Prayer* [1746] in Carroll, ed., *Religion and the Coming of the American Revolution*, p. 14.

32. Ezra Stiles, *A Discourse on the Christian Union*, in Carroll, ed., *Religion and the Coming of the American Revolution*, pp. 69–70.

33. See Morgan, "The Puritan Ethic and the American Revolution," *The William and Mary Quarterly*, 3rd series, 24 (1967), 3–7; Sacvan Bercovitch, "How the Puritans Won the American Revolution," *Massachusetts Review*, 17 (1976), 597–630, and Clark, *The Language of Liberty*, esp. p. 13.

34. Edmund Burke, "On Moving His Resolutions for Conciliation With The Colonies, March 22, 1775," *The Works of the Right Honourable Edmund Burke*, III: 52. Alexis de Tocqueville offered a comparable summary in 1835 when tracing "the origin of the Anglo-Americans." "It [the character of Anglo-American civilization] is the result. . .of two distinct elements. . . .I allude to *the spirit of religion* and *the spirit of liberty*." Alexis de Tocqueville, *Democracy in America*, trans. Phillips Bradley, 2 vols. (New York: Vintage Books, 1958), I: 45.

35. Benjamin Colman, *Government the Pillar of the Earth: A Sermon Preached at the Lecture in Boston, Before His Excellency, Jonathan Belcher, Esq; Captain General and Commander in Chief, August 13th, 1730* (Boston: T. Hancock, 1730).

36. Jonathan Mayhew, *A Discourse Concerning Unlimited Submission and Non-Resistance to the Higher Powers* [1750], in Carroll, ed., *Religion and the Coming of the American Revolution*, pp. 30, 41.

37. Samuel Davies, *On the Death of His Late Majesty, King George II*, in Carroll, ed., *Religion and the Coming of the American Revolution*, pp. 17–23. For the development of the assumption of happiness into a full-blown *right* to happiness by 1768, see Daniel Shute, *An Election Sermon* [1768] in Charles S. Hyneman and Donald S. Lutz, eds., *American Political Writing during the Founding Era, 1760–1805*, 2 vols. (Indianapolis: Liberty Press, 1983), I: 109–136.

38. Gad Hitchcock, *An Election Sermon* [1774] in Hyneman and Lutz, eds., *American Political Writing during the Founding Era*, I: 281–304.

39. For just a few of the more prominent uses of the passage, see John Dickinson, "Letter V," *Letters from a Farmer in Pennsylvania* [1768] in Forrest McDonald, ed., *Empire and Nation: Letters from a Farmer in Pennsylvania, John Dickinson and Letters from the Federal Farmer, Richard Henry Lee* (Indianapolis: Liberty Fund, 1999), p. 29; George Washington to the Hebrew Congregation in Newport [August], 1790, in W. B. Allen, ed., *George Washington, A Collection* (Indianapolis: Liberty Classics, 1988), p. 548; Paul F. Boller, Jr., "George Washington and Religious Liberty," *The William and Mary Quarterly*, 3rd series, 17 (October, 1960), 486, and Silas Downer, *A Discourse on the Dedication of the Tree of Liberty*" [1768], in Hyneman and Lutz, eds., *American Political Writing During the Founding Era*, I: 98.

40. Scholarly debates over how important Locke's actual writings were to American understandings seem pointless in the light of general dissemination of those ideas through newspaper and other popular accounts, but for a recent summary of these debates, see J. C. D. Clark, *The Language of Liberty*, pp. 24–27.

41. Montesquieu, *The Spirit of Laws*, p. 151 [Bk. XI, No.6]. The most prominent of many uses of Montesquieu's definition in the American Revolution was that of the Continental Congress in its *Appeal to the Inhabitants of Quebec* in 1774. See Hyneman and Lutz, eds., *Political Writings during the Founding Era*, I: 235–236.

42. The two most famous Revolutionary sermons of 1776, by Samuel West and Samuel Sherwood, both adopted this tactic. See West, *A Sermon Preached before the Honorable Council, and the Honorable House of Representatives of the Colony of the Massachusetts Bay, May 29th, 1776*, in Carroll, ed., *Religion and the Coming of the American Revolution*, p. 146, and Sherwood, *The Church's Flight Into The Wilderness: An Address On The Times* [1776], in Sandoz, ed., *Political Sermons of the American Founding Era*, pp. 523–525.

43. For good examples of ministerial exploitation of the phrase, see Samuel Langdon, *Government corrupted by Vice, and recovered by Righteousness, A Sermon Preached Before the Honorable Congress of the Colony of the Massachusetts-Bay in New England . . . the 31st Day of May, 1775*, and David Jones, *Defensive War in a just Cause SINLESS, A Sermon Preached On the Day of the Continental Fast* [1775], both in Carroll, ed., *Religion and the Coming of the American Revolution*, pp. 141, 146.

44. Nathaniel Niles, *Two Discourses on Liberty*, in Hyneman and Lutz, eds., *American Political Writing during the Founding Era*, I: 258–259, 270–274.

45. Joseph Emerson, *A Thanksgiving-Sermon Preach'd at Pepperrell, July 24, 1766 . . . On Account of the Repeal of the Stamp-Act*, in Carroll, ed., *Religion and the Coming of the American Revolution*, pp. 89–90.

46. For examples, see Samuel West, *On the Right to Rebel Against Governors* [1776], and Simeon Howard, *A Sermon Preached to the Ancient and Honorable Artillery Company in Boston* [1773], in Hyneman and Lutz, eds., *American Political Writing during the Founding Era*, I: 432, 200.

47. For these and other examples, see George F. Scheer and Hugh F. Rankin, eds., *Rebels and Redcoats: The American Revolution Through the Eyes of Those Who Fought and Lived It* (New York: World Publishing Co., 1957), pp. 66, 51, 40, 339, 428, 433.

48. Daniel Shute, *An Election Sermon* [1768], in Hyneman and Lutz, eds., *American Political Writing during the Founding Era*, I: 109–112.

49. Joseph Bellamy, *The Millennium* [1758], in Alan Heimert and Perry Miller, eds., *The Great Awakening : Documents Illustrating the Crisis and Its Consequences* (Indianapolis: Bobbs-Merrill, 1967), pp. 609–610, 620–623.

50. Colman, *Government the Pillar of the Earth*, p. 22.

51. For the best known discussion of distrust of the law in just these terms, see John Hart Ely, *Democracy and Distrust: A Theory of Judicial Review* (Cambridge: Harvard University Press, 1980), pp. 56–59.

52. See Ferguson, "The Literature of Public Documents," *The American Enlightenment 1750–1820*, pp. 124–149.

53. In the "Preface" to the most complete and influential theory of constitutionalism of the day, his three-volumed master work, *Defence of The Constitutions of the United States of America* [1787–1788], John Adams was quite certain that a proper constitution created virtue rather than the reverse. Adams, ed., *The Works of John Adams*, IV, 284–287, 292–294, 298.

54. In the most pointed version of the premise, Montesquieu wrote *"it is necessary People's Minds should be prepared for the Reception of the best Laws"* and "Liberty itself has appeared intolerable to those nations who have not been accustomed to it." Montesquieu, *The Spirit of the Laws*, p. 292 [Bk. 19, Sect. 2].

55. E. P. Thompson, "The Rule of Law," *Whigs and Hunters: The Origin of the Black Acts* (New York: Random House, 1975), pp. 258–269.

56. John Locke, *Two Treatises of Government*, student edition, ed. Peter Laslett (Cambridge, Cambridge University Press, 1988), pp. 76–79, 405, 418–422.

57. For how American legal understandings related to the concept of liberty, see Reid, *The Concept of Liberty in the Age of the American Revolution*, pp. 1–84.

58. Samuel Johnson, *Taxation No Tyranny; an Answer to the Resolutions and Address of the American Congress* [1775], in Donald J. Green, ed., *Political Writings: The Yale Edition of the Works of Samuel Johnson, Volume X* (New Haven: Yale University Press, 1977), p. 454.

59. The claim of preeminence for *Letters from a Farmer in Pennsylvania* and *The Federalist* can be justified in three ways. They were the most influential examples of pamphleteering by lawyers in context. They were the longest and most carefully constructed pamphlet series by lawyers (or any other American writer) of the day. They were written by the best-educated lawyers in America in Dickinson and Jay and by a leading practitioner in Hamilton. Even Madison, who alone of the four never practiced law, can be included as a leading legal theoretician and lawgiver in the Federal Convention of 1787.

60. For the conservatizing elements in capping the Revolution, see Gordon S. Wood, *The Radicalism of the American Revolution* (New York: Alfred A. Knopf, 1992).

61. For the identification of Dickinson as "the penman of the Revolution," for the influence of *Letters from a Farmer in Pennsylvania*, and for Dickinson's clever manipulation of the persona of the simple farmer, see Carl F. Kaestle, "The Public Reaction to John Dickinson's *Farmer's Letters*," *Proceedings of the American Antiquarian Society*, 78 (1969), 323–359; Pierre Marambaud, "Dickinson's *Letters from a Farmer in Pennsylvania* as Political Dis-

course: Ideology, Imagery, and Rhetoric," *Early American Literature*, 12 (1977), 63–72; and Stephen H. Browne, "The Pastoral Voice in John Dickinson's First *Letter from a Farmer in Pennsylvania*," *Quarterly Journal of Speech*, 76 (February, 1990), 46–56.

62. John Dickinson, "Letter I," *Letters from a Farmer in Pennsylvania to the Inhabitants of the British Colonies* [1767–68] in Forrest McDonald, ed., *Empire and Nation: Letters from a Farmer in Pennsylvania, John Dickinson and Letters from the Federal Farmer, Richard Henry Lee* (Indianapolis: Liberty Fund Inc., 1999), I:3. All further references to *Letters from a Farmer in Pennsylvania* in the text will be to this readily available edition and, as above, will be identified first by letter number (roman numerals) and then page number (arabic numerals) to this edition.

63. Samuel Johnson, *Taxation No Tyranny; an Answer to the Resolutions and Address of the American Congress* [1775], pp. 424–425, 429.

64. Daniel J. Boorstin has argued that William Blackstone's *Commentaries on the Laws of England* ranked second only to the Bible as a literary and intellectual influence on the history of early American institutions. See Boorstin, "Preface to the Beacon Press Edition," *The Mysterious Science of the Law: An Essay on Blackstone's Commentaries Showing How Blackstone . . . Made of the Law at Once a Conservative and a Mysterious Science* (Boston: Beacon Press, 1958).

65. William Blackstone, *Commentaries on the Laws of England*, [1765–1769], Facsimile of the First Edition, 4 vols. (1765–1769; Chicago: The University of Chicago Press, 1979), I: 140–141, 123. [Emphasis added.] In the quotation, Blackstone refers to Book XI ("Of The Laws Which Establish Political Liberty With Regard To The Constitution") of Montesquieu's *The Spirit of the Laws*. For Blackstone's optimistic overview of English history, paraphrased in the text, see *Commentaries*, IV: 400–435.

66. Blackstone, for example, rejected the legitimacy of the Puritan Revolution of the 1640s altogether, thought the Glorious Revolution of 1688 a dubious precedent, and refused to discuss a legal theory of rebellion ("since law and history are silent, it becomes us to be silent too"). *Commenataries on the Laws of England*, IV: 431; I: 238.

67. See Reid, *The Concept of Liberty in the Age of the American Revolution*, pp. 25–28; also Daniel T. Rogers, "Natural Rights," *Contested Truths: Keywords in American Politics Since Independence* (New York: Basic Books, 1987), pp. 45–66.

68. John Adams to William Tudor, June 1, 1818, in Adams, ed., *The Works of John Adams*, X: 317.

69. James Otis, *The Rights Of The British Colonies Asserted And Proved* [1764] in Bernard Bailyn, ed., *Pamphlets of the American Revolution, 1750–1776* (Cambridge: Harvard University Press, 1965), pp. 426, 442–444. For a parallel interpretation of this pamphlet, see Robert H. Webking, "James Otis," *The American Revolution and the Politics of Liberty* (Baton Rouge: Louisiana State University Press, 1988), pp. 16, 25.

70. Quoted from, Edmund S. Morgan, ed., *Prologue to Revolution: Sources and Documents on the Stamp Act* (Chapel Hill: University of North Carolina Press, 1959), p. 56.

71. John Adams, Diary, 8 Sept. 1774, and Autobiography, in L. C. Butterfield, ed., *Diary and Autobiography of John Adams*. 4 vols. (Cambridge: Harvard University Press, 1961), II: 128–130; III: 309.

72. In eighteenth-century legal practice, natural law was rarely, if ever, a viable response to the strictures of positive law in either a civil or a criminal context. See Reid, *The Concept of Liberty in the Age of the American Revolution*, pp. 23–27.

73. Samuel West, *On the Right to Rebel Against Governors*, in Hyneman and Lutz, eds., *American Political Writing During the Founding Era*, I: 414.

74. John Adams quotes Otis here on a lawyer's preferred reading, Adams to Hezekiah Niles, January 14, 1818, in Adams, ed., *The Works of John Adams*, X: 275. See, as well, Otis, *The Rights of the British Colonies Asserted and Proved*, in Bailyn, ed., *Pamphlets of the American Revolution*, pp. 423, 447, and J. C. D. Clark, *The Language of Liberty*, pp. 100, 117–118.

75. Theophilus Parsons, *The Essex Result* [1778], in Hyneman and Lutz, eds., *American Political Writing During the Founding Era*, I: 494, 510–511, and Theophilus Parsons, Jr., *Memoir of Theophilus Parsons, Chief Justice of the Supreme Judicial Court of Massachusetts; with Notices of Some of His Contemporaries* (Boston: Ticknor and Fields, 1859), pp. 156–157, 166, 206–208.

76. Theophilus Parsons, *The Essex Result*, in Hyneman and Lutz, eds., *American Political Writing During the Founding Era*, I: 486, 490–491.

77. The quotation is from Alexander Hamilton, "The Federalist No. 26," *The Federalist: A Commentary on The Constitution of the United States* (New York: Modern Library, 1937), 26:159, but similar sentiments abound elsewhere in the text. See for example, *The Federalist*, 10:55, 1:5 All further references to *The Federalist* in the text will be to this edition and will be noted there, as here, first by the number of the *Federalist* paper in which the reference appears and then by page number to the Modern Library edition.

78. Hamilton spoke for all three contributors in the last *Federalist* paper with an assertion that is implicit everywhere in their prose. "I shall not dissemble," he wrote, "that I feel an entire confidence in the arguments which recommend the proposed system to your adoption, and that I am unable to discern any real force in those by which it has been opposed. I am persuaded that it is the best which our political situation, habits, and opinions will admit, and superior to any the revolution has produced" (85:570).

79. Publius repeatedly claimed that "theoretic reasoning, in this as in most cases, must be qualified by the lessons of practice" *The Federalist* (43:284), and he was dismissive of those who had not had that practice (2:11, 37:231, 85:573). He was particularly impatient in dealing with abstract theoretical assertions against the federal plan (9:49–50, 47:313–315).

80. Madison invokes "a finger of that Almighty hand" to explain "the unanim-

ity almost as unprecedented as it was unexpected" in the Federal Convention (37:231), but he traces faction to religious zeal and rejects the adequacy of religious and moral arguments as political controls (10:55,58). Hamilton and Jay use similar references to providence but within the same spirit of restriction (1:5, 2:9).

81. Here, in "Federalist No. 35," "learned professions" becomes "the man of the learned profession," and, although the legal profession is not singled out, the context makes it clear that Hamilton is not speaking here of clergymen or academicians so much as he is identifying men of affairs who take on civic assignments, where lawyers predominated.

82. Blackstone, *Commentaries on the Laws of England,* I: 6, 119.

83. For a recent discussion and application of preinterpretive concepts of law, see Anthony J. Sebok, *Legal Positivism in American Jurisprudence* (Cambridge: Cambridge University Press, 1998), pp. 246–251.

84. Blackstone, *Commentaries on the Laws of England,* I: 119–120.

85. Ibid., 120–121.

86. John Locke, "Of the State of Nature," *The Second Treatise,* in *Two Treatises of Government,* ed. Peter Laslett (Cambridge: Cambridge University Press, 1988), p. 275 [ch. 2, sect. 11–12].

87. Blackstone, *Commentaries on the Laws of England,* I: 119.

88. Sebok, *Legal Positivism in American Jurisprudence,* p. 251.

89. John Hart Ely, *Democracy and Distrust,* p. 56.

90. The quotation is from Lloyd W. Weinreb, *Natural Law and Justice* (Cambridge: Harvard University Press, 1987), p. 125. My definition of legal positivism derives from Weinreb and the classic first study of this subject, Lon L. Fuller, *The Law in Quest of Itself* (Chicago: The Foundation Press, 1940), pp. 4–5, 16. For the predominance of legal positivism in modern law, see Heinrich A. Rommen, "The Victory of Positivism," *The Natural Law: A Study in Legal and Social History and Philosophy,* trans. Thomas R. Hanley (1947; Indianapolis: Liberty Fund, 1998), pp. 109–113. Fuller provided the original definition of legal positivism that all later discussions have had to cope with when he wrote "by legal positivism I mean that direction of legal thought which insists on drawing a sharp distinction between the law *that is* and the law *that ought to be.*" I rely here and in the next four paragraphs on the above sources for the philosophical differences between natural law and legal positivism; also on the recent defense of legal positivism in Sebok, *Legal Positivism in American Jurisprudence.*

91. *Olmstead v. United States,* 277 U.S. 438, 478 (1927). [Justice Louis Brandeis is dissenting in this opinion.]

92. *Meyer v. Nebraska,* 262 U.S. 390, 399 (1923).

93. The terminology, though not the application, in this sentence comes from Sebok, *Legal Positivism in American Jurisprudence,* p. 226.

94. Concern about the fragility of liberty and the need for special vigilance in protecting it is everywhere in Revolutionary rhetoric. Once again John

Dickinson presents the most articulate example of a general phenomenon. See *Letters from a Farmer in Pennsylvania*, I:3, II:14, VI:36.

95. Both the quotation and the description of how the Administration of George W. Bush "has encountered few obstacles from Congress or public opinion" while facing technical and highly contextual challenges from "federal judges, across the ideological spectrum" are from Linda Greenhouse, "The Imperial Presidency vs. the Imperial Judiciary," *The New York Times*, September 8, 2002.

96. Weinreb, *Natural Law and Justice*, p. 103

97. Ibid., p. 125. Lon Fuller's comparable version runs as follows: "The illusion characteristic of natural law is the belief that there is no limit to what human reason can accomplish in regulating the relations of men in society. The illusion characteristic of positivism is the belief that reason can deliberately set itself a limit and stop at this limit." See *The Law In Quest of Itself*, p. 110.

98. In this, Hamilton, Madison, and Jay are no different than other political theorists of their day and ours. For a general explanation of the phenomenon in these terms, see Weinreb, *Natural Law and Justice*, p. 67.

99. George M. Fredrickson traces this shift from revolution toward loyalty and toward a "new respect for nationalism and the positive state" through the ideological formations of the Civil War. See *The Inner Civil War: Northern Intellectuals And the Crisis Of The Union* (New York: Harper and Row, 1965), pp. 135, 184, 187, 191. I argue that some of the conditions enabling that shift came earlier.

3. The Commonalities of *Common Sense*

1. The divorce between historical claim and literary assessment is an interesting feature in the criticism of *Common Sense*. Historians emphasize its power as event, paraphrasing the language instead of analyzing it and tracing the presumed influences on Paine. Literary critics tend to ignore the implications and immediacy of a lost genre like the political pamphlet. Not surprisingly, the quoted literary assessment in the text comes from an historian who has studied the pamphlet tradition. See Bernard Bailyn, "Common Sense," *Fundamental Testaments of the American Revolution* (Washington, D.C.: Library of Congress, 1973), p. 7, and Bailyn, ed., *Pamphlets of the American Revolution, 1750–1776* (Cambridge: Harvard University Press, 1965).

2. Jefferson's Declaration of Independence (1776), Harriet Beecher Stowe's *Uncle Tom's Cabin* (1851–1852), and Abraham Lincoln's Gettysburg Address (1863) are other obvious candidates. But the Declaration, a composite document, and Lincoln's "remarks" at Gettysburg were not instantly recognized as controlling expressions in their own times. *Uncle Tom's Cabin* did have an immediate impact, and it is still avidly read, but aspects of its mes-

sage have been rejected by later Americans. Compare favorable contemporary usage of a phrase like "common sense" to pejorative evocations of
"uncle tom."

3. In the disputes over numbers of copies printed, I accept the guarded assessment of Paine's most thorough, recent biographer. See John Keane, *Tom
Paine, A Political Life* (London: Bloomsbury Publishing, 1995), pp. 108–
111, and also A. J. Ayer, *Thomas Paine* (New York: Atheneum, 1988),
p. 35, and Eric Foner, *Tom Paine and Revolutionary America* (New York:
Oxford University Press, 1976), p. 79. Some scholars have suggested up to
half a million copies in 1776, one for every four Americans then living. See
Arthur M. Schlesinger, *Prelude to Independence: The Newspaper War on
Britain 1764–1776* (New York: Alfred A. Knopf, 1958), p. 253. For Paine's
own comment, see Thomas Paine to Henry Laurens, January 14, 1779, in
Philip S. Foner, ed., *The Complete Writings of Thomas Paine*, 2 vols. (New
York: The Citadel Press, 1945), II: 1162–1163. [Hereinafter cited as *Com-
plete Writings of Paine*.] For a more conservative estimate of circulation, see
Patricia Loughran, "Virtual Nation: Local and National Cultures of Print,
1776–1850" (Ph.D. diss., University of Chicago, 1999).

4. For Washington's evaluation of *Common Sense*, see his letters to Colonel
Joseph Reed in January and March of 1776 quoted in *Complete Writings of
Paine*, I: 2. For the quotations from Franklin and Rush and a balanced sum-
mary of the overall impact of *Common Sense*, see Isaac Kramnick, "Editor's
Introduction," *Common Sense* (New York: Penguin Books, 1976), pp. 7–
10, and Keane, *Tom Paine, A Political Life*, pp. 103–114.

5. Eric Foner, *Tom Paine and Revolutionary America*, p. 74, xvi.

6. Manfred Pütz and Jon-K Adams, "Preface," *A Concordance to Thomas
Paine's Common Sense and The American Crisis* (New York and London:
Garland Publishing, 1989), vii.

7. *Common Sense* (New York: Penguin Books, 1976), pp. 82, 94. All further
references to *Common Sense*, unless otherwise noted, are to this readily
available Penguin edition.

8. Ibid., pp. 95–98, 118, 85.

9. Ibid., pp. 65, 100, 98.

10. Ibid., pp. 118–120, 70.

11. Ibid., pp. 100, 109–110, 88–89.

12. William L. Hedges, "Toward a Theory of American Literature, 1765–
1800," *Early American Literature*, 4 (1970), 5–14, and Hedges, "The Old
World Yet: Writers and Writing in Post-Revolutionary America," *Early
American Literature*, 16 (1981), 3–18.

13. *Common Sense*, pp. 88, 117–118.

14. Ibid., pp. 63, 82, 86.

15. Ibid., pp. 81, 64, 90, 99, 113.

16. Ibid., pp. 104–107, 120, 115, 86. For Paine's integrations of virtue and
prosperity, see David Wootton, "Introduction," *Republicanism, Liberty,*

and Commercial Society, 1649–1776 (Stanford: Stanford University Press, 1994), pp. 32–41, and Peter Messer, "Stories of Independence: Eighteenth-Century Narratives" (Ph.D. Diss., Rutgers University—New Brunswick, NJ, 1997).

17. *Common Sense,* pp. 95, 117–118.

18. We see this conflation most extensively in the long opening section that uses the First Book of Samuel to demonstrate "original sin and hereditary succession are parallels." Ibid., pp. 71–82.

19. For example, while insisting that he is "not inflaming or exaggerating matters," Paine also writes "the present winter is worth an age if rightly employed, but if lost or neglected the whole continent will partake of the misfortune." Ibid., p. 89.

20. Pocock, *Virtue, Commerce, and History: Essays on Political Thought and History* (Cambridge: Cambridge University Press, 1985), p. 276.

21. For the embroiled and thoughtless haranguer, see Howard Fast, *Citizen Tom Paine* (New York: Grove Press, 1943), pp. 18–19, 26–27, 47–48, 92–95. Eric Foner, among others, notes that Paine's originality lies not in his ideas, but in his innovative combination of others' ideas in an American context. Foner, *Tom Paine and Revolutionary America,* pp. 79–80. More recently, A. J. Ayer finds that Paine achieved his results "more by rhetoric, of which he was a master, than by force of argument"; David A. Wilson suggests "there was nothing particularly original about Paine's views" in placing him somewhere between philosopher and polemicist; and Jack T. Fruchtman, Jr. argues "Paine's life as a journalist, which was something he came to quite by accident in 1775, imparted to him much of his character and style." See, in order, Ayer, *Thomas Paine,* p. 36, Wilson, *Paine and Cobbett: The Transatlantic Connection* (Kingston and Montreal: McGill-Queen's University Press, 1988), pp. 48, 25, and Fruchtman, Jr., *Thomas Paine, Apostle of Freedom* (London: Four Walls Eight Windows, 1994), pp. 4–5.

22. *The Writings of Thomas Jefferson,* ed. H. A. Washington, 12 vols. (Washington, D.C.: Taylor and Maury, 1894), VII: 198.

23. Kenneth Burke uses the Aristotle quotation in discussing identification in rhetoric. See Burke, *A Rhetoric of Motives* (Berkeley: University of California Press, 1969), pp. 55–59.

24. Paine acknowledged his advantage in "bringing a knowledge of England with me to America." See *Complete Writings of Paine,* II: 1189.

25. Richard A. Lanham, *A Handlist of Rhetorical Terms,* 2nd ed. (Berkeley: University of California Press, 1991), pp. 131–135, and Kenneth Burke, *A Rhetoric of Motives,* pp. 49–50.

26. *Common Sense,* pp. 120, 89.

27. Benedict Anderson discounts philosophical coherence as a basis of national thinking in favor of language repetition in a print culture that encourages "deep, horizontal comradeship." A community is "imagined" in this pro-

cess of reiteration. See Anderson, *Imagined Communities: Reflections on the Origin and Spread of Nationalism* (London: Verso, 1983), pp. 13–16, 38–40.

28. Because of the controversies surrounding them, the biographical facts in the next five paragraphs have been winnowed from a consensus in five basic sources, all of which tend to repeat the same information in slightly different ways. Philip S. Foner, "Introduction," *Complete Writings of Paine*, I: ix–xii, Eric Foner, "The Making of a Radical," *Tom Paine and Revolutionary America*, pp. 1–17, A. J. Ayer, "The Years of Obscurity," *Tom Paine*, pp. 1–13, George Claeys, *Thomas Paine: Social and Political Thought* (Boston: Unwin Hyman, 1989), pp. 20–24, and John Keane, *Tom Paine, A Political Life*, pp. 3–71.

29. For Paine's account of his education and Christian upbringing, in *The Age of Reason*, see *Complete Writings of Paine*, I: 496–498. John Keane suggests that the tension between Quakerism and Anglicanism in Paine's upbringing not only led to early toleration of all religion but freed him rhetorically "by establishing nonreligious spaces of compromise." See *Tom Paine, A Political Life*, pp. 18–19. Jack Fruchtman, Jr. argues alternatively that the combination turned Paine into a secular preacher of sorts. Fruchtman, Jr., *Thomas Paine and the Religion of Nature* (Baltimore: Johns Hopkins University Press, 1993), pp. 172–175.

30. Eric Foner, *Tom Paine and Revolutionary America*, p. 3.

31. Maj. Gen. Charles Lee, second in command of the Revolutionary army, described Paine as one who "has genius in his eyes"; Lee to Benjamin Rush, February 25, 1776, in *Lee Papers*, 4 vols., *Collections of the New-York Historical Society for the Year 1871* (New York: New York Historical Society, 1872), I: 325, 312. John Adams, who introduced Paine to Lee in the first place as "a Citizen of the World," picked up and used Lee's phrase in his letters: Adams to Abigail Adams, April 28, 1776, in Charles Francis Adams, ed., *Familiar Letters of John Adams and His Wife Abigail Adams during the Revolution* (Freeport, N.Y., 1970; orig. pub. 1865), 167. In each instance, commentary implies the sudden appearance of a prodigy.

32. For accounts of these meetings and the scientific circles that Paine entered, see Keane, *Tom Paine, A Political Life*, pp. 42–43, 61, 79, 111.

33. *Complete Writings of Paine*, II: 3–15.

34. Paine in a reply to James Cheetham, August 21, 1807, quoted in Jack Fruchtman, "Nature and Revolution in Paine's *Common Sense*," *The History of Political Thought*, 10 (August 1989), 427 (28n). Scholars typically try to escape the dilemma of direct influence by arguing "Paine was, consciously or unconsciously, in agreement with Locke." See Ayer, *Thomas Paine*, p. 41, and Fruchtman, *Thomas Paine, Apostle of Freedom*, pp. 64–70.

35. Quoted in Philip S. Foner, "Introduction," *Complete Writings of Paine*, I: ix.

36. For Paine's Whig origins, see Claeys, *Thomas Paine: Social and Political Thought*, p. 20, and Eric Foner, *Tom Paine and Revolutionary America*, pp. 4–13. For different versions of the Quaker influence, see Moncure D. Conway, *The Life of Thomas Paine*, 2 vols. (New York: G. P. Putnam, 1892), and Harry Hayden Clark, "Introduction," *Thomas Paine: Representative Selections* (New York: American Book Company, 1944), xii–xv.

37. For arguments that use Paine's parents and marriages to "stretch Paine out on the couch," see Winthrop D. Jordan, "Familial Politics: Thomas Paine and the Killing of the King, 1776," *The Journal of American History*, 60 (September, 1973), 302–303.

38. See Isaac Kramnick, "Editor's Introduction," *Common Sense*, p. 27.

39. See Eric Foner, *Tom Paine and Revolutionary America*, xvii, 28–29, 32–43.

40. Joseph V. Metzgar, "The Cosmology of Thomas Paine," *Illinois Quarterly*, 37 (September, 1974), 47–63. See, as well, David A. Wilson, *Paine and Cobbett*, pp. 20–29.

41. See in order, Eric Foner, *Tom Paine and Revolutionary America*, pp. 4–13, Fruchtman, "Nature and Revolution in Paine's *Common Sense*," *The History of Political Thought*, 10 (Autumn 1989), 424–425, Ayer, *Thomas Paine*, pp. 17–23, J. C. D. Clark, *The Language of Liberty 1660–1832: Political Discourse and Social Dynamics in the Anglo-American World* (Cambridge: Cambridge University Press, 1994), pp. 30–38, 244, 329–338, and Wootton, "Introduction," *Republicanism, Liberty, and Commercial Society, 1649–1776*, pp. 32–39.

42. Quoted in Eric Foner, *Tom Paine and Revolutionary America*, p. 86.

43. "Independent Whig" to "The Printer," *New York Journal*, February 22, 1776.

44. I paraphrase and quote from Roger Shattuck, *Forbidden Knowledge: From Prometheus to Pornography* (New York: St. Martin's Press, 1996), p. 9.

45. Jack Fruchtman also sees, though with different implications, how Paine's political and social ideas "developed in ways that mirrored a wandering lifestyle" in *Thomas Paine, Apostle of Freedom*, p. 4.

46. The phrase came originally from the Latin poet Horace but was popularized by Immanuel Kant and other late eighteenth-century thinkers as the essential precondition in the spread of new knowledge or enlightenment. See Kant, "An Answer to the Question: 'What is Enlightenment?'" in Hans Reiss, ed. *Kant Political Writings*, trans. H. B. Nisbet (Cambridge, England: Cambridge University Press, 1970), p. 54.

47. For the quoted terminology and significance of the republic of letters, see Lewis P. Simpson, *The Brazen Face of History: Studies in the Literary Consciousness in America* (Baton Rouge: Louisiana State University Press, 1980) pp. 3–24. For the impact of the printing press on eighteenth-century Anglo-American culture, see Michael Warner, *The Letters of the Republic: Publication and the Public Sphere in Eighteenth-Century America* (Cambridge: Harvard University Press, 1990), and Larzer Ziff, *Writing in the*

New Nation: Prose, Print, and Politics in the Early United States (New Haven: Yale University Press, 1991).

48. *Common Sense*, p. 82.

49. See Robert A. Ferguson, "Writing the Revolution," in *The American Enlightenment, 1750–1820* (Cambridge: Harvard University Press, 1997), pp. 80–123.

50. *Common Sense*, p. 65.

51. Ibid., p. 65. The analogy of tyranny in government to original sin in humanity is kept afloat throughout "Of Monarchy and Hereditary Succession," where Paine concludes, "it unanswerably follows that original sin and hereditary succession are parallels" (p. 78).

52. Charles Inglis, "An American, The True Interest of America Impartially Stated" [1776], in Leslie F. S. Upton, ed., *Revolutionary Versus Loyalist: The First American Civil War, 1774–1784* (Waltham: Blaisdell Publishing Co., 1968), p. 73. Comparing Paine and Inglis, Stephen Newman argues that Paine's predictions tallied effectively with the eschatological framework of new world Calvinism. See Newman, "A Note on *Common Sense* and Christian Eschatology," *Political Theory,* 6 (February, 1978), 101–108.

53. The Whig Theory of History assumed that all of English history could be interpreted as a struggle to recover the lost rights of Anglo-Saxon times after they had been swept away by the Norman conquest in 1066. Magna Carta, the legal reforms of Edward the First, and the Glorious Revolution of 1688 became so many stepping stones along that path of recovery. For the most complete eighteenth-century version of this theory, one with which Americans were thoroughly familiar, see William Blackstone, "Chapter 33: Of the Rise, Progress, and Gradual Improvements, of the Laws of England," *Commentaries on the Laws of England,* 4 vols. (Oxford: Clarendon Press, 1765–1769), IV: 400–436.

54. *Common Sense*, pp. 69, 72, 78, 80.

55. Ibid., pp. 77, 80–81, 69.

56. Ibid., pp. 69–81.

57. Ibid., pp. 77, 80–81, 91.

58. Ibid., pp. 84, 89.

59. For the transformation from nature toward nurture in eighteenth-century notions of childhood, see Jay Fliegelman, *Prodigals and Pilgrims: The American Revolution against Patriarchal Authority, 1750–1800* (Cambridge: Cambridge University Press, 1982).

60. *Common Sense*, p. 108, but also pp. 87, 89, 99–100, 109, 114–115.

61. *Letter to the Abbé Raynal* in *Complete Writings of Paine,* II: 243. Written in 1782, this pamphlet gives Paine's most detailed account of the American Revolution.

62. Samuel Johnson, *Taxation No Tyranny: an Answer to the Resolutions and Address of the American Congress,* in Donald J. Greene, ed., *Samuel Johnson: Political Writings* (New Haven: Yale University Press, 1977), pp. 411–455. See, in particular, pp. 454, 428–429, 443, 417–418.

63. *Common Sense*, pp. 81–82.

64. Both the quoted phrase and the premise that "in the Age of Print a success-ful style involves a strategy of intimacy" are from Lewis P. Simpson, *The Brazen Face of History*, pp. 10–11.

65. *Common Sense*, p. 90.

66. Ibid., pp. 87–88.

67. Ibid., pp. 88–89. See, as well, p. 82.

68. Ibid., pp. 82, 85, 90, 93, 114, 121. The emphases on the word "now" in the quotations in the text are Paine's.

69. Ibid., pp. 89, 107, 108, 100. The emphases in these quotations are Paine's.

70. Ibid., p. 82.

71. Ibid., pp. 82, 120–121.

72. Ibid., p. 99. The biblical allusion is to Jesus, speaking as he is crucified, Luke 23:34.

73. Ibid., p. 87.

74. Ibid., p. 99–100.

75. For treatment of Paine's conflation of revealed and natural religion, see Fruchtman, *Thomas Paine and the Religion of Nature*, pp. 8ff.

76. *Common Sense*, p. 121.

77. Ibid., p. 81.

79. Putz and Adams, eds., *A Concordance to Thomas Paine's Common Sense and The American Crisis*, pp. 159, 331.

80. For Paine's "plain style," see Elaine K. Ginsberg, "Style and Identification in *Common Sense*," *Philological Papers: West Virginia University Bulletin*, 28 (1977), 26–36.

81. See James T. Boulton, *The Language of Politics in the Age of Wilkes and Burke* (London: Routledge and Kegan Paul, 1963), pp. 138–139.

82. L. H. Butterfield, ed., *The Diary and Autobiography of John Adams*, 4 vols. (New York, Atheneum, 1964), III: 333, and John Adams, *Thoughts on Government*, in Charles S. Hyneman and Donald S. Lutz, eds., *American Political Writing during the Founding Era*, 2 vols. (Indianapolis: Liberty Press, 1983), I: 403.

83. John Adams to Benjamin Waterhouse, October 29, 1805, in Worthington Chauncey Ford, ed., *Statesman and Friend: Correspondence of John Adams with Benjamin Waterhouse, 1784–1822* (Boston: Little, Brown, and Company, 1927), p. 31.

84. All sides predicted cultural collapse if the wrong choices were made in 1776. The one thing that Charles Ing is shared with Paine in his attack on *Common Sense* was his acceptance of a presumed threat to all of posterity. See Upton, ed., *Revolutionary versus Loyalist*, p. 83.

85. *Common Sense*, p. 68.

86. Ibid., pp. 71, 79. See, as well, pp. 78, 81, 87.

87. Ibid., p. 81.

88. Ibid., pp. 65–67.

89. In rhetorical terms, a parable involves "teaching a moral by means of an ex-

tended metaphor." See Lanham, *A Handlist of Rhetorical Terms*, pp. 106–107.

90. *Common Sense*, pp. 65–68.

91. Ibid., pp. 68–80, 81, 94.

92. Ibid., pp. 115, 117. See, as well, "The American Crisis, No. V," in *Complete Writings of Paine*, I: 125.

93. Ibid., p. 122.

94. See Martin Roth, "Tom Paine and American Loneliness," *Early American Literature*, 22 (Spring, 1987), 175–182.

95. *Common Sense*, p. 66.

96. Ibid., pp. 88–90. Paine quotes from Milton without revealing that it is Satan who is speaking in this passage from *Paradise Lost*. On the controlling importance of anger in *Common Sense*, see Roth, "Tom Paine and American Loneliness," p. 179.

97. *Common Sense*, p. 113.

98. "The Forester's Letters: No. III," April 22, 1776, in *Complete Writings of Paine*, II: 74.

99. Daniel Leonard, John Adams' leading opponent as Massachusettensis in 1775, supplies perhaps the best example of this call for calm in Loyalist rhetoric. See Upton, ed., *Revolutionary Versus Loyalist*, pp. 37–43.

100. For these qualities in Paine and for the quotation in this sentence, see Evelyn J. Hinz, "Thomas Paine," in Everett Emerson, ed., *American Literature, 1764–1789: The Revolutionary Years* (Madison: University of Wisconsin Press, 1977), pp. 48, 55–56.

101. Bernard Bailyn, *The Ideological Origins of the American Revolution* (Cambridge: Harvard University Press, 1967), pp. 25, 94–143, 17–19. Bailyn speculates that Paine brought his "daring impudence" and "uncommon frenzy" with him from England.

102. For treatments of the prevalence and general unruliness of mob behavior in eighteenth-century America, see Gordon S. Wood, "Notes and Documents: A Note on Mobs in the American Revolution," *William and Mary Quarterly*, 23 (October 1966), 635–642, Jesse Lemisch, "Jack Tar in the Streets: Merchant Seamen in the Politics of Revolutionary America," *William and Mary Quarterly*, 25 (July 1968), 371–407, Pauline Meier, "Popular Uprisings and Civil Authority in Eighteenth-Century America," *William and Mary Quarterly*, 26 (January 1970), 3–35, and Merrill Jensen, "The American People and the American Revolution," *The Journal of American History*, 57 (June 1970), 5–35.

103. Arthur M. Schlesinger, "Political Mobs and the American Revolution, 1765–1776," *Proceedings of the American Philosophical Society*, 99 (1955), 244.

104. John Dickinson, "Letter I," "Letter III," *Letters from a Farmer in Pennsylvania, to the Inhabitants of the British Colonies* (New York: Outlook Company, 1903), pp. 11, 29–30. See also Marc Egnal, *A Mighty Empire:*

The Origins of the American Revolution (Ithaca: Cornell University Press, 1988), pp. 213–214.

105. A large propertyless group of itinerant laborers, seamen, and artisans—men more or less in Paine's own first situation as an immigrant—constituted the rampaging mobs of the 1770s. The corset-maker from Thetford would have had more ties to these elements than Dickinson, the Philadelphia lawyer. See James Henretta, *The Evolution of American Society, 1700–1815* (Lexington, Mass.: D.C. Heath and Co., 1973), pp. 96–97.

106. *Common Sense*, p. 122.

107. As Merrill Jensen has argued, "some of the ordinary people in every colony were far ahead of their leaders in opposition to Britain." See Jensen, "The American People and the American Revolution," *The Journal of American History*, 57 (June 1970), 23.

108. Ibid., pp. 63–64, 72–81, 88–89, 99–100, 114–115.

109. *Common Sense*, p. 88. Elias Canetti, *Crowds and Power*, trans. Carol Stewart (New York: Farrar Straus Giroux, 1984; orig. pub. 1962), pp. 19–20.

110. *Common Sense*, pp. 72, 81, 114, 91, 93. Unlike Paine, Colonial American pamphleteers remain squeamish about assailing their king, preferring to blame British abuses on his ministers. As late as 1774, Thomas Jefferson, who goes farther than other Americans, still keeps his *A Summary View of the Rights of British America* "an humble and dutiful address to be presented to his Majesty." Jefferson and others attack the king directly only after learning the value of this lesson from *Common Sense*. See Adrienne Koch and William Peden, eds. *The Life and Selected Writings of Thomas Jefferson* (New York: Random House, 1944), pp. 22–26, 293.

111. *Common Sense*, pp. 88, 98, 114. See, as well, *Complete Writings of Paine*, I: 29.

112. In the first of *The American Crisis* pamphlets, also written in 1776, Paine justifies revenge and the right to exercise it as "the soft resentment of a suffering people." *Complete Writings of Paine*, I: 55.

113. *Common Sense*, pp. 89, 99, 121.

114. Ibid., p. 121.

115. Ibid., p. 100.

116. Ibid., p. 96.

117. Ibid., pp. 72, 76, 109, 95.

118. Ibid., pp. 117–118.

119. Ibid., p. 120.

120. Canetti, *Crowds and Power*, pp. 19–20, 29–30. See, as well, J. S. McClelland, *The Crowd and the Mob: From Plato to Canetti* (London: Unwin Hyman, 1989), pp. 1–33, 327–335.

121. For a parallel description of the same phenomenon with a different vocabulary, see Jack P. Greene, *Understanding the American Revolution: Issues and Actors* (Charlottesville: University Press of Virginia, 1995), pp. 285–286.

122. *Common Sense*, p. 112.

123. This bipolar anatomy of nationalist sentiment is the first premise in Ernest Gellner, *Nations and Nationalism* (Ithaca, N.Y.: Cornell University Press, 1983), p. 1.

124. Anderson, *Imagined Communities*, pp. 140, 12–15. See also E. J. Hobsbawm, *Nations and Nationalism since 1780* (Cambridge: Cambridge University Press, 1990), pp. 1–45.

125. For the terminology in this paragraph and a discussion of the ethnocentric against the cosmopolitan view of nationhood, see Jürgen Habermas, "The European Nation-State—Its Achievements and Its Limits: On the Past and Future of Sovereignty and Citizenship," in Gopal Balakrishnan, ed., *Mapping the Nation* (London: Verso, 1996), pp. 281–282, 286–288.

126. *Common Sense*, pp. 118.

127. "The American Crisis III," *Complete Writings of Paine*, I: 81.

128. *Common Sense*, p. 109.

129. David A. Wilson goes further when he argues that "it was characteristic of Paine not to leave things hanging; where there was room for concrete proposals, he would supply them," though the result might look like "a trail of contradictions." *Paine and Cobbett*, pp. 52–53.

130. *Common Sense*, p. 98. The Isaac Kramnick edition of *Common Sense* in Penguin Books, used here for general availability, leaves a blank space with a dash after the word "Royal" to indicate an unspoken pejorative noun for "King" in the quotation. I have substituted the word "Brute" for that dash, placing the word in brackets, relying on the use of that term in the Philip S. Foner edition of *Common Sense* in *Complete Writings of Paine*, I: 29.

131. See Robert N. Bellah, "Civil Religion in America," *Daedalus*, 96 (Winter, 1967), 1–21, and Bellah, *The Broken Covenant: American Civil Religion in Time of Trial*, 2nd ed. (Chicago: University of Chicago Press, 1992).

132. These distinctions between ritual and contest are elucidated by Claude Lévi-Strauss, *The Savage Mind* (Chicago: University of Chicago Press, 1962), p. 32.

133. For a balanced extrapolation of the rule of law used in this paragraph, see E. P. Thompson, "The Rule of Law," *Whigs and Hunters: The Origin of the Black Acts* (New York: Random House, 1975), pp. 258–269.

134. *Common Sense*, pp. 93, 120.

135. Thompson, *Whigs and Hunters*, p. 263.

136. *Common Sense*, p. 121.

4. Becoming American

1. John Locke, *The Second Treatise of Government: An Essay concerning the True Origin, Extent, and End of Civil Government*, in *Two Treatises of Government* [1690], ed. Peter Laslett (Cambridge: Cambridge University Press, 1988), p. 418 [sec. 230].

2. William Blackstone, *Commentaries on the Laws of England*, 4 vols. (Oxford: Clarendon Press, 1765–1769), IV: 92, 370, 374, 380–381.

3. For confirmation that "the American law of treason was the law of England transferred to a new home," see Bradley Chapin, *The American Law of Treason: Revolutionary and Early National Origins* (Seattle: University of Washington Press, 1964), pp. 3–9.

4. Jared Sparks, ed., *The Works of Benjamin Franklin*, 10 vols. (Boston: Hilliard, Gracy and Co., 1836–1840), I: 408.

5. Thomas Paine, *Common Sense* [1776], in Philip S. Foner, ed., *The Complete Writings of Thomas Paine*, 2 vols. (New York: Citadel Press, 1945), I: 43–44.

6. James Thomas Flexner, *Washington, the Indispensable Man* (Boston: Little, Brown, 1909), p. 145.

7. Quoted in James Thomas Flexner, *The Traitor and the Spy: Benedict Arnold and John Andre* (1953; Boston: Little, Brown, 1975), p. 372.

8. See Brander Matthews, ed., "Introduction," William Dunlap, *André: A Tragedy in Five Acts*, (New York: Dunlap Society, 1887), vii–xxiv, and William Gilmore Simms, "Benedict Arnold as a Subject for Fictitious Story," *Southern and Western Magazine*, 1 (April 1845), 257.

9. The following facts are taken from Frances Vivian, "The Capture and Death of Major André," *History Today*, 12 (December 1957), p. 813; Flexner, *Traitor and Spy*; and J. E. Morpurgo, *Treason at West Point: The Arnold-André Conspiracy* (New York: Mason/Charter Publishing, 1975).

10. Quoted from Noemie Emery, *Washington: A Biography* (New York: Putnam's Sons, 1976), p. 266.

11. Charles Royster, "The Nature of Treason: Revolutionary Virtue and American Reactions to Benedict Arnold," *William and Mary Quarterly*, 3d series, 36 (April 1979), 163–193.

12. "Narrative of General Lafayette," Marquis de Lafayette to the Chevalier de la Luzerne, September 26, 1780; Lafayette to Madame de Sesse, October 4, 1780; Lafayette to Madame de Lafayette, October 8, 1780, in *Papers concerning The Capture and Detention of Major John André*, ed. Henry B. Dawson (Yonkers: The Gazette, 1866), pp. 204–209. Where possible, references to primary materials are to the Dawson edition because of its complete collection of official and popular materials involving the event. [Hereinafter referred to as Dawson, *Papers*.]

13. Quoted in Vivian, "Capture and Death," p. 813.

14. Dawson, *Papers*, pp. 105–106.

15. Jeremiah Dummer, *A Defence of the New-England Charters* (Boston: B. Green and Company, 1745), pp. 22, 32.

16. John Adams to William Tudor, August 11, 1818, in *The Works of John Adams, Second President of the United States*, ed. Charles Francis Adams, 10 vols. (1850–1856; rpt. New York: Books for Libraries Press, 1960), X: 343.

17. Jonathan Mayhew, *A Discourse Concerning Unlimited Submisson And*

Nonresistance to the Higher Powers: With Some Reflections on the Resistance made to King Charles I. And on the Anniversary of his Death (Boston: D. Fowle and D. Gookin, 1750), p. 54.

18. Locke, *Two Treatises of Government*, pp. 418–419 [sec. 230–232].

19. For Patrick Henry's words and their context, see Norine Dickson Campbell, *Patrick Henry: Patriot and Statesman* (Old Greenwich, Conn.: Devin-Adair, 1969), pp. 56–61.

20. Merrill Jensen, *The Founding of a Nation: A History of the American Revolution, 1763–1776* (New York: Oxford University Press, 1968), pp. 103–104.

21. Evidence for this shift is based on content analyses of newspapers cited by Charles S. Hyneman and Donald S. Lutz in their edited collection, *American Political Writing during the Founding Era, 1760–1805*, 2 vols. (Indianapolis: Liberty Press, 1983), I: 656.

22. John Dickinson, "Letter III," *Letters from a Farmer in Pennsylvania* in *Empire and Nation*, ed. Forrest McDonald (Englewood Cliffs, N.J.: Prentice-Hall, 1962), pp. 17–18. The *Letters* first appeared between December 2, 1767 and February 15, 1768.

23. The right of resistance through natural law was everywhere in American pamphleteering after it was raised in 1750 by Jonathan Mayhew in *Discourse Concerning Unlimited Submission*, pp. 29–30, 38–40, 44–45.

24. The motto itself reached back to the Puritan Revolution of the 1640s, where John Bradshaw, the regicide judge, first used it against Charles I in the legal proceedings against the king. See George Earlie Shankle, *American Mottoes and Slogans* (New York: H. W. Wilson, 1941), p. 146.

25. Nathaniel Niles, *Two Discourses on Liberty*, in Hyneman and Lutz, eds., *American Political Writing*, I: 271.

26. *Essex Gazette*, July 13, 1775. See also Philip Davidson, *Propaganda and the American Revolution, 1763–1783* (Chapel Hill: University of North Carolina Press, 1941), pp. 22–23.

27. *Common Sense*, in Foner, ed., *The Complete Writings of Thomas Paine*, I: 43–44.

28. See Henry F. May, *The Enlightenment in America* (New York: Oxford University Press, 1976), pp. 42–65.

29. Lieutenant-Colonel Alexander Hamilton to Lieutenant-Colonel John Laurens, October 1780, in Dawson, *Papers*, p. 101.

30. Alexander Hamilton to Elizabeth Schuyler, October 2, 1780, and Alexander Hamilton to John Laurens, both in Dawson, *Papers*, pp. 94, 95.

31. Major Benjamin Tallmadge, "Narrative of the Detention of Major André," in Dawson, *Papers*, pp. 12–13.

32. "Narrative of Dr. James Thacher, of the Army of the Revolution, Concerning the Execution of Major André," in Dawson, *Papers*, pp. 131–133.

33. For an account of these elements as well as the quotation in this sentence, see Robert D. Arner, "The Death of Major André," *Early American Litera-*

ture, 9 (Spring, 1976), 52. See also Caleb Crain, "Introduction: The Ghost of André," *American Sympathy: Men, Friendship and Literature in the New Nation* (New Haven: Yale University Press, 2001), pp. 1–15.

34. See the account of Major Benjamin Talmadge, the presiding officer of the troops who captured André, in Dawson, *Papers*, pp. 9–10, and James Fenimore Cooper, *The Spy: A Tale of the Neutral Ground*, ed. James H. Pickering (Schenectady, N.Y.: New College and University Press, 1971), pp. 54, 68 [chs. 2 and 4].

35. Major John André to Commander George Washington, September 24, 1780, in *Proceedings of a Board of General Officers Held By Order of His Excellency Gen. Washington, Commander in Chief of the Army of the United States of America, Respecting Major John André, Adjutant General of the British Army, September 29, 1780* (Philadelphia: Francis Bailey, 1780) as reprinted in Dawson, *Papers*, pp. 20–22. All further references to the trial transcript will be to this source, hereinafter referred to as *Proceedings against Major André*.

36. *Proceedings against Major André*, pp. 20, 41.

37. John Laurens to George Washington, October 4, 1780, and George Washington to John Laurens, October 13, 1780, quoted in Saul K. Padover, ed., *The Washington Papers: Basic Selections from the Public and Private Writings of George Washington* (New York: Grosset and Dunlap, 1955), p. 367.

38. Hamilton to Elizabeth Schuyler, October 2, 1780, in Dawson, *Papers*, p. 94.

39. *Proceedings against Major André*, pp. 17–41, especially pp. 19–20, 22–26, 29–30.

40. William C. Dowling argues convincingly for "the eighteenth century as a literary moment dominated by epistolarity" in *The Epistolary Moment: The Poetics of the Eighteenth-Century Verse Epistle* (Princeton: Princeton University Press, 1991), pp. 21–25.

41. *Proceedings against Major André*, pp. 29–30.

42. Janet Gurkin Altman, *Epistolarity: Approaches to a Form* (Columbus: Ohio State University Press, 1982), p. 207.

43. John André to George Washington, October 1, 1780, *Proceedings against Major André*, p. 40.

44. See Altman, *Epistolarity: Approaches to a Form*, pp. 87–88.

45. For the most dramatic reworking of this theme, see William Dunlap, *André: A Tragedy in Five Acts: As Performed by the Old American Company, New-York, March 30, 1798* (New York: T. and J. Swords, 1798), but every major eyewitness account also raised the matter in excruciating detail. See Dawson, *Papers*, pp. 94, 103, 112, 132.

46. Alexander Hamilton to Elizabeth Schuyler, October 2, 1780, in Dawson, *Papers*, p. 94. Hamilton's public version of the André affair appeared in the *The Pennsylvania Gazette* on October 25, 1780. For his break with Washington in early 1781, see Alexander Hamilton to Philip Schuyler, February

18, 1781. *The Works of Alexander Hamilton*, ed. Henry Cabot Lodge, 12 vols. (New York: Putnam, 1904), IX: 232–236.

47. George Washington to Lieutenant-Colonel James Jameson, September 25, 1780, in Dawson, *Papers*, p. 74.

48. The debate over the issue is an extensive one. See Flexner, *Washington, the Indispensable Man*, pp. 147–148, and Flexner, *Traitor and Spy*, pp. 386–393, for arguments that "Washington had no choice." But see, as well, Morpurgo, *Treason at West Point*, pp. 134–146, 158–160, and Vivian, "Capture and Death,"p. 818, for comments that, in Vivian's words, "Washington, perhaps, in ignoring the young man's request went too far."

49. For the Cincinnatus image in Washington, see Garry Wills, *Cincinnatus: George Washington and the Enlightenment* (Garden City, N.Y.: Doubleday and Co., 1984). Washington's comments are contained in "General Orders, Headquarters, January 1, 1776," "General Orders, Headquarters, July 2, 1776," and "To the President of Congress, February 9, 1776," all in *George Washington: A Collection*, ed. W. B. Allen (Indianapolis: Liberty Classics, 1988), pp. 55, 71–72, 63. For a more general comment on discipline in the Revolutionary army and on Washington's belief in its efficacy, see Jensen, *The Founding of a Nation*, pp. 634–638.

50. "The Rules of Civility and Decent Behavior in Company and Conversation," in Allen, ed., *Washington, A Collection*, pp. 6–13. For a good analysis of Washington's overriding concern with duty and obligation, see Edmund S. Morgan, *The Meaning of Independence: John Adams, Thomas Jefferson, George Washington* (1976; New York: W. W. Norton, 1978), pp. 29–55.

51. The inability of later generations to comprehend Washington the disciplinarian is part of what Edmund S. Morgan calls "the story of how the American Revolution transformed some of the least lovable traits of a seemingly ordinary man into national assets." Morgan, *The Meaning of Independence*, p. 30. See also Michael Kammen, *A Season of Youth: The American Revolution and the Historical Imagination* (1978; New York: Oxford University Press, 1980), pp. 105–106, 118.

52. Dunlap, *André: A Tragedy in Five Acts*, p. 67.

53. Cooper, *The Spy*, pp. 221 [chap. 17], 337 [chap. 26], 356 [chap. 28], 383–388 [chap. 30]. See also James Fenimore Cooper, *Notions of the Americans: Picked Up by a Travelling Bachelor*, 2 vols. (1828; New York: Frederick Ungar, 1963), I: 217–222.

54. *The Ballad of Major André* in Dawson, *Papers*, pp. 236–239.

55. Paul M. Sniderman, *A Question of Loyalty* (Berkeley and Los Angeles: University of California Press, 1981), pp. 166–170.

56. *Proceedings against Major André*, pp. 18, 29–30.

57. Joel Barlow to Ruth Baldwin, October 2, 1780, quoted in Charles Burr Todd, *Life and Letters of Joel Barlow, L.L.D.: Poet, Statesman, Philosopher* (New York: Burt Franklin, 1972), p. 35; Arthur L. Ford, *Joel Barlow*

(New York: Twayne Publishers, 1971), p. 19; Joel Barlow, *The Columbiad* [1825], Bk. 6, lines 350–360, 549–610, 699–712 in *The Works of John Barlow* (Gainesville: Scholar's Facsimiles & Reprints, 1970), pp. 621, 630–637.

58. Charles Royster makes and documents these claims in "The Nature of Treason," pp. 164, 188. See also *The New-Jersey Journal*, November 21, 1781.

59. Morpurgo, *Treason at West Point*, p. 165, and Kammen, *A Season of Youth*, pp. 133–134.

60. Benedict Arnold to George Washington, September 25, 1780, and Arnold to Washington, October 1, 1780, in *Proceedings against Major André*, pp. 26, 36.

61. See Morpurgo, *Treason at West Point*, pp. 163–164.

62. *The New-Jersey Journal*, August 1, 1781; *The Providence Gazette*, August 11, 1781; *The New-Jersey Gazette*, July 25, 1781.

63. *A Representation of the Figures exhibited and paraded through the Streets of Philadelphia, on Saturday, the 30th of September 1780*, quoted in Royster, "The Nature of Treason," p. 164, 188–189.

64. John André to George Washington, September 24, 1780, and Benedict Arnold to George Washington, October 1, 1780, in *Proceedings against Major André*, pp. 20–21, 38–40.

65. Paine, *Common Sense* in *Complete Writings*, I: 43.

66. The most famous and influential of these treatments are those of James Fenimore Cooper in *Notions of the Americans*, I: 208–223, and William Gilmore Simms in "Benedict Arnold," *Views and Reviews in American Literature, History, and Fiction*, ed. C. Hugh Holman (Cambridge: Harvard University Press, 1962), pp. 55–75.

67. *Proceedings against Major André*, p. 41.

68. Arnold to Washington, September 25, 1780, in Dawson, *Papers*, pp. 117–118.

69. Hamilton to Elizabeth Schuyler, September 25, 1780, in Dawson, *Papers*, pp. 92–93.

70. Flexner, *Washington, The Indispensable Man*, p. 141. For the facts about Arnold in this paragraph and the next, I rely on Flexner, *Traitor and Spy*, and Morpurgo, *Treason at West Point*, pp. 48–86.

71. Royster, "The Nature of Treason," pp. 174–178.

72. Letter of General Anthony Wayne, September 27, 1780, in Dawson, *Papers*, p. 69.

73. Quoted in Morpurgo, *Treason at West Point*, p. 164.

74. See Flexner, *Traitor and Spy*, p. 392, and Colonel Alexander Scammell to Colonel Peabody, October 3, 1780, in Dawson, *Papers*, pp. 66–67.

75. Editorial from *The Pennsylvania Packet*, September 30, 1780, in Dawson, *Papers*, p. 228.

76. *The Pennsylvania Packet*, September 25, 1781. See, as well, Royster, "The Nature of Treason," pp. 163–193.

77. *The Pennsylvania Gazette*, September 30, 1780, in Dawson, *Papers,* p. 91.

78. Colonel Alexander Scammell to Colonel Peabody, October 3, 1780, in Dawson, *Papers,* p. 66.

79. "General Orders to the Army, Headquarters Orange Town, September 26, 1780," in Dawson, *Papers,* p. 64.

80. William Livingston to George Washington, October 7, 1780, in Dawson, *Papers,* p. 83; Abigail Adams to John Adams, October 15, 1780, *Letters of Mrs. Adams, The Wife of John Adams,* ed. Charles Francis Adams, 4th edition (Boston: Wilkins, Carter, 1848), p. 119.

81. See Baron De Montesquieu, *The Spirit of the Laws* [1748], trans. Thomas Nugent, 2 vols. (New York: Hafner Publishing Co., 1949), I: 190.

82. That the framers meant to curb excesses in dealing with the crime of treason is clear from Madison's discussion of the crime in "The Federalist No. 43," *The Federalist: A Commentary on the Constitution of the United States* [1787–1788] (New York: Modern Library, 1937), pp. 280–282.

83. For the power of Burr's Edwardsian connection, see John Adams to Thomas Jefferson, November 15, 1813, in *The Adams-Jefferson Letters: The Complete Correspondence between Thomas Jefferson and Abigail and John Adams,* ed. Lester J. Cappon, 2 vols. (Chapel Hill: University of North Carolina Press, 1959), II: 399.

84. See David Robertson, *Reports Of The Trials of Colonel Aaron Burr In The Circuit Court of the United States, Summer Term, 1807,* 2 vols. (Philadelphia: Hopkins and Earle, 1808), II: 95–101. For the demonization of Aaron Burr across the nineteenth century, see Charles F. Nolan, *Aaron Burr and the American Literary Imagination* (Westport, Conn.: Greenwood Press, 1980).

5. The Forgotten Publius

1. For the naming of Jay as "the third" or "forgotten Publius," see Garry Wills, "Chapter 30: The Third Publius," *Explaining America: The Federalist* (1981; rpt. New York: Penguin Books, 1982), pp. 248–253.

2. Quoted in Frank Monaghan, *John Jay* (New York: Bobbs-Merrill, 1935), p. 284.

3. See Monaghan, *John Jay,* pp. 292–294.

4. John Jay to James Lowell, May 10, 1785, in Henry P. Johnston, ed., *The Correspondence and Public Papers of John Jay,* 4 vols. (New York: G. P. Putnam's Sons, 1890–1893), III: 143.

5. John Jay to George Washington, June 27, 1786, and January 7, 1787, in *The Correspondence and Public Papers of John Jay,* III: 204, 226–227.

6. John Jay to John Adams, October 14, 1785, November 1, 1785, November 1, 1786, July 25, 1787, in *The Correspondence and Public Papers of John Jay,* III: 172–174, 175–178, 214–215, 250–251.

7. John Jay to Thomas Jefferson, January 9, 1786, August 18, 1786, Septem-

ber 8, 1787, in *The Correspondence and Public Papers of John Jay*, III: 178–180, 210, 253.

8. George Washington to John Jay, March 10, 1787, and May 18, 1786, John Jay to George Washington, March 16, 1786, June 27, 1786, January 7, 1787, July 25, 1787, in *The Correspondence and Public Papers of John Jay*, III: 238–240, 195–196, 186–187, 203–205, 226–229, 250.

9. John Jay to John Adams, October 14, 1785, and May 4, 1786, in *The Correspondence and Public Papers of John Jay*, III: 172, 194–195.

10. John Jay to Thomas Jefferson, October 27, 1786, in *The Correspondence and Public Papers of John Jay*, III: 212.

11. John Jay to John Adams, July 25, 1787, and John Adams to John Jay, September 22, 1787, in *The Correspondence and Public Papers of John Jay*, III: 250–251, 253–255.

12. For this controversy and the quotations, see Richard Morris, *Witnesses at the Creation: Hamilton, Madison, Jay and the Constitution* (New York: Holt, Rinehart and Winston, 1985), pp. 7–11.

13. Alexander Hamilton, John Jay, and James Madison, *The Federalist: A Commentary on the Constitution of the United States, Being a Collection of Essays written in Support of the Constitution agreed upon September 17, 1787, by the Federal Convention*, ed. Edward Meade Earle (New York: Modern Library, 1937), pp. 3–7. [Cited hereafter as *The Federalist* and by particular paper.]

14. "The Federalist No. 1," *The Federalist*, pp. 3–7.

15. "The Federalist No. 2," *The Federalist*, 8–11.

16. Ibid., pp. 9–10.

17. Ibid., pp. 8–9.

18. John Jay to James Lowell, May 20, 1786, in *The Correspondence and Public Papers of John Jay*, III: 143.

19. Each of the three premises is important to *The Federalist*, but all three achieve their logical maturation as stylistic devices five months later in Jay's longer pamphlet, printed by Samuel and John Loudon, "Printers to the State," in the Spring of 1788 under the full title of *An Address to the People of the State of New York, on the Subject of the Constitution, Agreed upon at Philadelphia, the 17th of September, 1787*. Accordingly, I pair prominent references from *The Federalist* with their subsequent exposition in *An Address to the People of the State of New York*.

20. *An Address to the People of the State of New York* in *The Correspondence and Public Papers of John Jay*, III: 318; "The Federalist No. 4," *The Federalist*, p. 19; "The Federalist No. 64," *The Federalist*, p. 422.

21. See, for example, Jonathan Edwards, in *An Humble Attempt to Promote Explicit Agreement and Visible Union of God's People, in Extraordinary Prayer* (1746), or Ezra Stiles, in *A Discourse on the Christian Union* (1761), in Peter N Carroll, ed., *Religion and the Coming of the American Revolution* (Waltham, Mass: Ginn-Blaisdell, 1970), pp. 13–15, 76–79.

22. *The Federalist,* pp. 9–10.
23. *The Correspondence and Public Papers of John Jay,* III: 295–296.
24. *The Federalist,* pp. 10–12. For these theories of linkage, see Arthur O. Lovejoy, *The Great Chain of Being: A Study of the History of an Idea* (Cambridge, Mass.: Harvard University Press, 1936). For the authority of *The Federalist* residing in comprehensiveness of view, see Albert Furtwangler, *The Authority of Publius: A Reading of the Federalist Papers* (Ithaca: Cornell University Press, 1984), pp. 80–97.
25. *The Correspondence and Public Papers of John Jay,* III: 295, and *The Federalist,* pp. 14, 16–17, 20, 23.
26. For Jay's subtlety on the concept of union, see Morton White, *Philosophy, The Federalist, and the Constitution* (New York: Oxford University Press, 1987), pp. 150–155.
27. *An Address to the People of the State of New York* in *The Correspondence and Public Papers of John Jay,* III: 312, 304–305.
28. *The Federalist,* pp. 24–26.
29. *The Correspondence and Public Papers of John Jay,* III: 311, 295–296, 315.
30. "The Federalist No. 2," "The Federalist No. 4," *The Federalist,* pp. 12, 22; also William Shakespeare, *King Henry the Eighth* [Act 3, scene 2, line 351].
31. *An Address to the People of the State of New York* in *The Correspondence and Public Papers of John Jay,* III: 316.
32. "The Federalist No. 2," *The Federalist,* p. 11. Jay as Publius parallels the earlier Continental Congress with current opponents of the Constitutional Convention in this passage, and subsequent *Federalist* papers make it clear that the analogy holds.
33. "The Federalist No. 2," *The Federalist,* p. 11–12.
34. *An Address to the People of the State of New York* in *The Correspondence and Public Papers of John Jay,* III: 295, 307.
35. Ibid., 295, 307, 317.
36. For example, the first page of every brief submitted to the Supreme Court of the United States contains just one sentence: the precise question that legal counsel want the Court to answer in a form that will lead to the answer counsel desire.
37. "The Federalist No. 2," *The Federalist,* p. 8.
38. "The Federalist No. 3" *The Federalist,* p. 14.
39. "The Federalist No. 4," *The Federalist,* p. 22.
40. *An Address to the People of the State of New York* in *The Correspondence and Public Papers of John Jay,* III: 307.
41. Ibid., 314–315.
42. Alexander Hamilton introduces the entire pamphlet series with this claim in "The Federalist No. 1," *The Federalist,* p. 3. See, as well, Robert A. Ferguson, *Law and Letters in American Culture* (Cambridge: Harvard University Press, 1984), pp. 1–33.
43. Francis Bacon, "Of Honor and Reputation" [1625], *The Essays or Coun-*

sels, Civil and Moral, in the Works of Francis Bacon, 10 vols. (London; W. Baynes and Son, 1824), II: 381–382.

44. "The Federalist No. 2," *The Federalist,* p. 10.

45. For the fascination with classical lawgivers, see "The Federalist No. 38," *The Federalist,* pp. 233–234, and David F. Epstein, *The Political Theory of The Federalist* (Chicago: The University of Chicago Press, 1984), pp. 25–26.

46. Arthur Hugh Clough, *Plutarch's Lives,* Dryden Edition, 3 vols. (New York: E. P. Dutton & Co.), I: 130, 142, 151, 161–164.

47. "The Federalist No. 2," *The Federalist,* p. 10.

48. *An Address to the People of the State of New York* in *The Correspondence and Public Papers of John Jay,* III: 301–305, 308–310. [Emphasis added.]

49. Ibid., 295, 305.

50. "The Federalist No. 2," *The Federalist,* pp. 9–12.

51. Ibid.

52. Quoted in Richard B. Morris, *Witness at the Creation: Hamilton, Jay, and the Constitution* (New York: Holt, Rinehart, and Winston, 1985), p. 62.

53. Richard B. Morris, *John Jay, The Nation, and The Court* (Boston: Boston University Press, 1967), p. 35.

54. Morris, *Witness at the Creation,* pp. 240–243.

55. Francis Hutcheson, *An Essay on the Nature and Conduct of the Passions and Affections* [1742], ed. Paul McReynolds (Gainesville: Scholars' Facsimiles and Reprints, 1969), p. 185. For the nature of these influences and the direct relevance of Hutcheson and moral sense philosophy to the writing of *The Federalist,* see Daniel Howe, ' The Political Psychology of *The Federalist, William and Mary Quarterly,* 44 (July 1987), 485–509.

56. *An Address to the People of the State of New York* in *The Correspondence and Public Papers of John Jay,* III: 294, 319.

6. Finding Rome in America

1. See Bernard Bailyn, *The Ideological Origins of the American Revolution* (Cambridge, Mass.: Harvard University Press, 1967), pp. 23–26. Bailyn concludes "the classics of the ancient world are everywhere in the literature of the Revolution, but they are everywhere illustrative, not determinative, of thought." From the other side, see Carl J. Richard, *The Founders and the Classics: Greece, Rome, and the American Enlightenment* (Cambridge: Harvard University Press, 1994), pp. 232–243. Richard argues "it is clear that the classics exerted a formative influence upon the founders."

2. For a functional approach, see *Classical Humanities in the American Republic: Final Report of the Committee of the American Philological Association to the Division of Education Programs of the National Endowment for the Humanities on the Completion of the Three Year Program under Grant EH-9601–74–321* (February 1, 1977), pp. 6–10, 17–27.

3. Stephen Botein in *Classical Humanities in the American Republic: Final Report*, pp. 6–10, 17–24, and Meyer Reinhold, *Classica Americana: The Greek and Roman Heritage in the United States* (Detroit: Wayne State University Press, 1984), and Reinhold, ed., *The Classick Pages: Classical Reading of Eighteenth-Century Americans* (University Park, Pa.: American Philological Association, 1975).

4. See Henry Steele Commager, "The American Enlightenment and the Ancient World: A Study in Paradox," *Proceedings of the Massachusetts Historical Society*, 83 (1971), 3–15, especially pp. 7, 9–11.

5. See George Earlie Shankle, *American Mottoes and Slogans* (New York: H. W. Wilson Co., 1941) pp. 49–50, and "Report on a Seal for the United States, with Related Papers" in Julian Boyd, ed., *The Papers of Thomas Jefferson*, 30 vols.— (Princeton: Princeton University Press, 1950—2003), I: 494–497.

6. Bates Lowry, *Building A National Image: Architectural Drawings For The American Democracy, 1789–1912* (Washington, D.C.: National Building Museum, 1985), p. 10.

7. *The Aeneid* [bk ix, line 625] in Virgil [Works], ed. H. Rushton Fairclough, Loeb Classical Library, 2 vols. (Cambridge: Harvard University, 1930), II: 154; Virgil, *The Pastoral Poems*, trans. E. V. Rieu (1949; Middlesex, England: Penguin Classics, 1972), pp. 52–53; and Virgil, *Eclogue Four* [line 5], in Virgil, *Opera*, ed. R. A. B. Mynors (Oxford: Clarendon Press, 1969), p. 10. [Emphasis added in the English translations.] Charles Thomson, secretary to Congress from its inception in 1774 until 1789, gives the eighteenth-century signification of *Annuit Coeptis*. See http://www.greatseal.com

8. For Enlightenment thought and the national anthem, see Robert A. Ferguson, "What Is Enlightenment?': Some American Answers," *American Literary History*, 1 (Summer, 1989), 249–256.

9. See Fred Somkin, *Unquiet Eagle: Memory and Desire in the Idea of American Freedom, 1815–1860* (Ithaca, N.Y.: Cornell University Press, 1967), pp. 55–130.

10. Seymour Martin Lipset, *The First New Nation: The United States in Historical and Comparative Perspective* (1963; rpt. Garden City, N.Y.: Anchor Books, 1967), pp. 17–18, 38–40.

11. See Joyce Appleby, *Inheriting the Revolution: The First Generation of Americans* (Cambridge: Harvard University Press, 2000), p. 240.

12. See Edwin A. Miles, "The Whig Party and the Menace of Caesar," *Tennessee Historical Quarterly*, 27 (Winter, 1968), 361–379.

13. Alexander Hamilton in "The Federalist No. 9," and James Madison, "The Federalist No. 14," in Edward Mead Earle, ed., *The Federalist: A Commentary on The Constitution of The United States* (New York: Random House, 1937), pp. 47, 81, 85, 80.

14. Douglass Adair, "Experience Must Be Our Only Guide," *Fame And The*

Founding Fathers, ed. Trevor Colbourn (New York: W. W. Norton & Co., 1974), pp. 106–123.

15. John Adams to Benjamin Rush, December 4, 1805, in John A. Schutz and Douglass Adair, eds., *The Spur of Fame: Dialogues of John Adams and Benjamin Rush, 1805–1813* (San Marino: The Huntington Library, 1966), p. 44. See as well *The Oxford Classical Dictionary*, 2nd edition (London: Oxford University Press, 1970), pp. 234–236, 648, 928–930, and Reinhold, *Classica Americana*, pp. 94–100, 156–157.

16. For a knowing comparison of early republicans to the classical lawgivers, see James Madison, "The Federalist No. 38," *The Federalist*, pp. 233–235.

17. See William Smith, *An Oration of General Montgomery and of the Officers and Soldiers Who Fell with Him, December 31, 1775, before Quebec, Drawn Up (and Delivered February 19th, 1776) at the Desire of the Honourable Continental Congress*, 2nd ed. (Philadelphia, 1776), pp. 1–3, 20, 12, and Michael T. Gilmore, "Eulogy as Symbolic Biography: The Iconography of Revolutionary Leadership, 1776–1826," *Harvard English Studies*, 18 (1978), 131–135.

18. See Garry Wills, *Cincinnatus: George Washington & The Enlightenment* (Garden City, N.Y.: Doubleday, 1984).

19. See Howard Mumford Jones, "Roman Virtue," *O Strange New World: American Culture: The Formative Years* (1963; rpt. New York: Viking Press, 1968), pp. 227–272.

20. Stephen Botein, "Cicero As Role Model For Early American Lawyers: A Case Study in Classical 'Influence'," *Classical Journal*, 73 (Spring, 1978), 314, and Francis Bacon, "Of Honor And Reputation" [1625], *The Essays or Counsels, Civil and Moral*, in *The Works of Francis Bacon*, 10 vols. (London: W. Baynes and Son, 1824), II: 381–382.

21. Charles F. Montgomery and Patricia E. Kane, eds., *American Art: 1750–1800, Towards Independence* (Boston: New York Graphic Society, 1976), pp. 95–105.

22. John Adams to Thomas Jefferson, May 1, 1812, and Thomas Jefferson to John Adams, February 28, 1796, in Lester J. Cappon, ed. *The Adams-Jefferson Letters: The Complete Correspondence Between Thomas Jefferson and Abigail and John Adams*, 2 vols. (Chapel Hill: University of North Carolina Press, 1959), II: 301, I: 260. [Emphasis added.]

23. See Max Farrand, ed., *The Records of the Federal Convention of 1787*, rev. ed., 4 vols. (New Haven: Yale University Press, 1966), I: 49, II: 36, 93.

24. Jefferson to Adams, June 27, 1813, in Cappon, ed., *The Adams-Jefferson Letters*, II: 335–336. For the split between Federalists and Republicans, see Daniel Sisson, *The American Revolution of 1800* (New York: Alfred A. Knopf, 1974).

25. See Pauline Maier, "Popular Uprisings and Civil Authority in Eighteenth-Century America," *William and Mary Quarterly*, 3rd ser., 27 (1970), 3–35, and J. S. McClelland, "The Crowd and Liberty: Machiavelli, Montesquieu,

and America," *The Crowd And The Mob: From Plato to Canetti* (London, Unwin Hyman, 1989), pp. 93–109.

26. Charles Lee to Robert Morris, August 15, 1782, quoted in Reinhold, ed., *The Classick Pages*, pp. 20, 40.

27. John Adams, *A Defence of the Constitutions of the United States of America*, in Charles Francis Adams, ed., *The Works of John Adams*, 10 vols. (Boston: Little and Brown, 1851), IV: 469.

28. John Adams to Benjamin Rush, September 30, 1805, *The Spur of Fame*, pp. 42–43. ["The Scenery of the Business" refers to Napoleon.]

29. Quoted in Reinhold, ed., *The Classick Pages*, pp. 82–83.

30. For these artistic influences, see Peter Gay, *The Enlightenment*, 2 vols. (1966; rpt. New York: Norton Library, 1977), I: 46, 84–85, 120, and II: 231, 293–298.

31. Gay, *The Enlightenment*, II: 293–298, and James Thomas Flexner, *America's Old Masters*, rev. ed. (Garden City, N.Y.: Doubleday & Co., 1980), pp. 45–47, 339–340. Flexner quotes Winckelmann.

32. Joshua Reynolds delivered his famous discourses between 1769 and 1790, and they were published in regular editions, starting in 1778. The influence of Winckelmann is clear. Reynolds argued in "Discourse III" that the artist must "become possessed of the idea of that central form . . . by a careful study of the works of the ancient sculptors." In "Discourse IV" "grandeur of design" took precedence over "strict historical truth" in "History Painting." "Discourse VIII" placed "repose" over "novelty" and ruled out contrast and "excesses of all kinds." Joshua Reynolds, *Discourses On Art*, ed. Robert R. Wark (San Marino: Huntington Library, 1959), pp. 45. 59–60, 73, 77, 146–147, 154–155.

33. See Flexner, "Benjamin West's American Neo-Classicism," *America's Old Masters*, pp. 315–340, and Jules David Prown, "Benjamin West and the Use of Antiquity," *American Art*, 10 (Summer, 1996), 29.

34. Joel Barlow, *The Columbiad* [1828], Bk. 8, lines 587–604 and note 45, in *The Works of Joel Barlow*, 2 vols. (Gainesville: Scholars' Facsimiles & Reprints, 1970), II: 290, 417–425.

35. For political placement of West, see William L. Vance, *America's Rome*, 2 vols. (New Haven: Yale University Press, 1989), I: 15–17.

36. Tacitus, *The Annals*, Bk. 2: 69–88, and Bk. 3: 1–5, in Moses Hadas, ed., *Complete Works of Tacitus* (New York: Modern Library, 1942), pp. 92–104. See, as well, Kenneth Silverman, *A Cultural History of the American Revolution* (New York: Thomas Y. Crowell Co., 1976), pp. 118–130.

37. *The Odes of Horace*, trans. James Michie (1964; rpt. London: Penguin Books, 1967), pp. 152–155 [Bk. 3, No. 5].

38. See Bailyn, *The Ideological Origins of the American Revolution*; J. G. A. Pocock, *The Machiavellian Moment: Florentine Political Thought and the Atlantic Republican Tradition* (Princeton: Princeton University Press, 1975), pp. 462–552, and Gordon S. Wood, *The Creation of the American*

Republic, 1776–1787 (1969; rpt. New York: W. W. Norton, 1972), pp. 1–124. For the English context, see Prown, "Benjamin West and the Use of Antiquity," pp. 41–43.

39. Tacitus, *The Annals*, p. 102 [Bk 3: 1], and *The Odes of Horace*, p. 155.

40. Joyce Appleby describes this problem of "an unpoliced public sphere" in *Inheriting the Revolution*, pp. 35, 148–150.

41. Reynolds, *Discourses on Art*, p. 78 ["Discourse V"].

42. "In the eighteenth century, politicians and political commentators on both sides of the Atlantic shared the fear that the mob would 'get out of hand'." John S. McClelland, *The Crowd and the Mob*, pp. 2, 102–104, 111. See, as well, Bailyn, *The Ordeal of Thomas Hutchinson* (Cambridge: Harvard University Press, 1974), pp. 35–69, 109–155; and James A. Henretta and Gregory H. Nobles, *Evolution and Revolution: American Society, 1600–1820* (Lexington, Mass.: D.C. Heath and Co., 1987), pp. 129–132, 138–139.

43. Elias Canetti, *Crowds and Power,* trans. Carol Stewart (New York: Farrar Straus Giroux, 1984), pp. 16–19, 27–28.

44. Edward G. Parker, *The Golden Age of Oratory* (Boston: Whittenmore, Niles, and Hall, 1857), p. 1.

45. Robert A. Ferguson, *Law and Letters in American Culture* (Cambridge: Harvard University Press, 1984), pp. 77–84, 207–240.

46. Fisher Ames, "A Sketch of the Character of Alexander Hamilton" [1804], *Works of Fisher Ames,* ed. W. B. Allen, 2 vols. (Indianapolis: Liberty Classics, 1983), I: 510–511, 516, 518.

47. Fisher Ames, "Eulogy on Washington," "A Sketch of the Character of Alexander Hamilton," "The Dangers of American Liberty," "The Republic No. 1," *Works of Fisher Ames*, I: 537, 515, 128–130, 152, 86–89.

48. "The Dangers of American Liberty," *Works of Fisher Ames*, I: 129, 130, 153, 168.

49. "American Literature," *Works of Fisher Ames*, I: 22–37. [Emphasis added.]

50. See Botein, "Cicero As Role Model For Early American Lawyers: A Case Study in Classical 'Influence,'" *Classical Journal*, 73 (Spring, 1978), 313–321; Reinhold, ed., "Cicero," *The Classick Pages*, pp. 49–63; and Ferguson, *Law and Letters in American Culture*, pp. 20–21, 74–76.

51. John Quincy Adams, "July 31, 1826," *The Diary of John Quincy Adams: American Diplomacy, and Political, Social, and Intellectual Life from Washington to Polk,* ed. Allen Nevins (New York: Frederick Ungar, 1969), p. 363. See, as well, John Quincy Adams, *Lectures on Rhetoric and Oratory delivered to the Classes of Senior and Junior Sophisters in Harvard University,* 2 vols. (Cambridge: Hilliard and Metcalf, 1810), I: 128, 133.

52. Adams, *Lectures on Rhetoric and Oratory*, I: 108–110.

53. Alexis de Tocqueville, *Democracy in America* [1835–1840], ed. Phillips Bradley, 2 vols. (New York: Vintage Books, 1958), II: 66–67.

54. Adams, *Lectures on Rhetoric and Oratory*, I: 16–17, 71, 30.

55. Daniel Webster, "A Discourse in Commemoration of the Lives and Services

of John Adams and Thomas Jefferson, delivered in Faneuil Hall, on August 2, 1826," *The Writings and Speeches of Daniel Webster,* 18 vols. (Boston: Little, Brown, 1903), I: 307.

56. "The Character of Washington, A Speech delivered . . . on the 22nd of February, 1832," *The Writings and Speeches of Daniel Webster,* II: 71.

57. See Vance, *America's Rome,* I: 15, and Montgomery and Kane, eds., *American Art: 1750–1800, Toward Independence,* p. 36.

58. Lowry, *Building A National Image,* pp. 10–47, and James Sterling Young, *The Washington Community 1800–1828* (New York: Columbia University Press, 1966), pp. 1–37.

59. Thomas Jefferson to Charles L'Enfant, April 10, 1791, *The Papers of Thomas Jefferson,* XX: 86, and Thomas Jefferson to Benjamin H. Latrobe, July 12, 1812, quoted in Lowry, *Building A National Image,* p. 30.

60. Jefferson, *Notes on the State of Virginia* [1787], ed. William Peden (1954; rpt. New York: W. W. Norton, 1972), pp. 153–154.

61. See William H. Pierson, Jr., *American Buildings And Their Architects,* 5 vols. (New York: Oxford University Press, 1970), I: 211–212, 215–216, and Lowry, "Public Architecture and the Well-being of the State," *Building A National Image,* pp. 36–47.

62. Allen Nevins, ed., *The Diary of Philip Hone 1828–1851,* 2 vols. (New York: Dodd, Mead and Co., 1927), I: 302.

63. Adams, *Lectures on Rhetoric and Oratory,* I: 45.

64. *The Writings and Speeches of Daniel Webster,* I: 319, VIII: 238–239, X: 101; Edward G. Parker, *The Golden Age of Oratory,* pp. 95–98; Barnet Baskerville, *The People's Voice: The Orator in American Society* (Lexington: The University of Kentucky Press, 1979), pp. 58, 41; Peter Harvey, *Reminiscences and Anecdotes of Daniel Webster* (Boston: Little, Brown and Co., 1877), pp. 161–163.

65. Irving H. Bartlett, *Daniel Webster* (New York: W. W. Norton, 1978), p. 10; *The Writings and Speeches of Daniel Webster,* I: 289–290, 245–246, 220–221; Edwin P. Whipple, "Daniel Webster as a Master of English Style," *The Great Speeches and Orations of Daniel Webster* (Boston: Little, Brown and Co., 1889), p. 49.

66. *The Writings and Speeches of Daniel Webster,* I: 308–312, 262–263.

67. Ralph Waldo Emerson, "June 18, 1843," "August 18, 1843," *The Heart of Emerson's Journals,* ed. Bliss Perry (Boston: Houghton Mifflin Co., 1926), pp. 199, 201.

68. Edward G. Parker, *The Golden Age of Oratory,* p. 84; Adams, *Lectures on Rhetoric and Oratory,* I: 136–138.

69. William Kent, ed., *Memoirs and Letters of Chancellor James Kent* (Boston: Little, Brown, 1898), pp. 24–27.

70. Daniel Boorstin, *The Americans: The National Experience* (New York: Random House, 1965), pp. 307–314.

71. Cicero, *De Officiis*, trans. Walter Miller (1913; rpt. Cambridge: Harvard University Press, 1961), p. 161. [1.44.156–157]

72. George Lukacs, *The Theory of the Novel*, trans. Anna Bostock (1916; rpt. Cambridge: M.I.T. Press, 1968), p. 29.

73. Jean Starobinski, "The Idea of Nostalgia," *Diogenes: An International Review of Philosophy and Humanistic Studies*, 54 (Summer 1966), 84–89. I take the distinction between "restorative nostalgia" and "reflective nostalgia" from Svetlana Boym, *The Future of Nostalgia* (New York: Basic Books, 2001), pp. xiii–xix, 24–25, 49–55.

74. I paraphrase from Nicholas Dames, *Amnesiac Selves: Nostalgia, Forgetting, and British Fiction, 1810–1870* (Oxford: Oxford University Press, 2001), pp. 7, 14, 236, and Jonathan Steinwand, "The Future of Nostalgia in Friedrich Schlegel's Gender Theory: Casting German Aesthetics Beyond Ancient Greece and Modern Europe," in Jean Pickering and Suzanne Kehde, ed., *Narratives of Nostalgia, Gender, and Nationalism* (New York: New York University Press, 1997), p. 9.

75. Dames, *Amnesiac Selves*, pp. 18, 238. For how nostalgia works, see also Boym, *The Future of Nostalgia*, pp. 41–55.

76. Stephanie Coontz, *The Way We Never Were: American Families and the Nostalgia Trap* (New York: Basic Books, 1992).

7. Gabriel's Rebellion

1. See Walter Benjamin, *Illuminations*, trans. Harry Zohn (New York: Schocken Books, 1969), p. 256.

2. This phrase, from the Pledge of Allegiance in the United States Code, first published in 1892, has been a part of national understandings since the inception of the republic.

3. Don E. Fehrenbacher, *The Slaveholding Republic: An Account of the United States Government's Relations to Slavery* (Oxford: Oxford University Press, 2001), p. 113.

4. Quoted in Robert Sutcliff, *Travels in Some Parts of North America, in the Years 1804, 1805, and 1806* (York, England: C. Peacock, 1811), p. 50.

5. James Monroe to Joseph Cabell, February 8, 1823, quoted in Douglas R. Egerton, *Gabriel's Rebellion: The Virginia Slave Conspiracies of 1800 and 1802* (Chapel Hill: University of North Carolina Press, 1993), p. 112; James Monroe to Thomas Jefferson, September 15, 1800, in Stanislaus Murray Hamilton, ed., *The Writings of James Monroe*, 7 vols. (New York: G. P. Putnam's Sons, 1900), III: 208–209; and Thomas Jefferson to James Monroe, September 20, 1800, in Paul Leicester Ford, ed., *The Writings of Thomas Jefferson*, 12 vols. (New York: G. P. Putnam's Sons, 1896), VII: 457–458. For the most reliable record of formal executions and other punishments administered by the Henrico County slave courts after the rebel-

lion of 1800, see Philip J. Schwartz, *Twice Condemned: Slaves and the Criminal Laws of Virginia, 1705–1865* (Baton Rouge: Louisiana State University Press, 1988), pp. 324–327.

6. For these measures, see Egerton, *Gabriel's Rebellion*, pp. 88, 141, 164–168.

7. Daniel Sisson, *The American Revolution of 1800* (New York: Knopf, 1974).

8. Sigmund Freud, *Civilization and Its Discontents*, in James Strachey, ed., *The Standard Edition of the Complete Psychological Works of Sigmund Freud*, 24 vols. (London: Hogarth Press, 1961), XXI: 141, 95–97, 60, 69–70.

9. Freud, "The Uncanny," in Strachey. ed., *Standard Edition of the Works of Freud*, XVII: 219–220, 241, 245.

10. Mary Douglas, *How Institutions Think* (Syracuse, N.Y.: Syracuse University Press, 1986), pp. 69–70, 76, 90.

11. "The Trial of Gabriel," "Confessions of Ben Alias Ben Woolfolk," and "The Trial of Gilbert, the Property of Wm. Young," in H. W. Flournoy, ed., *Calendar of Virginia State Papers and Other Manuscripts from January 1, 1799, to December 31, 1807; Preserved in the Capitol at Richmond*, vol. 9 (Richmond: Virginia State Library, 1890), pp. 164–165, 150–153. All trial records of the slave rebellion are from this source, pp. 140–174, hereinafter cited as "Gabriel's Rebellion," in *Calendar of Virginia State Papers*.

12. Sutcliff, *Travels in Some Parts of North America*, p. 50.

13. Arthur Lee, "Address on Slavery," *Virginia Gazette* (March 19, 1767).

14. Thomas Jefferson, "Query XVIII: Manners," in Jefferson, *Notes on the State of Virginia*, ed. William Peden (Chapel Hill: University of North Carolina Press, 1955), pp. 162–163; Thomas Jefferson to St. George Tucker, August 28, 1797, in Ford, ed., *Writings of Thomas Jefferson*, VII, 168; Thomas Jefferson to John Holmes, April 22, 1820, in Merrill Peterson, ed., *Thomas Jefferson Writings: Autobiography, A Summary View of the Rights of British America, Notes on the State of Virginia, Public Papers, Addresses, Messages, and Replies, Miscellany, Letters* (New York: Library of America, 1984), p. 1434.[Hereinafter, Jefferson, *Writings*.]

15. Douglas, *How Institutions Think*, p. 90.

16. George Earlie Shanke, *State Names, Flags, Seals, Songs, Birds, Flowers, and Other Symbols* (New York: H. W. Wilson, 1934), pp. 215–218. See also Benjamin F. Shearer and Barbara S. Shearer, *State Names, Seals, Flags, and Symbols: A Historical Guide* (Westport, Conn.: Greenwood Press, 1987), pp. 30, 59.

17. John Locke, chapter 4 of *An Essay Concerning the True Original, Extent, and End of Civil Government* (1690) in Peter Laslett, ed., *Two Treatises of Government*, 2nd critical ed. (Cambridge: Cambridge University Press, 1967), p. 302.

18. Freud, "The Uncanny," in Strachey, ed., *Standard Edition of the Works of Freud*, XVII: 220–225, 241. See, as well, Priscilla Wald, *Constituting Amer-*

icans: Cultural Anxiety and Narrative Form (Durhan, N.C.: Duke University Press, 1995).

19. Lee, "Address on Slavery," Jefferson, *Notes on the State of Virginia,* pp. 163, 138–143.

20. Thomas Roderick Dew in *The American Quarterly Review* [1832] in Drew Gilpin Faust, ed., *The Ideology of Slavery: Proslavery Thought in the Antebellum South, 1830–1860* (Baton Rouge: Louisiana State University Press, 1981), pp. 60 ff.

21. *A Narrative of the Life and Adventures of Venture, a Native of Africa, but Resident Above Sixty Years in the United States of America* (1798; rpt. Middletown, Conn.: J. S. Stewart, 1897), p. 2. Herman Melville, "Chapter Ten: A Bosom Friend," *Moby-Dick or The Whale* [1851], ed. Harrison Hayford, Hershel Parker, and G. Thomas Tanselle (Evanston and Chicago: Northwestern University Press and The Newberry Library, 1988), p. 50.

22. John Randolph to Joseph H. Nicholson, September 26, 1800, quoted in William Cabell Bruce, *John Randolph of Roanoke, 1773–1833* 2 vols. (New York: G. P. Putnam's Sons, 1922), II: 250–251.

23. For the military organization of the slave conspirators, see "Gabriel's Rebellion," in *Calendar of Virginia State Papers,* pp. 141, 144–145, 146, 151–153, 159–160, 164–165, 168, 170–171. For frightened slave owners who knew the "execution of [Gabriel's] purpose was frustrated only by a heavy fall of rain which made the water courses impassable," see Egerton, *Gabriel's Rebellion,* p. 77.

24. George Washington, "To the President of Congress, Cambridge, February 9, 1776," "General Orders, January 1, 1776," and "To the President of Congress, September 24, 1776," in William B. Allen, ed., *George Washington: A Collection* (Indianapolis: Liberty Classics, 1988), pp. 63, 56, 80. See also George F. Scheer and Hugh F. Rankin, eds., *Rebels and Redcoats: The American Revolution Through the Eyes of Those Who Fought and Lived It* (New York: World Publishing Co., 1957), pp. 304–305; and James Thomas Flexner, *Washington: The Indispensable Man* (Boston: Little, Brown, 1969), pp. 37, 68–69.

25. Thomas Jefferson to Dr. Walter Jones, January 2, 1814, in Jefferson, *Writings,* pp. 1318–1319.

26. Washington's Last Will and Testament, in Allen, ed., *George Washington: A Collection,* pp. 667–679.

27. Sutcliff, *Travels in Some Parts of North America,* p. 50.

28. Claude Lévi-Strauss, *The Savage Mind* (Chicago: University of Chicago Press, 1962), p. 32.

29. Douglas, *How Institutions Think,* p. 102.

30. Gayatri Chakravorty Spivak, "Can the Subaltern Speak?" in Cary Nelson and Lawrence Grossberg, eds., *Marxism and the Interpretation of Culture* (Urbana and Chicago: University of Illinois Press, 1988), pp. 280, 285, 287, 294.

31. For the legal repression of slavery issues in the United States, see Robert M. Cover, *Justice Accused: Antislavery and the Judicial Process* (New Haven: Yale University Press, 1975).

32. There are many examples of this relatively new scholarship, but the most trenchant possibility, quoted in the text, can be found in the groundbreaking work of Patricia Williams. See, in particular, *The Alchemy of Race and Rights* (Cambridge: Harvard University Press, 1991), pp. 4, 119–120, 129, 183, 191.

33. James Monroe to Colonel Thomas Newton, October 5, 1800, in Hamilton, ed., *Writings of James Monroe*, III: 213.

34. Quoted from "Mrs. Price's John," one of the slave conspirators, in the trial of Gabriel's second in command, Jack Bowler, "Gabriel's Rebellion," in *Calendar of Virginia State Papers*, p. 159.

35. Jean-Francois Lyotard, *Le différend* (Paris: Minuit, 1984).

36. Freud, "The Uncanny," in Strachey, ed., *Standard Edition of the Works of Freud*, XVII: 249.

37. Herman Melville, *Benito Cereno*, in Harrison Hayford, Alma A. MacDougall, and G. Thomas Tanselle, eds., *The Piazza Tales and Other Prose Pieces, 1839–1860*, n *The Writings of Herman Melville* (Evanston and Chicago: Northwestern University Press and the Newberry Library, 1987), IX: 37–117, 116, 112. See, as well, Eric J. Sundquist, *To Wake the Nations: Race in the Making of American Literature* (Cambridge: Harvard University Press, 1993), pp. 135–189; Susan Weiner, "'Benito Cereno' and the Failure of Law," *Arizona Quarterly*, 47 (Summer, 1991), 1–28; and, more generally, Carlyn L. Karcher, *Shadow over the Promised Land: Slavery, Race, and Violence in Melville's America* (Baton Rouge: Louisiana State University Press, 1980).

38. William Styron, *The Confessions of Nat Turner* (New York: Random House, 1966). For negative reactions, particularly from African-American critics, see John Henry Clarke, ed., *William Styron's Nat Turner: The Black Writers Respond* (Boston: Beacon Press, 1968).

39. Clarke, ed., *William Styron's Nat Turner*, x. Clarke adds that "our Nat is still waiting." For some attempts to find him, see John B. Duff and Peter M. Mitchell, eds., *The Nat Turner Rebellion: The Historical Event and the Modern Controversy* (New York: Harper and Row, 1971); Eric Foner, ed., *Nat Turner: Great Lives Observed* (Englewood Cliffs, N.J.: Prentice-Hall, 1971); Henry Irving Tragle, *The Southampton Slave Revolt of 1831: A Compilation of Source Material* (Amherst: University of Massachusetts Press, 1971); and Albert E. Stone, *The Return of Nat Turner: History, Literature, and Cultural Politics in Sixties America* (Athens: University of Georgia Press, 1992).

40. Arna Bontemps, *Black Thunder* (1936; rpt. Boston: Beacon Press, 1968), vii.

41. Nathaniel Hawthorne, "Chapter XV: The Scowl and Smile," *The House of*

the Seven Gables in William Charvat et al., eds., *The Centenary Edition of the Works of Nathaniel Hawthorne*, 23 vols. (Columbus: Ohio State University Press, 1962–1994), II: 231–232.

42. Cleaver, *Soul on Ice* (New York: McGraw-Hill, 1968), pp. 205, 208, 61.

43. Melville, *Benito Cereno* in *The Writings of Herman Melville*, IX: 98.

44. "Gabriel's Rebellion," in *Calendar of Virginia State Papers*, pp. 153, 164.

8. Jefferson at Monticello

1. William Howard Adams, *Jefferson's Monticello* (New York: Abbeville Press, 1983), p. 226; quotation from *Thomas Jefferson and the Design of Monticello*, Museum Exhibit, Equitable Gallery, New York, December 18, 1993.

2. Bettina K. Knapp, *Archetype, Architecture, and the Writer* (Bloomington: Indiana University Press, 1986), v.

3. See Marilyn R. Chandler, *Dwelling in the Text: Houses in American Fiction* (Berkeley: University of California Press, 1991), pp. 1–9.

4. For the centrality of the plantation in Southern culture, see Charles S. Sydnor, *American Revolutionaries in the Making: Political Practices in Washington's Virginia* (New York: The Free Press, 1952), and Lewis P. Simpson, *The Dispossessed Garden: Pastoral and History in Southern Literature* (Athens, Ga.: University of Georgia Press, 1975).

5. See "Query XII" and "Query XV" in Jefferson, *Notes on the State of Virginia*, ed. William Peden (New York: W. W. Norton and Co., 1972), pp. 108–109 and 151–155.

6. The biblical reference appears in Luke 11:17. Abraham Lincoln makes the phrase famous, but see Thomas Paine and others. Roy P. Basler, ed., *The Collected Works of Abraham Lincoln*, 8 vols. (New Brunswick: Rutgers University Press, 1953), II: 461, and Paine, *Common Sense*, in Philip S. Foner, ed., *The Complete Writings of Thomas Paine*, 2 vols. (New York: The Citadel Press, 1945), I: 8.

7. Jack McLaughlin, *Jefferson and Monticello: A Biography of a Builder* (New York: Henry Holt & Co., 1988), pp. 20–21, and more generally, 1–32.

8. See McLaughlin, *Jefferson and Monticello*, pp. 72–80.

9. Robert A. Ferguson, "'What Is Enlightenment?' Some American Answers," *American Literary History*, 1 (Summer, 1989), 245–272.

10. Immanuel Kant, "An Answer to the Question: 'What Is Enlightenment?'" in Hans Reiss, ed., *Kant's Political Writings*, 2nd ed., trans. H. B. Nisbet (Cambridge: Cambridge University Press, 1991), pp. 54–55.

11. Henry James, "Preface to The Portrait of a Lady" [1908], *The Art of Fiction* (New York: Charles Scribner's Sons, 1962), pp. 46ff.

12. McLaughlin, *Jefferson and Monticello*, pp. 5–7.

13. Quoted in Adams, *Jefferson's Monticello*, p. 100.

14. See TJ to Robert Skipwith, August 3, 1771 and editor's note in Julian P.

Boyd, ed., *The Papers of Thomas Jefferson*, 30 vols. (Princeton: Princeton University Press, 1950–2003), I: 78–81. "The New Rowanty" in Jefferson's terminology "associates Monticello with 'The mountain of the world,' or Rowandiz, the Accadian Olympos . . . believed to be the pivot on which the heaven rested."

15. TJ to Roger C. Weightman, June 24, 1826, in Thomas Jefferson, *Writings: Autobiography, A Summary View of the Rights of British America, Notes on the State of Virginia, Public Papers, Addresses, Messages, and Replies, Miscellany, Letters*, ed. Merrill Peterson (New York: Library of America, 1984), pp. 1516–1517. [Hereinafter Jefferson, *Writings*.]

16. Quoted in McLaughlin, *Jefferson and Monticello*, p. 203.

17. TJ to JA, August 1, 1816, and TJ to JA, October 23, 1823, in Lester J. Cappon, ed., *The Adams-Jefferson Correspondence: The Complete Correspondence Between Thomas Jefferson and Abigail and John Adams*, 2 vols. (Chapel Hill: The University of North Carolina Press, 1959), II: 484, 599.

18. TJ to Martha Jefferson, March 28, 1787, and TJ to Martha Jefferson, May 21, 1787, in Adrienne Koch and William Peden, eds., *The Life and Selected Writings of Thomas Jefferson* (New York: Random House, 1944), p. 417, and Jefferson, *Writings*, p. 896.

19. See Adams, *Jefferson's Monticello*, p. 229.

20. See Sarah Randolph, *The Domestic Life of Thomas Jefferson*, 3rd ed. (Charlottesville, Va.: Thomas Jefferson Memorial Foundation, 1947) p. 290, and Adams, *Jefferson's Monticello*, pp. 213, 226.

21. Adams, *Jefferson's Monticello*, p. 112.

22. For Jefferson's careful obelisk design, see TJ to William Short, April 6, 1790, in Boyd, ed. *The Papers of Thomas Jefferson*, 16: 321. See also Adams, *Jefferson's Monticello*, pp. 196, 213.

23. McLaughlin, *Jefferson and Monticello*, pp. 36, 252–253, 426–427.

24. McLaughlin, *Jefferson and Monticello*, pp. 111–119, 262.

25. Michel Foucault, *Discipline and Punish: The Birth of the Prison*, trans. Alan Sheridan (New York: Random House, 1979), pp. 195–228.

26. Gaston Bachelard, *The Poetics of Space*, trans. Maria Jolas (New York: Orion Press, 1964), pp. 232–239.

27. TJ to James Oldham, January 19, 1805, quoted in McLaughlin, *Jefferson and Monticello*, p. 290.

28. Quoted in McLaughlin, *Jefferson and Monticello*, pp. 54, 251.

29. Edwin H. Cady, *The Gentleman in America: A Literary Study in American Culture* (Syracuse, N.Y.: Syracuse University Press, 1949), pp. 1–27.

30. McLaughlin, *Jefferson and Monticello*, pp. 376–378.

31. See Emerson's *Nature* ["III. Beauty"] and the beginning of the essay "Circles," in Stephen E. Whicher, ed., *Selections from Ralph Waldo Emerson: An Organic Anthology* (Boston: Houghton Mifflin, 1960), pp. 27, 33, 168. "We are never tired, so long as we can see far enough," Emerson wrote in

Nature. In "Circles" he added "the eye is the first circle; the horizon which it forms is the second."

32. TJ to the Marquis de Chastellux, June 7, 1785, and TJ to Edward Coles, August 25, 1814, in Jefferson, *Writings,* pp. 799–800, 1343–1345.

33. *Notes on the State of Virginia,* p. 166 [Query XX: Subjects of Commerce].

34. Quoted in Adams, *Jefferson's Monticello,* pp. 80–81.

35. TJ to Martha Jefferson Randolph, February 5, 1805, quoted in McLaughlin, *Jefferson and Monticello,* p. 269.

36. *Notes on the State of Virginia,* pp. 80–81 [Query VII: Climate]; TJ to Maria Cosway, October 12, 1786, in Jefferson, *Writings,* pp. 866–877; and Adams, ed., *Jefferson and Monticello,* pp. 115–116.

37. Bachelard, *The Poetics of Space,* pp. 227–228 and, generally, 211–231.

38. TJ to George Gilmer, August 12, 1787, in Boyd, ed., *The Papers of Thomas Jefferson,* 12: 26.

9. Charity in the City of Brotherly Love

1. *Vidal et al. v. Girard's Executors,* 2 Howard's Reports 126–202 (The Supreme Court of the United States, January Term, 1844); Carl Zollman, *American Law of Charities* (Milwaukee: Bruce Publishing Co., 1924), pp. 6–9, 31; George Gleason Bogert, *Handbook of the Law of Trusts,* 3rd edition, Hornbook series (St. Paul: West Publishing Co., 1952), pp. 239, 252; Maurice G. Baxter, *Daniel Webster & The Supreme Court* (Amherst: The University of Massachusetts Press, 1966), pp. 167–168; Robert H. Bremner, *American Philanthropy* (Chicago: The University of Chicago Press, 1960), pp. 38–40, 95. [The quotation is from Baxter.]

2. Henry A. Wise, *Seven Decades of the Union* (Philadelphia: J. B. Lippincott and Co., 1872), pp. 216–220; Charles Warren, *The Supreme Court in United States History,* 3 vols. (Boston: Little Brown, and Co., 1923), II: 398.

3. Fred Somkin, *Unquiet Eagle: Memory and Desire in the Idea of American Freedom, 1815–1860* (Ithaca: Cornell University Press, 1967), pp. 38–48, and Marvin Meyers, *The Jacksonian Persuasion: Political and Belief* (Stanford: Stanford University Press, 1957), p. 115.

4. Walter Benjamin, *Illuminations,* trans. Harry Zohn (New York: Shocken Books, 1969), pp. 255–258.

5. Howard S. Miller, *The Legal Foundations of American Philanthropy* (Madison: The State Historical Society of Wisconsin, 1961), pp. xi–xii, 3–8, 18–19.

6. Arthur Schlesinger, Sr., "The True American Way of Life," *St. Louis Post-Dispatch,* Part Two (December 13, 1953), p. 3.

7. *The Trustees of the Philadelphia Baptist Association et al. v. Hart's Executors,* 4 Wheaton's Reports 1–51 (The Supreme Court of the United States,

February Term, 1819). For the history of this shift, I rely on Miller, *The Legal Foundations of American Philanthropy.*

8. Bremner, *American Philanthropy*, pp. 2–3. See also Merle Curti, "American Philanthropy and the National Character," *American Quarterly*, 10 (Winter, 1958), 420–437.

9. See Miller, *The Legal Foundations of American Philanthropy*, pp. 7–8, 42–43, and Lawrence M. Friedman, *A History of American Law* (New York: Simon and Schuster, 1973), pp. 223–224.

10. Story, "Appendix: Note 1, On Charitable Bequests," 4 Wheaton's Reports 3–23, and Story, "On Chancery Jurisdiction," *The North American Review*, 11 (July 1820), 146–148.

11. See Perry Miller, *The Life of the Mind in America from the Revolution to the Civil War* (New York: Harcourt, Brace and World, Inc., 1965).

12. Joseph Story to James Kent, August 21, 1819 and March 2, 1844, in *Life and Letters of Joseph Story*, ed. William W. Story, 2 vols. (Boston: Charles Little and James Brown, 1851), I: 33–332, II: 480. See also James Kent to Joseph Story, April 11, 1834, October 5, 1842, April 18, 1844, and June 17, 1845, all in *The Joseph Story Papers, 1808–1845*, ed. Waldo Story [The Massachusetts Historical Society].

13. Quoted in Dixan Ryan Fox, *The Decline of Aristocracy in the Politics of New York [Studies in History, Economics and Public Law*, vol. 86] (New York: Columbia University Press, 1919), pp. 254–255.

14. Morton J. Horwitz, *The Transformation of American Law, 1780–1860* (Cambridge: Harvard University Press, 1977), pp. 48, 50–51, and J. G. A. Pocock, "Authority and Property: The Question of Liberal Origins," *Virtue, Commerce, and History* (Cambridge: Cambridge University Press, 1985), p. 69. See, as well, Brook Thomas, *Cross-Examinations of Law and Literature: Readings of Selected Works by Cooper, Hawthorne, Stowe, and Melville* (Cambridge: Cambridge University Press, 1987).

15. Somkin, *Unquiet Eagle*, pp. 166–171. See, as well, George B. Forgie, *Patricide in the House Divided: A Psychological Interpretation of Lincoln and His Age* (New York: W. W. Norton, 1979).

16. Alexis de Tocqueville, *Democracy in America*, Vintage Edition, 2 vols. (New York: Alfred Knopf, 1954), II: 105, and Quentin Anderson, *The Imperial Self: An Essay in American Literary and Cultural History* (New York: Alfred Knopf, 1971).

17. *First Settlement of New England, A Discourse Delivered at Plymouth, on the 22nd of December, 1820*, in *The Writings and Speeches of Daniel Webster*, ed. James W. McIntyre, 18 vols. (Boston: Little, Brown and Co., 1903), I: 181–186, 211–215.

18. *The Writings and Speeches of Daniel Webster*, I: 183, 220, 225.

19. James Fenimore Cooper, *The Pioneers* (New York: Holt, Rinehart and Winston,1964), pp. 16–17, 285–286, 414–416, and Nathaniel Hawthorne, *The House of the Seven Gables* in William Charvat et al., eds., *The Cente-*

nary Edition of the Works of Nathaniel Hawthorne, 23 vols. (Columbus: Ohio State University Press, 1962–1994), II: 38–45, 122, 130, 272.

20. My account of the *Girard* Will case in the next three paragraphs relies on the court record, newspaper accounts, and the descriptions of Charles Warren, *The Supreme Court in United States History,* II: 398–407, Miller, *The Legal Foundations of American Philanthropy,* pp. 36–39, and Baxter, *Daniel Webster & the Supreme Court,* pp. 156–168.

21. *The New York Herald,* Thursday, February 8, 1844.

22. For the biographical facts about Girard, see Harry Emerson Wildes, *Lonely Midas: The Story of Stephen Girard* (New York: Farrar and Rinehart, 1943).

23. Wise, *Seven Decades of the Union,* p. 218. *The New York Herald,* February 8 and 10, 1844.

24. *Philadelphia Baptist Association v. Hart's Executors,* 43. 49–50.

25. *Vidal v. Girard,* 195, 193. For the role of *Magill v. Brown* in Story's *Girard* opinion, see Irvin G. Wyllie, "The Search for an American Law of Charity, 1776–1844," *Mississippi Valley Historical Review,* 46 (September 1959), 203–221.

26. The *Girard Will* Case," *Writings and Speeches of Daniel Webster,* XI: 139, 144, 149, 167–168.

27. Ibid., 145, 164–168, 176.

28. Joseph Story to James Kent, August 31, 1844, and Joseph Story to Mrs. Joseph Story, February 7, 1844, in *Life and Letters of Story,* II: 469, 468.

29. *Vidal v. Girard,* 198–199.

30. Joseph Story to Mrs. Joseph Story, March 3, 1844, in *Life and Letters of Story,* II: 473.

31. Joseph Story, *Commentaries on Equity Jurisprudence, as Administered in England and America,* 3rd edition, 2 vols. (Boston: Charles Little and James Brown, 1843), II: 493–494, 503–510. See also Bogert, *On Trusts,* p. 239.

32. Quoted in Miller, *The Life of the Mind in America,* p. 215. Also, Joseph Story to James Kent, August 31, 1844, *Joseph Story Papers* [Massachusetts Historical Society].

33. "Literary Tendencies of the Times," in William W. Story, ed., *The Miscellaneous Writings of Joseph Story* (Boston: Charles Little and James Brown, 1852), pp. 743, 747–750. 776–777.

34. *Vidal v. Girard,* 190, 186–187. Also Joseph Story to James Kent, August 31, 1844, in *Life and Letters of Story,* II: 469.

35. Peter Dobkin Hall, *The Organization of American Culture, 1700–1900: Private Institutions, Elites, and The Origins of American Nationality* (New York: New York University Press, 1984), pp. 114, 96.

36. Friedman, *A History of American Law,* pp. 174–186, 445.

37. "Progress of Jurisprudence," *The Miscellaneous Writings of Story,* pp. 231–232.

38. Charles Francis Adams, ed., *Memoirs of John Quincy Adams,* 12 vols. (Philadelphia: J. B. Lippincott, 1874–1877), XI: 510.
39. See Stanley N. Katz, Barry Sullivan, and C. Paul Beach, "Legal Change and Legal Autonomy: Charitable Trusts in New York, 1777–1893," *Law and History Review,* 3 (Spring, 1985), 51–89.
40. Bremner, *American Philanthropy,* pp. 40–41, 105.
41. Miller, *The Legal Foundations of American Philanthropy,* p. 4; Bremner, *American Philanthropy,* p. 24; Curti, *American Philanthropy and the National Character,* pp. 427–437.
42. Katz, Sullivan, and Beach, *Law and History Review,* p. 51.

10. The Last Early Republican Text

1. See Brian W. Dipple, *The Vanishing American: White Attitudes and U.S. Indian Policy* (Middletown, Conn.: Wesleyan University Press, 1982), p. 2, and Alden T. Vaughan, "From White Man to Redskin: Changing Anglo-American Perceptions of the American Indian," *The American Historical Review,* 87 (October 1982), 917–953.
2. For criticism of periodization as a concept, see Susanne K. Langer, *Philosophy in a New Key: A Study in Symbolism, Reason, Rite, and Art,* 3rd ed. (1957; Cambridge, Mass.: Harvard University Press, 1969), pp. 3–8; Robert Rehder, "Periodization and the Theory of Literary History," *Colloquium Helveticum,* 22 (1995), 118, 120–124; and Lawrence Besserman, ed., *The Challenge of Periodization: Old Paradigms and New Perspectives* (New York: Garland, 1996), 3–27. The quotations are from Fredric Jameson, *The Political Unconscious* (London: Methuen, 1981; rpt. London: Routledge, 1989), p. 27, and from J. Hillis Miller in *The Challenge of Periodization,* p. 197.
3. For these generic problems, see Donald A. Ringe, "Mode and Meaning in *The Last of the Mohicans,*" in W. M. Verhoeven, ed., *James Fenimore Cooper: New Historical and Literary Contexts: Studies in Literature 12* (Amsterdam and Atlanta: Editions Rodopi B. U., 1993), pp. 109–124.
4. Cooper's use of ambiguity will become a celebrated vehicle amongst successors like Nathaniel Hawthorne and Herman Melville, but in 1826, this practice violated two of the six principles identified by William Charvat as central to the writing of American literature. Cooper was skeptical and pessimistic where he was supposed to be optimistic (rule four), and he was obscure in not always explaining himself (rule five). See Charvat, *The Origins of American Critical Thought 1810–1835* (1936; rpt. New York: Russell & Russell, 1968), pp. 7–26, and more generally James D. Wallace, *Early Cooper and His Audience* (New York: Columbia University Press, 1986).
5. Cooper, "Preface [1826]," in *The Last of the Mohicans: A Narrative of 1757,* eds. James A. Sappenfield and E. N. Feltskog (Albany: State Univer-

sity of New York Press, 1983), pp. 1, 4.[All further parenthetical references to the novel in the text will be to this standard scholarly edition.]

6. James Fenimore Cooper, *Gleanings in Europe* [1837], ed. Robert E. Spiller, 2 vols. (New York: Oxford University Press, 1928–1930), II: 153. See, as well, Robert E. Spiller, "Introduction," *James Fenimore Cooper: Representative Selections, with Introduction, Bibliography, and Notes* (New York: American Book Company, 1936), xi–xxv. [Cited henceforth as *Cooper: Representative Selections.*]

7. *Letter to His Countrymen* [1834], quoted in *Cooper: Representative Selections*, p. 181.

8. Carl E. Schorske. *Thinking With History: Explorations in the Passage to Modernism* (Princeton: Princeton University Press, 1998), pp. 4–6, 224–226.

9. Georg Lukács, *The Theory of the Novel: A historico-philosophical essay on the forms of great epic literature*, trans. Anna Bostock (Cambridge, Mass.: The MIT Press, 1983), pp. 84–85, 146.

10. Fred Somkin, *Unquiet Eagle: Memory and Desire in the Idea of American Freedom, 1815–1860* (Ithaca, N.Y.: Cornell University Press, 1967), pp. 34–38.

11. John Adams to Thomas Jefferson, June 28, 1812, *The Adams-Jefferson Letters: The Complete Correspondence between Thomas Jefferson and Abigail and John Adams*, 2 vols. (Chapel Hill: The University of North Carolina Press, 1959), II: 311.

12. John Quincy Adams to James Lloyd, October 1, 1822, in Worthington C. Ford, ed., *Writings of John Quincy Adams*, 7 vols. (New York: Macmillan, 1913–1917), VII: 311–313.

13. See Seymour Martin Lipset, *The First New Nation: The United States in Historical and Comparative Perspective* (1963; rpt. Garden City, N.Y.: Doubleday, 1967), pp. 17–38.

14. Daniel Webster, *The Bunker Hill Monument: An Address delivered at the Laying of the Corner-stone of the Bunker Hill Monument at Charlestown, Massachusetts on the 17th of June, 1825, and Adams and Jefferson: A Discourse in Commemoration of the Lives and Services of John Adams and Thomas Jefferson, delivered in Faneuil Hall, Boston, on the 2d of August, 1826*, in James W. McIntyre, ed., *The Writings and Speeches of Daniel Webster*, 18 vols. (Boston: Little, Brown, & Co., 1903), I: 253–254, and I: 289.

15. Rufus Choate, *The Importance Of Illustrating New-England History By A Series Of Romances Like The Waverly Novels* [1833], in *The Works of Rufus Choate with a Memoir of His Life*, ed. Samuel Gilman Brown, 2 vols. (Boston: Little, Brown, 1862), I: 319–320, 323–324, 340–344.

16. James Fenimore Cooper, "Letter 30: Prophecy," *Notions of the Americans*, 2 vols. (New York: Frederick Ungar Publishing Co., 1963), II: 333.

17. James Fenimore Cooper, *The American Democrat, or Hints on the Social and Civic Relations of The United States of America* (New York: Vintage Books, 1956), pp. 156–157, 162. These comments are from 1838, but the same views are already apparent in Cooper's first Leatherstocking tale, *The Pioneers* from 1823.

18. For these claims about romanticism and their use as early as 1820, see René Wellek, "The Concept of Romanticism," *Concepts of Criticism* (New Haven: Yale University Press, 1963), pp. 128–198 and G. Harrison Orians, "The Rise of Romanticism, 1805–1855," in Harry Hayden Clark, ed., *Transitions in American Literary History* (New York: Octagon Books, 1975), pp. 51–244. For applications to Cooper's early career and his plans as a novelist, see George Dekker, *James Fenimore Cooper, The American Scott* (New York: Barnes & Noble, 1967), pp. 20–21, 43–44, 64–70.

19. William L. Hedges, "The Old World Yet: Writers and Writings in Post-Revolutionary America," *Early American Literature,* 16 (Spring, 1981), pp. 16–17.

20. Cooper's Indian plot with Uncas as Tamenund's anointed successor only makes sense through the theory of the cycles of history (pp. 309–310, 307, 304–306, 350). The pivotal text on the pessimism inherent to such a cyclical view on which Cooper draws was Edward Gibbons, *The History of the Decline and Fall of the Roman Empire* [1776 to 1788].

21. See James Franklin Beard, "Historical Introduction," *The Last of the Mohicans: A Narrative of 1757* (Albany: State University of New York Press, 1983), xv–xlviii, and, more generally, Jill Lepore, "Remembering American Frontiers: King Philip's War and the American Imagination," in Andrew R. L. Cayton and Fredrika J. Teute, eds., *Contact Points: American Frontiers from the Mohawk Valley to the Mississippi, 1750–1830* (Chapel Hill: University of North Carolina Press, 1998), pp. 327–360.

22. For Cooper's accuracy and the controversies surrounding his use of the massacre of Fort William Henry, see John McWilliams, *The Last of the Mohicans: Civil Savagery and Savage Civility* (New York: Twayne Publishers, 1995), pp. 92–102.

23. Lukács, *The Theory of the Novel*, p. 90.

24. For accounts of this disservice, see Steven Blackmore, "'Without a Cross': The Cultural Significance of the Sublime and Beautiful in Cooper's *The Last of the Mohicans*," *Nineteenth-Century Literature,* 52 (June 1997), 47–57, and McWilliams, *The Last of the Mohicans: Civil Savagery and Savage Civility* (New York: Twayne Publishers, 1995), pp. 52–80. For the prominence of the dark heroine, see Janet E. Dean, "The Marriage Plot and National Myth in *The Pioneers*," *The Arizona Quarterly,* 52 (Winter, 1996), 1–29, and Terence Martin, "From the Ruins of History: *The Last of the Mohicans*," *Novel,* 2 (Spring, 1969), 228–229.

25. In this quotation and in my treatment of Cora Munro, I follow Robert

Milder, "*The Last of the Mohicans* and the New World Fall," *American Literature*, 52 (November 1980), 426–429.

26. The count of uses of "blood" and "bloody" is noted in Thomas Philbrick, "*The Last of the Mohicans* and the Sounds of Discord," *American Literature*, 43 (March 1971), 28, 39. Philbrick associates Cooper's use of the term in the novel to his "demoniac frenzy" and "nearly pornographic obsession with violence."

27. David Haberly claims that *The Last of the Mohicans* "is above all a captivity narrative" with Cora as "prey to the [genre's] three important moral perils—defeminization, rape, and Indianization" in "Women and Indians: *The Last of the Mohicans* and the Captivity Tradition," *American Quarterly*, 28 (Fall 1976), 431–444.

28. Thomas Cole's two paintings from 1827, both entitled *Cora Kneeling at the Feet of Tamenund*, are now at the Wadsworth Atheneum in Hartford, Connecticut and The New York State Historical Association in Cooperstown, New York.

29. See Vaughan, "From White Man to Redskin: Changing Anglo-American Perceptions of the American Indian," 917–953.

30. Ian Dennis, "The Worthlessness of Duncan Heyward: A Waverley Hero in America," *Studies in the Novel*, 29 (Spring 1997), 13.

31. James Franklin Beard, ed., "Introduction," *The Letters and Journals of James Fenimore Cooper*, 6 vols. (Cambridge, Mass.: Harvard University Press, 1960), I: xxx–xxxi, and Jane Tompkins, "No Apologies for the Iroquois: A New Way to Read the Leatherstocking Novels," *Criticism: A Quarterly for Literature and the Arts*, 23 (Winter 1981), 35, 41.

32. For examples, see Joyce Appleby, *Inheriting The Revolution: The First Generation of Americans* (Cambridge: Harvard University Press, 2000), pp. 264–265.

33. The phrase "mediating woman" as applied to a series of Cooper's female protagonists is Janet Dean's in "The Marriage Plot and National Myth in *The Pioneers*," 1–29.

34. D. H. Lawrence, *Studies in Classic American Literature* (New York: Viking Press, 1966), p. 62. [Originally published in 1923.]

35. George Dekker first raises this troubling question in *James Fenimore Cooper: The American Scott*, pp. 74–75.

36. See Nancy Ruttenburg, *Democratic Personality: Popular Voice and the Trial of American Authorship* (Stanford: Stanford University Press, 1998), pp. 313–324. I differ from Ruttenburg only in assigning the "ultimate democratic personality" to Magua instead of Natty Bumppo, who always knows and keeps his place, deferring to his superiors, in the social hierarchy.

37. For Cooper's clearest statement on the ideal leader, on the need for deference to that leader, and on the dangers of demagoguery as the values of the

Revolution recede into history, see *The American Democrat, or Hints on the Social and Civic Relations of The United States of America* (New York: Vintage Books, 1956), pp. 4, 67–69, 70–71, 90–92, 99, 150–151, 156, 172. The same views can be found in dramatic form as early as *The Pioneers* in 1823.

38. James Fenimore Cooper, "Letter 23: Literature and National Taste," *Notions of the Americans*, 2 vols. (New York: Frederick Ungar Publishing Co., 1963), II: 108.

39. "Letter 28: George Washington, Man and Hero," *Notions of the Americans*, II: 187–188.

40. For an analysis of Heyward as the "naïve observer" and his "almost criminally inept" behavior, see Ian Dennis, "The Worthlessness of Duncan Heyward: A Waverly Hero in America," *Studies in the Novel*, 29 (Spring, 1997), 2, 1–16. See also Edward W. Pritcher, "Cooper's Cunning and Heyward as Cunning-Man in *The Last of the Mohicans, ANQ*, 9 (Winter, 1996), 10–17.

41. H. Daniel Peck, *A World by Itself: The Pastoral Moment in Cooper's Fiction* (New Haven: Yale University Press, 1977), p. 141.

42. An allegory, from the Greek *allegoria* for "speaking otherwise," is a story with two or more levels of distinct meaning, a primary or surface meaning that elucidates through parallelism a secondary or under-the-surface meaning. See J. A. Cuddon, *A Dictionary of Literary Terms* (Garden City, N.Y.: Doubleday, 1977), pp. 23–26.

43. For the confusions in language that lead to civil war in the Native American world of the novel, see Dennis W. Allen, "'By All The Truth Of Signs': James Fenimore Cooper's *The Last of the Mohicans*," *Studies in American Fiction*, 9 (Autumn, 1981), 159–179, and Steven Blackmore, "Strange Tongues: Cooper's Fiction of Language in *The Last of the Mohicans, Early American Literature*, 19 (Spring, 1984), 21–41.

44. Isaiah Berlin uses these terms to designate "turning points" in the history of thought in *The Sense of Reality: Studies in Ideas and their History* (New York: Farrar, Straus and Giroux, 1996), pp. 17, 168–170.

45. Walter Benjamin, "Theses on the Philosophy of History: IX," *Illuminations*, trans. Harry Zohn (New York: Schocken Books, 1969), pp. 257–258. Benjamin takes this image from Paul Klee's modernist painting entitled "Angelus Novus."

46. E. L. Doctorow, in another dark book about American culture, puts the issue as a question: "Why is straight shooting a metaphor for honesty?" See Doctorow, *The Book of Daniel* (1971; rpt. New York: Random House, 1983), p. 84.

47. For Cooper's many invocations of Magua's alcoholism as a partial explanation of his villainy, see *The Last of the Mohicans*, pp. 20–21, 103–104, 170, 186, 249.

48. Herman Melville to Nathaniel Hawthorne, April[?] 16, 1851, and June 29,

1851, in Herman Melville, *Correspondence,* ed. Lynr Horth (Evanston: Northwestern University Press and Newberry Library, 1993), pp. 186, 196.

49. William L. Hedges, "Toward A Theory of American Literature, 1765–1800," *Early American Literature,* 4 (No. 1, 1970), pp. 7–10.

50. Gordon S. Wood, "The Democratization of Mind in the American Revolution," in *Leadership in the American Revolution: Library of Congress Symposia on the American Revolution* (Washington, D.C.: The Library of Congress, 1976), pp. 63–65.

51. Jean Starobinski, "The Idea of Nostalgia," *Diogenes: An International Review of Philosophy and Humanistic Studies,* 54 (Summer, 1966), 81–103.

52. For vocabulary here, I rely on Nicholas Dames, *Amnesiac Selves: Nostalgia, Forgetting, and British Fiction, 1810–1870* (Oxford: Oxford University Press, 2001), pp. 4–18, 236–243.

53. Mary Douglas, "Institutions Remember and Forget," *How Institutions Think* (Syracuse: Syracuse University Press, 1986), p. 69.

Epilogue

1. Giambattista Vico, *On the Study Methods of Our Time,* trans. E. Gianturco (Ithaca, N.Y.: Cornell University Press, 1990), p. 73. See as well, Anthony Grafton, "An Introduction to the *New Science* of Giambattista Vico," *Bring Out Your Dead: The Past as Revelation* (Cambridge: Harvard University Press, 2001), pp. 259–278.

2. Rinehart Koselleck, "The Eighteenth Century as the Beginning of Modernity," *The Practice of Conceptual History: Timing History, Spacing Concepts,* trans. Todd Samuel Presner (Stanford: Stanford University Press, 2002), pp. 154–169.

3. Thomas Paine, *Common Sense,* in Philip Foner, ed., *The Complete Writings of Thomas Paine,* 2 vols. (New York: The Citadel Press, 1945), I: 17, 45.

4. See Bernard Bailyn, *To Begin The World Anew: The Genius and Ambiguities of the American Founders* (New York: Alfred A. Knopf, 2003), pp. 4–6. I use Bailyn's terms here but extend his meaning.

5. See Gordon Wood, "A World Within Themselves," "Middle-Class Order," *The Radicalism of the American Revolution* (New York: Alfred A. Knopf, 1992) pp. 305–325, 365–368. Wood's thesis, which dominates scholarship today, is that "democratic society was not the society the revolutionary leaders had wanted or expected" (p. 365).

6. Thomas Carlyle, "On History," *Critical and Miscellaneous Essays: Collected and Republished,* 7 vols. (1839; London: Chapman and Hall, 1869), II: 257. ["On History" was written and first published in *Fraser's Magazine* in 1830.]

7. Henry Steele Commager, "Leadership in Eighteenth-Century America and Today," *Daedalus,* 90 (1961), 652; Adrienne Koch, "Introduction," in Koch, ed., *The American Enlightenment* (New York: George Braziller,

1965), p. 35; Gordon S. Wood, "The Democratizaton of Mind in the American Revolution," *Leadership in the American Revolution* (Washington, D.C.: Library of Congress Symposia on the American Revolution, 1976), pp. 63.

8. Wood, "The Democratization of Mind in the American Revolution," p. 64.

9. Bailyn, "Politics and the Creative Imagination, *To Begin the World Anew,* pp. 3–36.

10. Michael Warner, *The Letters of the Republic: Publication and the Public Sphere in Eighteenth-Century America* (Cambridge: Harvard University Press, 1990), pp. 1–33, 108; Larzer Ziff, *Writing in the New Nation: Prose, Print, and Politics in the Early United States* (New Haven: Yale University Press, 1991), x–xi, 83–106.

11. Christopher Looby, *Voicing America: Language, Literary Form, and the Origins of the United States* (Chicago: The University of Chicago, 1996), p. 5.

12. Rinehart Koselleck, "Historical Criteria of the Modern Concept of Revolution," *Futures Past: On the Semantics of Historical Time,* trans. Keith Tribe (Cambridge: The MIT Press, 1985), pp. 41–44.

13. Benjamin Franklin, "A Proposal for Promoting Useful Knowledge Among the British Plantations in America," in Franklin, *Writings,* ed. J. A. Leo Lemay (New York: Library of America, 1987), pp. 295–297; William Livingston, "Of Patriotism" [May 3, 1753], *The Independent Reflector or Weekly Essays on Sundry Important Subjects More particularly adapted to the Province of New York,* ed. Milton M. Klein (Cambridge: Harvard University Press, 1963), p. 215; Thomas Jefferson to George Wythe, August 13, 1786, *The Papers of Thomas Jefferson,* 30 vols. (Princeton: Princeton University Press, 1950–2003), X: 244–245; James Savage, "The Patronage of Letters and National Prosperity," *Monthly Anthology and Boston Review,* 4 (May 1807), 243–245; and Arthur Maynard Walter, "A Century of Literature and Revolutions," *Monthly Anthology and Boston Review,* 2 (April 1805), 199–200.

14. Jefferson, *A Bill for Establishing Religious Freedom,* in Thomas Jefferson, *Writings: Autobiography, A Summary View of the Rights of British America, Notes on the State of Virginia, Public Papers, Addresses, Messages, and Replies, Miscellany, Letters,* ed. Merrill D. Peterson (New York: Library of America, 1984), p. 347.

15. John Dickinson, *The Letters of Fabius, in 1788 on the Federal Convention,* in *The Political Writings of John Dickinson, Esquire, Late President of the State of Delaware, and of the Commonwealth of Pennsylvania,* 2 vols. (Wilmington: Bonsal and Niles, 1801), II: 72–73, 115–116.

16. John Adams to Count Sarsfield, January 21, 1785, in Charles Francis Adams, ed., *The Life and Works of John Adams,* 10 vols. (Boston: Little, Brown, 1850–1856), VIII: 370.

17. Thomas Jefferson to James Madison, January 30, 1787, in Boyd, ed., *The*

Papers of Thomas Jefferson, XI: 93; John Jay to Lansdowne [Second Earl of Shelburne], April 16, 1786, in Henry P. Johnston, ed., *The Correspondence and Public Papers of John Jay,* 4 vols. (New York: G. P. Putnam's Sons, 1891), III: 190.

18. Excerpts from Democratic Society of Pennsylvania minutes, Civic Festival, May 1, 1794, quoted in Sean Wilentz. ed., *Major Problems in the Early Republic, 1787–1848* (Lexington, Mass.: D.C. Heath and Co., 1992), p. 65.

19. "American Tract Society (1825) and Colporteur System," quoted in Edwin S. Gaustad, ed., *A Documentary History of Religion in America to the Civil War,* 2nd edition (Grand Rapids William B. Eerdmans Publishing, 1993), pp. 334–335.

20. Richard Allen, *The Life Experiences and Gospel Labors of the Rt. Rev. Richard Allen* [1793]; John Leland, "fashionable fast-day sermon" [1801]; Lyman Beecher, "Against Duelling" [1806]; and "Constitution of the American Bible Society" [May 1816], all quoted from Gaustad, ed., *A Documentary History of Religion in America to the Civil War,* pp. 302–303, 321, 323, 329.

21. "Free Blacks Appeal for Freedom and Christian Forbearance, 1794," "Tecumseh Confronts Governor William Henry Harrison, 1810", quoted in Wilentz, ed., *Major Problems in the Early Republic, 1787–1848,* pp. 127, 155; and [Anonymous], *The Female Advocate: Written by a Lady* (New Haven: Thomas Green and Son, 1801), p. 4.

22. Thomas Jefferson to Roger C. Weightman, June 24, 1826, in Jefferson, *Writings,* p. 1517.

23. See Chapter Seven at page 201 and Thomas Jefferson to William Henry Harrison, 1803, quoted in Wilentz, ed., *Major Problems in the Early Republic, 1787–1848,* p. 131.

24. Norbert Elias, *The Civilizing Process: The History of Manners and State Formation and Civilization,* trans. Edmund Jephcott (Oxford: Blackwell, 1994), pp. 6–7.

INDEX